DESIGNING MAGAZINES

D1568017

Designing Magazines

Inside Periodical Design, Redesign, and Branding

Edited by Jandos Rothstein

ALLWORTH PRESS
NEW YORK

11 10 09 08 07 5 4 3 2 1

Published by Allworth Press
An imprint of Allworth Communications, Inc.
10 East 23rd Street, New York, NY 10010

Cover design by Derek Bacchus
Interior design by SR Desktop Services, Ridge, NY
Page composition/typography by SR Desktop Services, Ridge, NY

Library of Congress Cataloging-in-Publication Data
Designing magazines : inside periodical design, redesign, and branding / edited by Jandos Rothstein.
p. cm.
Includes index.
ISBN-13: 978-1-58115-499-3 (pbk.)
ISBN-10: 1-58115-499-2 (pbk.)
1. Magazine design. I. Rothstein, Jandos.

Z246.D485 2007
741.6'5—dc22

2007021922

Printed in Canada

Sources

Chapter 1: "Redesign Anyone?" originally appeared in March 2006, *Folio Magazine*. © 2006 John Brady.
Chapter 3: "Imitation, Inc." originally appeared in August 2002, *Folio Magazine*.
Chapter 8: "Details" originally appeared in July/August 2001, *Print Magazine*. © 2001 Steven Heller.
Chapter 12: "Dialog" originally appeared on *speakmag.com*. © *Speak Magazine*, reproduced by permission.
Chapter 15: "Edward Leida" originally appeared on January 31, 2005, *MediaBistro*.
Chapter 21: "Home Erotic" originally appeared in November/December 1998, *Print Magazine*. © 1998 Steven Heller.
Chapter 22: "Left Wanting" appeared in shorter form, in *I.D. Magazine*, February 2007. © 2007 David Barringer.
Chapter 24: "Bored at 40,000 Feet" originally appeared on December 5, 2005, *MediaBistro*.
Chapter 29: "The ABC's of ASFs" originally appeared, in slightly different form, in October 2006, *SND Update*.
Chapter 30: "Cover Lines" originally appeared in July/August 1997, *Print Magazine*. © 1997 Steven Heller.
Chapter 34: "Art and Design Won't Save Publishing" originally appeared, in slightly different form, in August 2006, *Nieman Watchdog*.

Table of Contents

Introduction

MAGAZINES AND REDESIGNS

Life offers the graphic designer no other project quite like a magazine or newspaper redesign or launch. Most designers are concerned with finished products—posters, advertisements, Web sites, or single issues of a publication. The designer undertaking a redesign is more concerned with the potential of the format. It's sort of like building a set for an improvised play—the redesign specialist builds a structure within which the real action—written and visual storytelling—can take place. This structure must be familiar enough to be understandable, bold enough to be engaging, and flexible enough to accommodate unexpected twists and turns in the plot. Unless the publication is dismally and predictably edited, it is impossible to take everything that might run within the format into account.

A set designer, a director, and an actor all have a different understanding of what's involved in making a play, but each must be empathetic toward the views and concerns of the others. Their collaborative understanding both enriches the expertise of each and allows all to work within an environment of mutual respect and industry. Likewise, magazines are collaborative enterprises. Launching or redesigning a publication must emerge from a shared vision that incorporates editorial, design, and (usually) business interests. This book has views from editors, redesign specialists, and in-house art directors. It is my hope that readers who hold, or aspire to, any of these job titles will find value in these pages.

Even more than their editorial and business-side colleagues, designers approaching a redesign must have an empathetic outlook. You cannot address the needs of a publication without being, or quickly becoming, a generalist, able to translate various management, editorial, and design concerns into a functioning structure. Whether working from a staff position or as an outside consultant, the principal manager of a redesign must be part salesperson, encouraging other stakeholders to consider significant changes, and part marriage counselor, finding common ground between colleagues who may see the redesign as an opportunity to advance their personal aspirations for the magazine. The hardest part for many staff designers is giving fair—but not more than fair—attention to what naturally interests them most: their own aspirations for the magazine. At presentation time when mocked-up pages for the new format come out, the author of the new approach must step down into the role of client—equal to the other clients in the room. He or she must somehow abandon the role of proud parent and look at his or her work critically.

The redesigner must also be a good and questioning listener. Many of the nondesign staff members involved in a redesign—even visually astute staff members—do not always have the vocabulary to articulate what concerns them about an approach. An editor may offer, "I don't like that typeface," but often will not be able to explain why without prodding. Only questioning the comment will result in the possibility of consensus, either to accept the font as is or as modified, or about desirable qualities in an alternative.

Alas, we are all human, and one of the frailties that goes along with the human condition is that we tend, usually subconsciously, to respect most the skills that we best understand. (One editor I used to work with paid me the highest compliment he knew to give an art director: "You could be a writer," he said.) Within the hierarchy of most magazines, the art director reports to the editor in chief. Design and art direction are largely responsive to and supportive of the editorial mission. The redesign turns that relationship upside down. During a redesign, designers provide some of the ideas for new features, new ways to divide up content—shortening some things, lengthening others. Long-standing ways of working are held up for scrutiny and sometimes rejected. For editors—particularly strong editors—this can be an uncomfortable process. For staff designers, who must rise above their traditional position in the organization to claim new authority, it can be a difficult time as well. This book will look at the politics of redesigns and strategies for handling them from several perspectives.

The first order of business when contemplating a redesign is deciding whether a new format is warranted at all. A redesign is not a panacea, and a new format, by itself, will not enliven a staff that has grown tired of the topic and predictable in the information it presents. In short, a redesign does not replace a long vacation, if one is needed.

For other magazines, though, whose format is laden with long-out-of-fashion fonts, no-longer-hip colors, and regular features that have grown stale, it is well past time. It is often such magazines that find the prospect of reinvention most difficult, however. Why? They lack the expertise or the resources to redesign; otherwise they would have done it before they got to such a desperate state. The desktop-publishing revolution (and then the switch to digital photography and PDF workflow) allowed many magazines to trim their staffs. The advertising drought after 9/11 and a paper market in flux has since forced many more to do so. While some of the hardest-hit magazines have managed to keep publishing, they do so in a diminished form. Small titles with staffs of three or four do not have a lot of extra time for the significant extraproduction cycle effort required for even the smoothest of reinventions.

Other magazines—particularly large newsstand titles—seem to change design every three or four years. Even daily newspapers, once icons of stability (and for which a redesign is a truly Herculean effort) have caught the bug. The credit (or the blame) for this quickening of the redesign cycle goes to the Web, according to many of the experts I've talked to. The Internet, with its vast variety, has raised the overall level of visual literacy and created an expectation for freshness among readers. Magazines must run to stay in place. Personally, I think the fear that motivates frequent reinvention is an overreaction, albeit one with which we can all sympathize. Traditional magazine publishing is adapting—sometimes painfully—to the existence of unwanted competition from a new medium (which even now has not reached its full potential). However, publishing once adapted to radio and the movies. All of these adapted to television and then cable television, and no deaths yet under the media big top. Magazines (and newspapers) are, however, going through an uncomfortable transitional period.

In truth, there are no hard and fast rules about how often to redesign. *Magazineland* is full of monuments to stability and consistency—publications that remain essentially unchanged for years or decades and prosper. Word-driven publications such as *Harper's*, the *Week*, and the *Economist* fit into this category. Stalwarts *National Geographic* and the *New Yorker*, likewise, have evolved slowly enough not to shake up readers. Other magazines, such as *Zoetrope: All-Story*, have no consistent format issue-to-issue. Readers seem to be adaptable to both approaches.

Because every redesign comes with risk as well as promise, the decision to redesign should be entered with eyes open. There are always reasons to redesign now, but the reasons to proceed rarely come without a counterargument. Changing with the times is essential for survival, but in the short term it can alienate the current readership and create an opening for a competitor—both worrisome prospects, particularly for small special-interest titles that may rely on a market too small for division.

Bad Reasons to Redesign

STAFF BOREDOM. There is no better reason to redesign than reader boredom. Staff boredom, on the other hand, is best ignored—at least for a while. A typical staff member devotes anywhere from 160 to 200 hours a month working to put out each monthly issue. The typical reader will spend anywhere from fifteen minutes to three hours with the printed artifact of that process. It is even likely that the staff will be a little tired of a new design before its premiere, thanks to all the hours that went into the format's preparation. Under the best of circumstances, staff instinct about when a format has passed its sell-by date will be distorted; it should not be trusted as the only indicator of when to make a change.

STAFF CHANGES. There are lots of times when a new publisher, editor, or design director will come into an organization and leverage his or her outsider perspective and energy to become the driving force for an overdue or otherwise needed redesign. There are other times when a new person advocates changes to make the publication more personally comfortable or simply to be able to point to a major accomplishment under his or her stewardship. Because a redesign can come at the expense of a possibly fragile reader relationship, the "accomplishment" of a redesign can be more perception than reality.

How can you tell the difference between ego and vision? It is tempting to suggest that it is a bad sign if a magazine is being pushed toward the new staffer's previous publication, but it's likely that the new staffer has been hired, in part, because of his or her success in a past job. If the two magazines have or seek comparable readerships, the re-creation of some aspect of a previous tenure may be what's called for. It is also tempting to suggest that the new staffer take some time before proceeding—really get to understand the magazine before instituting any changes. This cautious approach is workable at most special-topic and controlled-circulation titles, where the staff members tend to have specialized expertise and long tenures. In the go-go New York publishing world, where staffers are fired and replacements hired in a matter of days, the reflective approach can be deadly.

However, it must be said that arbitrary changes are likely to be poor changes. This is not a design example, but it serves to illustrate the point: One editor I knew attempted to switch his new magazine's stylebook (the agreed-upon collection of grammar and usage rules) from University of Chicago to Associated Press in the middle of his first production cycle. The two standards are roughly comparable, but very different in application. It was a change meant to benefit the new staffer, not the publication. The disruption caused by one person adapting (even a high-level staffer) is less than the havoc caused by the forced and abrupt derangement of an entire staff. Style changes—whether visual or textural—often result in a period of uncertainty during which mistakes can more easily make it into print.

When staffers get together to determine the direction of a redesign, there is a mute personality in the room as significant as anyone's: the personality of the magazine. Even publications with similar readerships can have very different souls. If the new staffer is an advocate for respecting that essence and attitude (which is deeper than the list of departments, the typeface, and the color palette), a redesign is more likely to be solid.

Looking Beyond the Printed Page

I started this book not entirely certain that the topic of magazine design would fill an entire volume. Now, I can't help thinking about all the viewpoints that could not be part of this dialogue because there wasn't room. However, magazines tend to fall into a few broad areas regardless of topic and target audience. I have tried to bring a range of voices from magazines at different places on the publishing spectrum.

BUDGET. Most publications are not *Vanity Fair.* The big New York–based newsstand magazines have large staffs, vast art budgets, and long production cycles; these publications typically have several issues in progress at once. Some smaller magazines have little or no money for art, and only a few days to turn edited text into inviting pages. When redesigning a magazine, designers need to pay attention to the realities of budget and schedule; although some of those realities may be open to adjustment during the process.

MOTIVATION. Everyone hopes his or her magazine will prosper. Nevertheless, financial success (or even remaining in business in a year's time) is unlikely enough for most start-ups that profit is rarely the sole motivating factor. Passion for the topic or the community being served, plus faith that what interests the staff will break through the noise and connect to a larger audience, is what drives the phenomenal amount of research, planning, and work necessary for the typical launch. Passion is power: it has driven many of the most successful publications against long odds.

Passionate publications exist in sharp contrast to many of the largest newsstand magazines, where there is scant difference between the advertising and the editorial content. "Special deals" drive the advertiser–publisher relationship at large publishing houses, as does product placement—the paid appearance of products and services within an editorial context. At many national magazines—particularly at gender-specific magazines—the firewall has been entirely shattered. I do not mean to suggest that big magazines do not offer value; product placements and special deals fuel some sumptuous photo shoots, breathtaking designs, and, in exceptional cases, ambitious and enterprising journalism. Deals have also helped keep large national titles affordable. One shudders at what the September *Vogue* would cost if the reader paid the full cost of producing it. On the other hand, it seems clear that special deals have blunted some diversity of editorial voice.

BUSINESS MODEL. A trip to Borders reveals a breathtaking array of publications. These range from titles that sell more than a million each month, such as *People*, to magazines that sell only a few thousand on the newsstand, such as the *Bulletin of the Atomic Scientists.* Some have huge budgets; others rely on volunteer contributors and free art. From the richest to the poorest, these are all consumer magazines available to anyone who cares to dig an issue out of the rack and pay for it. Of course, you must also find it. Even a well-stocked Borders has only a fraction of available consumer titles.

But these titles represent a tiny percentage of publishing; most magazines are controlled-circulation titles, so called because they are available free, but only to readers who meet a specific profile—usually because of what they do for a living. Instead of a subscription fee, these publications require readers to fill out and sign a survey asking about the size of their organization and their influence over purchasing decisions. Controlled-circulation publications are successful because they offer a great deal to both readers and advertisers: readers get monthly news and information about their field for free, and advertisers get to hawk their wares specifically to customers who might be interested. The value of such "precision media buys" is obvious when you look at the range of publications within a single field. Medicines are promoted through titles aimed at doctors; multi-million-dollar medical equipment is sold through titles aimed at hospital administrators.

In addition to business-to-business publications, the other major category of controlled-circulation publication is membership or association based. Some association magazines serve roughly the same purpose as business-to-business titles, providing news about goings-on within an industry; others build affinity around political, social, or cultural concerns. As a rule, the production values at a controlled-circulation publication are lower than for a successful consumer title, but that's not always the case. *National Geographic* is probably the most obvious example of an expensively produced controlled-circulation title. Although it is now available on the newsstand, for years the magazine was the principal benefit of membership in the National Geographic Society. Many of the best-controlled titles are good enough to have a secondary life on the newsstand, and some do—*Preservation*, *AARP*, and *Smithsonian*, for example. Also, a number of newsstand magazines—particularly business titles—round out their readerships with a small, often highly prosperous controlled readership that sometimes gets copies with ads just for them.

Finally, a growing sector of the magazine world is referred to as "custom publishing." Custom magazines are produced or distributed by companies whose principal business is something other than publishing. While many custom publications accept advertising and are profitable in and of themselves, they are usually motivated primarily by a desire to maintain and build consumer loyalty or otherwise advance the objectives of the parent company. Airline magazines are among the most familiar custom publications, but car companies and other manufacturers, hotel chains, cable companies, large hospitals, shopping malls, and other kinds of entities have custom magazines.

Many if not most custom magazines are editorially limp—they speak in a voice blunted by public-relations departments that excise the slightest whiff of offense or controversy from the pages. These magazines end up closer to brochures or long advertisements than magazines. However, some custom publications are fine magazines, which rise above what is often a limited mission to publish engaging articles on a range of topics. Air Canada's *enRoute* and the recently revived Benetton *Colors* come to mind.

The best part about editing this book was that it gave me a reason to call many of my heroes in publishing and design. Despite starting each conversation just short of coherence, I invariably found a warm, knowledgeable person on the other end of the phone line, willing to discuss design and magazine issues with a stranger. Many agreed (despite the demands of working for a monthly title or running a business) to contribute an essay or sit for an interview; others informed and expanded on my views. I want to thank the contributors first of all for making this project possible.

A special thanks to my longtime friend and editor Caroline Schweiter who gave careful attention to the chapters I wrote. Any mistakes, however, are fully my own responsibility.

I'd also like to give thanks to Peter Harkness who dismissed any concerns about printing an internal document and allowed me to reproduce the design brief for *Governing*, as well as the rest of my colleagues at the magazine, who were supportive despite my occasional distraction as I worked on this book—especially Alan Ehrenhalt, Bonnie Becker, Anne Jordan, Pam Johnson, Elder Witt, and Jennifer Royal Anderson.

Thanks are due to Sarah and Adam Horowitz and Herbert Winkler for the use of archival material, and additional gratitude goes to all my colleagues at George Mason University, particularly my former chairman, Scott Martin, who encouraged my writing, and my current chairman, Harold Linton, who expedited my study leave to give me the time to complete the book. Thanks also go to so many others who offered me support and encouragement, among them Tom Ashcroft, Lynn Constantine, Walter Kravitz, Helen Fredrick, Shanshan Cui, Peggy Fenwick, Gail Scott White, Renee Sandell, Don Starr, Paula Crawford, Suzanne Carbonneau, Chawky Frenn, Suzanne Scott, Kirby Malone, Maria Karametou, Sue Wrbican, and Peter Winant.

Is it appropriate to write a mushy personal dedication to an edited volume? Alas, I think not, but I would be remiss if I didn't also give loving thanks to my family—Jan, Sarah, Emily, Stanley, Linda, and Jason—for everything.

SECTION 1

Beginning

I've never seen a publication's staff decide to undertake a redesign without some doubts. In most cases, there's general agreement that something needs to be done, that the old design is dated or is no longer serving the content. But, as in any marriage, knowing that it's over doesn't make the divorce any less messy, nor the search for a new partner any less of a journey into the unknown. Other major initiatives, a lack of time or resources, or a shortage of in-house talent can all postpone the decision to begin the process.

Caution is often justified. If the written content of a publication is in flux, if budget necessitates that an inexperienced in-house designer would be revisiting a dated but otherwise effective format, or if upper-masthead staff changes are on the horizon, the time may not be right. It's better to postpone than do two redesigns in quick succession—the first one will be perceived by readers as a failure.

There is a boatload of magazines that never find the time or the resources to undertake a redesign. But for most publications, a regular redesign has become a part of life. Timing will always be a factor, however. The staff should have a clear idea of what they hope the redesign will accomplish and how and if the essence of the magazine will change before there's any thought of colors or typefaces.

Redesign, Anyone? 1

JOHN BRADY

I CAN REMEMBER WHEN A MAGAZINE DESIGN WAS good for five to seven years. Some publishers liked to extend that even further. "If it ain't broke, don't fix it," was the standard attitude. Not today.

More than ever before, a magazine is a work in progress. If your book looks the same as it did three years ago, it's probably time to consider a new look. If you are editing for a high tech or youthful audience, two years is the norm. The mantra has become, "If it ain't broke, improve it anyway."

We live in an age of tremendous change, and many readers lose interest in a publication that looks as though it is standing still. There are other reasons for considering a redesign as well. In the past three years, have you noticed any of the following?

1. Has your editorial message changed? A magazine can stumble if there is a lack of focus and the old editorial game plan is just that: old.

2. Has your audience changed? If so, bring current and future readers into the plan. Remember, many young members of your audience today are visual learners. Measure your editorial/visual ratio, for instance. How much of each editorial page is devoted to text? How much to visuals?

3. Has your staff changed? This may be an opportunity to take advantage of incoming talent for new design ideas.

4. Have your production or distribution methods changed? If you are changing from Quark to InDesign, for instance, you might as well take a fresh look at the design as you go about the task of creating new templates. If you are going to newsstand or display racks, likewise, you will need to rethink your cover design.

5. Have reader attitudes changed? If readership starts to slip, do a survey. Find out why readers are dropping and if there are things that can be done in a redesign to keep everyone in their seats.

6. Have advertiser attitudes changed? If reps come back with complaints from advertisers or with "no thanks" from prospects because you don't look quite cool enough, you've got a problem that is anything but cool.

7. Has your competition changed? A dozing competitor can transform overnight with fresh ideas and a new design, thus competing more aggressively for ad revenue.

Notice that change is part of every question. If you answered "yes" to any of the seven, a redesign may be in your future. Even if you answered "no" and are leading your category, a redesign may be a smart strategy for staying ahead. Leaders are proactive. They deal with a problem before it becomes one.

A Few More Points to Ponder

Should the new design be implemented piecemeal or all at once? A redesign is best done all at once, with much editorial thunder. I have found that the notion that piecemeal is easier doesn't hold up. Problems abound when you are implementing the old along with the new, not to mention the schizoid effect it can have on readers.

In-house or out? A redesign can be done in-house if you have the talent and the time, but you may not get the best work from an exhausted staff. Teaming with an outside designer can become a collaborative experience. Also, the outsider can see what others are blinded to by familiarity.

How much time will it take? Four to six months, start to finish. For your "premier" issue, allow twice the normal production time for the learning curve of a new design.

What will it cost? Some redesigns may require focus groups (which are expensive). Some call for testing a prototype among advertisers before rolling out the premier issue. Other variables include new media kits, letterhead, business cards, and design changes on the Web site. A lean and mean guesstimate: Take two to three months of your editor's salary plus benefits, add it to your art director's salary plus benefits for the same period, and that is the approximate cost of going from an idea to a totally new look.

Designing Small Magazines of Ideas

2

ALISSA LEVIN

All magazines are unique, but small magazines of ideas—literary journals, academic publications, and independent political and culture magazines—have design and production challenges all their own. When embarking on a redesign, these small magazines share many of the same goals as large publications: developing a stronger editorial voice, updating their look and feel, broadening their readerships, improving their work flow. But small, independent magazines are defined by having small staffs and limited (or nonexistent) art budgets. Fortunately, they are also blessed with passionate editors and specialized content, and are not censured or limited by the demands of advertisers.

A small publication is also identified by its loyal audience—a small but truly engaged group of readers with significant personal or professional interest in the content. The design's priority is to create an environment that is accessible and respectful of the reader. When a design is quietly restrained—drawing the attention to the *ideas* in the magazine—it is the most successful.

Below is a list of design strategies for these niche magazines. Addressed individually, each can improve a publication tremendously. Tackled together, the list represents a full-scale redesign.

Define Mission and Editorial Direction

Before publishers, editors, and designers analyze a magazine's look and feel, the mission and goals of the magazine must be established. Regardless of a publication's size and subject, critical questions need to be answered: How has the content evolved over the years? Who is the current competition? How has the readership changed? How has the publication's Web presence affected the print edition? And finally: Does the design of the magazine reflect its editorial voice?

Armed with the responses to these questions, the redesign process can begin.

Examine Size, Paper, and Use of Color

At the earliest stage of a redesign, it is wise to explore three production specifications: trim size, paper stock, and use of color. Even the slightest reduction in trim can yield significant savings, both in paper cost and in mailing. Often the paper stock's weight, color, and texture are taken for granted, but it is worthwhile to investigate alternatives not only for cost, but for look and feel as well. Even when the decision to change the trim or paper has cost-saving origins, both changes can help redefine the magazine's identity. For example, a smaller size becomes a distinctive characteristic, helping set apart the magazine from its competition.

It is also important to evaluate the use of color. For most large magazines, and even for some small magazines, four-color (CMYK) printing is an assumed production expense. Publications with smaller printing budgets tend to use two colors throughout (generally black and a spot color), yet a second color is usually unnecessary. It often feels tacked on or is poorly integrated into the layout. With the right typography, black ink alone can create color on the page. And if the budget is limited, investing in one or two full-color signatures to reproduce some art in full color gives a stronger visual impact than sprinkling a single color throughout. Black-and-white art can be used to illustrate departments, while full-color art is best saved for the feature well, where more space can be devoted to it.

Maximize the Art Budget

It is not unusual for the staff of a small magazine to work without a predetermined art budget. When art is purchased without a budget in mind, magazines often end up spending more than they expect due to inaccurate estimates and hasty decisions. Stock art can be deceptively expensive and rates vary greatly from agency to agency. Another common though well-intentioned mistake is using free art (publicity photos, head shots, or reproductions of book jackets, for example), which usually adds pointless clutter and lends a feeling of desperation to the pages. Regardless of its size, a budget must be established in order to develop a realistic strategy for art direction and art research.

It is also imperative that the magazine is designed with its art budget in mind, taking into consideration the rhythm and flow of an entire issue. With a modest budget, less is more. Art direction should focus on commissioning a few spectacular pieces rather than spreading the budget too thin. Consider whether each feature needs to have a piece of art, and if standing art can be commissioned for recurring departments. Illustration and photography provide natural resting places for the reader, and their placement is an opportunity to highlight an important feature. Innovative typographic solutions for headlines can also provide drama to significant features without the expense of purchasing art. Departments, and shorter features that do not have artwork, should have uniform treatments for headlines, subheads, and pull quotes, establishing a consistent look and feel to the magazine.

Create Hierarchy

The pacing of the magazine must express the editorial hierarchy. Designers and editors work closely to decide where the visual emphasis should be and how best to organize the various departments and sections. Meanwhile, all the elements of the magazine should be evaluated:

LOGO. The logo sets the tone of the magazine and should inspire the design of both the cover and the interior. Often the logos of small intellectual magazines, especially academic journals, do not provide a strong enough anchor for the cover: The typography is frequently poorly executed or too delicate. If this is the case, it is preferable for a publication to develop a new or updated logo in conjunction with a redesign.

COVER. The logo and the cover fonts must complement each other—it is important that they work together to create both contrast and balance. Consistent use of typography and art on the cover strengthens the magazine's recognition factor, which is critical on the newsstand. Also, the cover art should not attempt to portray every article in the magazine; instead, it should have a strong focal point expressing the main feature article or overall theme of the issue. Finally, continuity in mood and style between the cover and the interior is also important.

DEPARTMENTS AND FEATURES. Departments are short sections that provide information in brief, while the feature well is an opportunity to slow down the pace and pull the reader into longer articles. One of the most common mistakes small intellectual magazines make is a lack of visual differentiation between departments and features. Often, departments have no clear entry points and no graphic indications signaling a new section. As a result, columns, departments, and features all blend into each other. This lack of discernible organization is confusing for the reader and gives the magazine a feeling of disorder. Consistent openers and dedicated layouts for columns and departments help distinguish departments from features. A redesign is also an ideal time to create new sections that bookend each issue. For example, several short articles can be joined together to create a department in the front of the magazine, creating a space for different points of view and breathing a new life into the magazine.

TABLE OF CONTENTS. Readers should be able to easily locate everything they are looking for in the table of contents, including their favorite writers. For many small magazines, the design of the table of contents is an afterthought, but even for readers who do not dwell on the page, it is valuable for establishing the hierarchy and tone of the magazine.

Establish an Interior Grid

Another typical mistake of small magazines is an inconsistent or limited grid. Single-, two-, three-, and four-column layouts may not maintain the same margins. Or the entire magazine might be designed on a single column width, resulting in mechanical, monotonous pacing.

The grid should be the foundation of the design. Regular margins and different column widths for departments and features yield a more thoughtful and dynamic magazine. Inexperienced designers often think of the grid as limiting, but once the structure is established, it is possible to use it to create limitless variety, for example adding white space to create breath and color on the pages. This is especially true of the feature well, where there is more freedom to loosen certain design constraints while maintaining the grid.

Refine Typography

The typography is the soul of the magazine and requires the most nurturing. The lack of typographic standards, superfluous fonts, and awkwardly paired typefaces are a few of the offenses often committed. Magazines with thoughtless type can look unkempt, distracting readers and making them uncomfortable. Badly styled type is hard to read.

Fortunately, with the proper attention to detail, order can be restored. After the selection of an appropriate body typeface—a typeface that is well matched to the spirit of the magazine—its proportions and styling must be carefully considered: its weight and leading, as well as hyphenation and justification. It is also essential that the body text use proper small caps and old-style numbers (their ascenders and descenders blend more evenly into the rest of the text). Attention to these details improves the legibility of the page and keeps the reader engaged and focused on the content.

The integration of a secondary typeface (usually a sans serif) and display fonts rounds out the typographic essentials. Drop caps, pull quotes, folios, slugs, and other type elements, used consistently, can also help give the magazine a distinct graphic personality.

Use Ads Strategically

Small, independent magazines often have a large number of partial ads combined with an overall layout that fails to distinguish between the ads and the editorial content. This problem occurs when a magazine's grid is ill-defined and the partial ads are placed haphazardly, wherever they fit.

The placement of ads (partial and full-page) should enhance the rhythm and pacing of the magazine, not interfere with it. Ads should be placed opposite the openers to departments or sections, and never in the middle of a section or in the feature well. Half-page ads should be stacked together to create full pages, and quarter-page ads should be paired to create half-pagers. Redundant ad sizes should be eliminated; for example, there is no need to offer a half-page vertical ad size in addition to a half-page horizontal.

Organize Work Flow

Small magazines frequently work with outside design consultants or design studios that help editors not only navigate the redesign process, but streamline the production of each issue as well. After the redesign, a design studio often continues to provide ongoing art direction and design for subsequent issues. Alternately, the redesign can be conceived with the goal of making the magazine entirely self-sufficient in its design and production. Regardless of which route the magazine takes for subsequent issues, the consultant can provide training and job descriptions for in-house staff, outlining design and production responsibilities. More efficient work flow can save valuable time and resources for a small staff.

Other production improvements that should be evaluated include updating technology and software (switching from Quark to InDesign, for example), sending hi-res PDFs directly to the printer, and streamlining how content is published to the Web.

Just as all magazines are unique, the redesign process must be customized to fit a publication's individual needs and resources. The strategies outlined in this article are a starting point when considering how to improve the look and feel of small magazines of ideas.

Imitation, Inc. 3

Gallagher Paper Collectibles Offers Design Ideas for Magazine Publishers

GREG LINDSAY

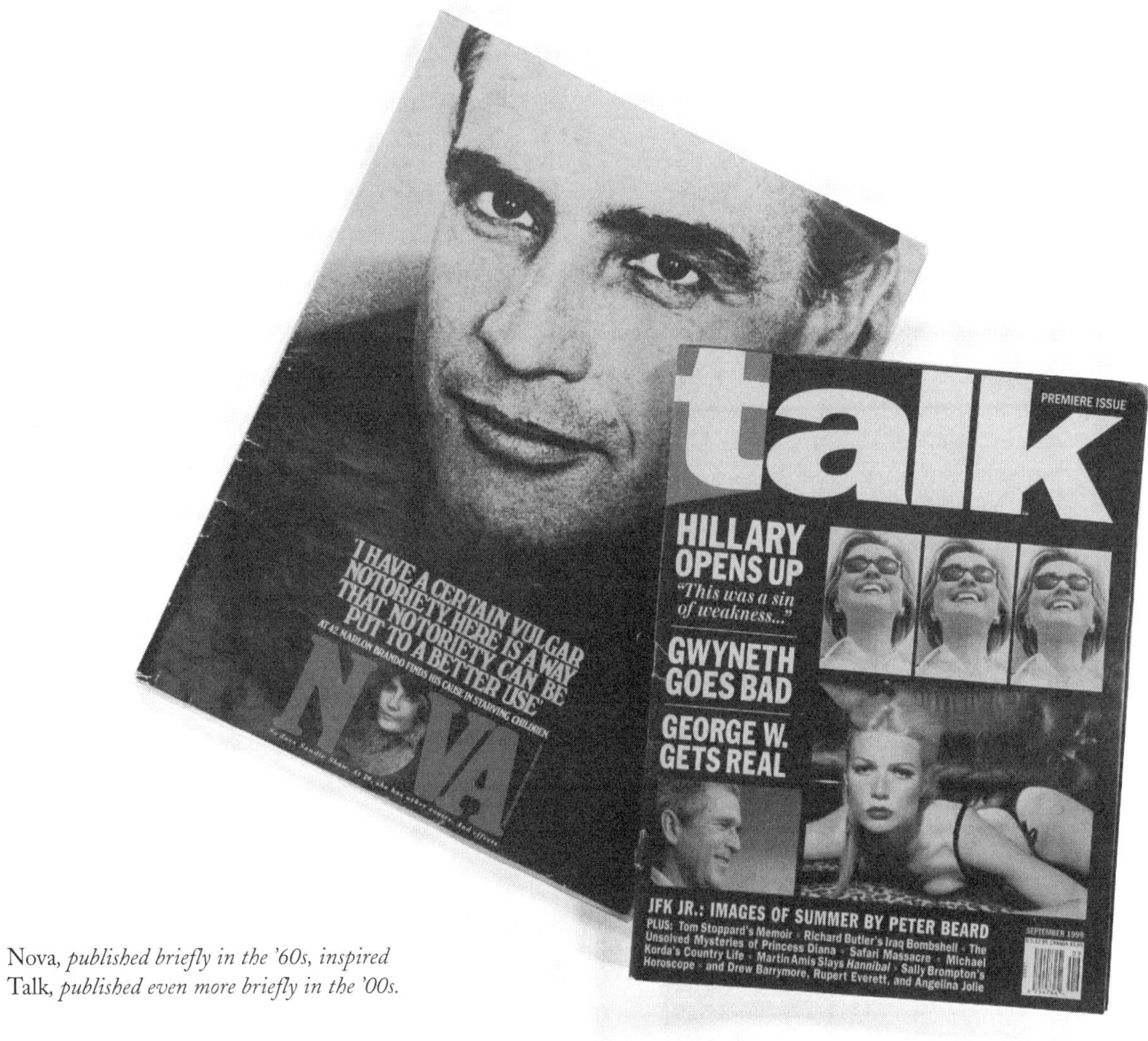

Nova, *published briefly in the '60s, inspired* Talk, *published even more briefly in the '00s.*

ON A QUIET STREET IN THE EAST VILLAGE, UNDER a metal sidewalk grate, lies the magazine industry's not-so-best-kept design secret: Gallagher Paper Collectibles. This store below the street houses a dizzying archive of vintage magazines—everything from one-hundred-year-old *Harper's Bazaars* to a complete collection of *Flair*, a lushly produced magazine from the fifties. But the buzz about Gallagher's has less to do with the actual stash and more to do with who's been in to riffle through it. Considered the muse of the fashion and design worlds, this is the place to spend an afternoon if you're dying to get a read on the next big design trend, or if you just enjoy gossip about who's stealing what from whom.

So which magazine czars have been spotted there recently? Designer Raul Martinez (formerly of *Vogue* fame); ex-*Mademoiselle* editor Gabe Doppelt; fashion photographer Steven Meisel; *Harper's Bazaar*'s creative director Stephen Gan; and *Another Magazine*'s creative director Alex Wiederin. Word is they're buying lots of

European men's and women's fashion magazines from the sixties—obscure titles such as *Nova, Twen,* and *Town. Real Simple*'s creative director Robert Newman also dropped by to pick up back issues of *House and Garden* and an array of women's service magazines from the fifties. Newman, like his peers, says he was shopping for inspiration. The Seven Sisters magazines from half a century ago "have these huge, oversize lush drawings, as elegant as they could be," he says. "They really were escapism. To that extent, we try to copy that with *Real Simple*."

The design genius buried in Gallagher's stacks can often be rediscovered on today's magazine racks. But in this postmodern age, judicious recycling isn't about shameless copying. It's a knowing wink to pop culture or an honest homage to great magazine art directors from the past. It's about riffing off what's worked. And when you consider the incredible pressure on newsstand performance, it's easy to see why everyone from *Vogue* photographer Richard Avedon to *Harper's Bazaar*'s ex-editor Kate Betts has sat in Gallagher's basement searching for layouts and logos that once reigned at the newsstand.

"Why not reinvent what was beautiful?" asks the store's owner, Mike Gallagher. "Why not look back at something brilliant and put a twist on it?" A forty-one-year-old, garrulous, charming, and very well-connected former child actor, Gallagher founded his business in 1990 when he realized he could make a living selling old issues of fashion classics. In this dank retail shop, a 1960s *Vogue* goes for $75 and a copy of *Twen* will cost you $125. One year, fashion designer Donna Karan dropped $150,000 on what amounts to old newsprint.

Gallagher's encyclopedic knowledge of his inventory has made him a valuable asset to the fashion world's monied and fabulously chic. His elite clientele of fashion designers, such as Karan, Marc Jacobs, and Anna Sui, make sure he has a front-row seat to their shows. He's on the guest list of the best parties in and out of town. (He was recently invited to a soiree in Paris thrown by American *Vogue* creative director Grace Coddington.) Gallagher reveres his customers and, as such, Carrie Donovan, once an editor for the *New York Times Magazine* and *Vogue*, bequeathed to the collector eleven hundred documents from her personal archives before she died last year. "Half that went straight into my personal library," Gallagher says. The rest was scattered around his subterranean maze of musty photography books and magazines.

A shameless name-dropper, Gallagher loves to let you know who he knows, and isn't shy about telling tales, especially if they're about him. He describes the time one budding fashionista met him at the Paris shows and stared blankly, having never heard of his store. Fashion journalist Tim Blanks rescued him when, upon spotting him, began yelling, "Gallagher's! My favorite store!" "Then some guy from Bergdorf's started saying the same thing. Then somebody else," Gallagher says. Fashion's corporate players certainly know who he is: The fashion conglomerate LVMH recently made Gallagher a seven-figure offer for the entire store. He turned it down.

But the role he most relishes is historian. Gallagher can trace the lineage of the most obscure design trends, and he takes pride in connecting the past with the present. "I went in there once," Stephen Gan says, "and [Gallagher] said, 'I heard you're doing *Bazaar* now—let me show you the magazine where Kate Betts's logo came from.'"

Gallagher, like most students of magazine design, knows that *Harper's Bazaar* has a long history of borrowing from the past—mainly its own. When Liz Tilberis took over in 1992, she brought creative director Fabien Baron with her. In an effort to restore the magazine to its former glory, Baron looked back to the techniques of famed art director Alexey Brodovitch, who steered the title's creative direction from the thirties through the fifties. Baron commissioned a modern updating of the title's signature logo, reconstructed a modernized version of Didot typeface, and drew upon Brodovitch's designs to give his own work continuity while dragging it into the nineties.

When Kate Betts stepped in as editor, she hired design consultant Michael Grossman, who at her direction shelved the logo and filled in Baron's white space. The goal, says Grossman, was a "newsier" look. Today, Glenda Bailey and her design team are again glancing over their shoulders to the old *Bazaar*. Gan has revived the logo and is sticking to its classical past—but with restraint. Gan says only 10 percent of the present design winks backward. When it comes to borrowing, he stresses, "If you overdo it, you'll be massacred."

Referencing the past is paying off, Gan claims. After a decade of sliding newsstand sales, he reports that single-copy figures are up for the first half of the year, although he won't say by how much.

How Much Is Too Much?

Artful adoption can be especially beneficial when constructing a new magazine. A flip through musty classics can provide a touchstone for the next generation, says Newman, who, before joining the cast at *Real Simple*, designed the now-defunct *Inside* magazine. In one development session, Newman sat down with *Inside* cochairman Kurt Andersen to brainstorm the architecture of the front-of-book section. "And the first thing Kurt said was 'I want it to be like *Time* was in the sixties,' where they did small headlines and snaked text all the way through," Newman says. "That got me thinking about sixties magazines." So he sought out ancient issues of *Ramparts* and *Fact*—a pair of more left-leaning newsmagazines from that decade. "That was definitely an inspiration," he says. "To me, that's the most perfect kind of legitimate reference, where you look at stuff and adapt it to the modern-day experience of reading a magazine."

Those who fail to graft modern techniques onto the borrowed past, however, risk alienating audiences. Magazine design has changed drastically in the past ten years, due to the full flowering of desktop publishing. Today's page-layout software allows designers to create graphically dense spreads with minimal extra effort. In contrast, designs that predate the Macintosh are sparse in appearance and can look basic and unrefined next to contemporary layouts. "Referencing the visual past makes sense as a jumping-off point," says *Esquire*'s design director John Korpics. "But an art director can't ignore the problems and needs of the present." In fact, Korpics believes *Bazaar*'s Gan is guilty of this very mistake. "He seems to be doing yet another incarnation of the original *Bazaar*, again ignoring the readers."

A recent and memorable example of a magazine that many say borrowed too deeply and paid the price is Tina Brown's *Talk*. Design insiders love to dish about the remarkable similarities between the magazine's original design and *Twen*, an influential women's magazine published in 1960s Germany. According to *Talk*'s original associate art director, Teresa Fernandes, Brown instructed the staff to choose typefaces that matched *Twen* as closely as possible and would present designers with copies of the publication, telling them to simply copy. "I remember Tina coming to me, opening a page of *Twen* and telling me 'Duplicate this exactly,'" she says.

Brown readily admits to borrowing heavily from *Twen*'s logo and covers. "That was absolutely intentional. I loved the *Twen* covers," Brown says. "It was very classy. It was powerful. It looked intelligent. It was probably too smart for its day." But she says ideas for *Talk*'s interior design came from elsewhere. "We were always swiping spreads out of different things," she says, particularly from *Nova*, also from the sixties, and Italian *Vogue*. "[Talk's design staff] would always come to me with these huge folders of potential inspirations."

Talk's dark, dense, and highly touted "European-influenced" design was a disappointment on the newsstand. The magazine sold an average of just 150,164 single copies each month in 2000, well below the 247,000 copies promised in 1999 by publisher Ron Galotti. And its sell-through was just 19 percent. "*Talk* sucked," Gallagher snarls. "It reappropriated the past without adding anything new. They just ripped it off."

Modern Problems

While magazine art directors will undoubtedly continue to debate the appropriate, tactful, and judicious practices of plundering from history, there are larger issues afoot, Korpics says. "Trust me, the industry has much bigger problems than a few magazine designers ripping off old looks," he says.

"Today it's the pressure of the bottom line that most impacts the look of a magazine. It's the pressure to sell newsstand copies, please advertisers, use thinner and cheaper paper, use less editorial pages, reduce overall size to fit into newsstand racks and make them cheaper to mail. People can look to the past all they want, but a lot of what worked just won't work today," he says.

In Style's design director Rip Georges agrees. "Much more important than winning design awards is winning at the newsstand. We spent a lot of time trying to make the magazine beautiful, but we also make it work on the newsstand. The solutions are much less artistic than they are commercial. With *In Style*, we were trying to recreate the notion of a woman's magazine, and create something that is not all intimidating." The results have been a hit with readers and advertisers alike.

But the economic pressure to commercialize design may have lasting and damaging consequences, some say. If art-driven titles are pushed out of newsstands or fall victim to advertising shortages, then where will the up-and-coming designers experiment and innovate? "This country has become very unsophisticated visually," says Steven Baillie, creative director of *Surface*. "And I'm not a snob—I grew up in New Jersey. It's all about money here. In Europe, it's about pushing yourself as far as you can go creatively. I keep walking out of every magazine I go to. Nobody can judge creativity in this country."

Still, not all the latest trends are necessarily negative, at least from a design perspective, says David Carson, the famed former art director of *Raygun*. In many ways, mainstream magazines are becoming much more visually driven than they were. For instance, he says, it will be interesting to see how the attention-deficit style of lad magazines such as *Maxim* and *FHM* play out in *Rolling Stone*. "The fact that they've purposely gotten away from good writing and are going to a tabloid feel to keep their audience is, to me, not surprising," Carson says. "That audience is visually oriented, and if you give them five pages of gray type, there's a good chance they won't go through it. That's really a monumental thing."

So far, no lookouts have spotted Jann Wenner leaving Gallagher's with vintage *Maxims* under his arm. But it might not be long before he joins the regulars.

SECTION 2

Restructuring and Updating

How much does a magazine need to change for it to count as a redesign? That depends on the standards you apply. While a change in color palette and signage can do wonders, in many cases such changes are only skin-deep. Once you get used to what's new, you notice that sections have the same names and the same locations. The same old ways of presenting information are still employed.

Such a redesign is not a bad thing—the publication gets to play the role of dear Uncle Ned, a beloved member of the clan, spiffier now that he's abandoned the clothes he'd been wearing since 1970. For publications that function as they should and are growing (or at least not dropping) in circulation, but are a bit out of sync with visual trends, a cosmetic approach to a redesign—a freshening rather than an extreme makeover—can be the right way to go.

But some magazine staffs bring a larger list of objectives to a redesign than just an updating. For them, goals may include recapturing advertisers or readers who have drifted off, reordering a format that has become unwieldy or ineffective in places, or introducing new ways of presenting information. Even so, with this kind of structural redesign there is faith in the fundamental value of the magazine's content. The emphasis is on making the content more inviting and more accessible and revitalized—not in jettisoning it for something new.

There isn't a hard line between a cosmetic updating and a deeper, structural approach—most redesigns come with elements of both. They are both motivated by a desire to keep and expand the current readership, making them distinct from a repositioning which seeks to reach out and capture a fundamentally different market.

Of course, even a purely cosmetic redesign isn't always a simple matter of modifying style sheets—take out Garamond, pop in Century and you're done. Magazine designs are carefully balanced ecosystems, and it can be hard to make minor adjustments without setting off a cascade of visual issues, from leading to word counts to the problem of just how far to go once you get started. However, as exercises in aesthetics rather than strategy, cosmetic redesigns tend to require fewer meetings and less groundwork to get started.

As publications look to redesigns as a way to get some attention in the press and capture the notice of new readers, it's certain that the days of quietly shuffling features in and out of a stable format over the course of decades is gone.

Outside Magazine

4

KATHY MARTIN O'NEIL

IT NEVER MADE SENSE TO READERS—OR TO US editors, for that matter—that the creative juices of *Outside Magazine*, circa 1990, flowed from a jumble of cubicles above an Osco drugstore north of Chicago's Loop. From the late 1970s to the early 1990s, the nation's leading publication for sports, fitness, and adventure travel was conceived, written, designed, and edited not in an al fresco playground like San Francisco or Portland or Denver, but just a few steps from the Clark Street subway and the Cabrini Green housing projects. You're published in Chicago? dumbfounded readers would ask. And then we'd have to recount the story of how Chicagoan publisher Larry Burke launched a magazine named *Mariah*, finagled a deal to buy rival *Outside* from *Rolling Stone* publisher Jann Wenner in 1978, and merged the two. He published the first several issues from the offices of his grandfather's Chicago printing company with, he'll tell you himself, an unauthorized company check or two.

When I joined *Outside* in 1989, many of the editors were Chicagoans—maybe not originally, but we were rooted there. We urban writers and editors could talk the talk of the great outdoors quite convincingly, even without mountains or an ocean in our backyard. We were outdoorsy when and where we could be: We rode our bikes to work, ran marathons, and spent our vacations skiing or hiking. But around the magazine's fifteenth anniversary, Larry Burke decided that we should also walk the walk. We would actually live and create our pages in a setting more representative of the outdoor ethos we preached. In other words, the editors—and the accountants and the ad reps and the circulation gurus—would get out from behind our desks and bike the singletrack, tromp the trails, paddle the whitewater, ski the powder, and bag the peaks we wrote about.

The early nineties were heady times at the office: *Outside* stacked up National Magazine Award nominations for general excellence and rumors flew about Larry's frequent trips to Jackson Hole, Boulder, and Santa Fe. Many of us hoped he would choose Boulder because it was a university town with urban conveniences, intelligentsia, and a potential intern pool, in addition to the requisite opportunities to get vertical in the Rockies. We spent months on tenterhooks, huddled over tables in the art department or over beers at the Dearborn Social Club, speculating on where we'd be next year and which of us would be there: Who would pack up and go West with the magazine, and who would choose to stay in Chicago or head to New York for other magazine jobs? It was more than a matter of our social lives; a magazine like *Outside* is a pretty transparent product of the particular mindsets, personality quirks, and passions of its editors and writers. And the product in 1993 was so, so good. What would it be in 1995 with new editors in the mix? Who would they be? Could we do without key editors who had been with the magazine for years? Could we attract experienced editors from New York–based magazines to some rugged outpost in the West?

The announcement finally came: We were moving to Santa Fe, New Mexico, in May 1994. Burke had bought a ranch and a couple horses, and was scouting land for our new offices. He started wearing cowboy boots and a bolo tie to the office and announced that there would be two organized trips to New Mexico for each employee before the actual move—one to acquaint us with the place and the other for house-hunting.

The first trip came soon, before anyone had tipped his or her hand about whether or not they were willing to move with the magazine—and before editor Mark Bryant had let us know which of us were invited to go. So the editors traveled together as a familiar, established team on what seemed more like a vacation junket than a preview of what life might actually be like if we moved there. We dubbed that trip "the Woo": four fabulous days and nights of fully outfitted adventures, four-star amenities, Santa Fe's best grub, and all-you-could-drink margaritas and beer. We raced bikes up and down thousand-foot inclines. We paddled the Rio Grande and dunked ourselves in its swimming holes. We hiked through clouds above tree line, and drove the High Road up to Taos to shop for coyote art and other Southwestern tchotchkes. We sampled green chiles and black beans at Pascual's, the Coyote Café Cantina, and El Farol. On the last evening, we drove the dirt roads north of Santa Fe to Larry Burke's ranch for a barbecue. Out of the dust kicked up by our rental cars and vans came a sight we'd seen only in spaghetti westerns:

a man in a black Stetson and glinting silver belt buckle, galloping across the piñon and juniper hills on horseback. It was Larry Burke, welcoming us to our new home in the Wild West. Most of us giggled, but you had to admire the man's efforts to show us, in high dramatic style, his vision of an *Outside* lifestyle.

Back in Chicago, many of us started packing, mostly excited about the prospects of a life that would soon include skiing and hiking and rafting and mountain biking. It was hard to get any work done while announcements were made right and left about who was moving to Santa Fe and who was not. Editor Mark Bryant interviewed candidates to replace nearly half of our editorial staff who were switching to writing and consulting editor relationships with *Outside* or setting out for larger prospects in New York City magazines. There were no real hard feelings, since nearly all the editors were invited to go, but there was a fair amount of lame duck falloff in our editing and writing work. For months we attended parties celebrating the arrival of new editors and art staff (Susan Casey, Hampton Sides, Leslie Weeden, and Mike Paterniti, among others), and the departure of old friends (Dan Ferrara, Lisa Chase, Dan Coyle, Don Webster, Pat Prather . . .). To the chagrin of the writing community in Santa Fe who expected to have opportunities to join our staff, we hired all our editors and art staff before the move—most of them from New York or other urban areas. (The only jobs eventually offered to New Mexicans at the time of the move were clerical or business-side.) Many of our new editors moved temporarily to Chicago for a few months before the move so we could get to know each other and gel as an editorial unit. We took our apartment-hunting trips in small groups and often overlapped each other's appointments as we looked at the dismally few Santa Fe casitas affordable on an editor's salary.

There was no letup in our publication timetable. We still worked long hours on Clark Street trying to stockpile stories for that issue we would have to produce during our move. In our personal lives we were busy saying goodbye to Chicago, but at work we were even more busy integrating new people and a magazine redesign that made its debut in stages over the months just before or after the move. To boot we were switching to desktop publishing—no more cutting and pasting text and photos with Exacto knives on light tables. We went all-electronic, however, with just a single freelance Quark typesetter who went home at five. For years after the switch, most of us editors still edited and proofread on paper rather than computer screen, just for peace of mind, since there was no IT person on staff after hours to fix glitches or rescue snatches of text lost in cyberspace.

The wagon train of moving trucks left Chicago on Memorial Day weekend of 1994 and we followed in our cars and trucks. Most of us drove the route in two days via St. Louis and Springfield, Missouri, and then Arkansas, Oklahoma, and the Texas Panhandle across the old Route 66. We trickled into Santa Fe and camped out at the Homewood Suites until our furniture and belongings would arrive. As sad as it was to leave my home and life and the man I would eventually marry in Chicago, I felt nothing but relief to arrive in Santa Fe. The current issue of *Outside*, on disk and in paper proofs, had traveled cross-country on the passenger seat of my Blazer. The editors had joked about handcuffing the issue in a briefcase to my wrist for the move, but it was no joke that I was anxious to hand over the only copy of our precious pages.

We discovered immediately that we'd be camping out not only in our hotel suites, but also at work. Our office building, under construction in an old railyard southwest of the Santa Fe Plaza, wasn't inhabitable yet. But the issue was still due at the printers, so a makeshift office was set up in the basement of our architect's office. The editors, designers, and production department shared one big underground cavern we called "the Bunker," furnished with long cafeteria tables, folding chairs, computers, phones, and a carpet of wires and duct tape. There were no windows, not even a cubicle wall for privacy, and as you walked through the room you could hear all manner of conversations: fact-checkers researching minutiae like what color the truck driven by the mailman in Haines, Alaska, was; editors discussing sensitive word changes with writers; and production managers wrangling over the high cost of paper and deadlines we were probably going to miss. One enduring legend from the Bunker: Amid all that chaos and noise, editor Michael Paterniti was able to finesse Sebastian Junger's reporting and writing of the great *Outside* story that later became the movie *The Perfect Storm*.

One by one, each of us got a call in the Bunker that the moving trucks had arrived at our new homes, and so people would disappear for a few hours to unload, but inevitably return because there was so much work to do. All the promise of a new life in the great outdoors seemed like a tease at first—we barely saw the Sangre de Cristo Mountains in daylight for the first couple of weeks. The Chicago tensions of long hours and frantic deadlines were transferred to Santa Fe, where we had little support system beyond each other. We spent days in the Bunker, focusing intently on the issue at hand, until we would emerge, hungry, in the bright desert evening to explore restaurants and bars and local hiking trails and our friends' cute new adobe apartments and houses.

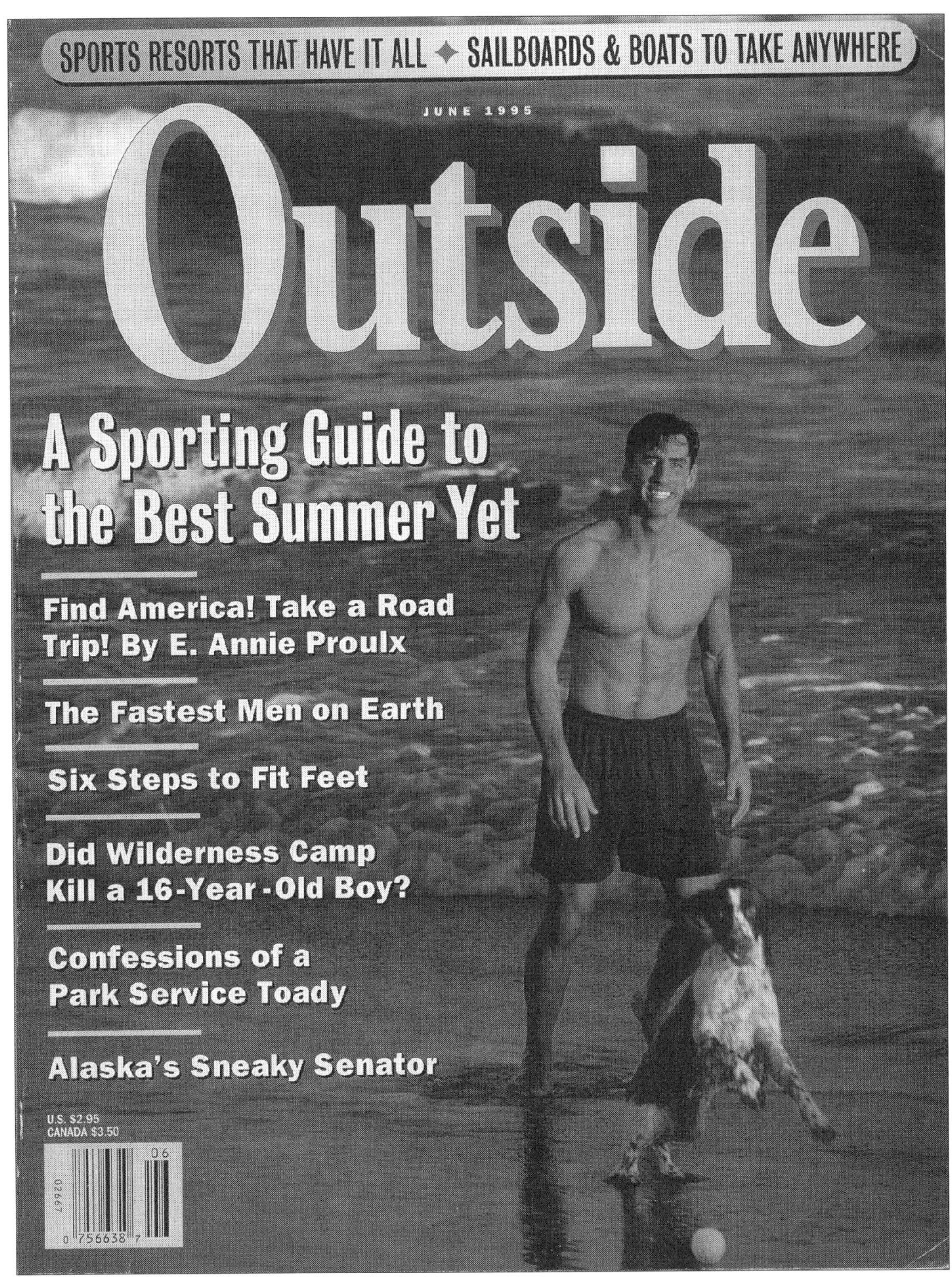

Santa Fe

Culture shocks were inevitable, not just because of the geographical differences between Chicago and Santa Fe, but because it was downright difficult to work in such a small town with such limited business services. On deadline in Chicago we had until 7 p.m. for the last Fed-Ex pickup to take our pages from the office to the printer. That time could be stretched to 9 p.m. if we were willing to drive the package downtown, or 11 p.m. if someone could drive it to the airport. These are important options in a deadline-driven business. In Santa Fe in 1994, the drop-dead last Fed-Ex pickup was at 4:30 p.m. Likewise, in Chicago we were used to leaving work at 9 or 10 p.m. and grabbing a beer or a bite to eat just about anywhere. In Santa Fe, the sidewalks rolled up much earlier and your options for takeout food were about nil after 9 p.m. unless you were willing to drive several miles down commercial Cerrillos Road toward the airport.

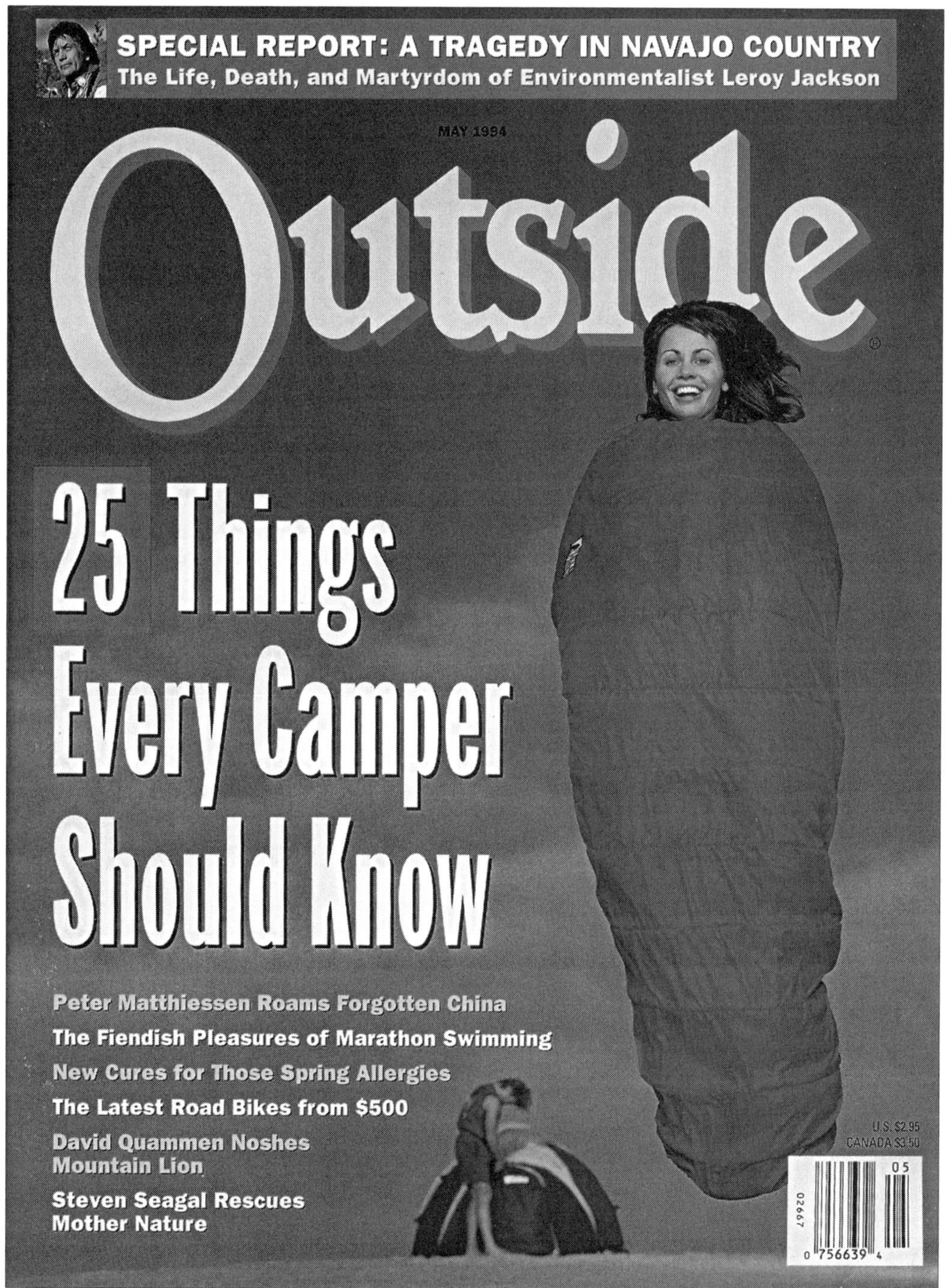

SPECIAL REPORT: A TRAGEDY IN NAVAJO COUNTRY
The Life, Death, and Martyrdom of Environmentalist Leroy Jackson
MAY 1994
Outside
25 Things Every Camper Should Know
Peter Matthiessen Roams Forgotten China
The Fiendish Pleasures of Marathon Swimming
New Cures for Those Spring Allergies
The Latest Road Bikes from $500
David Quammen Noshes Mountain Lion
Steven Seagal Rescues Mother Nature
U.S. $2.95
CANADA $3.50

Chicago

Eventually our office building was completed: a gorgeous two-story adobe castle with balconies and viga ceilings and sturdy Mexican wood tables and chairs in the meeting rooms and a library and windows that actually opened—some to far-off views of the Jemez or Sangre de Cristo Mountains. There was a fireplace in the lobby and a fitness center with a climbing wall and a bike rack in the parking lot. We still worked longish Chicago hours in the early months of our move, but our surroundings were inspirational, we got outside to play more, and pretty soon people were coming back from weekends touting recommendations for new trails to run or bike, great rocks to climb, and cool camping spots to check out.

It's hard to say exactly how much *Outside*'s move to Santa Fe affected the actual writing and appearance of the magazine. The tone of any magazine, the breadth of its content, and the look and feel of its pages are so much more a product of the individuals working on it than the surroundings in which they work. It's the alchemy of the editors' and art staff's minds and sensibilities that ring out on the page. The particular team that made the move from Chicago to Santa Fe was so talented and ambitious that it could be argued that they would have created the same great issues from Chicago or Pittsburgh or Kokomo, Indiana, just as easily as they did from Santa Fe.

But certainly the move had clear and definite value to readers, who no longer shook their heads about the "disconnect" between the lifestyle we touted in our pages and where we wrote those pages from. We finally fit with the perception that *Outside* should be published from somewhere like Santa Fe, and that probably boosted staff creativity and morale through

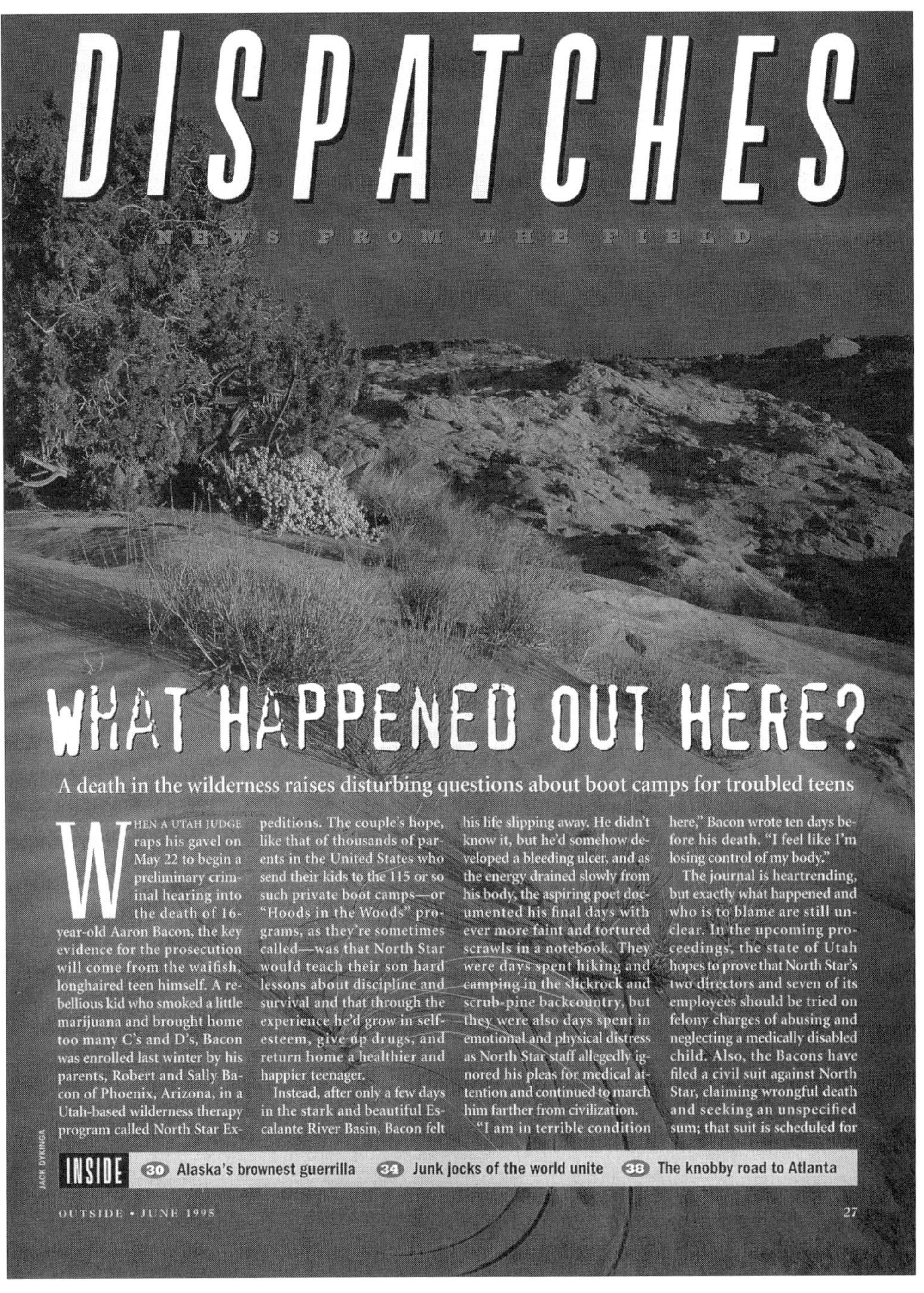

DISPATCHES

NEWS FROM THE FIELD

WHAT HAPPENED OUT HERE?

A death in the wilderness raises disturbing questions about boot camps for troubled teens

When a Utah judge raps his gavel on May 22 to begin a preliminary criminal hearing into the death of 16-year-old Aaron Bacon, the key evidence for the prosecution will come from the waifish, longhaired teen himself. A rebellious kid who smoked a little marijuana and brought home too many C's and D's, Bacon was enrolled last winter by his parents, Robert and Sally Bacon of Phoenix, Arizona, in a Utah-based wilderness therapy program called North Star Expeditions. The couple's hope, like that of thousands of parents in the United States who send their kids to the 115 or so such private boot camps—or "Hoods in the Woods" programs, as they're sometimes called—was that North Star would teach their son hard lessons about discipline and survival and that through the experience he'd grow in self-esteem, give up drugs, and return home a healthier and happier teenager.

Instead, after only a few days in the stark and beautiful Escalante River Basin, Bacon felt his life slipping away. He didn't know it, but he'd somehow developed a bleeding ulcer, and as the energy drained slowly from his body, the aspiring poet documented his final days with ever more faint and tortured scrawls in a notebook. They were days spent hiking and camping in the slickrock and scrub-pine backcountry, but they were also days spent in emotional and physical distress as North Star staff allegedly ignored his pleas for medical attention and continued to march him farther from civilization.

"I am in terrible condition here," Bacon wrote ten days before his death. "I feel like I'm losing control of my body."

The journal is heartrending, but exactly what happened and who is to blame are still unclear. In the upcoming proceedings, the state of Utah hopes to prove that North Star's two directors and seven of its employees should be tried on felony charges of abusing and neglecting a medically disabled child. Also, the Bacons have filed a civil suit against North Star, claiming wrongful death and seeking an unspecified sum; that suit is scheduled for

JACK DYKINGA

INSIDE 30 Alaska's brownest guerrilla 34 Junk jocks of the world unite 38 The knobby road to Atlanta

OUTSIDE • JUNE 1995 27

Santa Fe

all the difficulties and growing pains of a cross-country move. At the most practical level, the move was also *Outside*'s opportunity to make some great hires, to ratchet up the experience base of its editors and designers. The magazine continued to enjoy great success in ad page growth and especially in editorial kudos, racking up National Magazine Award nominations each year, with wins for general excellence three years in a row (1996–1998).

Over the next five or six years, nearly the entire editorial and art staff turned over, but that's a pretty normal lifespan for any magazine staff. A great many of us left Santa Fe; there were no other decent magazine jobs in New Mexico. Some of us moved back home, wherever that was, to get married, start families, or move on to other jobs. It wasn't necessarily that Santa Fe was too limited in size or too crunchy or too remote, though some of us did find out, after a year or

NEWS FROM THE FIELD

LAW

Who's to Blame for Kolob Creek?

Survivors of a fatal Utah canyon trip point the finger at "the people who were supposed to know"

MARK BREWER still has nightmares about Kolob Creek, but he has no doubt about this: Neither he nor his two friends who died there in a July 1993 canyoneering mishap did anything wrong. "We knew if the water was high the canyon wouldn't be safe," says Brewer, a 36-year-old advertising executive from Salt Lake City. "The park said it was fine. It wasn't."

To underscore that point, Brewer, along with four of the five teenage boys who made the trip and the survivors of the two victims, has filed 13 wrongful-death and personal-injury claims against the U.S. Department of the Interior and Zion National Park, whose northern boundary abuts the brief stretch of Kolob Creek Canyon where the tragedy played out. At the heart of what is believed to be a multimillion-dollar claim (neither side will reveal the amount) is a big difference of opinion about who screwed up. Brewer says Zion rangers should have warned his group that spring-runoff release from an upstream dam had made their planned route unsafe. Park officials are under orders not to talk, but in the past Zion spokesmen have been adamant that the park told the group to expect "high, cold water." Some experienced observers—such as Salt Lake City–based guide Dennis Turville, who made the first descent into Kolob Creek Canyon in 1978—are taking an equally dim view of the charges, for reasons that are partially driven by fears that, as canyoneering attracts more participants, other beginners will get into the same kind of trouble.

"Anyone with half a brain wouldn't have brought those kids in there," says Turville. "And once they got there, they made a series of stupid mistakes."

More than likely, the entire debate will wind up before a jury. The Interior Department has until July to respond to the filing, which is required by the Federal Tort Claims Act before Brewer and company can go to civil court. (Their attorneys say that if the claims aren't paid in full, the group will sue.) Meanwhile, the case is being watched at other federal sites where canyoneering is popular. According to Jeff Riffer, a liability expert and author of *Sports and Recreational Injuries*, this is the first canyoneering-related liability action against a national park, and a large cash award could influence permit policies across the West. At the moment these tend to be based on general assessments of whether hikers are equipped to go into the backcountry areas where canyons are found, but Riffer says a high-profile win by Brewer's side might inspire

INSIDE

Misled or misleadered, hiker Shayne Ellis needed an airlift from last summer's whirlpool zone.

OUTSIDE • MAY 1994 27

Chicago

two, that we were more urban at heart. Rather, most of us just came to natural crossroads in our lives and careers. Some of us moved on to other magazine jobs in New York or San Francisco, but many of us turned to writing. That's an obvious career progression for young editors, but I think it might have been heightened by living in such an arts community and being surrounded by natural beauty and an exciting subject area we could specialize in because now we lived and breathed it: the outdoor lifestyle, sports, adventure,

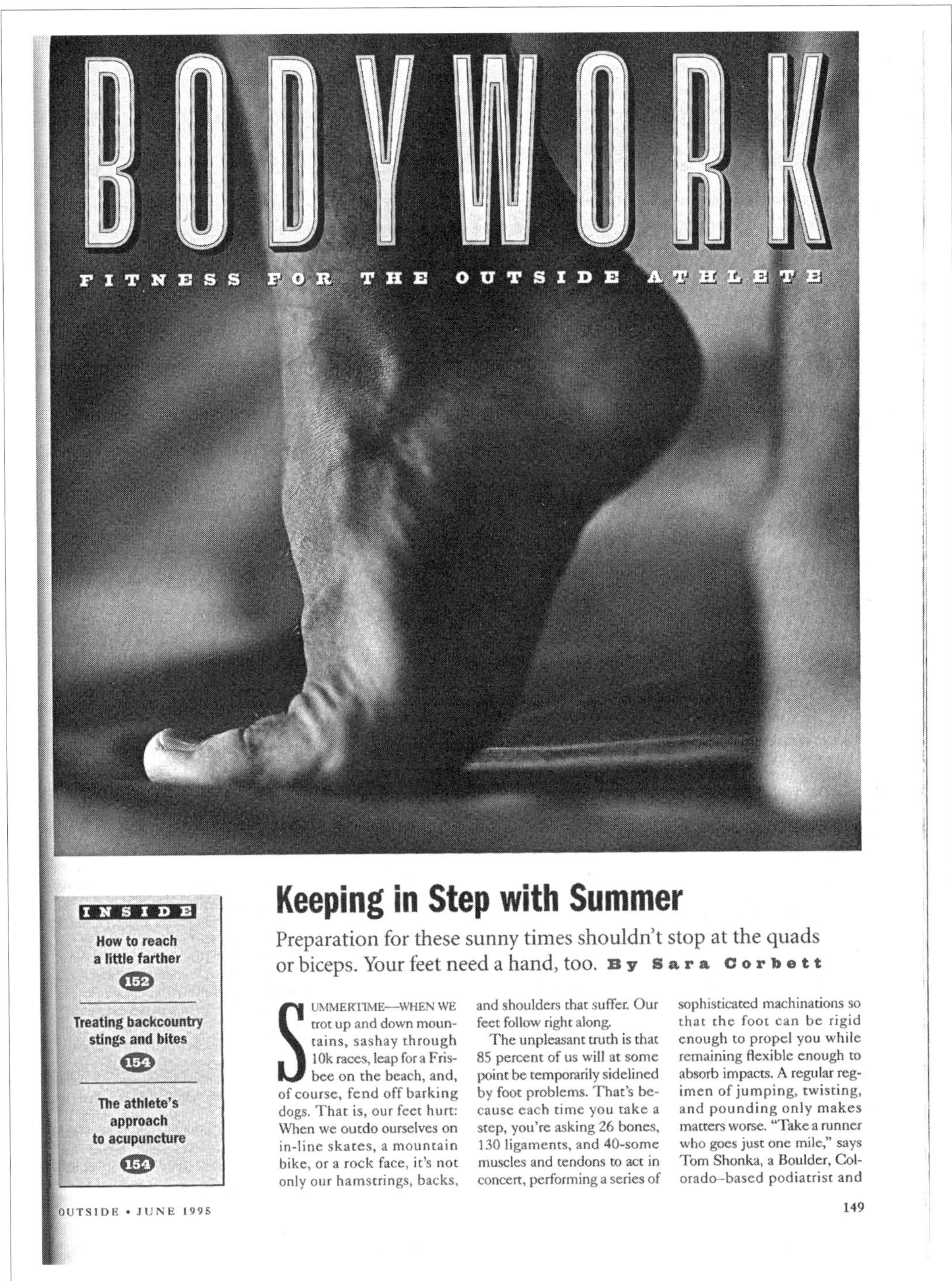
BODYWORK

FITNESS FOR THE OUTSIDE ATHLETE

INSIDE

How to reach a little farther 152

Treating backcountry stings and bites 154

The athlete's approach to acupuncture 154

Keeping in Step with Summer

Preparation for these sunny times shouldn't stop at the quads or biceps. Your feet need a hand, too. By Sara Corbett

SUMMERTIME—WHEN WE trot up and down mountains, sashay through 10k races, leap for a Frisbee on the beach, and, of course, fend off barking dogs. That is, our feet hurt: When we outdo ourselves on in-line skates, a mountain bike, or a rock face, it's not only our hamstrings, backs, and shoulders that suffer. Our feet follow right along.

The unpleasant truth is that 85 percent of us will at some point be temporarily sidelined by foot problems. That's because each time you take a step, you're asking 26 bones, 130 ligaments, and 40-some muscles and tendons to act in concert, performing a series of sophisticated machinations so that the foot can be rigid enough to propel you while remaining flexible enough to absorb impacts. A regular regimen of jumping, twisting, and pounding only makes matters worse. "Take a runner who goes just one mile," says Tom Shonka, a Boulder, Colorado–based podiatrist and

OUTSIDE • JUNE 1995 149

Santa Fe

and the environment. Of the staff that made the 1994 move to Santa Fe from Chicago, only two still work at the magazine, but an additional three still live and work in Santa Fe. For them, walking the walk of an outdoor lifestyle changed not only the public perception of the magazine where they worked, but it changed their lives and their home.

BODYWORK

COUNSEL FOR THE OUTDOOR ATHLETE

Some Things to Sneeze At

The pollen is flying this time of year, so make peace with your antibodies

By Elizabeth Kaufmann

IT'S THE DAY YOU'VE BEEN DYING for—bright, warm, a little breezy—and yet you feel like you're dying *from* it. You woke up sneezing half a dozen times in rapid succession. Your eyes water continuously, your throat itches, your brain feels like it's awash in Crisco. Rejoice! It's spring, the allergy season.

What allergy sufferers have done to deserve this—and about one out of five of us endures springtime hay fever—is simply to be born with a paranoid immune system. Our befuddled bodies mount a tremendous defense against a supposed poison (pollen!) every time we breathe, and as athletes we only make things worse by sucking in extraordinary amounts of air—and the poison with it. Since breathing is not optional, allergy victims have but two ways to seek relief: Find some way to avoid the poison, or try to calm a whacked-out bunch of antibodies.

It wasn't always like this. Nobody knows exactly why allergies evolved in humans. Physicians first noted them in England during that first great wave of air pollution, the Industrial Revolution. Some experts now speculate that airborne pollutants either broke down natural barriers in the nose and lungs or somehow altered the immune system. Then there's the parasite theory. Researchers at the National Institute of Allergy and Infectious Diseases in Bethesda, Maryland, have noted that populations with a high level of parasites—like the residents of some worm-infested islands in the South Pacific, hotbeds of parasite research—have a low incidence of allergies, and vice versa. The thinking goes that some of us have a misguided and rather overreactive immune system that, in the absence of truly dangerous parasites, mobilizes its forces against harmless pollen.

And pollen is everywhere, courtesy of a botanical sex-fest that kicks off every year when the snow finally melts. "Pollen is like sperm," says William Storms, an allergist who is an associate clinical professor at the University of Colorado Health Sciences Center in Denver. "It's the way the wind-pollinated plants mate. Those are the plants we need to worry about, not the insect-pollinated ones." So while flowers probably won't make you sneeze, the more prevalent trees, grasses, and weeds will. A maple tree, for example, puts forth thousands of grains of pollen each spring morning, which then blow in the wind, ideally landing where they can do their reproductive work. Why do the trees feel so sprightly only in warm, sunny, spring weather? "It's hard to get those answers out of a maple," says Storms.

If you came into this world with a predisposition to allergies—it's an inherited trait—then the first time you ever inhaled pollen (or animal dander or dust, for that matter) your immune system responded. Blood cells called lymphocytes produced a large quantity of antibodies known as immunoglobulin E, or IgE. These defenders latched on to your mast cells, which are found in high concentrations in

OUTSIDE • MAY 1994 179

Chicago

Change Is Hard 5

AN INTERVIEW WITH JULIE ANN MILLER, EDITOR, AND ERIC R. ROELL, DESIGN/PRODUCTION DIRECTOR, OF *SCIENCE NEWS*

Science News, *based in Washington, D.C., was founded in 1921 as a once-a-week service for newspapers. Providing packages of information on research across the sciences, the service became so popular that it was launched in 1922 as a black-and-white newsletter available to individual subscribers. Today the four-color, sixteen-page magazine reaches 140,000 scientists, educated lay readers, and libraries. It was redesigned in 2002, with updated typography, color palette, and revised contents page.*

When we spoke a few years ago—before your redesign—one of the things you said that fascinated me was that if there was a little bit of white space on a page, readers wrote in and complained. Apparently there's a consensus among your readership that every square centimeter of space should be filled with words. Most editors would envy such a passionate readership; on the other hand you were justifiably apprehensive about messing with your format.

JULIE ANN MILLER: Well, that's our readers—they want our words. We did go to something that has more art in it, and we did get complaints about it. They eventually simmered down. We're trying to appeal to a broader audience; we had to make the magazine visually appealing.

Before the redesign, there was a growing feeling that it was time to make a change, but if there was a decisive moment, it happened in New York. I go to the Folio meeting nearly every year, and that year [2001] I went to sessions on design. [I was] participating in a roundtable, and everyone showed their magazines. The woman directing the session would look at magazines and say, "This looks this very nice," and she got to mine and said, "Oh, no." It had a fifties look, and even then most of the parts didn't go together.

Can you tell me more about the magazine before the redesign?

MILLER: There hadn't been a redesign in at least seventy-five years. Once in a while the logo would change, or the table of contents would change, but nobody ever looked at the whole magazine at once and said, "Let's pull this together and do something." When we did redesign, it was also a good time for us because we were changing our production—we were bringing it in-house—and we just thought that the world of magazines had evolved and we needed to catch up.

What was the range of responses you got?

MILLER: We didn't get that many canceled subscriptions [laughs], but we probably got a couple. We did get a lot of noise.

ERIC ROELL: The readers wanted more text—they thought they were being cheated. Some of the readers think if you're using more pictures or more color it's taking away from something else.

MILLER: One of my favorite letters was from someone who wrote in that he knew blue ink was more expensive than the other colors and he thought we were wasting his money by using so much blue in the magazine.

ROELL: But we did get positive feedback, too. A lot of readers told us it was about time.

MILLER: However, I must say we got a letter yesterday—four years after the redesign. And someone called to complain about something that had been driving him crazy all that time: He wanted punctuation after the subheads. He kept reading them as a complete sentence even though the type was completely different.

What has happened to your subscriber base since the redesign?

MILLER: Up until last year it was going down slightly. Certainly the redesign didn't make any noticeable difference in circulation, but as with most magazines, ours was going down slightly. It's been going down more since last year, when we started to reduce the amount of direct mail.

Were you concerned about an aging readership—is that part of what drove the redesign?

MILLER: Yes, we definitely have an aging readership, but I have to tell you that ten years ago, when I started as editor, I sent out a quick postcard survey, asking people what they thought of the magazine, and

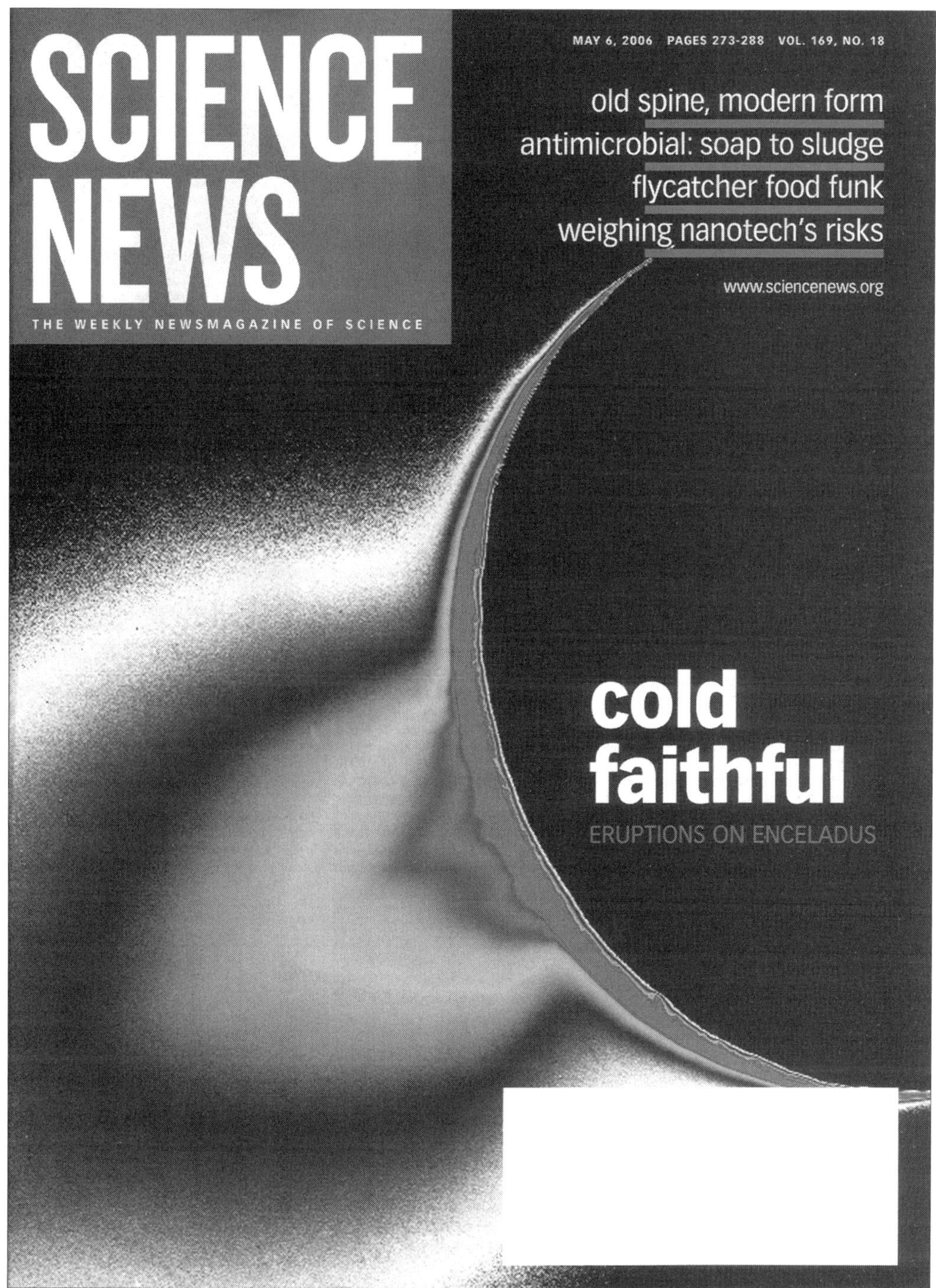

SCIENCE NEWS
THE WEEKLY NEWSMAGAZINE OF SCIENCE
MAY 6, 2006 PAGES 273-288 VOL. 169, NO. 18
old spine, modern form
antimicrobial: soap to sludge
flycatcher food funk
weighing nanotech's risks
www.sciencenews.org
cold faithful
ERUPTIONS ON ENCELADUS

Science News, *after the redesign*

one of the questions on it was "Is the type too small?" And I got a postcard back from some ninety-eight-year-old woman, who wrote, "Don't make the type bigger; it's fine." In fact, when we redesigned, we did make the type a little bit smaller, though it's in a different font.

Our current readership inhibits us from making any gross attempts to appeal to a younger audience. We did a couple of cartoony covers that we thought were great, but we got complaints. I won't say we'll never take an approach like that again, but we won't do three within two months.

We do pick up some younger readers. We know of cases where people start reading in high school and keep subscribing. But because we're only sixteen pages we don't have room to experiment. We once issued a

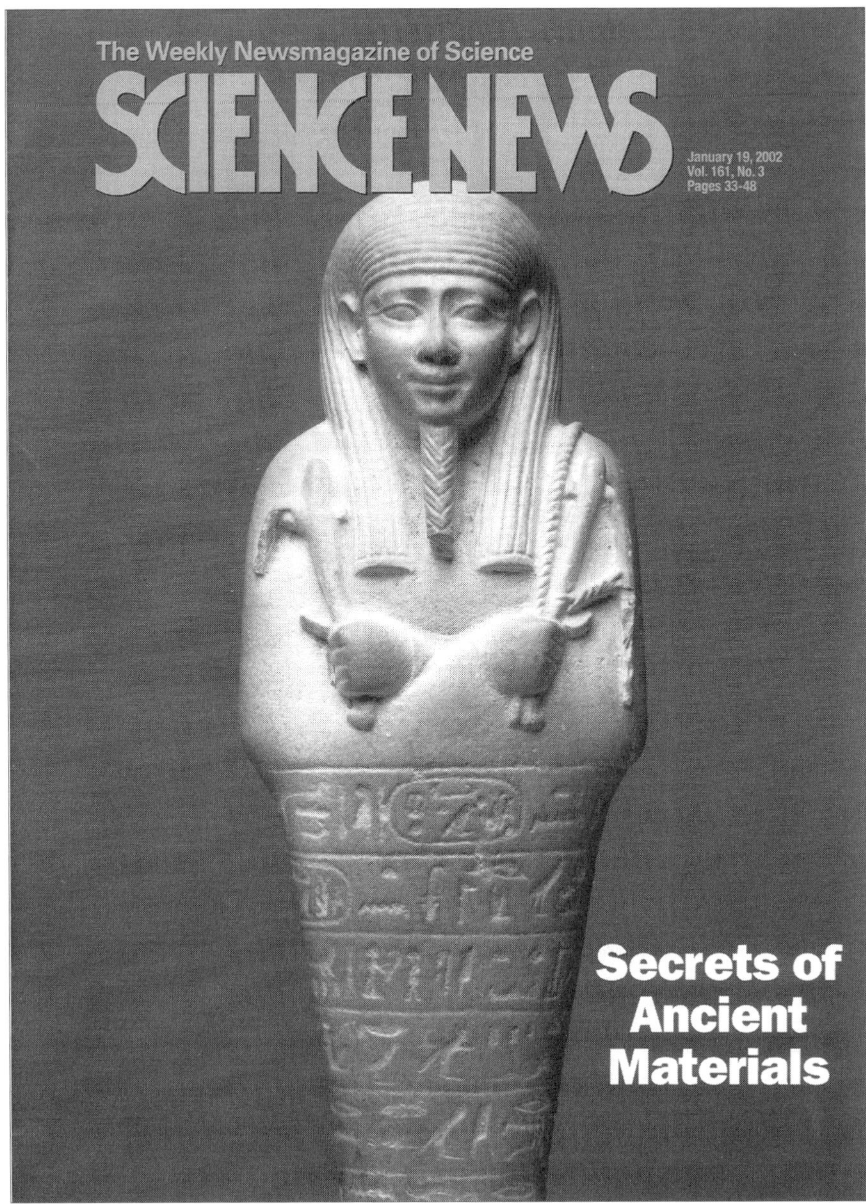

The old look

survey asking readers if they would be interested in reading different sorts of articles—things that focus on scientists rather than science results, for example. Younger people and women were more open to a broader approach in reporting, but our majority-middle-age-male readership wasn't. We're thinking in general terms about adding pages so we can broaden our approach. We also try to attract younger readers through a youth Web site and by participating in science fairs, though I don't know how successful we've been.

ROELL: We have a particularly loyal readership. I hear from people who say, "I subscribe, and my father subscribed, and my grandfather subscribed." A lot of people have been subscribers for a long time; they feel a unique ownership over the magazine. They're loyal to it, and they don't want to see it degraded in any way. It makes it difficult to make any changes or try anything new.

Did the redesign have any unforeseen consequences?

MILLER: One of the things that came up with the redesign was that we had to make some of the types of stories shorter. That was a problem for the writers—the news stories got shorter, and it took a year or so for them to settle down. Writing shorter is harder.

ROELL: We have readers wanting us to fill up every column—but the writers want to fill up the space between the columns, too! So that's another thing. But our surveys have shown in the past that people want short bits of news. The shorter the pieces we provide them with, the more variety of pieces we can give them.

The writers find the discipline the new format imposes difficult in other ways, too. I had a conversation just a month ago: that there are various rules we have to follow and I just can't put a picture behind the headline—that's not part of our design. I had to explain that I'm not just being stubborn or difficult—there are reasons why the design functions as it does. As the art director, I feel I have a responsibility to respect the format. Getting everyone to understand that is kind of a challenge.

MILLER: Readers want us to find out everything, then just tell them the most interesting part.

ROELL: And just because a writer wants to write 1,000 words about a topic doesn't mean a reader wants more than 450. So that's—I don't know if the writers have gotten that.

Did you do the redesign in-house?

ROELL: No, we hired an outside designer. Actually the project was already underway when I started. When I was hired, the designer had already been chosen and we were going through different proposals.

MILLER: We went to an outside designer in part because we didn't have anyone in-house yet. . . . We interviewed a bunch of different people, and we decided at that time on Maryanne Oches, who was then living in New York. We had a series of amazing disasters with her coming down: The first day we were scheduled to meet was September 11th. Her train left New York, got one station out, and turned around and went back. Another time there was a suicide on the train. Another time I had driven her to [D.C.'s] Union Station and dropped her off [to go home], and then a tornado came through. She also did the redesign for [the weekly glossy] *Chemical and Engineering News*—they're doing some tweaking now.

Did you feel she got it right away, or did it take her a while to find your visual voice?

MILLER: I think she was pretty close. I remember that there were things she was surprised about—for one, that our table of contents is on Page 3, and that was something she wasn't used to—[and] being able to use Covers 2 and 3 [the inside front and inside back covers]. We don't have a lot of advertising. With the redesign, we moved the table of contents to Cover 2.

ROELL: So that's where I came in. She brought in a bunch of samples, and from my point of view she was 90 percent of the way there. I really liked the concepts she came up with. [Working with her] from the staff we had Julie, me, [and managing editor] Keith Haglund, and we had a writer's representative involved.

MILLER: The other thing she had to take into account is how quickly we have to put the magazine together. We finish writing our stories Tuesday night. We have one round of pages that everyone looks at Wednesday morning, and then the pages go to the printer Wednesday afternoon. We really needed a format that wouldn't require a lot of fussing at the end.

Eric, can you tell me a bit about your background and what attracted you to this magazine as a designer?

ROELL: I have a degree in journalism—I thought I was going to write for newspapers but never did. My previous magazine was a monthly—the *American Spectator*—where I was the art director. It went through a bunch of changes, and I ended up leaving a little bit before I came here. It was hard going from a monthly to a weekly, getting used to the rapid pace and also the size of the magazine—it's only sixteen pages, compared with well over a hundred. I used to have the resources to design twelve-page features; here I do two two-pagers every week. Time is something I struggle with. I can't be creative every week; sometimes it's more a matter of getting it done.

MILLER: The other thing it means is, being a newsmagazine, everything can change at the last minute. Not every week, but no matter how much beautiful design you put into something, out in the world, events might force you to rip it up.

ROELL: We get a lot of our art from researchers, so we're always dependent on writers or someone else out in the field for illustration. A lot of times, I don't know until the day of whether I'm going to have art or not. I can't do what I did when I had a $10,000-a-month art budget. I miss being able to try different layouts, but I like the faster pace.

MILLER: There was a week when we didn't have a picture. The story was about dark energy, so we just thought we'd run the cover black, and we did get a couple of letters from readers asking why we didn't put a picture on the cover. I don't know how you show dark energy.

Are most of your readers professional scientists?

MILLER: Forty percent of our readers are scientists—you know, they self-identify as scientists. And then the next-largest group are teachers, and after that it just breaks up into many different groups.

SCIENCE NEWS BOOKS

To order these books or any other book in print, call 1-800-BOOKS-NOW (266-5766) ext. 1494. Visa, MasterCard, and American Express accepted. Send checks or money orders plus $4.95 shipping and handling ($2.50 for each additional item) to Books Now, 400 Morris Avenue, Long Branch, NJ 07740. Or see our Web site at www.sciencenewsbooks.org. This service is provided in conjunction with Science News Books.

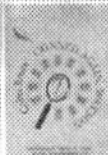

Conned Again, Watson: Cautionary Tales of Logic, Math, and Probability—Colin Bruce. In a follow-up to his book *The Einstein Paradox*, Bruce again employs Sherlock Holmes and his trusty sidekick Watson to present 12 new tales that illustrate how mathematical ignorance can have dreadful consequences. In these cases, Holmes draws on a deep understanding of probability, statistics, and game theory to enlighten greedy gamblers, reckless businessmen, and unsuspecting dupes of statistics-wielding con artists. Each story has a lesson about a scam or a calculated risk, presented in the style of an Aesop's fable. Originally published in hardcover in 2001. Perseus, 2001, 290 p., b&w illus., paperback, $15.00.

Herbs: The Complete Gardener's Guide—Patrick Lima with photographs by Turid Forsyth. By definition, an herb is a "plant of which leaves, seeds, or roots are used for food, medicine, scent, or flavor." Lima tours an extensive herb garden to explore these uses. His explanations of how to cultivate and reap herbs accompany Forsyth's spectacular photographs. These images grace every page in the book and help readers identify herbs and realize the beauty and versatility of these plants. Profiles offer a little history of each herb, its uses, and a word on how it prospers in the garden. Chapters devoted specifically to herbs for salads, for fragrance, for blending and brewing, and for growing in a shady garden help to distinguish varieties. Firefly, 2001, 222 p., paperback, color photos/illus., paperback, $24.95.

Making Babies: The Science of Pregnancy—David Bainbridge. Reproductive biologist Bainbridge offers the scientific counterpart to the popular book *What to Expect When You're Expecting*. This lucid and engaging text covers childbirth from conception to lactation and examines the complex biology of human gestation. Bainbridge asks and answers five big questions of pregnancy in five chapters. Why do we reproduce sexually? The answer is, for the sake of genetic variation. How does a mother know she's pregnant? Bainbridge explains how the embryo implants itself in the uterine wall and produces a hormone that stops the mother from menstruating. How does a baby get ready to live outside the womb? The author recounts the processes that take the fertilized egg from a single cell to fully developed fetus. Why does the mother accept the "foreign" baby? Bainbridge explores how mother and fetus coexist without the baby being mistaken for a parasite by the mother's body. How do mother and baby survive birth? Both do almost miraculous physical feats during labor and delivery. Overall, *Making Babies* is an accessible, insightful, and mesmerizing tour of our beginnings. Originally published in the United Kingdom in 2000. HUP, 2001, 292 p., b&w plates, hardcover, $26.00.

Naturally Dangerous: Surprising Facts About Food, Health, and the Environment—James P. Collman. In 1989, news broke that researchers had linked alar, a chemical used to control the ripening of apples, to childhood cancer. The chemical was pulled from the market and the apple industry lost millions of dollars. However, subsequent research revealed that alar was a cancer risk only at doses of 100,000 to 200,000 times the amount a child would likely consume in a day, Collman reports. He asserts that chemicals are often unfairly maligned in this way largely because of misleading statistics and public ignorance of how chemical compounds work. Moreover, Collman, a professor of chemistry at Stanford University, writes that the public is too trusting of the label "natural" and that people routinely and unwittingly put themselves at risk believing that natural chemicals are better than synthetic chemicals. His discussion extends to trans fats and fat substitutes, herbal remedies, designer drugs, mad cow disease, global warming, and acid rain, as he relates the inherent risk in almost anything. University Science Books, 2001, 270 p., color plates/b&w illus., hardcover, $29.00.

Nothingness: The Science of Empty Space—Henning Genz. Genz tracks the scientific quest to define nothing. Does empty space have matter within it, and if that matter were removed, what would be left? This seemingly immaterial problem, so to speak, has vexed many physicists and philosophers. Its solution charges the most cutting-edge endeavors of modern cosmology and quantum mechanics. Genz is of the belief that ancient Greek naturalists conceived the concepts that continue to inspire the moderns. In this book, Evangelista Torricelli and Plato are central characters alongside Werner Heisenberg and Albert Einstein. Originally published in hardcover in 1999. Perseus, 2001, 340 p., b&w photos/illus., paperback, $20.00.

The Science of Life: Projects and Principles for Beginning Biologists—Frank G. Bottone Jr. Young biologists who work through this set of 25 interactive experiments will come away with an understanding of the scientific method as well as a keen sense of the life of bacteria, fungi, protozoa, plants, and animals. Each experiment has a clearly defined objective, a list of materials, suggestions for what to look for, and instructions on how to record the results. One experiment is to grow carnivorous plants in order to discover how they capture and eat prey. Other projects ask junior biologists to compare compost heaps with and without worms, germinate seeds in sand and backyard soil, and clone a mushroom from a piece of its own tissue. In all, this is a serious but enjoyable book that illustrates the subtle ways in which biology affects our lives every day. Recommended for age 9 and up. Chicago Review Pr, 2001, 126 p., b&w illus., paperback, $14.95.

Science News (ISSN 0036-8423) is published weekly on Saturday, except the last week in December, for $54.50 for 1 year or $98.00 for 2 years (foreign postage is $18.00 additional per year) by Science Service, 1719 N Street, N.W., Washington, D.C. 20036. Preferred Periodicals postage paid at Washington, D.C., and additional mailing office. **POSTMASTER**: Send address changes to Science News, P.O. Box 1925, Marion, Ohio 43305. Change of address: Four to six weeks' notice is required—old and new addresses, including zip codes, must be provided.

Editorial, Business, and Advertising Offices
1719 N St. N.W., Washington, D.C. 20036
202-785-2255; scinews@sciserv.org

Subscription Department
P.O. Box 1925, Marion, Ohio 43305
For new subscriptions and customer service, call 1-800-552-4412.

Science News is published by Science Service, a nonprofit corporation founded in 1921. The mission of Science Service is to advance the understanding and appreciation of science through publications and educational programs.

Visit Science Service on the World Wide Web: http://www.sciserv.org

SCIENCE NEWS

The Weekly Newsmagazine of Science

Volume 161, No. 3, January 19, 2002

This Week

Articles

Research Notes

Departments

Cover: An ancient funerary figurine of Egypt's King Nectanebo II is made of faience, a glazed quartz. Recent analysis and replication experiments show that the detailed carving was possible because the piece was created from a finer paste that contained more lime, as compared with faience made 600 years earlier. **Page 45** (Photo: © The Cleveland Museum of Art, Gift of John Huntington Art and Polytechnic Trust)

Visit SCIENCE NEWS ONLINE for special features, columns, and references.
http://www.sciencenews.org

Editor's Letter

We have a pleasing surprise in store for you next week. It's a new look for SCIENCE NEWS. While we will continue to provide stories that are timely, concise, accurate, and engaging, our appearance will be easier on the eyes and give you more-efficient access to our valuable content.

We don't take this step lightly. We recognize that many readers have been satisfied with our classic look, which evolved gradually over almost 80 years of publication. In 1926, SCIENCE NEWS underwent its greatest change when it transformed from a mimeographed sheaf of pages to a printed newsletter that included photos. Since then, there have been occasional alterations in the table of contents, interior pages, logo, and cover. Among the recent notable changes were a cover update in 1978 and a new style for the table of contents in 1997.

With recent changes in magazine-production capabilities, we can now create a livelier look that conveys scientific findings to more people than ever and gives us more flexibility to inform you of the latest research from all fields. The design that will launch next week was created by Mariana Ochs of modesign in Rio de Janeiro. The mock cover at left gives you a preview of our new look.

However the appearance changes, the staff of SCIENCE NEWS is committed to keeping you informed of what's new to know in science each week. We look forward to continuing to provide valuable, information-packed issues.

—*Julie Ann Miller*

Before

Is there anything else challenging about the design?

ROELL: Mostly the feature stories. Even with time, it's very limited what you can do with them—which is both a strength and a weakness. I really have to fight every week to make it creative when I have three square images and maybe two-and-a-half pages. But it's also a strength, because readers are comfortable with it, and I have to work within that structure to keep it as creative as possible.

MILLER: What happened before is that everyone who had Eric's job did it differently and made up their own rules. One designer I remember, she really thought that science was boring and it was unfair to present it in any other way, so she just always did the same thing. And then there was the person who liked to put a picture behind the headline—if we had a good enough picture. But the space is really constricting. In some magazines you open up a story and there's a whole page of picture, and on the next just a column of text, and then the story starts—oh, that would be luxury. With some science magazines, you come to the middle of the story and there's a two-page picture of a whale with all the parts labeled. We could never do that.

THE WEEKLY NEWSMAGAZINE OF SCIENCE

SCIENCE NEWS

MAY 6, 2006 VOL. 169, NO. 18

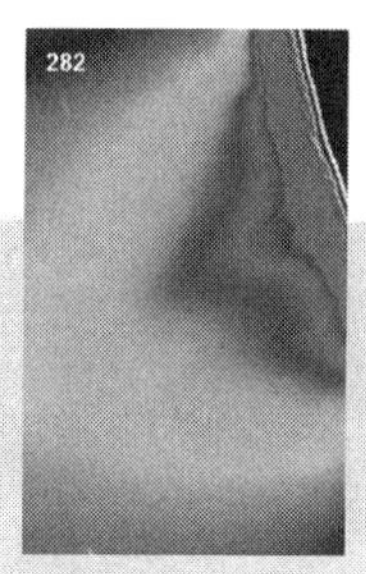

Features

This Week

Of Note

Departments

Cover Researchers last year discovered a geyser of water vapor and ice on Saturn's moon Enceladus. The finding spotlights this small moon as a new place to look for liquid water and other signs of life in the outer solar system. (JPL/NASA, Space Science Institute) Page 282

SCIENCE NEWS

This Week

Tainted by Cleanser

Antimicrobial agent persists in sludge

About 76 percent of a commonly used antimicrobial agent exits sewage-treatment plants as a component of the sludge that's often used as a farm fertilizer, according to the first study to track the chemical through a typical plant. The finding raises questions as to the ultimate fate of the antimicrobial in the environment, the study's authors say.

U.S. manufacturers add 500,000 to 1 million pounds of the chemical triclocarban each year to personal-care products, such as antimicrobial soaps. Past toxicological studies have linked the chemical to decreases in birthweight and survival in rats and rabbits, says Rolf U. Halden of Johns Hopkins University in Baltimore.

Halden and his colleagues followed triclocarban through a treatment plant that takes in 680 million liters of wastewater per day produced by 1.3 million residents of a city in the mid-Atlantic region. The plant separates the sewage into liquid and solid streams, and microbes break down much of the organic content of those flows.

According to the National Academies in Washington, D.C., U.S. treatment plants send about 60 percent of the solid sludge that they generate to agricultural fields and other land as fertilizer. Liquids leaving the plants typically flow into streams or other bodies of water.

The group determined the quantity of triclocarban in samples of the incoming sewage and outgoing liquid and sludge. "It's difficult analyzing the sludge," says Halden. "In the past decade, the appropriate instrumentation has become available."

In an upcoming *Environmental Science & Technology*, the team reports that microbes broke down only about 21 percent of the triclocarban entering the treatment plant. About 76 percent accumulated in the sludge, and another 3 percent remained in the liquid stream.

"If a consumer goes to the supermarket and buys a bar of soap, three-quarters of the active ingredient could end up in agriculture because the sludge is being recycled," says Halden.

The researchers estimate that from sludge released solely by the plant that they studied, more than 1,000 kilograms of triclocarban enter the environment each year. Scientists haven't yet discerned whether the chemical degrades or accumulates in soils or what its effects are on natural soil microbes, says Halden. "We don't know if it's being taken up by plants and migrating into the food supply," he adds.

QUOTE

"If a consumer ... buys a bar of soap, three-quarters of the active ingredient could end up in agriculture."

ROLF U. HALDEN, Johns Hopkins University

"This finding suggests potential problems due to the high usage rate of triclocarban in the U.S.," says Craig D. Adams, an environmental engineer at the University of Missouri-Rolla.

With the new insight on what quantities can be expected in the environment, researchers can now turn to assessing the chemical's risk, says chemist Diana Aga of the State University of New York at Buffalo.

Although the Environment Protection Agency hasn't endorsed a method for detecting triclocarban in sludge, Rick Stevens, EPA's national biosolids coordinator, says that the results "are the kind of thing that raises interest." —A. CUNNINGHAM

Evolutionary Back Story

Thoroughly modern spine supported human ancestor

Bones from a spinal column discovered at a nearly 1.8-million-year-old site in central Asia support the controversial possibility that ancient human ancestors spoke to one another.

Excavations in 2005 at Dmanisi, Georgia, yielded five vertebrae from a *Homo erectus* individual, says anthropologist Marc R. Meyer of the University of Pennsylvania in Philadelphia. The finds occurred in previously dated sediment that has yielded several skulls now attributed to *H. erectus* (*SN: 5/13/00, p. 308*).

The new discoveries represent the oldest known vertebrae for the genus *Homo*, Meyer announced last week at the annual meeting of the Paleoanthropology Society in San Juan, Puerto Rico. The fossils consist of one lumbar, two thoracic, and two cervical vertebrae.

Meyer and his colleagues—David Lordkipanidze and Abesalom Vekua, both of the Georgian State Museum in Tbilisi—compared the size, shape, and volume of the Dmanisi vertebrae with more than 2,200 corresponding bones from people, chimpanzees, and gorillas.

"The Dmanisi spinal column falls within the human range and would have comfortably accommodated a modern human spinal cord," Meyer says.

Moreover, the fossil vertebrae would have provided ample structural support for the respiratory muscles needed to articulate words, he asserts. Although it's impossible to confirm that our prehistoric ancestors talked, Meyer notes, *H. erectus* at Dmanisi faced no respiratory limitations on speech.

In contrast, the 1984 discovery in Kenya of a boy's 1.6-million-year-old skeleton, identified by some researchers as *H. erectus* and by others as *Homo ergaster*, yielded small, chimplike vertebrae. Researchers initially suspected that the ancient youth and his presumably small-spined com-

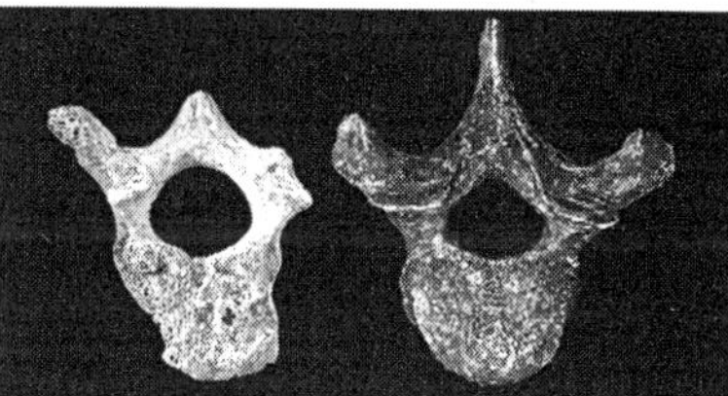

MEYER

WIDE OPEN A recently discovered *Homo erectus* vertebra from central Asia (left) displays a larger spinal cord canal than does a corresponding bone (right) from a skeleton that had been found in Kenya.

After

Print Magazine

6

JOYCE RUTTER KAYE

WITH ITS JANUARY 2005 ISSUE, *PRINT* MAGAZINE launched a cover-to-cover redesign that took the sixty-five-year-old bimonthly and effectively shook out any dust and cobwebs clinging to its pages. While readers had long respected the magazine for its eclectic, critical reporting on visual culture, we believed an aging design was limiting their access to content. In addition, circulation and advertising figures had dipped in the early 2000s as a result of an uneven publication schedule under a previous owner. After *Print* regained traction in 2003/2004 with a new publisher, a regular delivery schedule, and a fresh influx of acclaimed cultural writers and editorial awards, it was time to signify that a new era for the magazine had arrived.

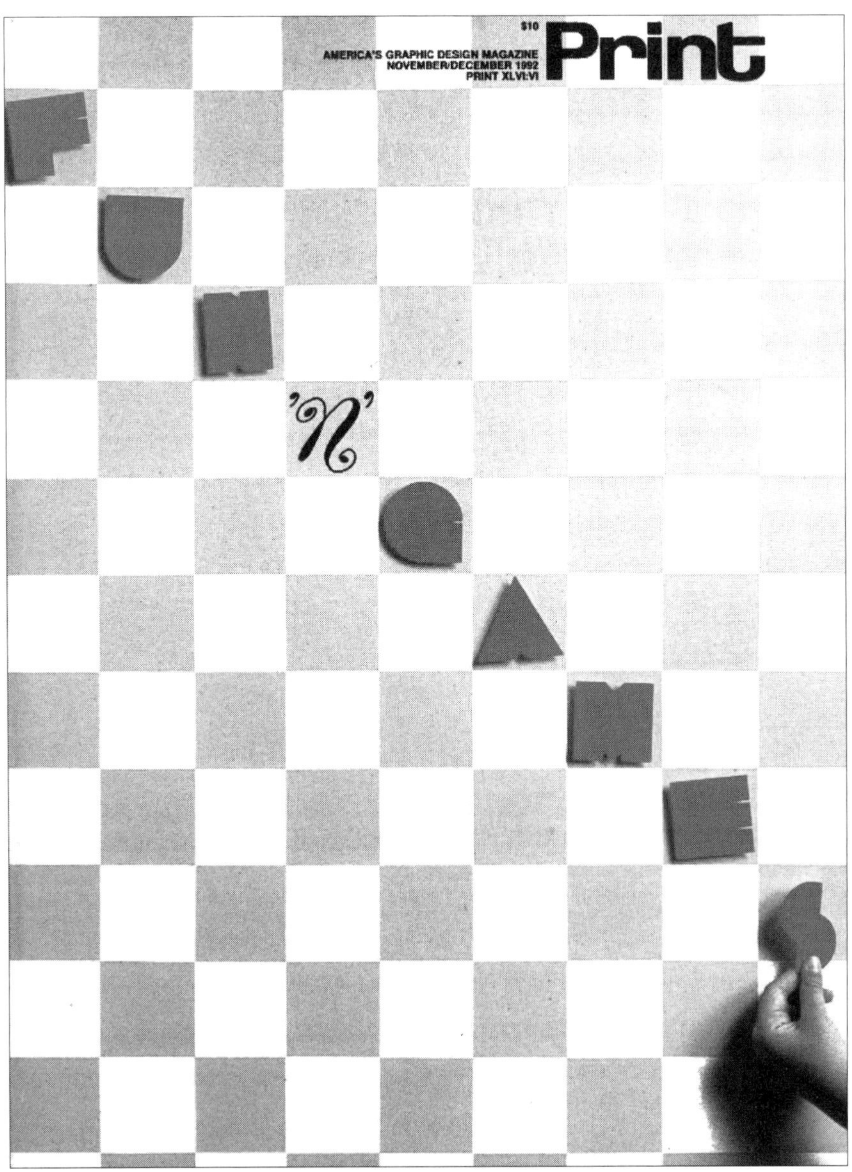

Print *in 1992*

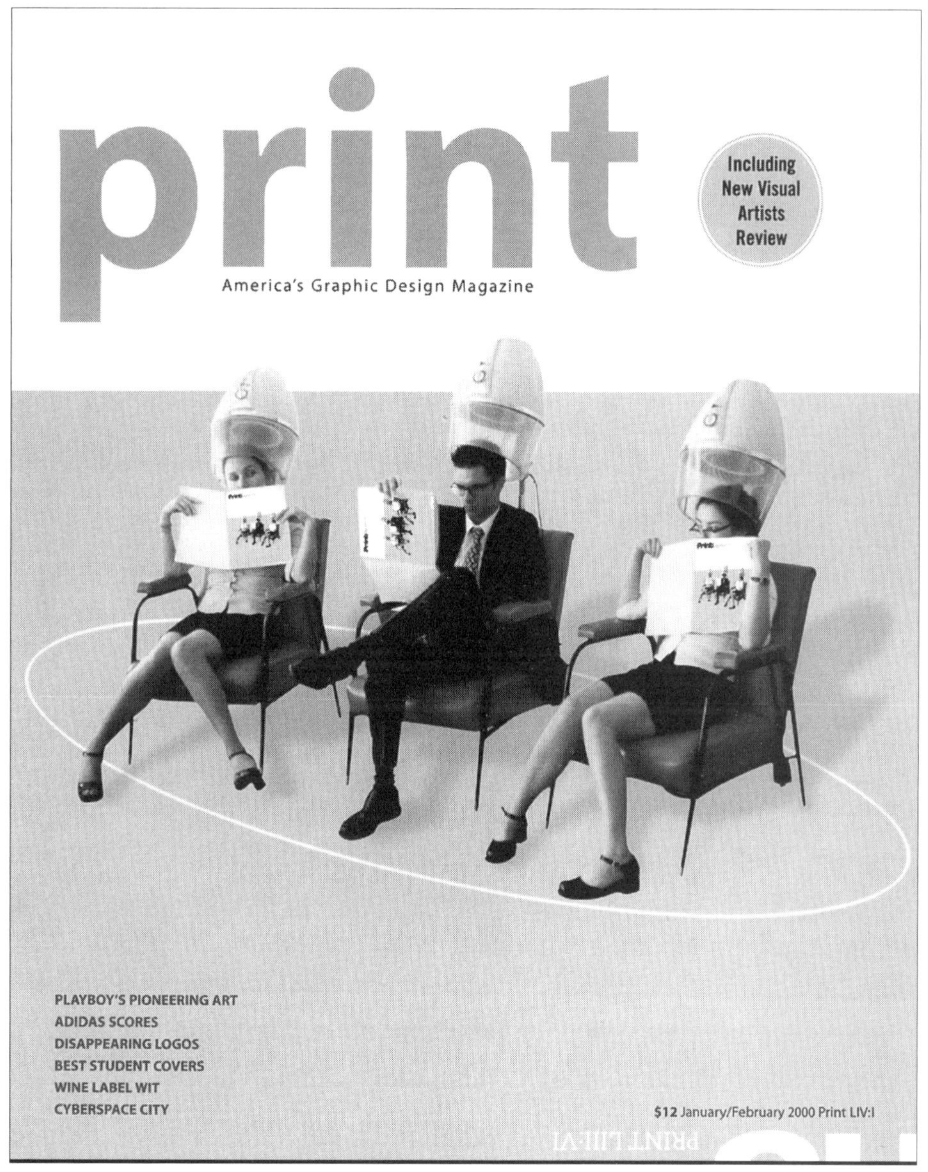

The 2000 redesign

Print's previous redesign in 2000 by art director Steven Brower had made many improvements. It replaced Herbert Bayer's diminutive cover logo from 1960 with a bold new one in lowercase Myriad. It created a new energy for the front and back of the book with a typographic emphasis on opening pages of columns. Features were designed with a more conceptual approach than the somewhat conservative look they had had before. But the makeover still largely maintained many vestiges of a design from 1996. Text from long features as well as front-of-book columns ran over into the back of the book, and technical and practical information in the back section was rather spare and unimaginatively presented. Our layouts used a riot of different typefaces and design approaches, making them rich individually, but adding up to a visual cacophony. By 2004 the look was becoming dated, especially with the clean, modern influences of magazines like *Wallpaper*, *Eye*, and *I.D.* Abbott Miller, partner of Pentagram New York, whom we hired to do the 2005 design, also saw this as a problem: "*Print*'s previous [feature well] did not always make it obvious that a feature was indeed opening because the interpretive typography often got lost within the visuals being shown."

In addition, the design of the front of the book created an environment that was simultaneously too constraining and too permissive for editorial content. Starting columns with large-size text meant pushing

Most of us grew up with comic books that were three-color offset printed on cheap yellowish newsprint stock of a quality one notch above toilet paper. Easy to roll up and stuff in a back pocket or hide between the pages of a schoolbook, they were a disposable pleasure. It was the stories inside that mattered, and they were devoured without regard to how they were packaged—that would be like caring who designed your TV set when your favorite show came on.

Over the years, the art and lit crowd has periodically acknowledged comics. The last wave of serious attention was in the late 1980s, mostly due to the deeply intelligent and evocative content—*Watchmen*, *Dark Night*, and *Sandman* from the mainstream; *Maus*, *American Splendor*, and "rediscoveries" such as R. Crumb and Will Eisner's *Spirit* from the small-press world—but also to the design of the packaging. Fancy, square-bound prestige editions and oversize graphic novels became all the rage, and casual critics of the medium issued yet another spate of articles about "comics as art, comics as literature." But the most inventive aspects of comic book design still took place within the page and panel layout, as artists exploded out of the tiered, square-panel grid.

We've seen many comics anthologies that package a variety of comic stories, often commissioning work around a

2001

massive amounts of runover into the back of the book. It limited the amount of text on the page (and sometimes we could have only one page per column up front, not two) and therefore made editors a little sloppier about cutting the piece down to its appropriate size. We are fairly generous with our writers because we do like pieces to be substantive, but the design was making it harder to be as concise as we should be, and we suspected that we were losing readers in the jumps. With feature jumps incorporated into the rear ghetto, our back of the book was a patchwork of story endings. The only content that originated in the back was "Tech and Techniques," a column about new products that was woefully undesigned.

My main goals with the redesign were to make the magazine a more seamless experience so readers would not be as aware of traditional divisions between front, middle, and end of book; to update and energize the design and make it more consistent overall; to incorporate new content addressing expanding areas of interest in design such as graphic novels, animation, interaction, and sustainability; to make the magazine more useful by enriching stories with resource boxes and other supplemental information; and to explore design's history more thoroughly though *Print*'s own rich archives.

I wanted there to be more immediacy with the book, to allow our great writing to come through. I wanted the design and content to come together as a seamless whole. I knew Abbott Miller was the right person to help us realize these goals. His work—for *2wice*, *Exhibition Design*, and *Dance Ink*—is truly like a performance on the page. He thinks as a writer and designer (he's coauthor of *Design Writing Research*), and I knew he would clarify *Print* but not tip the balance toward being either too trendy or too stodgy.

After hiring Miller in March 2004 over lunch (it was "yes" on the spot—fortunate, because I had no other designers in mind), *Print*'s staff set about planning the January/February 2005 "Global Design" issue's contents, assigning the articles, and also rethinking every element of the book. This involved several daylong retreats, followed by me sitting for many hours at my desk or kitchen table to work through all of the details that needed to be considered, page by page. This ranged from the large—*Print*'s editorial mission, content menu, voice, tone, style, and, of course, visual presentation—to the small, including word counts, end slugs, folios, resource boxes, department names, bio lines, pull quotes, and marginalia. Needless it say, it was a challenge for me and for the rest of our tiny staff of seven to shift from the practical requirements of pulling together some of our biggest issues of the year (including the 348-page *Regional Design Annual*) to envisioning a brand-new version of *Print* from scratch.

Miller did not begin the design process until June, when he was completely satisfied that he understood the goals and mission of the redesign. He achieved this by holding quite a few meetings with a core team consisting of art director Stephanie Skirvin, two senior-level editors—Todd Pruzan and Jeremy Lehrer—and

F.O.B.

twiggy stardust

If the Trajan Column is the wellspring of all Roman type, the mighty oak is another kind of font. The runic alphabet, after all, stems from twigs; one 19th-century typeface, Rustic (a.k.a. Log Cabin), was built with branches and boughs. The passion for sticks and stones (and vines and tendrils) that bloomed with Victorian and Art Nouveau design led to Stephen Doyle's 2002 jacket for *The Druid King*, a historical fantasy novel published by Knopf. Doyle began by placing twig type over a painting of Gallic general Vercingetorix, and he eventually stuck with sticks. "It's cheaper to spend 20 bucks on an armload of twigs at the flower market than to buy Jonathan Hoefler's newest font," he jokes. Last fall, Stefan Sagmeister replanted the motif on a poster for the School of Visual Arts, alluding to the life cycles of caterpillars and butterflies among the twigs. Sagmeister says he deliberately distanced himself from historical type to avoid its influence. "David Byrne issued a recent cover with twiggy type," Sagmeister says. "Twigs are in the air." STEVEN HELLER

the yellow pages

Who would've imagined that yellow, that golden hue of saffron-infused risottos and languorous afternoons en *Provence*, could stir up a hornet's nest of red-faced readers? In September, Houghton Mifflin's eagerly anticipated publication of *The Gourmet Cookbook*, a phone-book-size volume with 60 years of *Gourmet* magazine recipes, revealed that home cooks don't like it when they can't see the names of the recipes. For all its comprehensive scope, judicious use of type, and charming line drawings, it's the book's whipped-butter-yellow recipe-heading type—demanding a headache-inducing squint in any kitchen—that has galvanized the public. "Whoever is responsible deserves to be dipped like a crouton into hot sulphur," groused one Amazon.com customer, who called the "cheddar-cheesey typeface the essence of stupidity." Such gastronomic fury was countered by more coolheaded admonitions: "It's true the recipe titles are printed in yellow and are not easy to read under bright light. But GET OVER IT." The publisher, which didn't answer queries, is said to be considering a more legible color for the next printing. Meanwhile, a great debate keeps stirring. STEPHANIE SKIRVIN

about the type

soft

With this issue, *PRINT* is privileged to celebrate its redesign by introducing three precisionist typefaces: Gotham Rounded Book, Medium, and Light, created by Manhattan foundry Hoefler & Frere-Jones. The newest styles of the workmanlike Gotham family sprang from a fortuitous conversation between Abbott Miller (whose redesign of *PRINT* you're now reading) and Jonathan Hoefler. Miller sought a sans serif foil to Enschedé Font Foundry's Lexicon, his chosen serif body text, just as Hoefler and Tobias Frere-Jones were trying to create a gentler Gotham. Hoefler says: "We were going for a softness that was the product of an industrial process, rather than just an arbitrarily applied style." Miller asked Hoefler to develop the soft-edged Gotham further for *PRINT*. Frere-Jones, who created the original Gotham (see "Making the Cut," p. 64), developed the new faces' working prototypes, and he and Hoefler interpolated the three new intermediate weights for *PRINT*'s new logo and display type. "I think Gotham Rounded manages to be patently 'designed' without being overly stylized," Hoefler says. "It's articulate but not edgy. It also has a neutral effect appropriate to journalism that's driven by presentation and analysis rather than by a stylistic agenda." LISA TROLLBÄCK

hard

24 print JAN/FEB 2005

print JAN/FEB 2005 25

2005

me, during which he asked us many questions. Miller and his designers John Kudos and Jeremy Hoffman then developed a number of cover prototypes experimenting with logos of wildly varying styles. I was initially smitten by a dot-matrix version, probably because it hearkened back to our lowercase logo heritage but also was lighter, breezier, and very fresh. Other versions were a more traditional sans-serif logo mirroring the Myriad version, and a more playful one in Helvetica Rounded (HR). Our staff was fairly divided about what they liked, but we ultimately agreed that the Helvetica provided a nice foil to Lexicon, the serious-minded serif face Miller was working with for the text.

Reader focus groups were arranged by Debbie Millman, president of the Sterling Group, a branding design firm, who moderated sessions in the firm's offices in the Empire State Building. Our goal wasn't to have a beauty contest for the new designs, but to gather qualitative information about the magazine from our subscribers. It was a very instructive exercise. Many of our instincts about what should change were accurate. (One panelist memorably complained that our varying layout styles made her confused by "the whole big pie of it all.") We learned from our readers that it was important that we not compromise the integrity we had built up over sixty-five years in publication. If we were to redesign, they didn't want us to look as though we were trying too hard to come across as being cool or hip, so they disliked many of the new logos for that reason. Abbott took their comments to heart and reined in the logo design, keeping the Helvetica Rounded version but also playing with versions in Lexicon.

Issue prototypes were developed using those two main typeface choices. Front-of-book matter followed a three-column grid with cyan section titles set in lowercase HR and headlines in lowercase Lexicon. Miller wanted to streamline the magazine by limiting our typeface choices in the feature well. Heads would alternate between different weights of the same two typefaces, although he did suggest that further down the road we expand to additional typeface choices, but with a similar feel and flavor as these. At last we settled on a middle weight of HR for the cover logo.

When I first looked at the prototypes I felt a huge surge of relief that the magazine was calmer, but more energized at the same time. The new design offered many more entry points to draw readers in—more pull quotes, sidebars, resource boxes, marginalia—but it didn't seem cluttered. We had cut back on the amount of text to keep all columns and features contained within their sections, but added additional items, such as resource boxes, Web URL roundups, and a calendar

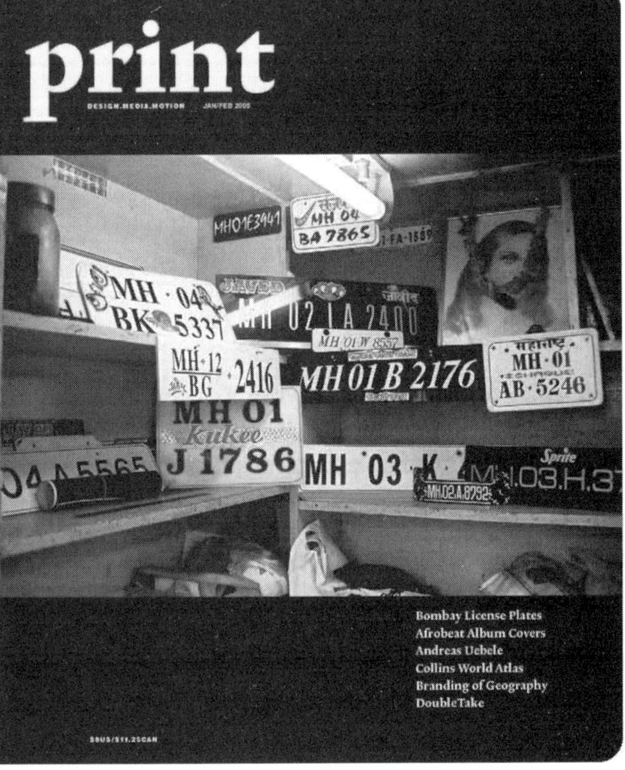

Logos under consideration

of events. This was part of making the magazine more useful and functional to readers. Eventually, we would also lead them to our Web site where we could show supplementary information to the articles and create a dialogue between the two media. The back of the book became as attractive as the front, which is good for readers as well as advertisers, who always want to be positioned near compelling-looking edit.

The prototype also incorporated rounded corners, because Miller envisioned the magazine to be a designed object. We were all for this until we found out the cost: $1 per issue, which meant $50,000 for the press run—an exorbitant expense for a smaller magazine with a limited budget.

As autumn arrived and our November 8 press deadline loomed closer, Miller contacted Jonathan Hoefler at Hoefler & Frere-Jones to find out whether they were working on developing a rounded version of their utilitarian typeface Gotham, and, as it happened, they were. Miller's inquiry accelerated the development of the typeface—they turned around three weights for us in literally three weeks. While it's not our own proprietary font, we were the first to debut it and use it until its commercial launch in 2006. It made for a very dicey first issue, though, especially for our art department as they worked on the production. With our deadline a mere four weeks away, they were swapping in versions of the new typeface on all the body text and captions. They were also struggling to adjust to a newer version of Quark that Pentagram was using. (A few months later we would switch to InDesign).

Once Gotham Rounded was in hand, Miller and his team (unbeknownst to us) began adjusting the logo size and weight once again, and surprised us with them at one of our final meetings at Pentagram's headquarters. A range of sizes were offered, and while we appreciated the drama of the larger versions, we all agreed something in between the small and large iterations would be best. The medium-size logo felt airy, sophisticated, yet still accessible, and had much more personality than the original Helvetica version. It just worked.

From that point on, we were revising layout designs and asking for design changes here and there. Some things still weren't working—the end slug, the size of type in our short-feature "FOB" section, and some headline choices. Miller was very accommodating to us because we had solid reasons for adjusting things. But the overall design was so well thought-out and appropriate from the beginning, we never really had to have him rethink anything on a major scale.

2005

The initial reaction from readers was overwhelmingly positive (save one letter writer who compared our new logo to that of IHOP, the International House of Pancakes). Miller feels that it was less a radical redesign than just making *Print* what it ought to be. "I am happy about the design, and how it works to really showcase the content. The most dramatic change we could have effected would have been to organize the heavy stock inserts and advertising so that they did not create such physical impediments to the reader. But we were not asked to come up with a new business plan." One year after its relaunch, the magazine's circulation rose 25 percent, from 38,000 to 47,000, and advertising revenue gained by 28 percent over 2004.

Now in its third year, the design continues to evolve and improve. In January 2006, after Stephanie Skirvin moved on to focus on freelancing, I hired Kristina DiMatteo as *Print*'s new art director. Over the course of the past year, DiMatteo has embraced Miller's design direction but has introduced a number of changes to make it her own. With associate art director Lindsay Ballant, she has simplified the feature well by creating more white space and removing various color blocks to help the artwork stand on its own while allowing the feature well to feel more cohesive. By building upon a type direction in each issue she is able to further explore the nuances of each typeface and how they work together while creating a visual brand for each issue's theme. She has also designed a system that brands our competitions, so they feel like special independent sections within the magazine. DiMatteo clearly enjoys the creative potential offered by working within a clean structure and dealing with a subject that's undeniably engaging to her. "The exciting thing about magazines is how they continuously grow," she observes. "After a redesign such as this, there's much room to explore all the decisions made and to expand on them in a way that can feel unexpected, when compared to the original direction." Two years after relaunching *Print*'s uncluttered new digs, and continually cleaning and refining, it's clear the days of "the whole big pie of it all" are gone for good.

SECTION 3

Repositioning

Few magazine staffs would undertake the investments in time and money that redesigns require without a list of objectives they hope those investments will achieve. For most magazines, the goals are fairly simple—they wish to excite their readers and advertisers, they want a format that reflects their evolving editorial direction or the changing world, or they simply wish to keep current. They are basically happy with what they are doing, but perhaps want to do it better. They like their readers and advertisers, but perhaps want more of them.

For other magazines, the redesign comes as part of an effort to "reposition"—to change not just the physical form of the publication but who is reading it as well. While any redesign will introduce a new look and may involve new approaches to storytelling, a repositioning alters the publication's DNA. The name may be the same, but the result of the redesign is a fundamentally different magazine.

Among the big national magazines, repositionings most often come in the form of a desire to reach a reader of a different age or income level than they currently attract. *Seventeen* may discover that its traditional twelve-year-old reader has turned to *Jane* and its core readership is now only an average age of ten—too young to have disposable income to spend at Delia's. A magazine in this position must decide either to keep its current editorial focus and change its marketing strategy, or to change the editorial focus to attract different readers. A repositioning could also become necessary if the magazine is acquired by a company that already produces a competing title.

When a big national magazine repositions, the message to current readers is very often that they're fired. The former readers may believe that their once-favorite magazine has become boring or juvenile—or just stopped meeting their needs—and all of these criticisms might be true. But, the magazine did not become bad. Turning-off old readers is a calculated decision—the publisher hopes that new enthusiastic readers will more than replace those who drift off.

Repositionings need not be so mercenary. For some magazines, repositionings are a matter of life and death—if a magazine has covered a topic that no longer resonates with a sustainable readership—the Cold War say—then it must expand or change its topic. If a readership is aging with the magazine, new readers must eventually be found.

While it's tempting to look at repositionings through a jaundiced eye, the fine-tuning of market position is responsible for the breadth of magazine choices. While the various women's or equestrian or log-home magazines look indistinguishable to my male, urban eyes, publications in each of these categories are actually holding a carefully carved niche on the newsstand. If they weren't, they wouldn't be there.

Out of Academia

7

AN INTERVIEW WITH MOISÉS NAÍM, EDITOR OF *FOREIGN POLICY*

Foreign Policy *was founded in 1970 as a scholarly journal on international politics and economics by the Carnegie Endowment for International Peace in Washington, D.C. In 2000, its mission expanded from the academic and diplomatic audience it had been serving to include a general audience. Reaching a larger audience required several changes in the design and editorial approach of the publication including increasing frequency from quarterly to bimonthly, increasing the physical size, and increasing the interior use of color.*

Could you tell me a bit about what you and other international-affairs journals were doing at the time you switched formats?

MOISÉS NAÍM: When I took over *Foreign Policy* in 1997, I did a study, and I discovered that there were literally hundreds of international-affairs magazines, although two were predominant: *Foreign Affairs* and *Foreign Policy*. So it was very clear that there was a market, but it was also clear to me that the market had been saturated by these highly specialized, more academic, more technical publications. I thought there was a place for a publication that would provide insights into how the world was changing, [for] readers who, while not experts, were still very interested in getting that kind of information—and without the acronyms and without the footnotes and the other academic affectations that general readers find off-putting. I was convinced that it was possible to retain intellectual rigor while making it more entertaining and easy to read.

Foreign Policy has always sought to get the best people in the world to write about what's going on and how they are thinking about what's going on. But, from the beginning of my editorship, we began to emphasize how the world is now connected in ways that are transforming life—our reader's family, company, town, and nation. We began to do the extra work necessary to show general readers why foreign affairs and politics affect them.

We have always had some of the best experts in the world, but we began working very closely with them to frame what they have to say in a way that is more accessible to nonexpert readers. After about a year of doing

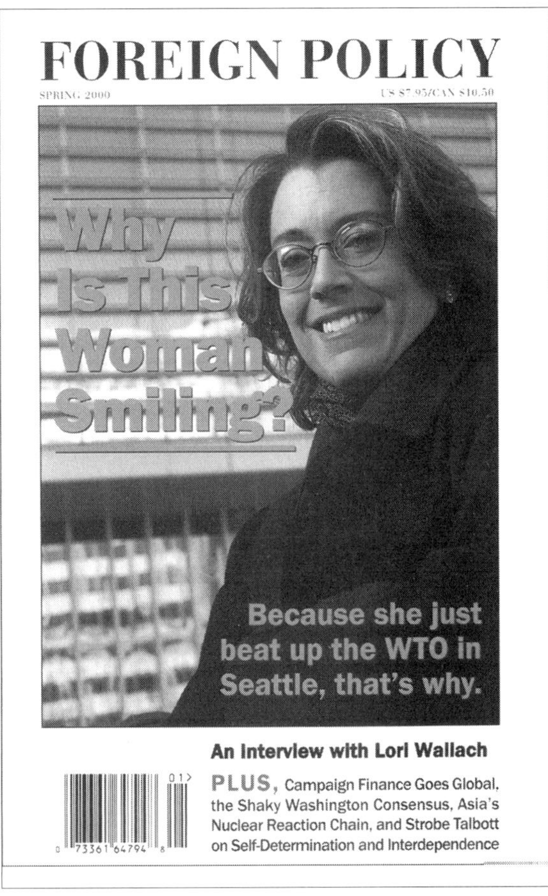

Before

this—we were then a quarterly—I discovered two things: The first is that we had become a general-circulation magazine and the second was that we were delivering this content through a publication that looked and felt like a specialized academic journal. My goal was to reach out and invite general readers to the conversation, but our vehicle inhibited that goal. Moreover, we were a quarterly, and we were black-and-white. We needed to be bolder.

We moved to bimonthly frequency and to a magazine format. We also started using the "FP" logo and brand, which is now well established. The goal was to visually communicate to the nonexpert that *FP* is not just for people who are in the business of foreign policy. If you are an interested reader of newspapers who wants

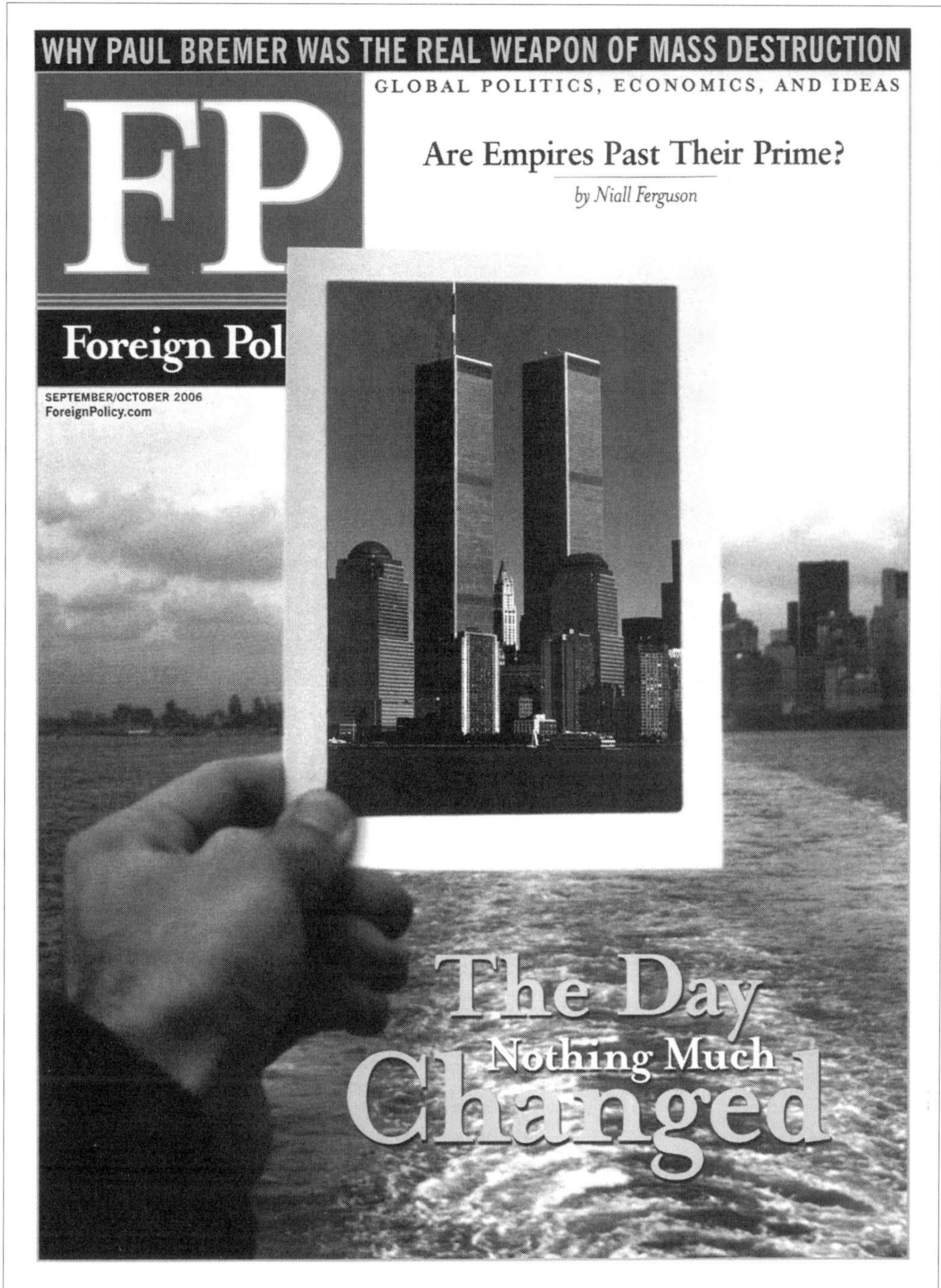

WHY PAUL BREMER WAS THE REAL WEAPON OF MASS DESTRUCTION
GLOBAL POLITICS, ECONOMICS, AND IDEAS
FP
Are Empires Past Their Prime?
by Niall Ferguson
Foreign Pol
SEPTEMBER/OCTOBER 2006
ForeignPolicy.com
The Day
Nothing Much
Changed

After

to know what is beyond the headlines and wants to understand more and know more about the world, then *FP* is for you.

Well, it's certainly true that if you read the *New York Times*, you get a lot of foreign policy and foreign news. If you read the *Des Moines Register* there's going to be nearly none.

Right, right. However, let me clarify: A huge number of our readers are also readers of the *New York Times*. They get the *Washington Post*; they watch CNN and the BBC. They are interested, but they feel that we provide value. We are growing quickly in circulation, and we're doing quite well at a time when growing circulation is a challenge for all print media. I think we were right in trying to position this magazine in a way that provides the best thinking in the world—state-of-the-art debates about international politics and economics—in a way that does not require readers to struggle with it.

A number of academic journals—and also literary magazines—have become visually friendlier, though most not to the degree *FP* has. Did you see yourself as part of this trend? Did you ultimately have this final result in mind, or did it just seem like the move from *Foreign Policy* to *FP* was a logical progression?

I don't claim to have had this perfect vision. This was an evolutionary concept. I inherited [the journal format], and I thought I could do a lot [within it], and then several things happened. I discovered that very often our advertisers did not have the art for the smaller format, and their advertising was not suited to it. I found that very often on newsstands this format tended to be overwhelmed and even covered up by magazines with larger formats. I also discovered that we would be included with the more academic group of publications when we were striving to reach out and cross over. Little by little, these concerns took us toward the changes we eventually made. What I knew—what I was certain of—was that the content had to change with the design. We worked on new content and began looking for a design that would fit it—form would work with function.

A lot of publications do what are called "repositionings," but it's along the lines of a magazine like *Mademoiselle* deciding that its readership has gotten two years too old, so it redesigns and adjusts to pick up younger readers. Your repositioning was far more dramatic. I can think of only one more example of an academic journal that became a popular magazine—*Psychology Today*, about twenty years ago now. It lasted for only a few years afterward, although the title is publishing again now after a long absence. What were your apprehensions?

Many. It was a big gamble, and I was very fortunate to have the support of the president and the board of trustees of the Carnegie Endowment, which owns the publication. But some skeptics said, "You're not going to get any of that new market that you dream of, because it does not exist. What you're going to do instead is alienate traditional readers—the experts, the ambassadors, the State Department types, the security wonks who want gravitas." And I kept saying, "My content is going to be as appealing to them as ever." If you talk to our writers, they will tell you we are rigorous, we are intellectually very demanding. Our arduous [editing] process does not aim at altering our

Lifting Asia's spirits: Wine is taking off in Japan and China.

Vintage Asia

What do you pair with Kung Pao chicken: Bordeaux or Chianti? These days, it's not uncommon for Asians to ask. Having adopted McDonald's and Coca-Cola, Asia is now developing a taste for the West's snobbiest beverage: wine. Denis Gastin, an Australian wine critic and authority on the Asian wine scene, says that the latest generation is particularly keen: "Younger people in the more affluent countries generally see wine as part of being 'international,' and many encountered the wine lifestyle while working or studying overseas." Japan is leading the way, followed by Hong Kong and Singapore, and China is catching up. According to the *Shanghai Daily*, wine imports surged 91 percent in the first three quarters of 2006. China now has some 500 wineries. The country's vineyards (almost half of which are planted with cabernet sauvignon) have grown so fast that China recently became one of the top 10 wine-producing nations by acreage.

The European wine industry is certainly not turning up its nose at the China market. Last year, French wine exports to China were expected to top $100 million, and many French companies are partnering with domestic Chinese wineries. Italy is aggressively marketing its wine in China, as well as investing in Chinese vintages. In 2005, the northern Italy-based liqueur producer Illva Saronno Group bought a 33 percent stake in ChangYu, China's oldest and largest wine producer.

Although many of the Asian wines lag behind their Western competitors, quality is on the rise. Some of them are even being exported to the United States and elsewhere, mostly finding their way onto the wine lists of ethnic eateries. So what goes best with Kung Pao chicken? Perhaps a nice glass of Dragon Seal Cabernet Sauvignon. *—Jim Clarke*

Money Talks

Is the global economy too hot, too cold, or just right? *FP* took its temperature by talking to one of Wall Street's most influential voices, Michael Klein, CEO of global banking at Citigroup and vice chairman of Citibank International.

FOREIGN POLICY: Which emerging markets have the best prospects in the short-to-medium term, from the position of an investor?

Michael Klein: Of course, it's impossible to look at the growth in India and China and not be impressed. However, the question as an investor is different. If you had invested in the Chinese stock markets over the past five or 10 years, you likely would not have made a significant amount of money. One of the least focused upon factors in these emerging markets is the money coming out. Investors need to focus far more on the capital leaving the emerging markets. There was a 12-month period [in 2005 when] there was more outbound capital from China than there was foreign direct investment.

FP: Which of the oil exporting countries is using its petrodollars most wisely?

MK: In 1998, [Russia was] a $200 billion economy. Today, it's about a $900 billion economy—part of that is chained to the ruble, but a fair bit of that is growth. They've paid off virtually all of their external debt. They've got $250 billion of reserves and substantial growth rates.

FP: How long can China continue posting double digit growth?

MK: It's clear that [the Chinese economy] has been growing more rapidly than most appreciated for 25 years. One has to assume that growth in China will continue in the intermediate term because when a government is spending 42 percent of [gross domestic product] on new capital into the economy—which would be equivalent to $5 trillion a year in the United States—it is going to have a continued drive toward development.

Buying in: China's economy will continue to roar.

22 Foreign Policy

Unskilled and in demand: Domestic workers boost rich countries' productivity.

Most Valuable Migrants

If the United States had to choose between letting in an Indian computer scientist or a nanny from Mexico, it might seem like a no-brainer. But, according to a new study by Harvard economists Michael Kremer and Stanley Watt, it's not so obvious. They found that unskilled immigrants, contrary to the conventional wisdom, can actually reduce wage inequality and make a country richer.

Kremer explains his findings by pointing out that domestic workers can increase a country's supply of highly skilled workers by allowing well-educated parents (generally mothers) to remain in the workforce. Household help is actually far more liberating to parents than day care, he argues, because nannies let them work the long hours required by many high-powered, high-paying jobs.

The findings aren't limited to the United States. According to the study, countries can boost their gross domestic product by as much as 1.2 percent by allowing foreign household workers to make up 7 percent of their labor force—just as Hong Kong (6.8 percent) and Singapore (7 percent) do. Not surprisingly, these economies have seen even higher rates of workforce participation among women between the ages of 25 and 34 than the United States, where foreign household workers account for only 0.3 percent of the country's workforce.

Not everyone, however, is convinced. Steven Camarota, director of research at the Center for Immigration Studies in Washington, D.C., disputes Kremer's conclusions, arguing that importing more household help will be a "double-whammy" that drives down wages for poor Americans and further burdens taxpayer-funded social services. He also notes survey data that suggest that "people want the ability to stay home, rather than the ability to hire someone to take care of their kids." But then again, with neither the demands of childrearing nor the rigors of corporate America on the decline, nanny might know best. *—James G. Forsyth*

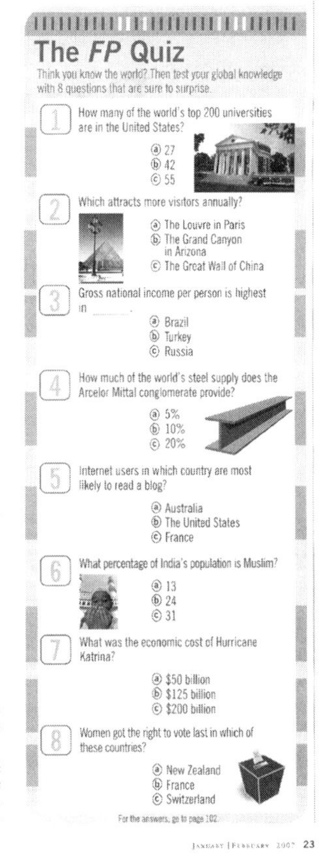

The *FP* Quiz

Think you know the world? Then test your global knowledge with 8 questions that are sure to surprise.

1. How many of the world's top 200 universities are in the United States?
   ⓐ 27
   ⓑ 42
   ⓒ 55
2. Which attracts more visitors annually?
   ⓐ The Louvre in Paris
   ⓑ The Grand Canyon in Arizona
   ⓒ The Great Wall of China
3. Gross national income per person is highest in ______.
   ⓐ Brazil
   ⓑ Turkey
   ⓒ Russia
4. How much of the world's steel supply does the Arcelor Mittal conglomerate provide?
   ⓐ 5%
   ⓑ 10%
   ⓒ 20%
5. Internet users in which country are most likely to read a blog?
   ⓐ Australia
   ⓑ The United States
   ⓒ France
6. What percentage of India's population is Muslim?
   ⓐ 13
   ⓑ 24
   ⓒ 31
7. What was the economic cost of Hurricane Katrina?
   ⓐ $50 billion
   ⓑ $125 billion
   ⓒ $200 billion
8. Women got the right to vote last in which of these countries?
   ⓐ New Zealand
   ⓑ France
   ⓒ Switzerland

For the answers, go to page 102.

January | February 2007 23

Foreign Policy's *front news section*

writer's ideas. It aims at making those ideas accessible to our readers. But that was our main apprehension—that the market we were trying to reach was not there, and by becoming more reader-friendly, we would be interpreted as being light.

In fact, if you look today, we have become better known and respected than ever. We have nothing to envy about anyone in terms of the world-class, worldwide personalities we have. We get literally hundreds of manuscripts a week, many of them from some of the most prominent thinkers, practitioners, and world leaders. Our traditional readers continue to like it, and we have been successful in importing readers to this field who otherwise would never read a journal called *Foreign Policy*.

What were some of the reactions of your longtime readers to the redesign? Did any of them write in or talk to you at conferences?

In the beginning people were perplexed, but very quickly they discovered there was something here that they had to read—that you could not afford to work in the field without subscribing to *Foreign Policy* magazine. Our first issue was dated September/October of 2000—that was a year before 9/11. Well, one article is "What Makes Suicide Terrorists Tick?"—a topic then under the radar, and that was written by one of the world's most respected experts in the field who had interviewed foiled suicide terrorists and others who had been tempted to become suicide terrorists. Another article—the cover story—was about the meltdown in the stock market, which had not yet happened, and it was a story about the global consequences if the stock market in the United States took a dip, which, in fact, it later did. So in every issue we are capable of surprising our readers with writing that is interesting, prescient, and pleasurable. *FP* is not taking your medicine. It's not even eating spinach. It is a magazine someone can take for a weekend and enjoy.

Can we talk about some of the specific things that the new format, with its meshing of content and form, allows you to do that you could not have done previously?

In every issue, we have a feature called "Prime Numbers," which is essentially a complex story told in

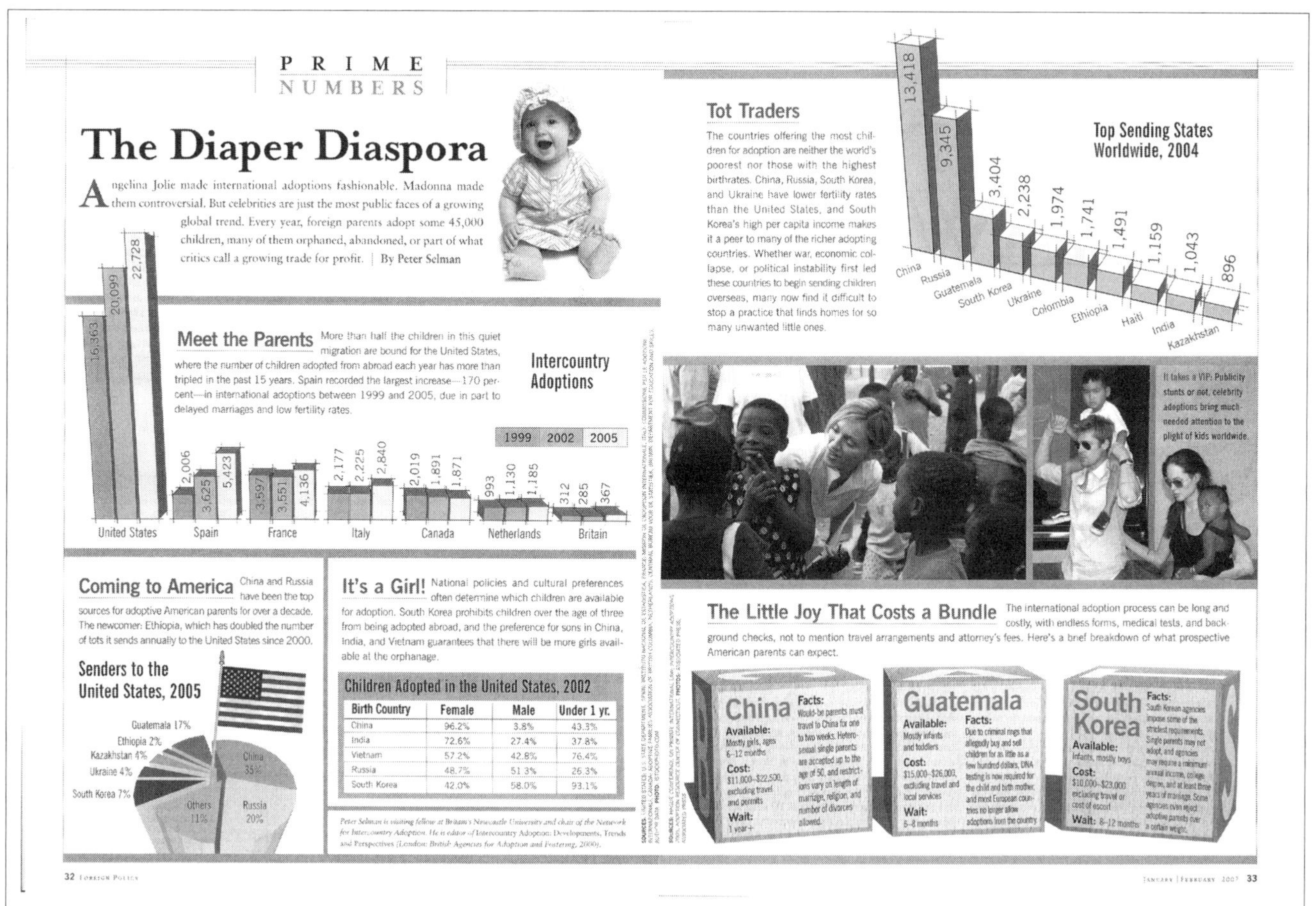
PRIME NUMBERS

The Diaper Diaspora

Angelina Jolie made international adoptions fashionable. Madonna made them controversial. But celebrities are just the most public faces of a growing global trend. Every year, foreign parents adopt some 45,000 children, many of them orphaned, abandoned, or part of what critics call a growing trade for profit. | By Peter Selman

Meet the Parents More than half the children in this quiet migration are bound for the United States, where the number of children adopted from abroad each year has more than tripled in the past 15 years. Spain recorded the largest increase—170 percent—in international adoptions between 1999 and 2005, due in part to delayed marriages and low fertility rates.

Intercountry Adoptions

	1999	2002	2005
United States	16,363	20,099	22,728
Spain	2,006	3,625	5,423
France	3,597	3,551	4,136
Italy	2,177	2,225	2,840
Canada	2,019	1,891	1,871
Netherlands	993	1,130	1,185
Britain	312	285	367

Tot Traders

The countries offering the most children for adoption are neither the world's poorest nor those with the highest birthrates. China, Russia, South Korea, and Ukraine have lower fertility rates than the United States, and South Korea's high per capita income makes it a peer to many of the richer adopting countries. Whether war, economic collapse, or political instability first led these countries to begin sending children overseas, many now find it difficult to stop a practice that finds homes for so many unwanted little ones.

Top Sending States Worldwide, 2004

China	13,418
Russia	9,345
Guatemala	3,404
South Korea	2,238
Ukraine	1,974
Colombia	1,741
Ethiopia	1,491
Haiti	1,159
India	1,043
Kazakhstan	896

It takes a VIP: Publicity stunts or not, celebrity adoptions bring much-needed attention to the plight of kids worldwide.

Coming to America China and Russia have been the top sources for adoptive American parents for over a decade. The newcomer: Ethiopia, which has doubled the number of tots it sends annually to the United States since 2000.

Senders to the United States, 2005

China 35%
Russia 20%
Others 11%
South Korea 7%
Ukraine 4%
Kazakhstan 4%
Ethiopia 2%
Guatemala 17%

It's a Girl! National policies and cultural preferences often determine which children are available for adoption. South Korea prohibits children over the age of three from being adopted abroad, and the preference for sons in China, India, and Vietnam guarantees that there will be more girls available at the orphanage.

Children Adopted in the United States, 2002

Birth Country	Female	Male	Under 1 yr.
China	96.2%	3.8%	43.3%
India	72.6%	27.4%	37.8%
Vietnam	57.2%	42.8%	76.4%
Russia	48.7%	51.3%	26.3%
South Korea	42.0%	58.0%	93.1%

Peter Selman is visiting fellow at Britain's Newcastle University and chair of the Network for Intercountry Adoption. He is editor of Intercountry Adoption: Developments, Trends and Perspectives *(London: British Agencies for Adoption and Fostering, 2000).*

The Little Joy That Costs a Bundle The international adoption process can be long and costly, with endless forms, medical tests, and background checks, not to mention travel arrangements and attorney's fees. Here's a brief breakdown of what prospective American parents can expect.

China
Available: Mostly girls, ages 6–12 months
Cost: \$11,000–\$22,500, excluding travel and permits
Wait: 1 year+
Facts: Would-be parents must travel to China for one to two weeks. Heterosexual single parents are accepted up to the age of 50, and restrictions vary on length of marriage, religion, and number of divorces allowed.

Guatemala
Available: Mostly infants and toddlers
Cost: \$15,000–\$26,000, excluding travel and local services
Wait: 6–8 months
Facts: Due to criminal rings that allegedly buy and sell children for as little as a few hundred dollars, DNA testing is now required for the child and birth mother, and most European countries no longer allow adoptions from the country.

South Korea
Available: Infants, mostly boys
Cost: \$10,000–\$23,000 excluding travel or cost of escort
Wait: 8–12 months
Facts: South Korean agencies impose some of the strictest requirements. Single parents may not adopt, and agencies may require a minimum annual income, college degree, and at least three years of marriage. Some agencies even reject adoptive parents over a certain weight.

32 FOREIGN POLICY

JANUARY | FEBRUARY 2007 33

Prime Numbers

a two-page spread with just statistics, presented through attractive, bold, and easy-to-understand charts. We take a complex theme, work with some of the best experts, and convert a vast amount of information into a two-page spread. It's a very popular feature, and it would not have been possible without this format.

The other is the use of design in a way academic journals can't. We want readers to be able to access the publication from many points of entry, not just the first page. We rely on irreverent captions and attractive pictures to do this.

You see, we know that the way we all read newspapers and magazines is that the first thing we look at is the headline, picture, and captions—they're often what get us to read. So, if I get a picture that attracts your attention to an article on public health in China, perhaps, and how that touches you and can threaten you. . . . It may be that that is not a topic a reader naturally finds compelling. But an engaging picture, a caption, and pullout quotes that provide layers of information; an interesting title and deck—that all creates a context that may tempt the reader to begin the article. If I get him or her to read the first two or three paragraphs, then it's very likely that I'm going to get him or her to read most of the article.

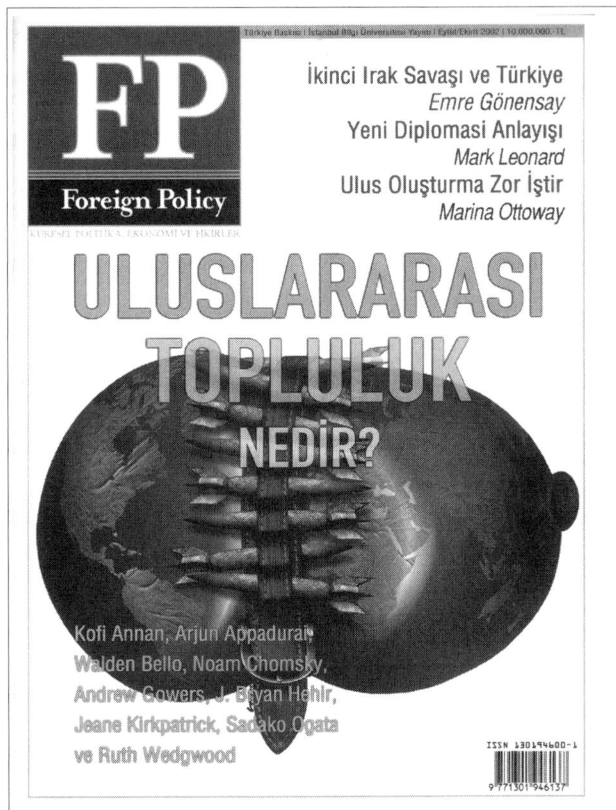

FP *foreign edition*

Is there anything you think you could have done with the old format that would be harder with the new format?

I'm tempted to say—but I would not agree with myself saying it—perhaps the ten-thousand- or fifteen-thousand-word pieces that we did we couldn't do [now], but that's not true. You see pieces of that length in the *Atlantic* or *Smithsonian* or the *New Yorker* all the time. So, no, it's not true.

But do you find yourself running fewer pieces of that length?

Yes, and by design. We do a lot of reader surveys, and uniformly we don't find there is much demand for those very long articles. And what we have found is that if you are a good editor, you can trim down a ten-thousand-, eight-thousand-word article into five thousand words and get the best and the essence of the argument. In every section and every article, one of our most popular features is titled "Want to Know More?" which is a narrated set of suggestions. It lists articles on our Web site and also discusses who else has written articles either challenging or supporting and extending the assertions made in our article. We give readers who want more information effective ways to find it.

You mentioned that your readership has gone up. Do you know how much?

We are at about a 110,000 circulation. We are also published in eleven other languages; if you add those we have about 100,000 more. We had approximately 20,000 readers when we switched, so it has been a great success, particularly if you take into account that this happened during an economic downturn and during the explosion of Internet material in which people—actually the kind of readers we have who are very Internet savvy—are gravitating toward nonpaid content. It also happened during what has been a complete collapse in the effectiveness of direct-mail advertising.

My magazine has also quit doing direct mail.

Everybody will tell you that you now get—and started getting in the late 1990s—many fewer responses from direct-mail campaigns, unless you put really a huge amount of money into it over a very long period and back it up with extensive statistical testing. Little by little, and almost inadvertently, we have had very organic growth, and the Web has been a friend to us; it has been a major source of paid subscribers for the print publication. We are not threatened by the Web. We are using it very happily, and it has been a major pillar of our increasing commercial success.

FP *foreign editions*

How does the Internet serve that purpose?

People discover us on the Web, particularly people in quantities and geographies that would have been prohibitive to get to through traditional means. Our Web site is very active. Recently we launched a blog that is also doing very well for us.

If this is a question you don't want to answer, I understand, but with all its success, has *FP* become a moneymaker for Carnegie?

No, and I don't mind saying it. The Carnegie Endowment's commitment is to try and promote peace in the world, and the board of trustees and the presidents of the endowment have interpreted that one way of creating a more peaceful world is by having a global dialogue about important ideas. And that fits perfectly with the mission of the magazine. We get a subsidy from the Carnegie Endowment—it's declining, and we are doing better. We could survive without the subsidy, but we would have to pare down—we would become a different magazine in a variety of ways. That's not in the cards, and there is strong support within Carnegie to continue the rapid expansion of the magazine.

When I look at the design, it's very friendly, readable, and elegant, but it also has a very conservative feel. Looking to the future, do you ever see *FP* getting yet more mainstream—I'm not suggesting you'd ever have the "Girls of the G8" featured on the cover . . .

No, the magazine has a feel and personality. People know what to expect from *Foreign Policy*. The genius behind the look is my colleague Travis Daub, who has been the art and design director [since we launched the new look], and he was and is a big part of our success. We will continue to innovate. . . . We have several innovations in the cards that will transform us even more. But those innovations are more in the realm of content—new features and new sections and new, interesting, and surprising ways of looking at the world. Some of these changes will come attached with changes in design, but the next challenge for us is to continue to appeal with innovation—we try to be innovative without changing the basic anchors that have served us so well.

We have proved that taking an academic publication mainstream is possible and that other journals can do it, too. One should not shy away from reaching out to broader segments of the market while retaining seriousness and rigor. We always say that we like rigor but not rigor mortis.

Details

8

STEVEN HELLER

In 1982, *Details* started life as a small, independent magazine covering the fashions and lifestyle of Manhattan's SoHo neighborhood. It soon acquired a hip, young downtowner following. Owing to this modest success, the magazine was bought by Condé Nast in 1988. But instead of being permitted to retain its identity, *Details* was relaunched as a large, uptown men's fashion magazine under the editorship of James Truman (who later replaced Alexander Liberman as creative czar of the publishing giant). After a few years

Details, before Condé Nast . . .

of editorial changes spurred by competition from hot, soft-core men's mags like *Maxim* (whose editor, Mark Golin, was eventually hired by *Details*) and the more entrenched, institutionally fashionable *GQ*, sales of the magazine faltered, and Condé Nast halted publication of *Details* in the spring of 2000.

That's where the story might have ended. Instead, the title was shuttled over to Condé Nast's sibling, Fairchild Publications (both now owned by Advance Publications), where *Details* was resurrected as a twentysomething men's lifestyle magazine and is currently struggling to find a viability in the market.

Since magazines tend to reflect their times and demographics, it puzzles me why *Details*, which made sense when it was "downtown," would be bought by Condé Nast only to be divested of what made it exciting and then killed for failing to live up to its imposed identity. And it's doubly puzzling that after tanking "uptown," it would emerge, phoenixlike, amid the tangle of trendy lifestyle magazines that currently clutter the field.

Condé Nast's *Details* never found its true focus, a fact evident in the design format. During the "downtown" phase, *Details* had been produced on a low budget with a fairly high degree of design acuity. Not being a downtown Gen Xer myself, I was not especially interested in the zeitgeist tips that were its regular fare, but I was certainly impressed by how the magazine was

. . . and after

art-directed and designed. The lively format was neither slavishly trendy nor vapidly retro. And the covers in particular always caught my attention because even when someone as personally unpalatable as Joan Rivers was featured, the approach was usually tongue in cheek. *Details* never took itself too seriously. Moreover, the logo was always being reconfigured, suggesting that someone was wide awake in the art department.

While Condé Nast is no stranger to making successful magazines, its publications invariably follow (even as they also initiate) editorial and design formulas. *Wired* is an example: When the magazine was acquired by Condé Nast in the late nineties, its edge was dulled—a result of its unique original design being blended with predictable contemporary conceits. Today, there is very little emblematic typographic sensibility in *Wired*'s pages.

Likewise in *Details*. After it was repositioned to compete with *Esquire*, *GQ*, and *Maxim*, its design became indistinguishable from the many publications vying with each other on the newsstand.

This is not to say that it was entirely bereft of visual interest. Tucked between stories about "peak performance sex," "peak performance health," and "peak performance fitness" were hype pieces about up-and-coming film stars (e.g., Ewan McGregor years before *Moulin Rouge*) photographed by stellar photographers like Herb Ritts, as well as superstar fashion spreads and sports exposés. And somewhere toward the back of each issue were brilliant comic-strip essays by the likes of Art Spiegelman, Kaz, Joe Sacco, and Peter Kuper, on themes as varied as rock festivals and war crimes. But to find these gems, you had to wade through a swamp of cluttered layouts and clunky type choices.

The major design flaw of Condé Nast's *Details* was that its appearance did not characterize the magazine clearly enough; it was too generic. In *Details*' original incarnation, the design was in sync with the readers' sensibilities—a bit untutored, somewhat brash, but confident—very downtown. The Condé Nast version was deliberately messy but with a professional sheen—very uptown. Its interior typographic scheme changed somewhat from issue to issue, but unlike, say, *Rolling Stone*, it lacked an overarching reason for this shifting.

In the November 1998 special music issue, for example, each front-of-the-book story was fitted with a different novelty typeface that sat at the top of the page as though taken arbitrarily from a seventies Typositor

I met with Aidan Quinn on the last day of 1987, sort of an early New Year's Eve date. Okay, it was only lunch, but it *felt* like a date. After a few preliminaries, he asked me my date of birth, did some quick calculations, and said that 1987 had probably not been an easy year for me. But he assured me that 1988 holds a lot more promise, and although I might feel boxed in, I have nowhere to go but up. Immediately I felt better.

Actually, it's easy to feel better just being in Aidan's company. The guy is relaxed and cheerful, and concerned with lots more than his image or star status: what we're doing to the water on this planet, the growing militancy of the Irish Republican Army, the role of healers, and his new dog Scamp.

Since we were both in upstate New York, I let Aidan choose the place—an omelette shop just outside Woodstock. There was a row of bells on the door, and it sounded like the North Pole during the Christmas rush. He came in looking rumpled and sleepy, carrying a worn copy of *A Streetcar Named Desire*. His new wife, Elizabeth Bracco, dropped him off and asked if I would mind taking him home after we talked. Mind?

Aidan is a regular here, so the waitress came by to apologize for being out of cheddar. Because he's trying to beef up for the role of Stanley Kowalski, he's given up smoking. He didn't seem to know what to do with his hands, and he chewed his gum ravenously.

While we ate, he kept his chewed gum stuck to the side of his plate ("You never know when you'll need it"). When his eggs came, he splashed ketchup over them, mounded them high on a piece of toast, and stuffed the whole mess into his mouth, talking and gesturing the whole time. Bits of egg and ketchup cascaded down his chin and onto his shirt. The pieces that remained on his plate he picked up with his fingers. I was transfixed.

When I told my friends I was interviewing him, all the men had questions. Did he do his own motorcycle riding in *Reckless*? ("Yeah," he said, "I did. I still have the bike. It's up at my house. Wanna see it?") What was it like doing *The Mission* with Robert De Niro? ("I'll tell you a funny story. Before I got into movies, I was maybe twenty-two, I took an acting class with Byrne Piven. He went off to do a movie, so Barbara Harris took over the class. I hadn't done anything yet, just a couple of little plays, and sometimes I was lazy and didn't show up for class. One day I skipped it, and my best friends called me up, yelling and carrying on. 'Hey Aidan, you really fucked up,' they said. 'Robert De Niro showed up today. You missed him, Aidan. You missed him 'cause you're lazy, you really blew it.' And they were going on and on, so goo-goo eyed, and I never liked that kind of adulation, plus I had moments of great arrogance in my youth, so I said, 'Yeah, that's no big deal. I don't want to see him in class, man, I'm going to *work* with the guy someday!' And then there I was down in Brazil, doing *The Mission* with Robert De Niro. The best part of working with him was watching how focused the man is. He actually transforms in front of your eyes. And then to discover that all those stories about him 'turning into his character,' and not being able to relate except as that character, well, that was total bullshit.") How was it working with Sam Shepard in *A Lie of the Mind*? ("I love his writing. I had done *Fool For Love*, which was a blast to do. It was very difficult, sometimes I'd feel just like the character: beat; bruised, burned-out and disgusting. And then the next night, you'd have just *so much fun*. The audience would be excited, emotional, laughing. With *A Lie of the Mind*, we had a luxurious, wonderful ten-week rehearsal. There was a terrific cast: Harvey Keitel, Amanda Plummer, Will Patton. There was tremendous freedom given to the actors within the context of the play.")

Yet a lot of my women friends said that they didn't really have anything to ask him, they just wanted to be in the same room and stare. Aidan seemed genuinely surprised when I told him this. "Nah," he said. "Is that for real?" I assured him that it was. Does that happen to him often? "Well, when you're in Sears, or in a supermarket, and these certain people look at you, because they recognize you, and they're women and young girls, and they're attracted to you . . . well, you could easily go 'umm-hmmm.' It's

Quintessential Quinn

Martha Frankel
photographed by Michael Tighe

110

A feature from before the redesign

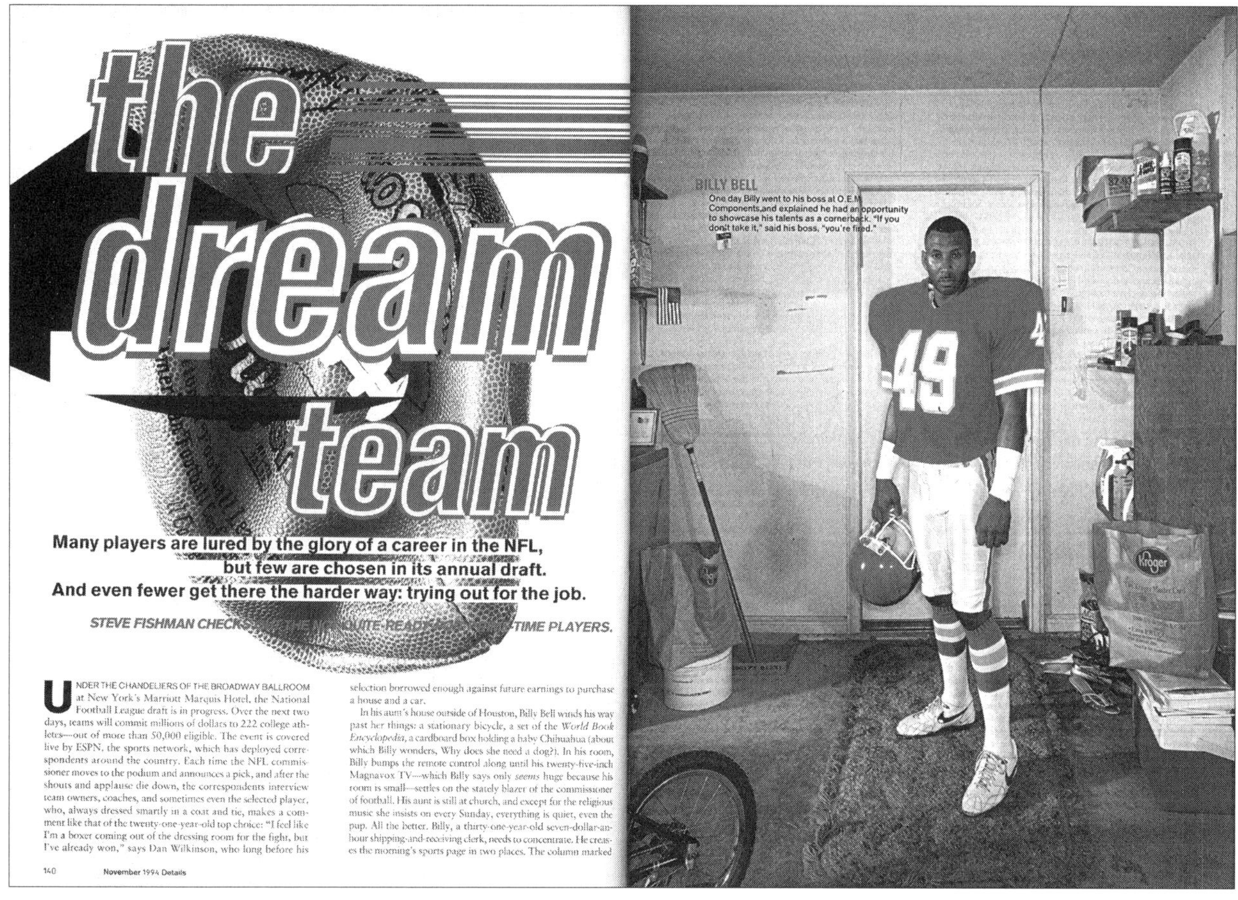

the dream team

Many players are lured by the glory of a career in the NFL, but few are chosen in its annual draft. And even fewer get there the harder way: trying out for the job.

STEVE FISHMAN CHECKS … QUITE-READY … -TIME PLAYERS.

UNDER THE CHANDELIERS OF THE BROADWAY BALLROOM at New York's Marriott Marquis Hotel, the National Football League draft is in progress. Over the next two days, teams will commit millions of dollars to 222 college athletes—out of more than 50,000 eligible. The event is covered live by ESPN, the sports network, which has deployed correspondents around the country. Each time the NFL commissioner moves to the podium and announces a pick, and after the shouts and applause die down, the correspondents interview team owners, coaches, and sometimes even the selected player, who, always dressed smartly in a coat and tie, makes a comment like that of the twenty-one-year-old top choice: "I feel like I'm a boxer coming out of the dressing room for the fight, but I've already won," says Dan Wilkinson, who long before his selection borrowed enough against future earnings to purchase a house and a car.

In his aunt's house outside of Houston, Billy Bell winds his way past her things: a stationary bicycle, a set of the *World Book Encyclopedia*, a cardboard box holding a baby Chihuahua (about which Billy wonders, Why does she need a dog?). In his room, Billy bumps the remote control along until his twenty-five-inch Magnavox TV—which Billy says only *seems* huge because his room is small—settles on the stately blazer of the commissioner of football. His aunt is still at church, and except for the religious music she insists on every Sunday, everything is quiet, even the pup. All the better. Billy, a thirty-one-year-old seven-dollar-an-hour shipping-and-receiving clerk, needs to concentrate. He creases the morning's sports page in two places. The column marked

140 November 1994 Details

BILLY BELL

One day Billy went to his boss at O.E.M Components,and explained he had an opportunity to showcase his talents as a cornerback. "If you don't take it," said his boss, "you're fired."

Details, 1994

specimen book. In this same issue, a feature on a sex party in Ibiza, Spain, shows a raunchy photograph of naked women smeared with blood (or red paint; it's hard to tell) and the layout is splattered with postpsychedelic sixties-style polka dots used as a design motif. I'm not sure why, but a few pages later, for an interview with Sheryl Crow, a clever headline, "Mason Vixen," is set in faux psychedelic lettering, which would have made sense if the very nineties Crow in any way recalled the sixties, which she doesn't.

Details ceased publication in the spring of 2000, its top editorial staff tossed from the Condé Nast stable. When Fairchild Publications reissued *Details* for its October 2000 issue, the magazine had a new logo, a new size, and a brand new contemporary format. While covering essentially the same subjects (though without the comic strip essays, which is truly a loss), it is more intelligently uniform and at the same time livelier than its predecessor.

This reincarnated *Details* clearly rejects the Condé Nast method of stuffing a great many stories into a given issue. The covers consequently sport fewer cover lines—the effect being that a beefcake portrait of Robert Downey Jr. on the premiere cover, for example, is not hidden behind a forest of Day-Glo type. So far, all the covers have featured hot male stars, unlike the emphasis on women of the Condé Nast *Details*. More refreshing, however, is the serious attempt at dynamic pacing in an uninterrupted editorial well that extends for a surprisingly large number of pages and for over a dozen features. If anything, the well goes on too long; because the text-heavy articles do not jump to the back, the result is a few large expanses of gray type.

Photography is *Details*' mainstay, and many of the images are provocative. Painted and drawn illustration, which has all but been eliminated in most fashion magazines, also makes a welcome, if limited, showing in the first few issues. Using real artists to create actual paintings rather than Photoshop collages is a virtue these days—and the illustrator credit is set nice and large.

The new and old *Details* share one element: those pesky polka dots mentioned above. In the new version, the type for all the regular department headings ("Vitals," "In the Works," etc.) is set in a dot-punch typeface, which at small sizes affords a typographic personality. Inside the well, the dot type is supplanted by gothic serif and sans-serif faces. The first five issues reviewed for this chapter reveal a much cleaner, smarter, and more rational format than was the case in the Condé Nast version. Rather than a hodgepodge, this is a magazine with a discernible beginning, middle, and end.

And yet I have an odd sense of déjà vu.

No, *Details* doesn't bear a resemblance to its predecessor. But it does resemble *Flaunt* and other contemporary lifestyle books on today's newsstand. Too many bits of other magazine formats mar its overall look. What's more, the typeface for the masthead—even granted that this is the most difficult of all design decisions—bears no relationship to any other typestyle in the magazine. Just as one can tell a lot about an artist by the way he draws hands, so does a logo's integration into a publication format say much about the designer.

Trading in the Condé Nast formula for what might be called "zeitgeist design" may have substantially improved *Details*—it's surely more readable and engaging than before—but a unique design experience it isn't.

Lost Equity

9

ROGER BLACK

THERE WAS A PERIOD IN AMERICAN MAGAZINE publishing when a redesign was built to last. The classic example is Walter Bernard's redesign of *Time* in 1977. Never mind the brilliant art direction and widely copied innovations in information graphics. The thing that stuck was the type. Bernard (who had won his stripes designing *New York* magazine) banished the modernist sans-serif typefaces used for headlines since the forties. The new design brought in Franklin Gothic, and after forty years, Franklin *is Time* magazine, and if you brought back Futura it would look wrong.

Few readers noticed that *Time* has been redesigned several times since. Another version was underway in early 2007, advised by Paula Scher and Luke Hayman of Pentagram. They would be mad to throw out the Franklin Gothic, no matter what else they change. That is part of the design equity of *Time*, and four decades of consistent typographical branding is a big asset.

In the sixties and seventies there were three other landmarks in redesign: *Esquire* (Sam Antupit), *Reader's Digest* (Bradbury Thompson), and *Rolling Stone* (starting with Robert Kingsbury and Mike Salisbury). Their designers thought long and hard about what made the visual style of the magazine—what photographers and artists could best create its look, what typefaces matched its voice.

The results fit so well that after those art directors moved on, their successors continued to work within the established styles. The result was evolutionary growth, not quick rehabilitation. Regular tweaks were made to the core design, however, to keep up with changing fashions.

In the nineties, magazines began to feel strong pressure, first from special-interest cable channels and then from the Web. When circulation and advertising sagged, publishers wanted a quick fix: something that would show up in the quarterly report for shareholders. They turned to quickie redesigns—solutions that most often came at the expense of long-term visual equity.

Frequent redesign became the fashion, a quick and nervous coating-over of magazines that most likely would not make a similarly impulsive editorial move. *Wired* and *Fast Company* made a big splash when introduced in the early nineties, in part because of their innovative designs. A few years later both titles jettisoned their distinctive looks in favor of something trendy—but generic. Why?

The danger in adopting a current fad is that the result will look like everything else. *BusinessWeek* and *Newsweek* both adopted the contemporary headline typeface—Champion, a powerful sans with wood-type origins. Unfortunately, Champion, which I dare say was first used by *Premiere*, had become the signature font of *Sports Illustrated*, one of the only other surviving weeklies. It became faddish, and *SI* moved to a serif-based "classic" design, partly in an effort to move away from *ESPN Magazine*, which had claimed the "contemporary" ground. The weeklies meanwhile had lost something of themselves.

The big women's magazines are no longer the original Seven Sisters (*McCall's*, once famous for its own design equity, is gone), and waves of editors with new editorial plans washed over them, bringing in new art directors with the tide. Once, each had its own feeling. You wouldn't mistake a page in *Ladies Home Journal* for one in *Good Housekeeping*. But as business and technology stresses affected their newsstand sales, they began to search for editorial formulae, cover headlines, and typography that would sell more copies. By 2000, they had copied each other so much that they all looked alike. Big numbers, type in colored circles, headlines about diet and sex—the same elements combined to make every cover generic. It didn't help (circulation continued to decline) in part because readers can now barely tell them apart.

Inevitably, new women's titles arrived to fill the personality gap. *O, The Oprah Magazine*, has come to occupy the narrative position of the old *McCall's*. *Martha Stewart Living* created a whole new design sensibility, with its calming pastels and refined custom typefaces. *Real Simple* is simpler still, but it's a big success.

All three have established a wealth of design equity. They've all been out long enough to undergo several mild redesigns. Meanwhile, readers, who have become remarkably sophisticated about design and redesign, followed the changes easily because they were natural improvements and not radical breaks. Now invited to interact with editors on magazine Web sites, readers are quick to point out when the design looks wrong for a magazine.

There are other titles that have tried to build on their design equity over the last fifteen years. *Rolling Stone* continues to evoke its legacy, and *New York* is reinvigorated through the combination of new ideas and classic elements from the past.

The *New Yorker* was brilliantly modernized by Massimo Vignellli, who adapted Rea Irwin's trademark custom typeface to a contemporary grid. *Texas Monthly*, through a series of art directors, continues to evolve (now with a fine set of slab-serif fonts by Champion's designer, Jonathan Hoefler) but has retained its energy, surprising illustrations, and a strong narrative style of photography. The result: It still looks like *Texas Monthly.* At a time of business crisis in publishing, the success of revived titles like *New York* should indicate how to build the design of a magazine, but most of the industry is still bobbing on the wavelets of fashion. They change it and then change it again. Instead of working with a visual foundation and redesigning gradually or restoring the enduring elements, many magazines change their looks every year. And they change their art directors, many of whom spend more time looking at the design annuals than reading the copy in their own magazines. So it is no surprise that they look alike. As a result, redesign is treated trivially, a kind of window dressing. Editors talk about doing a "makeover" as though the design of their magazines were no more fundamental than a haircut. It is true that improving layout software, inexpensive color printing, and larger design staffs have brought periodical design to a higher technical level, but the new polish cannot replace individuality or chance-taking.

Once committed to a redesign, editors and publishers have to decide whether to bring in an outside redesign expert or do it themselves. As someone who makes a living redesigning publications, you'd think I'd urge them to hire consultants, but I've done it both ways, and each way has advantages.

The staff art director of a magazine, assuming he reads the copy (it borders on malpractice if he doesn't), should know it better than any outsider. The insider knows the politics, knows the readers, and knows the advertising market. But sometimes all that knowledge gets in the way. The consultant is happily oblivious to all the rules the staffer has learned. ("We don't do it that way.")

Condé Nast magazines get around this problem by hiring new art directors (now called creative directors, like at ad agencies) every time they want a big change at a magazine. (They're not the only ones who work this way—that's also how I got hired at *New York*, the *New York Times Magazine*, and *Newsweek*.)

The first bit of advice I would give a new art director brought in under these circumstances is this: Don't detach yourself from the production of regular issues. You've got to get into the trenches to learn what you need to know about the title and the people. You've got to put out some markers and make some friends, particularly on the printing and production side.

Second: Move quickly. The honeymoon lasts about six months.

At *Newsweek* I learned a lot about how to do redesigns. The great Robert Priest, the previous art director, had also been hired to redesign the magazine and then run the art department. He sequestered himself in a handsome corner office at 444 Madison (the old Newsweek Building), doing exquisite old-fashioned pencil layouts for the new magazine. Dozens of alternative schemes were devised. "Comp'ed" covers were mounted on foam core and stacked up in the cabinets, while Bill Broyles, the editor, waited for the right moment to present the ideas to the formidable Katherine Graham, who had dispatched an editor every other year for the last ten years.

One of them, Ed Kosner, had undertaken the previous big redesign without involving Mrs. Graham, and she cited the result as one of the reasons for sacking him. Sadly, Broyles, too, was fired before the Priest design could be implemented. (Broyles landed on his feet in Hollywood, where he has written *Flags of Our Fathers*, among other screenplays.) Priest, after all this work, decided he didn't have the heart to start over with another editor, and moved on. (He, too, landed on his feet, of course. As of this writing, he is working on the launch of Condé Nast's new business magazine, *Portfolio*.)

Mrs. Graham hired Rick Smith, who had been at *Newsweek* since he interned there during college, and he hired me. In May 1985, I started to work in Priest's fine office, finding a treasure trove of covers and inside pages. There were a number of really great logo treatments, some of them recalling the *Newsweek* covers of the fifties, designed by the legendary M. F. Agha.

Rick Smith wanted to do the redesign methodically but fast, so the new format would hit the streets in three months. He proposed that we try two approaches—conservative and radical—and choose between them. We didn't have Macs in those days, so my layouts were handmade, although unlike Priest I

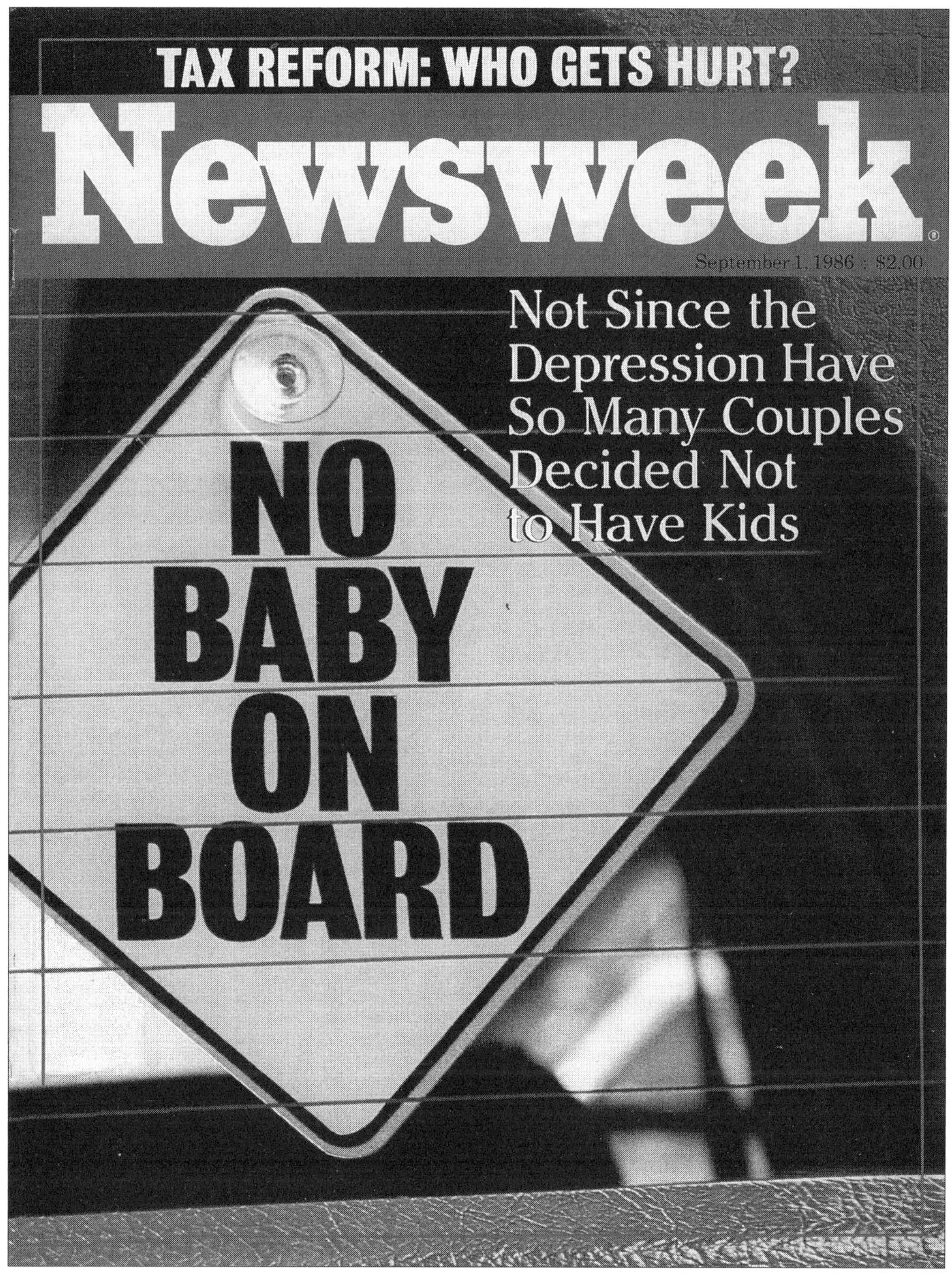

TAX REFORM: WHO GETS HURT?
Newsweek
September 1, 1986 : $2.00
Not Since the Depression Have So Many Couples Decided Not to Have Kids
NO BABY ON BOARD

Newsweek, 1986

didn't draw them all on vellum with a 6H pencil. Instead, I pasted together photocopies of type and pictures and reduced them to half size. Then I colored them in with Prisma colored pencils and glued them all into two half-size dummy books. Cute! The veteran editors were reminded of the old "pony edition" of *Newsweek*, sent to soldiers during World War II.

Now, at most magazines, the editor would have looked at the two versions and said, "that one" (or, more likely, "something in between"), and set a date for the relaunch. But Smith, while leaning toward radical, was very aware of the fate of recent *Newsweek* editors. He knew he had to bring Mrs. Graham in on the decision, but he also knew he could not show the owner of Post-Newsweek my crude little dummy. Instead, he ordered a full printed prototype of the more aggressive version.

Mimi Sheils, a senior editor who later went on to coedit *U.S. News*, was dragooned into writing all the

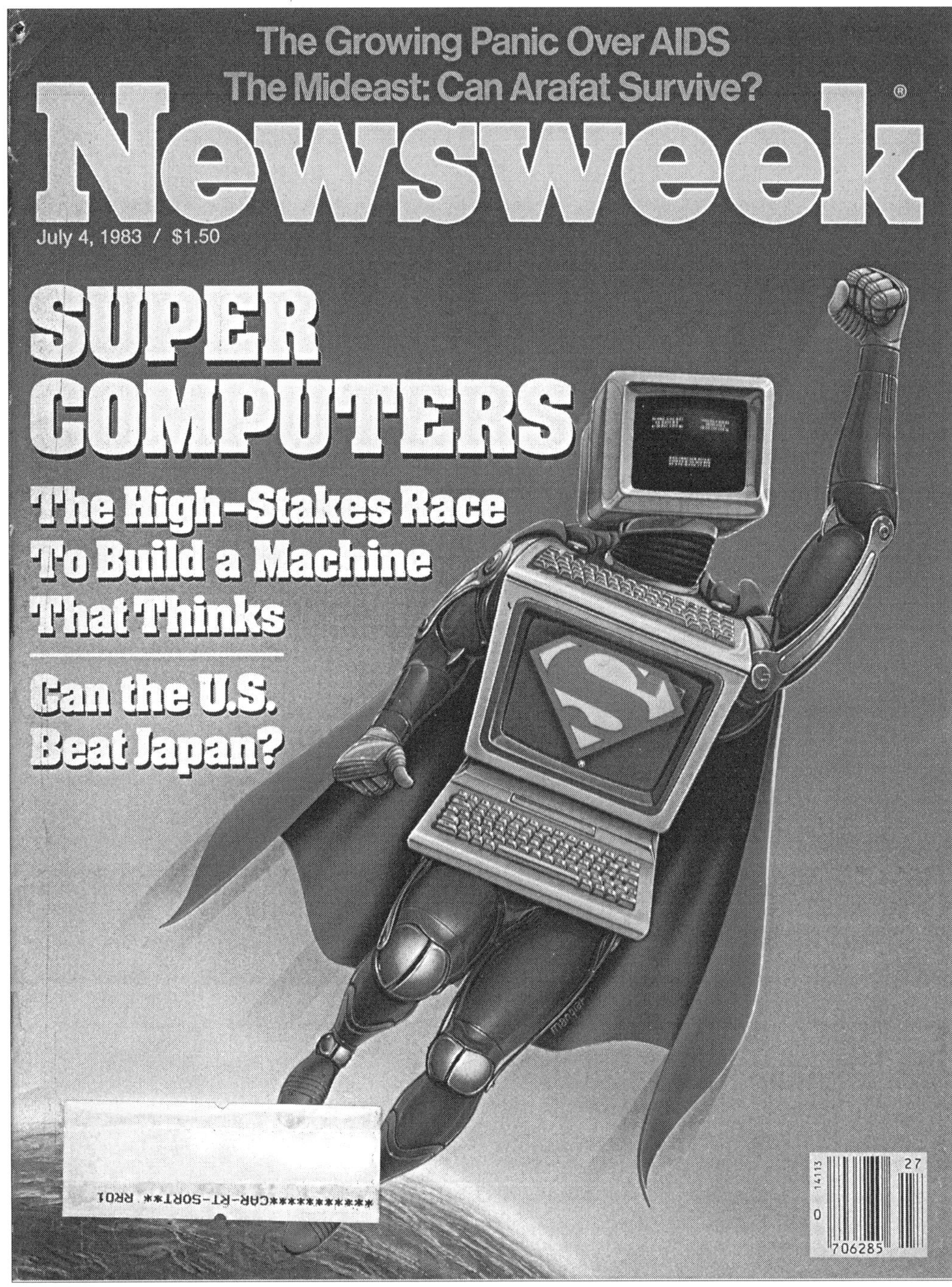

Newsweek, 1983

headlines, captions, and display copy. Karen Mullarkey, the photo editor, worked up all the images and in a matter of a month we went to press. We only needed a single copy, but we had to print the thing on a web because we wanted it to look right, and even in those days the paper at *Newsweek* was so thin it wouldn't go through a sheet-fed press without being wound around the cylinders.

Meanwhile, the editor called a series of meetings with small groups of staffers, presenting the dummy book and the full-size pages we were working on to get some feedback—and a bit of complicity. The groups came from every part of the magazine—edit, art, production, and the business side. He also ran down to Washington to let the columnist George Will, Mrs. Graham's confidant, and a few folks at the *Washington Post*, the parent company, take a look. One of those who gave us a green light was Ben Bradlee, the newspaper's editor and a former star correspondent at *Newsweek*.

UPDATE

Michael Schwarz—Gannett Rochester Newspapers

Feeding the hungry at a 'hospitality house': 'The challenge is greater than ever'

Rebirth of a Catholic Cause

Dorothy Day was perhaps the most influential U.S. Roman Catholic of her time—a pacifist and social visionary who, with French philosopher Peter Maurin, founded the **Catholic Worker movement** in New York City 50 years ago in the belief that the only true charity is service to the poor. Day edited the radical Catholic Worker newspaper and served as the spiritual force behind the communal farms, soup kitchens and "houses of hospitality" that dotted the United States during the Depression. When she died in 1980 at the age of 83, many people questioned whether the movement could survive without her. But today it is alive and flourishing as never before.

"There has been a renaissance of both interest and participation in our work," says Catherine Morris, who has been with the Catholic Worker community in Los Angeles for the past 11 years. New houses of hospitality, where society's down-and-outs can get a hot meal and a clean bed, are opening all the time, though no one knows exactly how many there are. "There's no master list," explains Brian Terrell, who with his wife operates the hospitality house in Davenport, Iowa. "It's not like a franchise operation." Those who come to work in the community receive room and board and sometimes a few dollars for pocket money. They do not sign any contract or even make a verbal promise to stay with the spartan life for any set period of time.

One reason for the movement's current strength is the weakness of the nation's economy. The Los Angeles Catholic Worker community, which runs a soup kitchen, a medical clinic and a law center specializing in getting federal aid for the needy, served almost 1,300 hot meals every day last winter—400 more than in the 1970s. "With increasing hunger, homelessness, unemployment, all kinds of oppression of the poor and—here in Los Angeles—radical cuts in health funds, our challenge is greater than ever," says Morris. "One thing our increased size has given us, though, is the durability to keep going."

Day's followers now face the delicate problem of "demythologizing" her—for the movement's own good. A recent editorial in the Catholic Agitator, a paper published by the Los Angeles Catholic Workers, observed that "a Dorothy Day cult movement would create a concomitant myth that once there was a 'Golden Age' of the Catholic Worker movement, a glorious past overshadowing the paltry present."

Faith: At the same time, many Catholic Workers would like to see Day considered as a candidate for sainthood. Father Philip Cioppa, a deacon at a seminary for American priests in Rome, claims that many churchmen recognize both the value and sincerity of the work she did, and he thinks there is a "great chance" she will be canonized someday. It probably won't be anytime soon, however, since as one Vatican priest points out, Day's "political radicalism is diametrically opposed to Pope John Paul's usual attitude that religion and politics should not be mixed." In any case, her followers will continue to feed the poor, shelter the homeless and not worry too much about the future. "The movement comes out of faith, out of the Gospel," says movement worker Geoffrey Gneuhs in New York City. "If it's supposed to go on, it will. If not, something else will rise up."

12

Mexico's Baby Panda: Bearing Up to Fame

This month, **Tohui**, the first panda to be born outside China and survive, will mark her second birthday at Mexico City's Chapultepec Zoo. "The whole zoo will celebrate—the entire staff and the family of animals," says administrator Maria Elena Hoyo, who has ordered ice cream and a cake decorated with two candles. Hoyo isn't the only one who has flipped over the cuddly, 242-pound cub. About 400,000 Mexicans and foreign tourists descend on the zoo every weekend to catch a glimpse of Tohui; singers have cut a dozen records about her, and she has even inspired a TV cartoon.

The panda's parents, Ying-Ying and Pe-Pe, were given to Mexico by the Chinese government in 1975. They produced their first offspring in 1980, but the cub died a week later when Ying-Ying crushed it in an excess of motherly love. Tohui escaped the same fate, but had to contend with another problem: a case of mistaken identity. Animal experts assumed that Tohui was a male, but now that the panda is maturing, they have concluded that he is a she.

Treasure: Most Western zoos, including the London Zoo and the National Zoo in Washington, have had no luck breeding pandas either naturally or by artificial insemination. Dr. Juan Téllez Giron, Tohui's veterinarian, attributes Mexico's success to the climate, which is similar to that of northwestern China, and to a special diet of apples, spinach, carrots, meat and bamboo shoots, all washed down with a milkshake.

Téllez also thinks it helps to house the adults in the same cage—something most zoos are afraid to do because of the animals' bellicose nature. "We were criticized at first," says Téllez, "but how can you breed animals that have never had a chance to get acquainted? It won't work." Zoo officials hope that when Tohui becomes an adult she will mate with Pe-Pe. In the meantime, however, the baby panda seems satisfied with her role as Mexico's national treasure.

EILEEN KEERDOJA with ELOISE SALHOLZ in New York, LINDA PROUT in Mexico City and bureau reports

Tohui: Meals washed down with milkshakes

Richard Cross

NEWSWEEK/JULY 4, 1983

My Mugging: Justice Is Done

MY TURN/DAVID SILVERBERG

On the night of Nov. 19, 1981, at about 10 o'clock, I was walking home in Silver Spring, Md., when I encountered two men coming toward me on a deserted side street.

I thought nothing about them—but almost as soon as I passed them I felt a blow to the back of my head. I whirled around to see both silhouetted against the street lamps, crouching slightly, waiting to spring, and I knew immediately, without a word being said, that I was being mugged.

I cursed, swung the only thing I had in my hands—a shopping bag full of books—and then threw it at them. They easily dodged the bag, and then I saw one of them raise a hammer over his head, poised to strike. Now weaponless, I decided on flight rather than fight, and I dashed down the street, bellowing for help at the top of my lungs.

When I regained consciousness, I was lying on the ground in a pool of blood alongside another man who I later discovered was a plainclothes police officer.

The Attack: As the events were reconstructed for me, I had been struck on the head with the hammer (which fractured my skull), knocked out and then struck again. A police team had been trailing the two men, and one of its members ran out from behind a building to stop the attack. He too was struck with the hammer, and his jaw was broken. Then the assailant charged the rest of the team. It took all of them, with an assist from a police car which knocked him off his feet, to finally subdue him.

The wielder of the hammer turned out to be 16 years old. His accomplice was 15.

When told of the assailant's arrest and his age, my first thought (and that of my family, friends and colleagues) was that he would immediately be released on bail.

He was not. The judge decided not to set bail for him.

We assumed he would be treated as a juvenile and would be sent to juvenile court.

He was not. Because he was charged with a capital crime (attempted murder), he was charged as an adult.

We thought he would plea-bargain.

He didn't. He pleaded guilty.

He came to trial. We thought he would get a light or suspended sentence.

He didn't. He was sentenced to 38 years altogether: 19 years for attempted murder, 19 years for assaulting a police officer.

The prosecuting attorney, a tough, gruff man who had seen a lot of trials, was jubilant. Even though the assailant is appealing the sentence, and even though he will eventually be eligible for parole, I, the victim, had the satisfaction of seeing justice done. (His accomplice's trial is still pending.)

In going back over the events of the case, however, I was taken aback by the cynicism with which I and everyone around me had approached the matter. This was a case where the system functioned properly. The police were present when the crime was committed. The arrest was properly made. I was allowed to make a "victim-impact statement" to the court. The judgment appeared fair, given the magnitude of the crime.

> Our perception of the criminal-justice system as inept encourages criminals and frightens the public.

In how many other cases does the criminal-justice system function as it ought to? And how often do we hear about it?

I don't know. And neither do most Americans. The impression that most of us have is that criminals slip through the cracks, first committing heinous crimes and then being released on technicalities. Or else that they are put back on the streets by lenient judges, crafty lawyers and sentimental psychiatrists. The prevailing conception of the norm is that the criminal-justice system is creaking and porous, overloaded, incompetent and overindulgent.

That is certainly *part* of the truth. And the people who function within the system are the first to admit it and point out its shortcomings.

But the criminal-justice system also has its successes and it does dispense justice. Its successes go unheralded and unrewarded, buried amid the paperwork and appeals, ignored by those angry at the system's failures and miscarriages.

It is not a mere matter of publicity—or lack of it. Our current perception of the criminal-justice system as lenient and inept has encouraged crime, giving criminals the idea that the odds are in their favor. Victims are left with a sense of despair at ever getting satisfaction and the public is left with a sense of vulnerability and fear.

Part of the rationale of our system of punishment is its ability to deter future crimes. Yet the general view of the system as dysfunctional is eroding that ability.

The current demands for stiffer sentencing, for consideration of victims' rights and for less reliance on the juvenile-court system are part of the solution, but by no means the whole solution. There has to be a change in the way we regard the criminal-justice system and part of that change has to be on the part of the media.

Newsworthy: As a journalist, I know how difficult it is to follow a single case through the courts, from indictment to sentencing, unless the case is highly publicized from the beginning. Severe miscarriages of justice and overly lenient sentences also make better stories and have a "man bites dog" quality which makes them newsworthy. Moreover, the long time between indictment and sentencing tends to dampen public interest in the ultimate outcome of any case.

Nonetheless, we have been so saturated with stories of court incompetence that just sentences and successful police work are now the "man bites dog" exceptions.

This is not to say that malfunctions in the system should not be publicized. Such publicity has its own deterrent effect and, combined with the public demand for stiffer sentences and victims' rights, makes judges think twice before sentencing. Nor is this a call for censorship or closed trials. It is simply an attempt to redress the balance.

In the past, criminals in America were depicted in the media and in popular entertainment as tragic heroes, people who defied the system only to face inevitable punishment because of the omnipotence and omniscience of the law. Today that sense of inevitable justice is gone and will probably never return. It is still possible, however, to reverse the sense of inevitable injustice which has replaced it.

Silverberg is assistant editor of the Near East Report.

NEWSWEEK/JULY 4, 1983

Front of the book, before the redesign

PERISCOPE

GREG DAVIS—BLACK STAR

'No conspiracy': *Mourners for KAL Flight 007 victims*

Murder by Bungle

Readers who expected investigative reporter Seymour Hersh to find a plot behind the Soviet destruction of Korean Air Lines Flight 007 in 1983 are in for a surprise. Conspiracy theorists have examined the scant evidence and concluded that foul play of some sort, most likely an American intelligence operation, caused the tragedy. But in "The Target Is Destroyed" Hersh concludes the cause was incompetence.

The book, due from Random House next month, with excerpts in The Atlantic Monthly, shows bungling at the start when a KAL crew member punched the wrong longitude—139 degrees west instead of 149 degrees—into the plane's navigation system. The Soviets goofed, mistaking it for an American reconnaissance plane. The U.S. National Security Agency not only recorded the Su-15 pilot as he chased the airliner, its instruments listened in when the deputy regional air-defense commander phoned Moscow for instructions. Hersh faults the Reagan administration for letting the world continue to believe the Soviets knew they were firing on an unarmed airliner. But he does not believe the United States could have warned the Korean pilot. By the time the U.S. surveillance network had analyzed the intercepted communications, the plane had been underwater four hours.

None of the principals will like Hersh's findings. The U.S. intelligence community won't be happy seeing some of its most secret capabilities discussed in print. The Soviets will also be disappointed. They gave Hersh access to major figures in the story, like ex-Chief of Staff Marshal Nikolai Ogarkov, in hopes that Hersh's book would support their charge that KAL 007 was a spy plane. "They simply wanted me to prove what they couldn't," he says. "There was no conspiracy."

Peking Toms

Diplomats in Peking are increasingly disturbed by stepped-up government harassment of foreigners and their Chinese associates. The new measures, by China's internal-security agencies, started after the arrest and expulsion last month of New York Times correspondent John Burns for entering an area off limits to foreigners. The Ministry of State Security—China's version of the Soviet KGB—charged that Burns was a spy. But Chinese Foreign Ministry officials have privately indicated that they opposed expelling him.

Since then, TV cameras have been installed to monitor movement inside foreign compounds in Peking. Phone calls of foreign residents are increasingly being tapped. And last week a Chinese security official entered the Swiss Embassy compound, interrupted a swimming party—and sent the Chinese guests scurrying for cover in the restrooms.

Diplomats speculate that hard-line security officials reflect the views of other conservatives in China's leadership, who fear that Deng Xiaoping's "open door" reforms are letting in spies and provocateurs. The harassment campaign could also undermine Deng's effort to attract foreign investment.

Clean Rock

Crusaders against so-called "porn rock" are planning to redouble their efforts to have the music industry clean up its act and eliminate lewd lyrics. After testy congressional hearings, 22 major companies last November agreed to put warning labels on sexually explicit records. But the Parents Music Resource Center complains that compliance has been "spotty"—with some companies blatantly promoting albums with dirty lyrics. "We're determined to wipe out the pervasive message in music that to be hip and cool you have to have sex," says PMRC leader Tipper Gore (wife of Tennessee Sen. Albert Gore Jr.). Under consideration: pressuring local authorities to bar youngsters under 18 from concerts by X-rated groups—unless they're accompanied by a parent.

LANA HARRIS—AP

Pressure tactics: *Gore*

JACK McKIGNEY—PICTURE GROUP

War games: *Guard in Honduras*

No Contest

A House-passed amendment would strip state governors of authority to block National Guard units from "training maneuvers" in Central America. But even governors opposed to such maneuvers—as obvious pressure on Nicaragua—probably won't fight the measure. Arizona Gov. Bruce Babbitt, who recently kept state troops from Honduras, is happy to see governors out of the chain of command. "My view is that the president already has the authority to call up guardsmen," he says. "I don't understand why he's hiding behind us."

■ A new flash point between the United States and Nicaragua may be shaping up on the Colombian island of San Andrés, 115 miles off Nicaragua's coast. During the regime of former Colombian President Julio César Turbay Ayala the Reagan administration explored the possibility of using the island for military operations, but the idea was dropped because of an outcry in the Colombian press. Now, Colombian sources say, informal discussions have been resumed with President Virgilio Barco Vargas about placing U.S. radar equipment on San Andrés. Though supposedly for use against drug smuggling, the system could be viewed as "hostile" by Nicaragua. The White House has "no comment."

LUCY HOWARD *with bureau reports*

NEWSWEEK · SEPTEMBER 1, 1986 5

After

PERSPECTIVES

Overheard

"First we dry up, and now we're going to drown."
South Carolina resident JEAN DAVIS, *on flash floods in the South*

. . .

"It had occurred to me that a whole lot of people were making a whole lot of money on Wall Street and that I wasn't one of them."
Convicted Wall Street Journal reporter R. FOSTER WINANS

. . .

"I never really had a drug problem, depending, of course, on what you call a problem. If smoking a joint some night is a problem . . ."
RON REAGAN JR.

H. PAYNE—SCRIPPS HOWARD

OHMAN—OREGONIAN

"Even if I talk to 'em, they write something bad. I'd rather just have them write something bad and not waste my time."
Tour de France winner GREG LEMOND, *a native Californian, on European journalists*

. . .

"Once an airplane comes out of the hangar, people find out about it."
Model-airplane designer JOHN ANDREWS, *explaining how he created a fast-selling plastic replica of the U.S. Air Force's supersecret Stealth fighter*

. . .

"You wonder how a little community with just 10 houses and a bus stop gets cocaine. But it's everywhere."
RICHARD KORBETT, *medical director at a hospital in rural Waterville, Maine*

"Leadership that's working."
Current campaign slogan for MARIO CUOMO *and, in 1984, for Ronald Reagan*

. . .

"I think there is a point, like with newspapers, where you start to want to censor stuff."
Former Beatle PAUL MCCARTNEY, *on offensive rock lyrics*

"The survey is an opportunity for the Geographic to make a significant scientific contribution to the understanding of smell."
National Geographic editor WILBUR GARRETT, *on a scratch-and-sniff test in the magazine's September issue*

DEORE—DALLAS MORNING NEWS

'DEA agents in Mexico were "tickled" to hear of Operation Alliance'

NEWSWEEK : SEPTEMBER 1, 1986 13

Perspectives

The benefit of a printed prototype was enormous. Not everyone can visualize an actual magazine from a dummy, but now we had a real magazine. Immediately, Smith showed it to Mrs. Graham. Second, it was shown by ad salespeople to drum up some enthusiasm on Madison Avenue. Then we showed it to readers in a series of "disaster check" focus groups, in case we were wrong.

All thumbs were up. Rick had built in a "launch hold" of a month, in case the owner changed her mind. We needed every day to get the specs all programmed into the clanking Atex system we used for setting type. During this time, he reconvened the little staff groups, and that was another good idea.

During a meeting with a group of young researchers (the people right out of college who did most of the grunt work at the magazine) one of them said, "I miss the political cartoons." (Coming from the *New York Times*, I had instinctively expunged the cartoons from the news sections as too opinionated.) In

Newsweek

Jean Louis Atlan—Sygma

Checks and balances: The legislative branch (House Speaker Tip O'Neill) greets the executive (State of the Union Message, 1982)

NATIONAL AFFAIRS

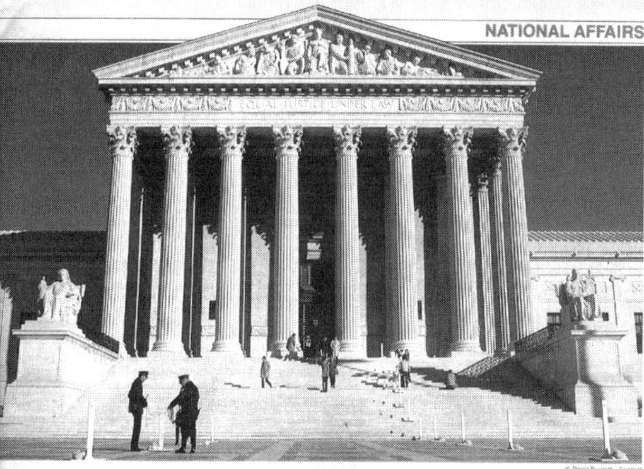

© David Burnett—Contact

Supreme Court Building: 'A fairly monumental change in the way the government does business'

The Court Vetoes the Veto

In a historic ruling, the executive branch regains power at the expense of Congress.

Justice Byron White usually does not say much on days when the U.S. Supreme Court announces its decisions, but last week he couldn't contain himself. "I have not spoken orally in dissent in many years," White began, "but this is no ordinary case. It is probably the most important case that the court has handed down in many years." Then for five minutes in a silent U.S. Supreme Court chamber White sharply criticized his colleagues for, as he put it, "in one fell swoop" readjusting the constitutional calculus between the president and Congress by striking down a device most Americans never heard of: the legislative veto.

In Washington, at least, White's criticism seemed understated. The ruling appeared to invalidate veto provisions tucked into nearly 200 laws—including major legislation giving Congress a measure of control over American troops involved in hostile actions abroad and allowing the House and Senate to make sure the president actually spends money they have appropriated (box, page 18). In so doing, the court struck down in one day more federal statutes than it has overturned in its history—and stripped Congress of an extremely powerful tool. Although it will be years before all the effects of the ruling are clear, it will change the way Washington does business and, in the short run, force Congress to write much stricter laws.

Shortcut: Invented as a simple way to keep an eye on the last gasps of Herbert Hoover's administration, the legislative veto has become Congress's desperate—and sometimes lazy—way of trying to check both an imperial presidency and a set of low-profile regulatory agencies with a taste for running amok. While it takes many forms, the veto typically works like this: Congress authorizes the White House to do something such as sell arms abroad, while reserving for itself the power to overrule any sale it doesn't like. By a 7-2 vote, the high court said that if Congress wants to thwart the president or a federal agency, it must pass another law. "The veto ... doubtless has been in many respects a convenient shortcut," wrote Chief Justice Warren Burger for the majority. "But it is crystal clear ... that the framers [of the Constitution] ranked other values higher than efficiency."

Congress responded with wounded cries. "It's a disaster," said Rep. Elliott Levitas of Georgia, sponsor of a bill to give Congress a veto over every new administrative-agency regulation. Both the House and Senate foreign-policy committees created task forces to explore the extent of the damage. And Sen. Charles E. Grassley of Iowa pledged to find new ways to curb presidents. The ruling was particularly stinging because it struck at the fruits of Congress's post-Watergate, post-Vietnam frenzy. Furious at presidents who either lied to or ignored them, a reassertive Congress has spent the past decade giving itself authority to, among other things, recall U.S. troops from hostile actions.

For the most part, the veto was useful simply as a bluff. While Congress approved 41 new provisions in 1980 alone, over the past five years it actually vetoed only 31 matters—and most of them were minor. In practice, the veto's existence helped stimulate compromise between legislative and executive branches unwilling to play a game of constitutional chicken. "The justices don't understand what it's like here," says Stanley Brand, counsel to the House of Representatives. "This is a fairly monumental change in the way the government does business." But, insists Brand, Congress may have the last laugh; without a veto the lawmakers may be less willing to dole out new authority to the executive branch: "Every time the president wants something he's going to have to come up here, hat in hand."

Excesses: A generation of White House staffers say they are willing to take their chances. Virtually every modern president has opposed the legislative veto; Jimmy Carter even asked his staff to find a test case that would challenge it. Candidate Ronald Reagan endorsed it as a way to check the excesses of the federal bureaucracy, but once in the White House he found the threat of congressional veto just as annoying as his predecessors had. Indeed, the bruising 1981 Senate battle over the sale of AWACS reconnaissance planes to Saudi Arabia was essentially a fight over the legislative veto; under the Arms Control Act of 1976, Congress could block the export of most military arms and equipment within 30 days after the president announced his plans. In fact, Congress never passed an arms-deal veto.

Like many other great cases, last week's landmark began as just another obscure dispute. At issue was whether one Jagdish Rai Chadha, an East Indian native of Kenya who came to the United States as a student, could be deported. Chadha overstayed his visa but argued he shouldn't be returned to Kenya because of that country's racial turmoil. Applying federal law, an immigration judge found that Chadha could stay in this country and suspended his deportation. However, 18 months later, for still unexplained reasons, the House of Representatives invoked its legislative veto power on immigration decisions and ordered Chadha and five others to leave. Chadha went to court, challenging the House action, and, in the process, the veto's very existence.

Burger: Striking down nearly 200 laws

© Evelyn Hofer

'Presentment': Last week's decision was surprising only for its great breadth. According to Burger's opinion, the Constitution requires that all valid acts of legislation must not only pass both houses of Congress, but also must be "presented" to the president for approval. The problem with the legislative veto, he concluded, was the absence of that "presentment" procedure.

For White the court's decision was simply too formalistic. In his view, the veto is entirely consistent with the separation-of-powers plan created by the Constitution. "Only within the last half-century has the complexity and size of the federal government's responsibilities grown so that the Congress must rely on the veto to ensure its

16 NEWSWEEK/JULY 4, 1983

NEWSWEEK/JULY 4, 1983 17

A feature spread from the redesigned Newsweek

the ensuing discussion, somebody else suggested, "What if we do a page with just cartoons?"

Smith thought about it for a second, and then said that they wouldn't quite fit together because we'd want at least three and they're all horizontals. Somebody else said, "What if we filled in the cracks with a few 'quotes of the week,' like the *Times*' 'Quote of the Day'?" So, a week before launch, the same researchers found themselves trying to make sure we could get reliably good cartoons and quotes on a weekly basis. The page, called "Perspectives," was put right before the opening of the news section opposite an ad, which made the sales department happy. And in the first Starch readership study of the magazine after the redesign, "Perspectives" was scored as the best-read page in the magazine.

The moral: When it comes to redesigns, many heads are better than one. A designer might have the instinct to chuck some fixture of the old design, but others might point out that those elements play an important role in the visual content of the magazine.

Fortunately, the late Mrs. Graham liked Rick Smith, who is still there, having moved up to CEO and chairman. She supported the design, which outlived her, and with continuing updates could still work today. It was successful not because the design was fashionable, but because it was a group effort by people who understood the magazine and wanted to reinforce it rather than fundamentally change it. It was a redesign that was right for *Newsweek*.

After Rick Smith moved on to the business side, I worked as a consultant with his successor, Maynard "Scramble-the-Jets" Parker, the last of a breed. Parker built on the framework, and readers came to accept that the magazine had "always looked this way," as I recall one readership survey found. After Parker's sudden death, I lost the will to do another design for *Newsweek*. A new editor and a new art director took over the next redesign. The trademark Grotesque No. 9 headline font was replaced by Champion (as we've seen). In order to appeal to an increasingly ADD audience, items became shorter and layouts trickier. While the magazine arguably still looked like *Newsweek*, it had lost something—not just gravitas but some self-awareness. At one time, I heard that they were planning to move the logo up, to bleed it off the top of the cover, and to remove the thin red rules on the sides and bottom, making it like any number of other cover designs. Wiser heads prevailed, but the magazine lost some of its identity, its design equity.

An interesting test of the idea of design equity is to look at a magazine's Web site. Does it look right? It's not that the site can or should mimic its parent, but it ought to carry some of the unique DNA. To do that, you have to find that uniqueness. With Newsweek.com (an early version of which I helped design), there is an appropriate family resemblance. In early 2007, after a redesign, Time.com was more generic. In some ways it looked more like the *New York Times'* Web site than *Time*. On the print side, steadier hands have held closer to the magazine's core identity.

In late 2006, *Newsweek* announced a new chief editor. An art director from the nineties was bought back. The rumor is that they're "channeling the ghost of Maynard Parker." This may be a good idea because Maynard was part of the historical spirit of the magazine, Hitler Diaries and all. This is why the 1985 redesign worked with readers. The logotype was changed, but the new drawing was derived from the 1950s logo.

The one project that I've done for *Time* was a logo redesign in the mid-nineties, after I left *Newsweek*. The new logo, still in use, actually interpolates a 1947 logo with the fatter one that Walter Bernard put on the magazine in 1977. The letter spacing was tightened, and the logo was made bigger. The result looked fresh. At the core, it was the historical design, not something new. By reviving the little white-and-black borders inside the big red border, we reminded the baby-boomer audience that *Time* is the magazine they grew up with.

Newsweek can do this, too. They can align a new design with the momentum built with readers over a lifetime. They can put visual equity to work for them again, and the readers will know it's still *Newsweek*. Then, when they do the redesign after this one, they won't have to start over. The work of many forgotten designers and editors can be the platform of a magazine that works for the future.

SECTION 4

The Soft Side of the Redesign Process

All graphic designers are collaborative by nature, but editorial designers are just a bit more collaborative. As a rule, designers work within a hierarchy in which they ultimately answer to a client—someone who controls the money and therefore the process. Publications are different in two important respects. First, at most magazines there is no one client, but a number of stakeholders. Second, magazine people see each other and must work together every day, whereas at design firms, teams and clients come and go. There are of course stories of impossibly difficult and controlling editors or prima donna art directors, but these stand out because they are the exceptions. Most magazine staffers know that while the issues go by, the people—at least for a time—remain the same. It doesn't pay to burn bridges.

At most magazines, designers and editors work as colleagues. Controversies in visual and written content are handled through discussion rather than by fiat, though the editor-in-chief holds ultimate responsibility and decides issues that aren't otherwise resolved.

Publications do tend to be competitive environments, whether the competition is to make the snarkiest remark or to create or shepherd the piece that gets the most attention. Designers' success is measured by how well they persuade, describe, and build consensus. Talented designers who operate effectively in this landscape control most of what they do. (And no, that doesn't mean emotions never run high.) But without people skills, a designer will find his or her talent is significantly less valuable.

This section is about the interpersonal aspects of the design and redesign process at a publication—working as a staffer or a consultant to establish authority and build consensus for a redesign. Much of what is here, of course, applies to regular operations as well as the special circumstances of a reinvention.

Clients and Cultures **10**

AN INTERVIEW WITH MARIO GARCIA, PRINCIPAL OF GARCIA MEDIA INC.

Garcia Media is a design consultancy focusing on newspaper and magazine redesigns. With offices in Tampa, Buenos Aires, and Hamburg, redesigns include the Wall Street Journal, der Zeit, Esquire, Vanity Fair, *and* TV Guide.

I wanted to focus on the political and interpersonal side of redesigns, the sort of issues that come up after you've been hired to do a job but before you've turned in a design, and what it takes to get it through the approvals process and win allies in an organization. Could you tell me a bit about the range of reactions you expect coming in as an outsider when you're meeting with the art director, editor, and advertising director for the first time?

MARIO GARCIA: Usually, by the time you have been hired, you have made it clear to them that this is going to be a collaboration—that's the key word. You cannot simply do a design from your studio and [expect] people will follow it—that would never fly. People inside the organization have to have ownership. You need the cooperation of the art director—he needs to be on board. The art director has to respect you, and you in turn have to respect the art director. If there is no mutual respect there, this also will never take off. Once this is established, you know that normally there is a project leader inside the organization, usually someone who has nothing to do with art direction—an editor type. He or she will deal with the logistics of the project from beginning to end.

So once you have the project leader in place, then the art director, the advertising director, the marketing director, and one or two editorial types become part of the project group—it is seldom more than eight people. However, I usually do the first phase of the project with my team and not with their team. If you start working with internal teams, they will censor you—they will say, "Oh, we will never be able to do this here," or "We don't have the machine to do that"—and I have learned that if you bring an idea from the outside and somebody in charge likes it, it will fly anyway.

By the time I come back to present the first two or three models of what I would do (which is completely new to them), then the art director comes into play, along with the internal team. I usually come back with three versions, A, B, and C. Then we begin to do D, or the prototype—which is really an outgrowth of all three versions. They may like the typography of A, the color palette of B, and the navigation system of C, for example. That's when the art director and the internal team move in to work with us. I like to say that the D version is like a "wet sculpture": We have the opportunity to turn the head down, right, up, whatever we want to do—there's nothing firm yet. I outline this procedure very clearly in my contract.

So that sounds like a very idealized process, and I would guess on occasion there's a bit of politicking you have to do to get there. I would imagine for some art directors it's a nervous-making process—they worry they won't be up to the demands of the new design.

Oh, it's worse than that. For many art directors the first real shock is that somebody at the top doesn't want them to do this themselves, and that they have hired outside help. This can be a blow to many art directors, and you can understand why. So you have to work very diplomatically, and that is also why you have to respect the art director. When I begin to work with them I tell them, "Listen, we all have our fortes," and I try to find out the forte of that art director. There are art directors who are very good with typography, for example, so I will make sure that anything typographic in this project, this person is going to have to have an OK. I'm the chief architect—that's what I've been hired to do—but I try to find out what it is that he or she has that can strengthen the result. In many cases, it's an area that's not my expertise. But, no matter what, you have to get the internal art director involved; you cannot simply do this without them. They must feel that they own it, because otherwise no one will protect the design later on. I work closely with this person for six to eight months, so they must also be someone who will be loyal to the company, and who will not fly away two months into the process.

The first thing I do to establish a relationship with the art director is to say, "Look, you could have done this yourself." And I always say that from the heart. If I think the internal art director cannot carry this out, I would tell the editors—and I have said this in the past—"Listen, you need to get another art director before we can get going here." And sometimes it has nothing to do with talent. Some art directors will not want to work with an outsider. I've had that happen too. They say, "Either I do this project or I'm out of here." They've been waiting for this moment, but the publisher thinks differently. The publisher says, "You've been here twenty-one years, and this is the way our pages look. Why should we believe now that you can do better?" All of the politics have to be out of the way before progress can be made.

I also imagine there are times when the editor and the publisher have agreed upon you, but they have a different vision of what will happen under your stewardship. How do you work those people toward a shared vision?

Well, you know, it takes many meetings, many briefings, but ultimately they've hired you because you bring something new to the table—they are aware that they need an outside vision. But at the end of the day, you also have to make sure that people remain within a certain comfort zone. It's critical to pay close attention to their aims, what they want this publication to be in five years and all of that. During this first step you clarify all of these objectives, and you listen to what they want. But I've learned that the reason they've hired you is they want to see something beyond what they want and what they've imagined. And many times at least 30 to 40 percent of that gets in.

But not all of it?

But not all of it. You very seldom get all of it in, because publication design is an exercise in compromise. It's just like an interior designer will do with the people who inhabit the house: Plans are shown, and if you're lucky, 60 to 70 percent of this will be executed for reasons that have to do with budgets, with taste, with whatever. It's the same in publications. Maybe they don't have the technology to do what you want yet. Maybe it has to do with people, maybe they don't have the courage to do it. Courage is always a very important factor. Courage, technology, and human resources: Those are the three things that become obstacles along the way.

So it's all up for grabs on both the editorial side and the design side when you come in. You're suggesting new features, new ways of doing things . . .

Oh, definitely, definitely—and story structure. I deal very much with the storytelling process. We are in the business of telling stories, so how do you tell stories, from a brief to a compact to a lead story? Design has a lot of components, but you begin with story structure—how this publication tells stories—and then you go into the typography, which is really what dresses these stories, and then you go into a color palette. And finally you go into an architecture. The grid, whether you are designing a Web site or a page: What are the physical qualities of it? Everything is different in every project except the method, which serves as a skeleton. If all you do is design, typography, and color, I think you're going to have a very limited scope. You have to become more of a fusionist.

Lately I work a lot with the telephone, how to translate a publication's format in a meaningful way to mobile-telephone screens. There are news prompts and all of that. And then you have the Internet and the printed version. Basically, "redesign" is not the word; it's more a rethinking. We come in there to help them rethink and approach their publication more like fusionists than designers.

At some publications, particularly at newspapers—but everywhere—I get a sense that advertising is becoming a bigger and bigger consideration. Whereas once there was that unyielding wall between edit and ad, the wall has become a little more porous. How do you find that affects the redesign process?

You cannot even begin a redesign project without the advertising director sitting in the room. Readers see advertising as information, and you now have all kinds of rich possibilities for advertising inspired by the Internet for different formats. You cannot bring those considerations in at the end of the process. I like to prototype using a variety of advertising positions—as we do the sketches, advertising is there from day one, the Web site is there from day one, marketing people are there from day one. The team is not just an editorial team at all.

You've also done a lot of international redesigns. How would you describe the character of the process, or staffs, or goals as you get into different locations?

Culture is culture, and there are going to be differences. I follow my same outline whether I'm in India or whether I'm someplace else, but there are differences. If you work with the Scandinavians, it's very different than working with the less organizationally inclined Brazilians. You have to make amends for delays, you have to make amends for. . . . You have to improvise; we're not machines.

Then you deal with training issues. I have to wear many hats, and the teacher's hat is a very important part of what I have done. Once the project is conceived you have to make sure that—before you leave for good—you have trained the key people to be your eyes and ears, your hands and your eyes and your brain. You have to do that; otherwise it will never fly. You have to be a mentor, you have to do hand-holding, and you have to do it without making anybody feel inferior—it has to be done in an atmosphere of equality.

How does it feel watching papers a couple of years after the launch, when that person does fly away, or start to drift in a different direction? Do you offer follow-up consulting?

My contracts always offer maintenance, and most clients do take this option. The first year I visit every ninety days; the second year, twice a year. Eventually, after three years people redesign again. But I am proud that in the majority of the projects—even when I find a paper in an airport or on a plane or whatever where they have not sent it to me (they always send you the best, or when they have a question)—if I see something that's not working, I write them a note. I just wrote a note to my clients in Sao Paulo because their Sunday Page One was wonderful. So you don't just shake them up when they're doing it wrong; you also send a note when they're doing it right, and it goes a long way. . . . I'll do this even for clients that do not opt for a maintenance contract. They have a great art director, and he invested so much of his time into this, so forget Mario and forget Garcia Media, he has invested enough that he's not going to let anybody torpedo it.

I'd like to talk about selling innovation. Right now you are quite established and people are coming to you because they like what you've done. And maybe they want something similar to an approach you've taken in the past but it's inappropriate for them. (Of course, less-experienced designers also face the same problem in the form of "We love X magazine. Will you do something like that for us?") How do you sell clients on something new and get them past a rote response about what's right for them?

I have a client who wants a cross between *La Révolution* and the *Wall Street Journal Europe.* This is like coming into Burger King and saying, "I want a mixture of your Whopper, but with a touch of turkey club thrown in." I don't want to make a client feel bad or stupid. I say, "Well, let's talk about what you want to be and where you want to be." Normally, there is always something you find where you can innovate—but you also follow your instincts. Some approaches occur to you in one place that would never occur to you in another place. It's very difficult to explain this to a client.

Can you give me an example of how you handled this one time?

Well, *de Morgen* is a newspaper I [redesigned] this year in Brussels: There we use a colorization process—it's like wallpaper. I have another client who doesn't have the same color capabilities for any of this, and he says, "Well, I like the wallpaper effect of *de Morgen.*" "Well, I'm not inspired to do this here. You don't have the press, you don't have the color palette, and this is not Brussels, so I will not be the one to wallpaper your pages with color and all that."

And the *Wall Street Journal* is the *Wall Street Journal.* We have another client in the United States that would like to look like my top newspaper in Germany, *der Zeit*, which has won a lot of design awards year after year, but it has twenty people in the art department. And how do you deal with this? "Well, OK, I want the Armani suit but I have a Kmart budget. And I don't have twenty designers in here to give it to me, but I like the Armani suit." Of course, we all do. So sometimes it's very difficult to get them to recognize that they can be who they should be and not copy. A suburban newspaper in California cannot be *der Zeit.*

It's a very touchy subject, because these clients mean well, and it happens with publishers who are very smart. "Oh, I love what you did here." At the first meeting, they already have three or four of your projects that they love, and you don't want them on the table—you want to have one blank page on the table. I usually remove the papers from the table very carefully and slowly, put them under the table or somewhere, and start with just a blank sheet of paper.

I take pride in the fact that my projects don't look like one another. If I am in America, I get inspired by the colors here. I am a runner—I run through the city. I also attend the local galleries, see how local people paint—if you take a train ride between two Swedish cities, all the curtains you see hanging in the windows are white. If you take the same train ride from Sao Paolo to Rio, there will not be a single white curtain. There, everybody's curtains are colorful. So how could you design newspapers in these two places that match each other? Impossible. I refuse to infuse something from one place into another simply because of a request.

Can a Redesign Improve the Design Staff? 11

DAN ZEDEK

A LOT OF CLAIMS ARE MADE FOR REDESIGNS: THAT they can woo new readers and make old ones fall in love with you all over again, that they can sharpen your editorial focus and blunt financial disadvantages. To this list add one more: a good redesign can actually improve the designers who execute it. A well-focused redesign uncovers the basic message of a publication. It also gives staff designers a set of guidelines to follow in everything they do.

Beyond what appears on the page, an effective redesign makes the most of the resources you have to connect with the reader. Design that reaches readers is not just good for the prestige of a publication—in a world where staffs are shrinking and readers have a growing number of choices in print and online, it's a good investment for the future.

While redesigns are outwardly about visual trappings, good ones are driven by a deep understanding of the editorial mission of the publication. Every effective redesign starts with an unflinching look in the mirror: Who reads the publication? Why and how do they read it? What are the strengths of the staff? What resources are available? Those questions seem so basic that they're often skipped over. Instead, many redesigns start with the wrong question: Who do we want to be?

The GQ Moment

It's a moment that's as comic as it is futile. The project is getting started and the publisher and the redesign consultant are getting to know each other. They're in the conference room of a weekly alternative newspaper or magazine in a mid-sized Southern city, or in a restaurant down the block from a big city daily. "Here are some publications that I'd like you to take a look at," says the publisher eagerly, "stuff I really like."

Out come one, two, many publications. Some are slick, some are trendy, one of them is usually *GQ*. None of them have anything in common with the publication to be redesigned.

At bottom, a successful redesign isn't about turning you into what you want to be, but about discovering what you do best and doing it better. When the design staff is clear on that, they will be more effective. For a designer there is no better route to being "good" than being "effective."

Getting to Know You

Begin with a frank and comprehensive look at who your readers are. The answers will be the cornerstone of a successful redesign:

- Who are your readers? What else do they read, what do they watch, how do they spend their time?
- Why do they read you? What unique information or perspective do you bring to them?
- How do they read you? Do they read through in one sitting or several short ones? How much time do they spend with the publication?
- Where do they find you? Do they buy you on a newsstand, receive you at home, or find you elsewhere?

Next take a hard look at yourself:

- What are the strengths of the design staff? What are their weaknesses?
- What resources does the staff have to draw on? What are the limitations of time, budget, experience, and training?

REAL WORLD EXAMPLE #1

Doing More with Less

The project was not a glamorous one: redesign the stock tables of the *Boston Globe* and give readers more while giving them . . . less. Our charge was to squeeze three pages of market listings into one to save space and, therefore, money. The designer in charge of creating the page each day was a former copy editor with only basic layout skills but a deep knowledge of subject matter, and experience searching the wire services for photos.

A previous redesign had taken the tables from four pages to three using all of the obvious tricks: fewer columns of information, more abbreviations, smaller type, fewer listings. It had cut a page, but it had also yielded a high volume of complaints from disgruntled readers. This time around, the reduction in space was much more dramatic, yet we received almost no complaints, and quite a few compliments. Here's how we did it:

We started by asking "how" readers used the tables, "who" they were as consumers of information, and "why" they chose us. Specifically, we were interested in the number of stocks they checked and what other ways they received information about stocks *besides* the daily newspaper.

We learned that, for the most part, they only checked on the stocks they owned, and that they also used the Internet and, to a lesser extent, television to check share prices throughout the day. Because these sources are both more complete (the Internet, in particular, is the source of almost endless statistical information) and more timely than a daily newspaper, we then asked: What content do we bring readers that's uniquely our own? We were pleased to learn that readers valued our knowledge and analysis, particularly of local companies.

The design that resulted from these discoveries completely dispensed with conventional tables. The answer to the "how" question had told us that we were using three pages of tables to display thousands of stocks each day, yet our readers only cared about the handful that they owned. Of course, it was a different handful for each reader, but none of them was using more than three column inches of information. The same went for the "who" question: Because readers relied on other sources for the raw numbers, a complete report of closing price, year-to-date performance, and so forth—even about stocks they owned—was not the primary way that we were useful to them.

The redesigned stock page features the same information about broad market trends as before, but displayed as charts rather than agate type. The heart of the page, though, is a tightly written analysis of ten companies in the news that day, half of them local, along with quick-read charts for each. We use photos to accompany two of these stories because we found that the designer could reliably locate that many strong images of relevant events, people, or products. Finally, we hired a programmer to write a computer script that automatically generates all of the charts on the page (programming cost a fraction of the savings realized by reducing the page count). The designer's job? He picks the companies (taking advantage of his knowledge of the subject matter), finds the photos (utilizing his strengths searching for images), runs the script, and builds a layout from a tight template. The result is a page that gives readers the information they want in an accessible and attractive format. The design is much improved, and so is the designer. We're giving the readers something that we alone offer in a form that best presents the content. And the designer is doing what he does well, too.

REAL WORLD EXAMPLE #2

The Babysitter Dilemma

Sometimes it's hard to focus on what's really important to readers and harder still to follow that knowledge to its logical conclusion. Case in point: the redesign of a weekly arts and entertainment newsmagazine in a large Southern city. Like many alternative papers around the country, it had built its readership and reputation on listings: It was the acknowledged best source for news and opinion on what to do and where to go in town. Over time, the paper had become more fully rounded, adding local political news and columns on subjects like architecture and development. In many ways, it did a better job on these topics than its competition at the monthly city magazine and the daily newspaper, a rightful source of pride for the editor and publisher.

The design staff was fairly small with the more experienced members assigned to the higher-prestige news and architecture pages and an inexperienced junior staffer handling all of the listings, even though they made up the most substantial part of the book.

The redesign was commissioned to give a new, more polished look that reflected the publication's growing prestige and to address reader complaints that the paper had become unwieldy as it grew. But a funny thing happened when we asked readers what they liked about the publication and how they used it. While everybody *liked* the news features and columns, everybody *used* the listings. Observations of readers in coffee shops and bookstores confirmed it: It was all about the listings.

The discovery that the listings had to look better and work better led us to ask more questions about how readers actually used them. They were the first thing that readers looked for, but they appeared on a different page each week. They were hard to read because they used a font that looked sharp and modern on news pages but was illegible at the smaller listings size. Finally, the listings felt unwieldy because they weren't organized in a way that reflected their use in the real world. In the end, the publisher summed up the concerns of many readers, who, like him, were in their thirties with children: "I don't get a babysitter that often and when I do, I can't figure out what's going on."

The realization that readers cared more about what was happening on the particular *day* they wanted to go out than what was happening in a particular *genre* over the course of a week led directly to the decision to reorganize the listings by date rather than by topic alone. The larger realization of the importance of listings led to staff shifts as well. The junior designer was reassigned to lay out the news columns, now created through the heavy use of templates, in keeping with her level of experience (she also continued to do some simple listings). A more experienced designer was put in charge of getting great art for the "going out" section and designing a splashy "critics' picks" spread, organized by date and always appearing in the same place in the book. When the redesign debuted, readers responded positively to the new look and structure of the listings and the designers responded to their new assignments with some of their best work. Were the listings better? No, but they were better organized. Were the designers better? It seemed as if they were, because they understood the publication better and were better utilized.

REAL WORLD EXAMPLE #3

"When I Look at You, I Want to See Myself"

For a designer, it seemed an assignment almost too good to be true. Take a magazine with a strong niche following—women interested in healthy food, fitness, and spirituality—and give it the cover gloss to sit next to mainstream fashion books on the newsstand. Out went the clunky logo redolent of the sixties and color photos of vegan meals; in came sleek typography promising "Five Steps to this" and "Ten Ways to Become that" and tightly cropped cover photos of attractive models.

Unfortunately, out went years of building a loyal readership, too. The readers noticed that the magazine looked better, they just thought it looked better in a way that made it look like every other magazine. And the problem started on the cover.

The readers didn't merely feel disappointed by the new covers, they felt betrayed. We'd spent a lot of our slender resources hiring photographers and stylists experienced in creating mainstream newsstand masterpieces—and models worthy of their attentions—but we were alienating our core readers without attracting significant numbers of new ones. When we listened to readers, we discovered a hard truth: Although we had fundamentally the same content as other women's magazines, our readers saw us as providing something quite different. The cover models personified the problem: They were too young, too made-up, and too skinny. Our readers didn't want to see a fantasy when they looked at us, they wanted to see themselves.

We set out to reengineer the cover design. We asked the agencies to send us models who were older and had more normal figures. We asked the photographers to go beyond their usual stock techniques. We asked stylists to show us looks with less makeup and more natural fabrics. In an industry with a narrow definition of what's beautiful, this was easier said than done. Yet the more difficult it was to find women with the right look for the cover, the more we came to realize the truth of our readers' criticisms. What we were looking for *was* different, and it would therefore be uniquely our own when we found it.

We started collecting images of women who seemed right for us wherever we found them, in ads, newspaper photos, and catalogs. When we contacted them, we found that they shared a common interest in—you guessed it—healthy food, fitness, and spirituality: all the things our magazine was about. They didn't just appeal to our ideal reader, they *were* our ideal reader.

The covers that followed were both better looking and better selling, more accessible to a broad audience while still appealing to our loyal readers. We never brought back the old logo, but we applied the lessons that we learned on the cover to the rest of the design in everything from typography to color palette to the styling of food photography. We developed a look that mirrored the naturalness and authenticity of our topic. As the mission became clearer, the design staff felt more confident and did better work.

Putting It All Together

A longtime copy editor laying out a groundbreaking new stocks and financial news page; a young designer in charge of a top-to-bottom reorganization of entertainment listings; a cover art director creating a unique look for a women's magazine. All were doing better work after their publications underwent a redesign. But was it the redesign that made them better designers? In each case, there were several interconnected factors that made them better and more effective. First, the staffs' strengths and skills were identified and drawn on in the redesign. Formats were simplified, templated, or automated to compensate for their weaknesses. Second, priorities were established and resources used accordingly. Finally and most importantly, the redesign process began with an unflinching appraisal of the publication's core mission and a deep understanding of the readership. Done together as part of a redesign, identifying and utilizing a staff's skills, prioritizing resources, and focusing on what's unique to a publication can create better and more effective designs—and designers.

Conversation

12

DAN ROLLERI

Speak's editor Dan Rolleri discusses the magazine's design and production with art director Martin Venezky.

DAN: *Speak*'s design is often the subject of discussion regarding the magazine. Yet it is rarely talked about in relation to the editorial, but almost as an isolated entity. One of the pleasures I take from the process is seeing how you will interpret each article, yet aside from the *Speak* writers, I never find myself in conversation with anyone about the words and the layouts. Has your experience been similar, and what do you make of it?

MARTIN: Yes, I've had similar feedback in the past. I think that in our current culture, magazines that are heavily visual are not usually expected to have strong literary impact. I have to admit that I am guilty of buying magazines for their visual sensibility and never get around to reading them. It pleases me as much as I know it pleases you when a design fancier proudly admits to having read the magazine cover to cover. They are aware that that is an unusual feat.

Although I do work hard to give articles, especially fiction and essays, a unique and surprising interpretation, I also try to make the pages enticing from a purely visual standpoint. So, if someone doesn't read an article—or doesn't care to finish it—there is still something for them on the pages. That a designer can interpret a text seriously and not just make it look "arty" or "hip" is not a common concept. In some circles, it would even be considered outrageous. I am lucky that I don't have to fight for the right to do this, that it is actually expected of me. I am curious what made you so open to this idea in the first place.

DAN: Before *Speak*, I bought certain magazines for their visual sensibility as well. But I also bought others to read. As my concept for *Speak* evolved, I thought a magazine that worked hard to excel editorially while not being constricted visually would be an unusual thing.

But it's frustrating when many people don't seem to get past the headlines and typefaces, and strangely are often critical of the design even though it's apparently the only reason they buy the magazine. On the other side, there are lots of traditionalists who are convinced that to make something visually compelling only undermines and distracts from its content. I'm sure there are lots of people who appreciate the design and the editorial, but I too notice a certain pride when a reader points out that he or she appreciates both.

Let's talk about your approach to laying out *Speak*. It seems that in a given issue there are at least two methodologies going on. Sometimes you work very instinctively where you have the entire layout visualized within moments of reading the text. But other times you're more thoughtful, going through a series of options, refining again and again. Does the latter approach only become necessary when there isn't an initial burst of inspiration, or do you consciously work in different ways just to keep things interesting? Also, do you find that you're typically more satisfied with layouts that come from one method or the other? Do you sometimes look back at something that came together quickly and wish you had spent more time on it?

MARTIN: First, I never really visualize how a page looks instantaneously. Typically, after reading the text, I'll let some time pass, then start rummaging through my collections of scrap, drawings, photos, etcetera, looking for something that connects to or resonates with the story. It has to really feel right before I take it any further. Often, immediately after reading the manuscript, a lot of potential metaphoric or suggestive images will come to mind. But, from experience, I always know that there is a good chance that these won't come off as well as I imagine they might. So I am always prepared to spend a lot of time on something that ultimately fails. Hopefully those ideas never make their way into print. But, I have to admit that many snuck in, in the earlier issues especially.

Only recently have I been able to look back through all the issues and pull out my favorite pages. I find that now I am drawn to the quieter ones that hinge on a single thought or relationship of forms or objects. Some of the jumpier pages still excite me, but many feel like overearnest attempts to be "radical" for its own sake. That isn't always a bad thing, it just doesn't always work in a magazine context.

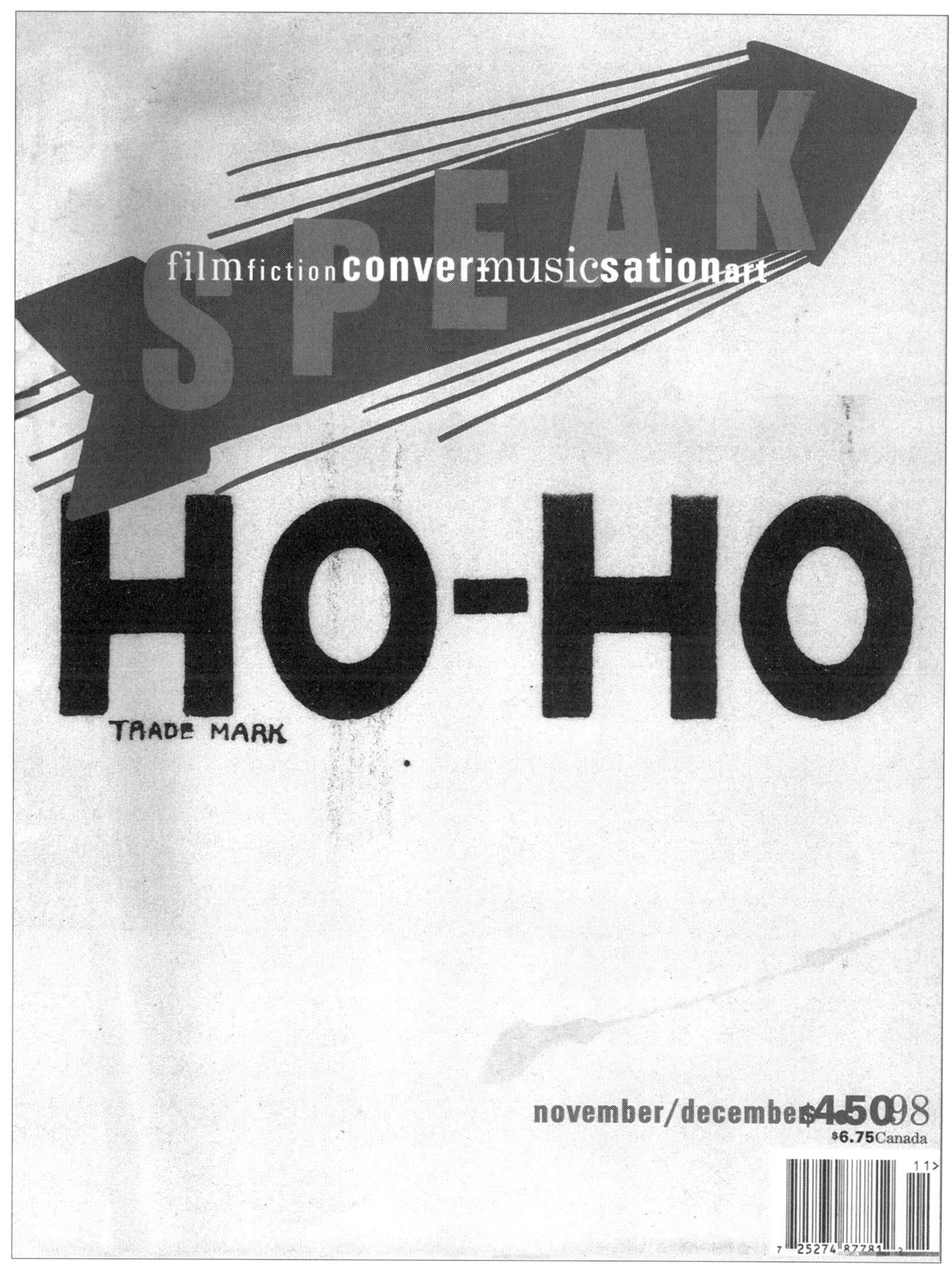

Speak, *1998*

I am always refining things to the last minute, and I am often very unsure of whether an idea should stay or be ditched. I like that feeling, though, because it suggests that I am trying new things. If I kept relying on surefire solutions, the project would probably bore me. I often surprise myself when images come together that I never expected to work. "The Plane" [*Speak* #10] or "Your Own Back Yard" [*Speak* #13] are good examples. I am especially pleased when I can take the same metaphor and make it work for two articles in the same issue, but in very different way. Using an orange for "Meditations on the Harp" and a few articles later for "Like Being Killed" [*Speak* #12] is a good example.

DAN: Your layouts for those articles are among my favorites too. In putting together a given issue, I'm

JOY division: Admire the Distance

by Roger Sabin

it's 1979: Joy Division is [illegible]ying at the Apollo Theatre, Manchester, [illegible]land. The show is a triumph. The band has come a long way since its early days as punk copyists, and tonight's show is proof that it has carved out its own distinctive ground. Playing songs from the new album, Unknown Pleasures, Joy Division has a live presence that is electrifying—transcendental, even. The singer, Ian Curtis, evidently in mental anguish, twitches around the stage, arms whirling like a marionette on wires. The rest of the band—looking for all the world like gangly Hitler Youth—keep things anchored in super-tight fashion. The music is sorrowful, haunting, disturbing and beautiful. It [illegible] Division has a great future.

It's 1998: New Order is playing the Apollo. The band which formed out of the ashes of Joy Division, following Curtis' suicide in 1980, and which itself disbanded four years ago, is back—reformed for tonight and possible future gigs. It's the first time they've played the Apollo since that night in 1979, and what's more, they're playing Joy Division songs—"Isolation," "Atmosphere," "Heart and Soul," "Love Will Tear Us Apart." Some things have changed: The band members are pudgy, more confident, and don't go for the Nazi chic any more. But the music is still sorrowful, haunting, disturbing and beautiful. And the crowd is ecstatic once more.

Why is New Order suddenly so keen to show off their roots—something it has never done before? There seems to be two reasons. One must certainly be financial. A lavish Joy Division box set, Heart and Soul, was released recently to a rapturous critical response, and this has led to a wave of fresh interest in the band. New Order's emphasis on Joy Division material is undoubtedly in part a reflection of its hope that back catalogue sales will be substantial. The second reason is less mercenary, but the members of New Order seem to have finally realized that they cannot compete with the myth of their previous band. New Order's legacy, impressive as it is, simply does not have the same hip cachet, and the band must know in its heart of hearts that the forthcoming follow-up box set of its own material is unlikely to cause the same stir as Heart and Soul. This despite the fact that New Order has released eight albums in its 18-year career to Joy Division's two.

Why the disparity? The missing link, of course, is the contribution of Ian Curtis. In 1977, when Joy Division formed, there was nothing about this skinny, fidgety individual that said "star quality," let alone indicated he could turn a band into a legend. Despite this, when Manchester teenagers Bernard Dicken (guitar) and Peter Hook (bass) were looking to complete the band, the punk imperative to get things moving was more important than waiting for the perfect frontman. Besides, they'd seen Curtis around at gigs (Dicken and Hook had been inspired to get together after seeing the Sex Pistols), and had been impressed by Curtis' (anti-) fashion sense: in DIY punk style, he was apt to wear a raincoat with the word HATE spelled out on the back in ticker-tape. This was enough to convince them that he had the right idea, and when he responded to their advert for a singer, he was hired.

With the completion of a few hastily-put-together songs, and the addition of drummer Steven Morris, the band first took the name Warsaw, and began to play live. In the beginning, the music was raw punk—too raw for many audiences. In tune with the times, early songs were a mix of distorted rama-lama guitars, and lyrics rooted in anger: "I've seen the troubles and the evils of this world/I've seen the color of corruption deep within" ("The Drawback"). But as Curtis gained confidence as a wordsmith, the band veered into more experimental waters. The early rants were replaced by increasingly introspective fare-songs about betrayal, doomed love, mental torture, and angst—while the music became more sophisticated—metronomic drumbeats with the bass played like a rhythm guitar. Gradually, the band developed a cult following in the Manchester area.

Curtis had ideas about fashioning the band's image, too. Indeed, he was the one who encouraged its Nazi craze—he had a Hitler fixation at the time, and collected books on the Third Reich—though it must be said that the others were hardly passive dupes (there was certainly an element of playing naughty schoolboys in it all). While Curtis claimed that the band's original moniker, Warsaw, was taken from a Bowie track, it also happened to be the name of the Polish city synonymous with a Nazi ghetto. When it came time to choose a new name (people were confusing them with the London band Warsaw Pakt), another extremely dubious one was adopted—Joy Division. Again, it had Holocaust connotations: specifically, the Joy Division was a group of female prisoners kept aside for the use of the SS.

The band pushed the image as far as it could go. The members started to dress like Hitler Youth (gleaming shoes, trousers with razor-sharp creases, scout shirts with the occasional thin black tie, short and parted hair); the first record ("An Ideal for Living") had a Hitler Youth drummer boy on the sleeve; Dicken took the more sinister-sounding name Albrecht; and Curtis started to make pro-Nazi comments on stage (see Speak, July/Aug 1998, p. 80). No wonder the music paper Sounds branded them "another outfit devoted to fascism and profit."

What are we to make of this with the benefit of hindsight? The very fact that Joy Division was another band flirting with Nazi imagery (like Siouxie and the Banshees and any number of other young punks) meant that it was spared wholesale condemnation. Indeed, biographers ever since have made excuses. The standard explanations include

3 4

3 5

BLACK ANGER
WHITE LIES
the case of stephen lawrence
by roger sabin

this is the story of a murder.

It's also the story of the British justice system's failure to find and punish those responsible. What makes it compelling is not the fact that the victim was black, and the murderers white—a depressingly common scenario—but that efforts to bring suspects to trial have exposed layer upon layer of racism within British society.

It is a case that will change the British judiciary system, the organs of law and order and, in particular, the London police force, forever. At a moment when America is in crisis over its own race relations—especially after the killing in Jaspar, Texas—it is sobering to reflect on events across the Atlantic where the racist threat is every bit as entrenched.

Stephen Lawrence was 18 when he was found bleeding to death near a south London bus stop on the night of April 22, 1993. He'd been stabbed twice, with downward thrusts to his upper torso, in an apparently unprovoked attack by a gang of white youths. His friend, Duwayne Brooks (also 18, also black), had managed to escape from the gang, but remembers their taunts of "nigger!" He returned to aid Lawrence once they fled (the whole attack only took a few seconds), and at first neither boy realized anything was seriously wrong. Lawrence got up, and started to walk home with Brooks. Then he stopped, and feeling his soaking chest, cried, "Look at me! Tell me what's wrong?" He collapsed, and died shortly thereafter. These are the facts of the murder insofar as they are known: They are horrific and tragic, without a doubt, but in no way indicate the subsequent celebrity of the case.

7 6

Feature opening spreads

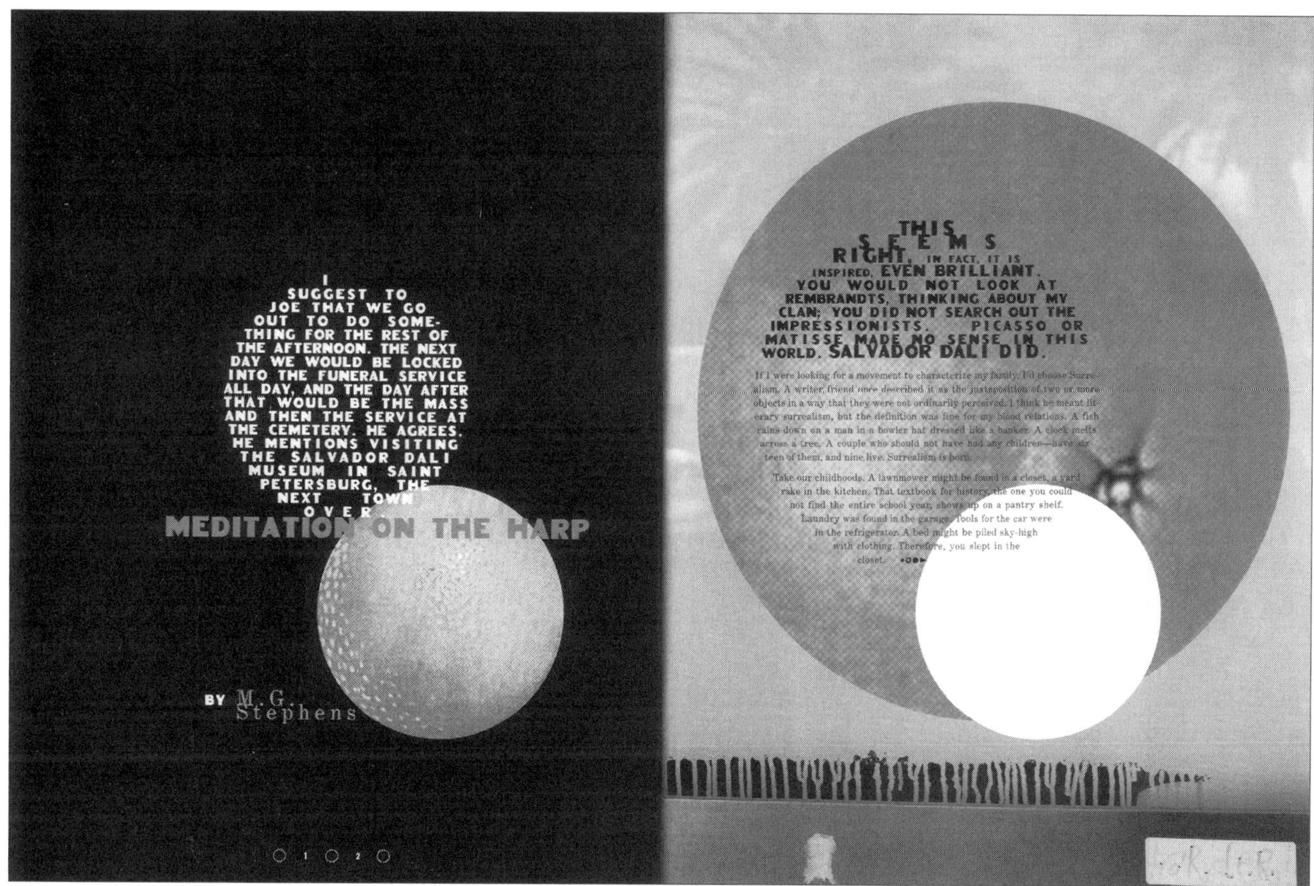

I SUGGEST TO JOE THAT WE GO OUT TO DO SOMETHING FOR THE REST OF THE AFTERNOON. THE NEXT DAY WE WOULD BE LOCKED INTO THE FUNERAL SERVICE ALL DAY, AND THE DAY AFTER THAT WOULD BE THE MASS AND THEN THE SERVICE AT THE CEMETERY. HE AGREES. HE MENTIONS VISITING THE SALVADOR DALI MUSEUM IN SAINT PETERSBURG, THE NEXT TOWN OVER.

MEDITATION ON THE HARP

BY M.G. Stephens

THIS SEEMS RIGHT. IN FACT, IT IS INSPIRED, EVEN BRILLIANT. YOU WOULD NOT LOOK AT REMBRANDTS, THINKING ABOUT MY CLAN; YOU DID NOT SEARCH OUT THE IMPRESSIONISTS. PICASSO OR MATISSE MADE NO SENSE IN THIS WORLD. SALVADOR DALI DID.

If I were looking for a movement to characterize my family, I'd choose Surrealism. A writer friend once described it as the juxtaposition of two or more objects in a way that they were not ordinarily perceived. I think he meant literary surrealism, but the definition was fine for my blood relations. A fish rains down on a man in a bowler hat dressed like a banker. A clock melts across a tree. A couple who should not have had any children—have sixteen of them, and nine live. Surrealism is born.

Take our childhoods. A lawnmower might be found in a closet, a yard rake in the kitchen. That textbook for history, the one you could not find the entire school year, shows up on a pantry shelf. Laundry was found in the garage. Tools for the car were in the refrigerator. A bed might be piled sky-high with clothing. Therefore, you slept in the closet.

Feature opening spread

always conscious of having things resonate editorially. It's probably too subtle for the casual reader to catch, but it's helpful to have you visually emphasize certain connections. Of course you often discover new links between articles that I hadn't even considered, like with "Meditations" and "Like Being Killed."

Many people might be surprised that you're more pleased with the quieter layouts. There was a period, as the magazine evolved editorially, that the design was downshifted to better suit the articles. During this time we received lots of negative feedback, mostly from designers, that the magazine had lost its spirit, that in producing stricter page formats and more readable text, it had sold out. It seems there were many designers for whom "being radical for its own sake" was a good thing. Funny also that we were simultaneously picking up new, more literary-minded readers who were probably more accustomed to the look of *Harper's* and *Utne*. These people seemed to view the magazine's appearance with suspicion and were often critical that the magazine was still too radical, that headlines weren't where they were supposed to be, etc. It was a period when I thought we were all doing our best work, yet we were being criticized in a way we hadn't been before.

You say that you've only recently been able to look back through all the issues. Is this just because of a lack of time, or is it frustrating to look back at your older work? While I make light of it in our back-issue ads, I personally can't open a *Speak* from its first two years. It just seems like one giant missed opportunity.

MARTIN: I remember when you made the decision to tone back the design. I think I was, at least in my mind, kind of resistant, but now I think it forced me to consider my choices more carefully. And that has helped me in all of my design projects. This way, when something feels completely off-the-wall, it stands out with much more impact, like "End of the World.com" in the latest issue.

I've redefined what "radical" means to myself and to the students I teach. It can be as much about making a dramatic and daring interpretation as it had been about sort of "non sequitur" design. It doesn't have to mean messy at all. I am not an especially big fan of the new "super cold, super corporate" style of design that has hit the airwaves. It seems just as gratuitous as the "wild style" of the earlier nineties.

To me it's less a question of "selling out" as it is about discovering new territory and keeping myself challenged. When you find that you can put any picture with any article and claim meaning, it stops being challenging.

Up until now I would hand out copies of the magazine to prospective clients. And because the earlier issues had more things I didn't like than pages that I did, I avoided giving them away. But I recently decided to put together a "greatest hits" series of portfolios. In doing so, I could pull out the pages that I especially liked and found quite a few in the first few issues. Seeing everything together gives me a better sense of the breadth of the work I've put into the magazine.

I know how you feel about the earlier issues and, at the risk of turning this into a public pep talk, I think that you are too hard on yourself. You were creating something concrete out of a vision in your mind. There are bound to be missteps. But I completely understand how you feel. By maintaining a rigid self-critical stance, it does make your work better. That is another thing I tell my students. They have to learn to be intensely self-critical. And regardless of how much work they put into an idea, they always have to be ready to accept the possibility that it just doesn't work.

I know there have been a lot of articles that you've worked hard editing that you ultimately had to give up on. That's a brave stance that too few people take.

DAN: It's self-serving enough to publish this conversation, but one more compliment and readers are going to be ill. On the issue of self-criticism, I must say that I am leery of consistently confident people. Not only do I find their self-satisfaction often unwarranted, I'm envious of their apparent well-adjustedness. At least in my case, my "rigid self-critical stance" is less a considered approach to my work, and more a psychological handicap. There are many days when I would rather be blissfully working in some dot-com marketing department, checking to see how I did on the weekend's office pool.

There was a stage when you became critical of your own work, and you put your design career on hold and went back to school. At the time, did you know exactly what you wanted to be doing, or was it just a matter of believing that there must be more to design than the mundane stuff you were working on at the time?

MARTIN: Ever since I was young, I have been skeptical of praise. I've found that it usually serves another purpose, and it rarely is to my benefit. At the firm where I was working before my return to school, I had been praised over and over as being "one of the best designers in San Francisco."

I knew it wasn't true, and I resented the motives behind it. My projects were very run-of-the-mill sales brochures for food companies, coupons, sell sheets, and point-of-purchase displays. I was neither proud of the work, nor felt that it made any difference in the world. Although I was making a reasonable salary, that was less important than being satisfied with the things I made. At the time, I had been seeing work by Rudy Vanderlans, Tom Bonauro, and others in the Bay Area. I thought it was wonderful, rich, and emotional, and I knew I could do work like that, too. Over time, though, I found that the divide between what I was doing and what I wanted to do was enormous. To be a generator of work and leader (rather than a follower of the trends of others), just wanting to do it was not enough. I needed to commit to my craft in a meaningful way. Therefore, I left work and studied at Cranbrook for two years.

To be honest, I had no idea what I was going to be doing or where my work was really heading. At the time, I had no special interest in editorial design work.

It was funny when you approached me right after graduation in 1993. I was extremely skeptical of the project—something that Cranbrook can do to you. You probably remember my questions about the integrity of the project. They must have seemed horribly self-important and rude.

DAN: My first direct contact with you was in the form of that letter you sent from the Netherlands, when you were working at Studio Dumbar the summer after graduation. It's one of my great regrets that I didn't save it.

Here you were, just out of Cranbrook, being offered the art directorship at an internationally distributed magazine. And you write this extremely pretentious letter outlining what the magazine should be, what it shouldn't be, and implying that you would only be interested if it scored high enough on your integrity meter.

In the meantime, I was this moron who just wanted to publish a cool magazine. I thought, Who is this guy? and immediately looked for P. Scott Makela's number. Still, I kept coming back to something Cranbrook's director Kathy McCoy said about you in her recommendation: that you were "without flaw." Between that and your letter, I imagined you to be some kind of supergenius designer. But, alas, you were merely a man, and your fancy talk was just a product of your fancy school.

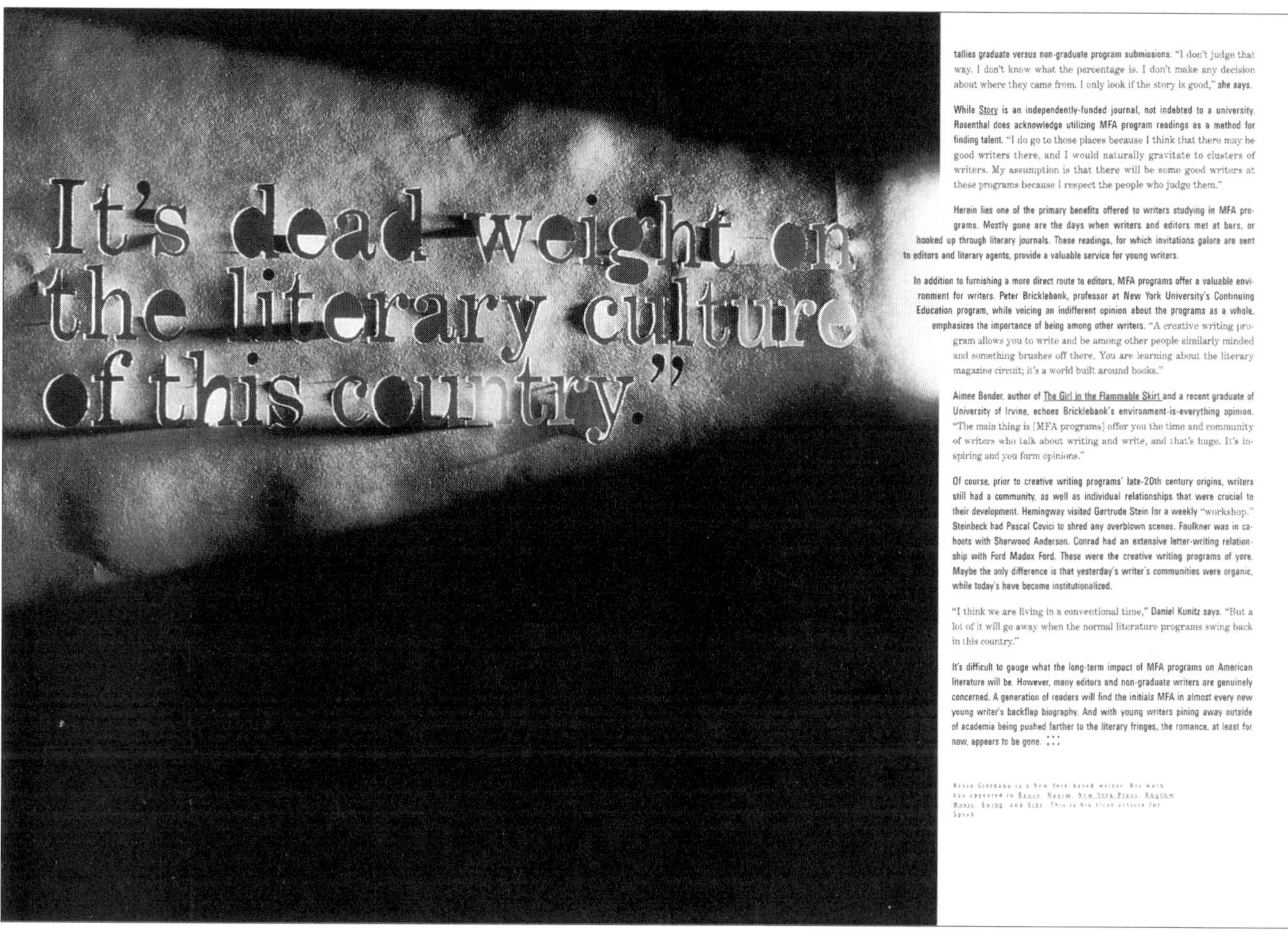
"It's dead weight on the literary culture of this country."

tallies graduate versus non-graduate program submissions. "I don't judge that way. I don't know what the percentage is. I don't make any decision about where they came from. I only look if the story is good," she says.

While Story is an independently-funded journal, not indebted to a university, Rosenthal does acknowledge utilizing MFA program readings as a method for finding talent. "I do go to those places because I think that there may be good writers there, and I would naturally gravitate to clusters of writers. My assumption is that there will be some good writers at these programs because I respect the people who judge them."

Herein lies one of the primary benefits offered to writers studying in MFA programs. Mostly gone are the days when writers and editors met at bars, or hooked up through literary journals. These readings, for which invitations galore are sent to editors and literary agents, provide a valuable service for young writers.

In addition to furnishing a more direct route to editors, MFA programs offer a valuable environment for writers. Peter Bricklebank, professor at New York University's Continuing Education program, while voicing an indifferent opinion about the programs as a whole, emphasizes the importance of being among other writers. "A creative writing program allows you to write and be among other people similarly minded and something brushes off there. You are learning about the literary magazine circuit; it's a world built around books."

Aimee Bender, author of The Girl in the Flammable Skirt and a recent graduate of University of Irvine, echoes Bricklebank's environment-is-everything opinion. "The main thing is [MFA programs] offer you the time and community of writers who talk about writing and write, and that's huge. It's inspiring and you form opinions."

Of course, prior to creative writing programs' late-20th century origins, writers still had a community, as well as individual relationships that were crucial to their development. Hemingway visited Gertrude Stein for a weekly "workshop." Steinbeck had Pascal Covici to shred any overblown scenes. Faulkner was in cahoots with Sherwood Anderson. Conrad had an extensive letter-writing relationship with Ford Madox Ford. These were the creative writing programs of yore. Maybe the only difference is that yesterday's writer's communities were organic, while today's have become institutionalized.

"I think we are living in a conventional time," Daniel Kunitz says. "But a lot of it will go away when the normal literature programs swing back in this country."

It's difficult to gauge what the long-term impact of MFA programs on American literature will be. However, many editors and non-graduate writers are genuinely concerned. A generation of readers will find the initials MFA in almost every new young writer's backflap biography. And with young writers pining away outside of academia being pushed farther to the literary fringes, the romance, at least for now, appears to be gone.

Pages from a feature

It is funny that *Speak* eventually became, at least to some degree, the magazine you originally envisioned it to be in that letter. That's not to say the same evolution would have taken place if the magazine were wildly successful in its early frivolous days.

Finally, let's talk about the evolution of *Speak*'s design. Sometimes I'm convinced the magazine needs to entirely rethink its visuals, yet your approach produces a sort of rethinking every issue. How restless do you feel with the look of the magazine? What's your thinking regarding a redesign?

MARTIN: One of the nice things about *Speak*, and our relationship, is that I never feel restless about the design at all. As both of our interests change and develop, so does the magazine. I've generally been given the power to reevaluate my work all the time, and to decide that I want to be more "raucous" in one section and more "reserved" in another. In fact, I think that the shifting moods within each issue and over time have become one of the signatures of the magazine.

As far as I can tell, the only disadvantage is that I get so tied to all of the nuances and changes that I can't easily hand over parts of the magazine for others to design. There are only a few areas that are specifically formatted, and even those pages reconfigure themselves over time. As each issue begins, there is both the exhilaration of getting to try new things, and the anxiety of reinvention.

I suspect that the only way to redesign the magazine would be to codify and regulate larger areas of it. It is tricky to harness such a beast. Either it could channel its strengths for more power, or it could trap the thing so that it withers and dies.

SECTION 5

In-House Designs

Most designers experience their first redesign as an in-house effort, and many who work for small or independent magazines are likely to have redesigns simply dumped in their laps. Some art directors get in the habit of revamping all the magazines for which they work. The reason for this has little to do with talent—there are many great editorial art directors who have little patience for the branding and minute structural concerns that go into a magazine format—and much to do with preference. Working within another designer's format represents, in most cases, a willingness and ability to speak a visual language invented by someone else. Some designers never work completely comfortably within another designer's structure.

An in-house design can be a struggle, requiring not just talent and motivation but also initiative and energy. It means finding time in the cracks of a regular production schedule to reimagine a magazine, it means finding a new visual vocabulary that is different from the one you speak daily, and it means guiding rather than merely following a process.

But those difficulties come with rewards. Designing a format in-house is a chance to work on a more generous schedule than the issue schedule, it's an opportunity to work with a different set of visual ideas, and it's a chance to design the running shoe you yourself will be racing in. A format can be altered to play to strengths of its author, to provide opportunities where wanted, and to save time and energy when useful.

The painter Chuck Close once said that if your own work looks like art to you, it must look like someone else's art, by which I think he meant that it's impossible to look at your own work without being overwhelmed by its flaws. Editorial designers rarely face the wholly personal creation in the same way a painter does—every page represents, in some measure, a collaboration with other talented people. Nevertheless, I've found it is harder to appreciate designs I've done for publications while I was also the art director. The formats I've made for myself, intentionally or not, do not push me out of my comfort zone. Nevertheless, I have always liked my publication more after the launch than before. If the new format didn't push me to be a better designer, it allowed me to be the best designer I am. An effective in-house design is a tool carefully crafted to the hand of its user.

Inside Magazine

13

ROBERT NEWMAN

IN THE SPRING OF 2000, I WAS WORKING AS DESIGN director at *Vibe* when I was called by Inside.com to design their new magazine. The magazine was a spin-off of a Web site started by some former print guys—Kurt Andersen and Michael Hirschorn—both of whom I had worked with at *New York* magazine. Their site was great, very forward, very smart—it dealt with media, entertainment, and technology. It was the forerunner of many of the blogs and news sites that are around now.

At some point they decided to start a print version of Inside.com. They originally hired Joe Dizney, who was then the design director of the *Wall Street Journal*. In fact, Joe called me at one point and asked my opinion about going there, because he knew I had worked with Kurt and Michael. Joe was hired, started staffing up, and contracted with Pentagram to work on a design for the magazine (they worked on the initial branding for the site). Then suddenly Joe got cold feet—he got a good counteroffer from the *Journal*—and backed out.

Without an art director and set to publish the first issue in about five weeks, Kurt called me and explained their situation. He said, basically, if you're interested, you have to decide tomorrow. I was very happy at *Vibe*. It was a great magazine, with an energetic young staff and a very smart new editor. But I loved the idea of working in an Internet environment. I told myself that I should experience the Internet boom at least once while it was at its peak. I also liked the idea of crafting a new magazine from the start. So the next day I told Kurt I was in. The day after that I was in the Inside.com office, meeting staff and starting work on the first issue (while still working full-time at *Vibe* for another two weeks).

I also liked the idea of working with Kurt again. He's smart, surrounds himself with talented people, and really gets publication design. He has a great eye for photos and understands the concept of developing an overall photo, illustration, and design aesthetic, something many editors do not. In addition, he is an extremely decisive and quick person, traits I love in editors. And he was very collaborative . . . at *New York* he and I would sit together at my computer and work on covers. Kurt was also a persuasive salesman—in terms of painting the opportunity at *Inside* as an adventure, something to be experienced—but he also was always up-front that the thing could go belly-up at any time.

The excitement of the times, the adventure of working in a new medium, a sense of being at the center of the media universe, and the energy that comes from working for a common goal with a group of smart, passionate, fun people made *Inside* a great place to be. The whole scene at *Inside* was very egalitarian and collaborative. There were no offices; everyone worked at desks in a giant room. In the art department, we literally sat together at a long table. There was barely enough room on either side to stretch out your arms. It sounds tough, but it was a great way to put out a magazine, without the layers of bureaucracy and departmentalization that usually exist.

As far as jumping to a business-to-business start-up from an established newsstand magazine, I didn't think it was much of a risk. The magazine business was booming at the time and there was unlimited work. When the time came to hire designers for *Inside*, we ended up in a bidding war with other publications. It was the ultimate boom time for publication designers. Lots of talent was going to the Web, and at the same time there were countless new magazine start-ups and spin-offs, and freelancers were being hired like crazy.

When I got to *Inside* there was already a deputy art director, Andrew Horton, who had been hired by Joe Dizney. We quickly hired a couple associates, Victor Williams from *Sports Illustrated* and Kate Elazegui, whom we lured out from the *Chicago Tribune*. We called her up and said, "How about moving to New York City in two weeks?" Fortunately she was up for the start-up. Andrew and I spent the first two weeks talking to a ton of people and just grabbed any promising people who were immediately available and threw them in a room and started working.

The directive for *Inside* was that it was supposed to both reflect and advance the Web site. Visually, it had to look connected, so we started with the basic site logo, which was [INSIDE]—caps inside blue brackets. The magazine was going to start as a biweekly, and ultimately come out as a weekly. The design needed to be

THE BUSINESS OF ENTERTAINMENT, MEDIA & TECHNOLOGY

AIMSTER! A NEW MUSIC BIZ NIGHTMARE

INSIDE

DECEMBER 12, 2000 / WWW.INSIDE.COM / $3.95

IN PARTNERSHIP WITH THE INDUSTRY STANDARD

THE NEW KILLER APP

Network TV's Surprisingly Crafty Plan to Win the Digital War

BY KYLE POPE AND SCOTT COLLINS

THE STUDIOS' VIDEO-GAME PROBLEM / AOL TIME WARNER'S BLOOD BUBBAS

BOB WRIGHT ON NBCi / LACHLAN MURDOCH'S PRIVATE BITS / e-BOOKS POWERHOUSE

PLUS: KURT ANDERSEN / ROGER PARLOFF / JEREMIAH CHECHIK IN HOLLYWOOD

Inside*'s debut issue, 2000*

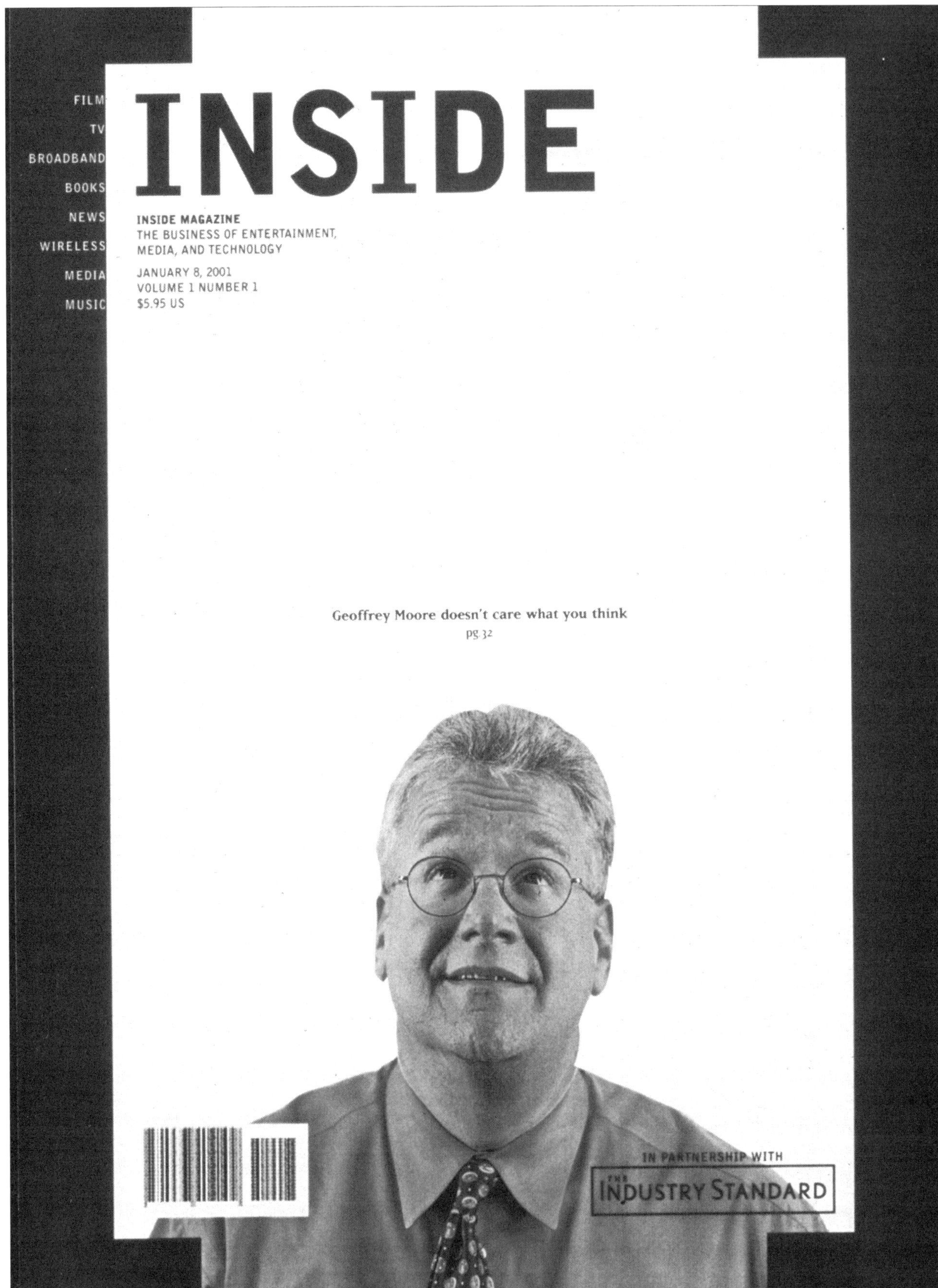

Proposed cover design

THE BUSINESS OF ENTERTAINMENT, MEDIA, AND TECHNOLOGY

INSIDE

FILM
TV
BROADBAND
BOOKS
NEWS
WIRELESS
MEDIA
MUSIC

Blood on the Titanium at Condé Nast

pg.55

JANUARY 8, 2001 VOLUME 1 NUMBER 1 $5.95 US

IN PARTNERSHIP WITH

THE INDUSTRY STANDARD

Proposed cover design

modern and elegant but also have an immediacy that spoke to its news content. At the same time, we had an extremely limited budget and resources, so we knew we had to come up with a design that would work without too much fussing and that wasn't too image-heavy. Not only did the design have to mirror the aesthetic and voice of the Web site, it also had to accommodate the production realities we were working with.

We had a little more than a month from start to hitting the streets with the first issue. Pentagram had worked on the initial Web site design and they came up with the *Inside* logo. When I got there, Pentagram had already started working on some designs for the magazine, but they were very loose. After talking with Kurt, Michael, and Richard Siklos, who was the magazine's editor (Kurt and Michael were more like editorial directors for the entire operation), I went to Pentagram with some very rough thoughts. For our first meeting, Andrew and I took along some sixties magazines—old copies of *Time*, *Fact*, and *Ramparts*. They were very simple, strong typographically, and they featured bold, full-page art. I also had in my head the idea to put the whole magazine on a seven-column grid. We sat with Michael Beirut and other designers from Pentagram and in about an hour sketched out the basic skeleton structure of the format and design of the magazine. Andrew and I went back to the office and started working on developing a photo, illustration, and graphics look (the magazine was to have a lot of charts), while Pentagram moved ahead executing ideas with the structure and fonts that we had talked about. At the same time, we had designers at *Inside* working on conceiving the nuts and bolts of how the sections and departments would work.

One of the other things we decided to do was to use only digital photographs and illustrations. That's pretty normal today, but back in 2000 the majority of freelancers were still working with film and paper. But we knew we didn't have the time to scan flat art or the resources to log, traffic, and return originals.

Our basic idea for the look of *Inside* was to keep it to two fonts. The display font was Bell—the logo font. Then we added a text/serif font, Scala. We wanted as little decoration and color as possible in the magazine . . . all the graphic punch and color was to be in the artwork. We wanted elegant, simple typography, generous white space, and a very clean, structured architecture.

I think we had a very successful collaboration with Pentagram, although it didn't work the way it usually does when a design firm delivers a finished magazine design. Most magazines come together over months—time we didn't have. In the end, we took what they had done, which was basically a bunch of sketches and ideas, very original and smart stuff, and plunked it onto a very formatted structure that we had created back in the office. We hired a couple of photo editors and a graphics person, and started working on the first issue on a two-week cycle. A lot of the departments and sections were worked out as we actually closed the magazine with real stories.

The big brackets Pentagram designed on the cover were really brilliant. These served as a *Time*-style frame, tied the magazine to the Web site, and gave the cover a distinctive look. The designers took those brackets and applied them throughout the sections of the magazine—sometimes as large borders on pages, other times as ways of organizing sidebars or subheads.

Pentagram also designed a horizon line around which we organized the pages. It runs all the way through the magazine about a third of the way down, and a lot of type, logos, and art start there. It's just an organizing device, but it's a really original idea. Initially, all the art was always going to be above the line, but that was too limiting. The horizon line is not on every page, but it appears often and was used in different ways. For example, text type might be big above the line and smaller below it. It gave the magazine a distinctive look and contributed to its overall cohesiveness.

To finalize the detailing of the design, we took each section and department and gave it to one of our *Inside* designers and said, "Here are the fonts, the basic structure, the column widths, and a story list; make this section real." And they just stretched it out, and we just sat there every day building it until we got to the real place of the finished magazine. It was all very organic.

We were hiring staff, getting in computers, working on the design, calling in photographs, setting up a color printer, all at the same time. The magazine was printed by the Industry Standard out on the West Coast. We would provide them with PDFs, and they would print off those. We didn't even get composed irises or Canon proofs of the pages. Our only proofer was a color printer.

The cover was the part that was never fully realized, partly because it wasn't clear how much we should be concerned about selling the magazine on the newsstand. The austere look that worked on the inside of the magazine didn't translate to the cover. I don't think we ever fully articulated a real voice there. The perfect manifestation of the look would have been to something like what the *Economist* is doing on their covers now—bold, provocative images and understated headlines with attitude. The first issue's cover was probably the closest we came to succeeding: a small, old-fashioned TV with a headline underneath that read, "The New Killer App." But the rest of the time we were just trying to be like any other magazine on the covers and didn't manage to develop our own unique voice in the way that the Web site did.

MEDIA

Over the next 10 years, employer-sponsored health plans will evolve en masse into defined-contribution formats, finally and irrevocably creating a consumer-driven health-care system in the United States. Over the next 10 years, employer-sponsored health plans will evolve en masse into defined-contribution formats, finally and irrevocably creating a consumer-driven health-care system in the United States. Over the next 10 years, employer-sponsored health plans will evolve en masse into defined-contribution formats, finally and irrevocably creating a consumer-driven health-care system in the United States. Over the next 10 years, employer-sponsored health plans will evolve en masse into defined-contribution formats, finally and

[HEADLINE]

Over the next 10 years, employer-sponsored health plans will evolve en masse into defined-contribution formats, finally and irrevocably creating a consumer-driven health-care system in the United States. Much as the defined-contribution model has placed individuals center stage in determining how to finance their own retirements, employees will soon be placMuch as the defined-contribution model has ed in the driver's seat for selecting their own health plans in an open market.

Economic, political, and social forces are starting to converge and a public dialogue is in the early stages of development. Health-care premiums, briefly under Much as the defined-contribution model has ers that participated in a Booz-Allen & Hamilton survey of leading companies express a nearly universal readiness to embrace new health-care benefits approaches that would limit their exposure to rising costs, and return choice and accountability to employee-consumers. Republicans and Democrats alike velopment. Health-care premiums, briefly under Much as the defined-contribution model has ers that participated in a Bvelopment. Health-care premiums, briefly under Much as the defined-contribution model has ers that participated in a Bhave presented election-year proposals addressing issues of access and cost via expanded enrollment in public risk pools (e.g., the Federal Employees

Health Benefits Program, or FEHB, and Me dicare), continued tax deductibility of benefits, and even tax credits. All of these developments support a defined-contribution approach. The recent success of similar changes in retirement benefits also augurs well for a fair hearing from consumers. en masse into defined-contribution formats, finally and irrevocably creating a consumer-driven health-care system in the United States. Much as the defined-contribution model has placed individuals center stage in determin-how to finance their own retire

[HEADLINE]

Over the next 10 years, employer-sponsored health plans will evolve en masse into defined-contribution formats, finally and irrevocably creating a consumer-driven health-care system in the United States. Much as the defined-contribution model has placed individuals center stage in determining how to finance their own retirements, employees will soon be placMuch as the defined-contribution model has ed in the driver's seat for selecting their own health plans in an open market.

Economic, political, and social forces are starting to converge and a public dialogue is in the early stages of development. Health-care premiums, briefly under Much as the defined-contribution model has ers that participated in a Booz-Allen & Hamilton survey of leading companies express a near-

[HEADLINE]

Over the next 10 years, employer-sponsored health plans will evolve en masse into defined-contribution formats, finally and irrevocably creating a consumer-driven health-care system in the United States. Much as the defined-contribution model has placed individuals center stage in determining how to finance their own retirements, employees will soon be placMuch as the defined-contribution model has ed in the driver's seat for selecting their own health plans in an open market.

Economic, political, and social forces are starting to converge and a public dialogue is in the early stages of development. Health-care premiums, briefly under Much as the defined-contribution model has ers that participated in a Booz-Allen & Hamilton survey of leading companies express a nearly universal readiness to embrace new health-care benefits approaches that would limit their exposure to rising costs, and return choice and accountability to employee-consumers. Republicans and Democrats alike velopment. Health-care premiums, briefly under Much as the defined-contribution model has ers that participated in a Bvelopment. Health-care premiums, briefly under Much as the defined-contribution model has ers thatdefined-contribution model has ers that participated in a Booz-Allen & Hamilton survey of participated defined-contribution model has ers that participated in a Booz-Allen & Hamilton survey of in a Bhave presented election-year proposals addressing issues of access and cost via expanded enrollment in public risk pools (e.g., thdefined-contribution model has ers that participated in a Booz-Allen & Hamilton survey

Health Benefits Program, or FEHB, and Me dicare), continued tax deductibility of benefits, and even tax credits. All of these developments support a defined-contribution approach. The recent success of similar changes in retirement benefits also augurs well for a fair hearing from consumers. en masse into defined-contribution driver's seat for selecting their own health plans in an open market.

Economic, political, and social forces are starting to converge and a public dialogue is in the early stages of development. Health-care premiums, briefly under Much as the defined-contribution model has ers that participated in a Booz-Allen & Hamilton survey of leading companies express a nearly universal readiness to embrace new health-care benefits approaches that would limit their exposure to rising costs, ande and a public dial-

[HEADLINE]

Over the next 10 years, employer-sponsored health plans will evolve en masse into defined-contribution formats, finally and irrevocably creating a consumer-driven health-care system in the United States. Much as the defined-contribution model has placed individuals center stage in determining how to finance their own retirements, employees will soon be placMuch as the defined-contribution model has ed in the driver's seat for selecting their own health plans in an open market.

Economic, political, and social forces are starting to creturn choice and accountability to employee-consumers. Republicans and Democrats alike velopment. Health-care premiums, briefly under Much as the defined-contribution model has ers that participated in a Bvelopment. Health-care premiums, briefly under Much as the defined-contribution model has ers that participated in a Bhave presented election-year proposals addressing issues of access and cost via expanded enrollment in public risk pools (e.g., the Federal Employees

Health Benefits Program, or FEHB, and Me dicare), continued tax deductibility of benefits, and even tax credits. All of these developments support a defined-contribu-

"The sleeping Music giant was only taking a Napster..."

Geoffrey Moore, Media Analyst

Employer Paid | Employer Paid
$50,000
Employer Assisted | Employer Assisted
$5,000
$500
Typical "Immortal" Male in His 20s | Typical Families
Risk Level | Normal | Catastrophic/ Extraordinary

Caption will go here to describe the image to the left of the text.

THE BIG

NEWS

[TV]

The Peacock is caught red-handed: NBC heads off to Court

Over the next 10 years, employer-sponsored health plans will evolve en masse into defined-contribution formats, finally and irrevocably creating a consumer-driven health-care system in the United States. Much as the de fined-contribution model has placed individuals center stage in determining how to finance their own retirements, employees will soon be placMuch as the defined-contribution model has ed in the driver's seat for selecting their own health plans.

Economic, political, and social forces are starting to converge and a public dialogue is in the early stages of development. Health-care premiums, briefly under Much as the defined-contribution model has ers that participated in a Booz-Allen & Hamilton survey of leading companies express a nearly universal readiness to embrace new health-care benefits approaches that would limit their exposure to rising costs, and return choice and accountability to employee-consumers. Republicans and Democrats alike velopment. Health-care premiums, briefly under Much as the defined-contribution model has ers that participated in a Bvelopment. Health-care premiums, briefly under Much as the defined-contribution model has ers that participated in a Bhave presented election-year proposals addressing issues

Caption will go here to describe the image to the left of the text.

Iceland
Finland | Sweden
Canada
Denmark
New Zealand | United Kingdom | Switzerland | Lu
Netherlands | Japan | Austria | Germany
Ireland | France | Belgium
Spain
Italy | Portugal | Greece
20 30 40 50 60 70 80 90

(BOOKS)

John Grisham goes crazy

Over the next 10 years, employer-sponsored health plans will evolve en masse into defined-contribution formats, finally and irrevocably creating a consumer-driven health-care system in the United States. Much as the defined-contribution model has placed individuals center stage in determining how to finance their own retirements, employees will soon be plac-Much as the defined-contribution model has ed in the driver's seat for selecting their own health plans.

Economic, political, and social forces are starting to converge and a public dialogue is in the early stages of development. Health-care premiums, briefly under Much as the defined-contribution model has ers that participated in a Booz-Allen & Hamilton survey of leading companies express a nearly universal readiness to embrace new health-care benefits approaches that would limit their exposure to rising costs, and return choice and accountability to employee-consumers. Republicans and Democrats alike velopment. Health-care premiums, briefly under Much as the defined-contribution model has ers that participated in a Bvelopment. Health-care premiums, briefly under Much as the defined-contribution model has ers that participated in a Bhave presented election-year proposals addressing issues of access and cost via expanded enrollment in public risk pools (e.g., the Federal Employees Health Benefits Program, or FEHB, and Me dicare), continued tax deductibility of benefits, and even tax credits. All of these developments support a defined-contribution approach. The recent success of similar changes in retirement benefits also augurs well for a fair hearing from consumers. en masse into defined-contribution for-

FILM

Information and Lists: Misc subjects relating to the film industry and data

Information and Lists: Misc subjects relating to the film industry and data

Information and Lists: Misc subjects relating to the film industry and data

continued tax over deduc tibility of benefits, and even tax credits. All of these developments support a defined-contribution approach. The recent success of similar changes in the retirement benefits also augurs well for a fair hearing from consumers. en masse into defined-contribution formats, finally and irrevocably creating a consumer-driven health-care system in the United States. Much

Proposed minimalist designs for Inside *sections*

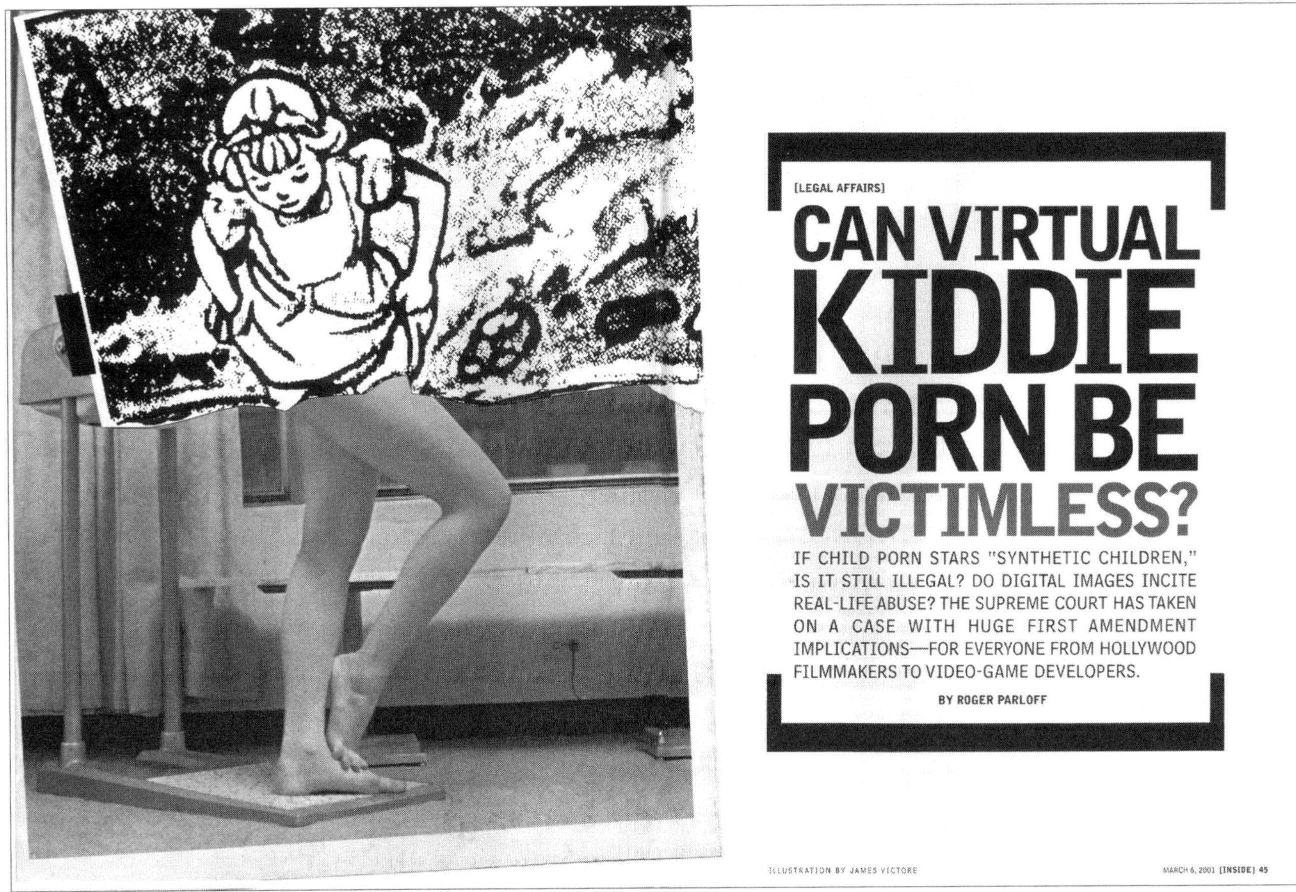
[LEGAL AFFAIRS]
CAN VIRTUAL KIDDIE PORN BE VICTIMLESS?
IF CHILD PORN STARS "SYNTHETIC CHILDREN," IS IT STILL ILLEGAL? DO DIGITAL IMAGES INCITE REAL-LIFE ABUSE? THE SUPREME COURT HAS TAKEN ON A CASE WITH HUGE FIRST AMENDMENT IMPLICATIONS—FOR EVERYONE FROM HOLLYWOOD FILMMAKERS TO VIDEO-GAME DEVELOPERS.
BY ROGER PARLOFF

Feature opening spread, 2001

In addition to *Inside*'s design, we came up with a pretty smart palette of illustrators. We were getting into a lot of the more modern, digital-styled illustrators like Peter Stemmler, Nana Rausch, Ulla Puggaard . . . a very cool, modern, stylish look.

Inside was different from any of the other magazines I've worked for because it was a Web site spin-off. It surprised some people that it didn't look like *Wired* or have a more "digital" or futuristic design. Actually, *Inside*, with its clean, sparse layout, was much more in keeping with the real spirit and look of the Web than publications that go into hyperdesign overload in an attempt to be "webby."

Inside came together fast. It also fell apart fast. Unlike a lot of Web sites, *Inside* didn't hype itself to its own employees; the management was very honest about the prospects of success. They paid well and created an environment that was really exciting and intelligent—it was a good place. Everyone was sad when it went under, but I don't think anyone was surprised. A couple of weeks before the end, they had a meeting and told us, "We're going to sell it," and they indicated it might be good or it might be nothing. When it was going to be sold they told us on Friday that we'd know what our situations were after the weekend. Monday morning, people came into work and Kurt said, "Go on upstairs and get your check," and it was over. Some people got to stay on the job with the new owner. But everyone who left got a severance check, and that's more than a lot of people got at dot-coms that folded owing them thousands of dollars.

After a summer at home with my young daughter, I landed at *Real Simple*. As a women's magazine, it was a whole different mindset from anywhere I had worked—particularly from *Inside*. At *Inside*, everything was fast and dirty, but at *Real Simple* everything was totally planned and meticulously thought out—every word and every picture. Nothing was put randomly into *Real Simple*. You couldn't just put a picture of a napkin in the magazine; it had to be a particular napkin for a particular reason, and it had to be available for purchase somewhere, because readers expected to be able to buy whatever they saw. You also couldn't use something that was too expensive, because the readers would complain about the prices.

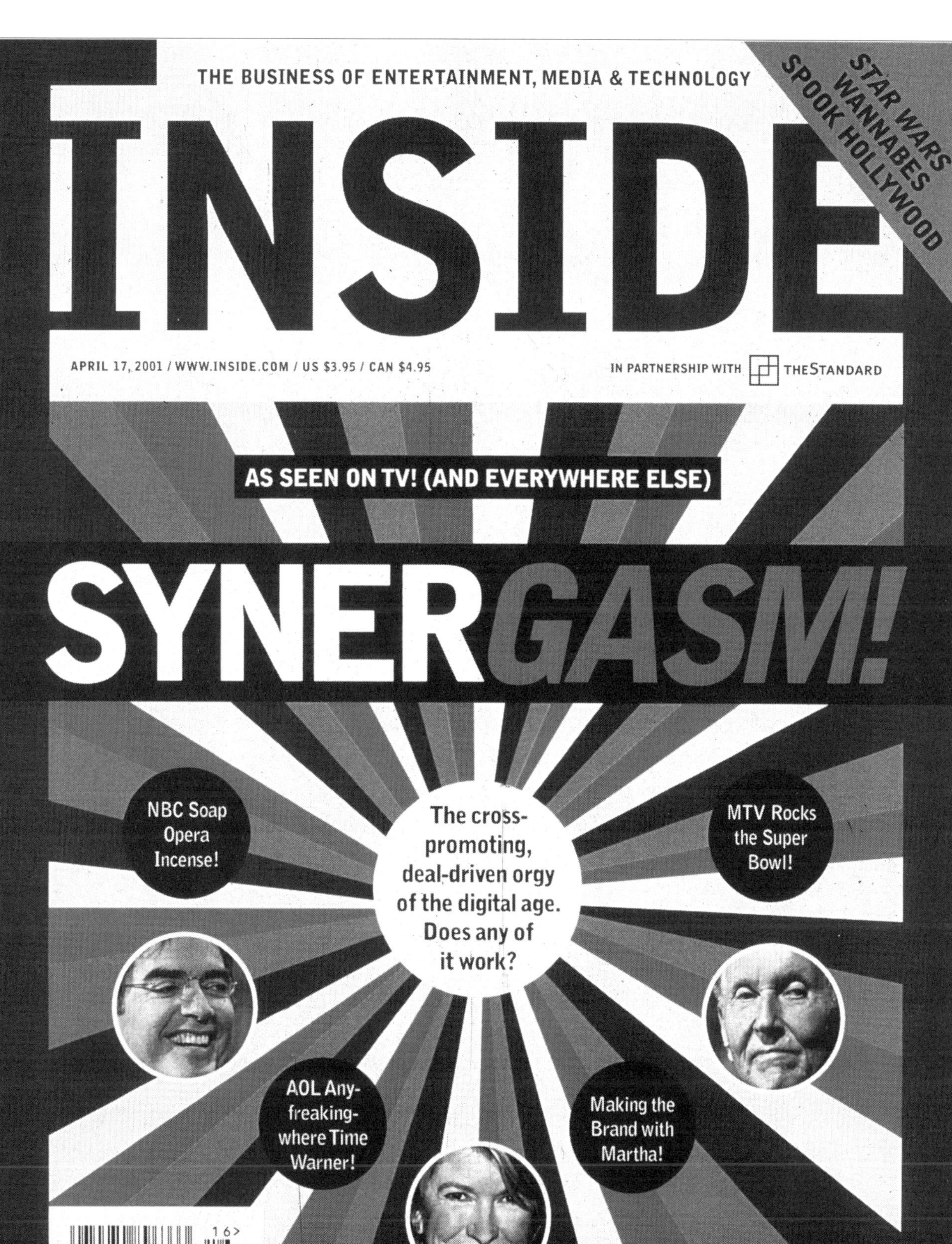

THE BUSINESS OF ENTERTAINMENT, MEDIA & TECHNOLOGY
STAR WARS WANNABES SPOOK HOLLYWOOD
INSIDE
APRIL 17, 2001 / WWW.INSIDE.COM / US $3.95 / CAN $4.95
IN PARTNERSHIP WITH THESTANDARD
AS SEEN ON TV! (AND EVERYWHERE ELSE)
SYNERGASM!
NBC Soap Opera Incense!
The cross-promoting, deal-driven orgy of the digital age. Does any of it work?
MTV Rocks the Super Bowl!
AOL Any-freaking-where Time Warner!
Making the Brand with Martha!
0 74470 89633 3
16>

The last, unpublished cover

Real Simple was the only magazine where I've worked out the features so far in advance. We did what we called "storyboarding." We'd sketch out and plot the photographs before they were shot. The sketch would be exactly as it was going to appear, complete with color swatches and photo reference of the products. Even when we did profiles—for example, we had a story about a woman who had cancer and moved out to a barn and started a business—we'd hire some kid or a local photographer to do a preliminary shoot and then use those pics as reference to storyboard the photos before we sent the real photographer. Then we would compress the woman's life into a couple days. Maybe she wouldn't have yoga on Wednesdays, but we'd make sure she'd schedule it for the Wednesday our photographer was there.

A lot of people editing and doing design in printed publications don't get the Web and never have. Bells and whistles and crazy Photoshop stuff don't really have a lot to do with the success of content on the Web. It's still all about content, no matter how it's delivered. Good design is just a way of making content more accessible to people. Visual storytelling is just making information something you can see. There are editors who want you to tart things up for no reason. A friend of mine speaks disdainfully of many art directors being "decorators," and by that he means designers who throw things on the page with no meaning and no content. The sad truth is that's really what a lot of editors want you to do. They get much more threatened when you're not a decorator—when the things you do impact the content and the basic DNA of the publication. I'm doing a redesign now, and we keep asking the editors fundamental questions about the content of the magazine and where it's going; they're always trying to deflect us over to the decoration side. "Let's talk about the colors; what fonts are you going to use?" Well, you know, we can't talk about that until we know what the overall direction is going to be. And, sad to say, many editors think a redesign is just all about shuffling things around. I've taken to calling it rearranging chairs on the deck of the Titanic, because at a time when drastic changes are needed to the way magazines present information, the editors are still just interested in a change of color and typefaces.

Governing Magazine

14

JANDOS ROTHSTEIN

Founded in 1987, Governing *is a controlled-circulation magazine for local government professionals. Covering innovation at the state, county, and municipal level through diverse topics (recent articles have covered law enforcement, health policy, early education, reservoir security, and library management, among other topics), the publication seeks to be the business magazine for elected and appointed officials.*

Of all the redesigns I've worked on, *Governing*'s went particularly smoothly, in part because I had great colleagues (though even great colleagues can disagree with one another), but also because everyone involved—all the stakeholders, if you prefer—had a clear and common understanding of the objectives for the redesign.

At a magazine, design has an impact on nearly everyone on staff. Editors and writers are concerned that the text be enhanced and readable but perhaps not upstaged, advertising representatives want something flashy they can take to the agencies, and the publisher wants to maintain or build circulation. And all of them, whether they are directly involved in making the magazine or not, want the public product that represents them to be, frankly, cool. If the staff members feel that they have been listened to during the planning stage and their concerns have been taken seriously (even if not always made manifest in the final), and if the designer has successfully banished the sort of vocabulary that can derail a plan (generally, any questions of "like" or "taste" should be avoided), then concepting, approval, and implementation can go smoothly.

Designers should be sympathetic to the inevitable apprehensions of their colleagues. A successful redesign can increase readership, advertising, or both. An unsuccessful redesign can have the opposite effect. Life and death? Hardly. But no one wants to see a publication's fortunes turn down under his or her stewardship. Magazines gain and lose ground for lots of reasons—design is just one factor—but everyone's professional reputation, comfort, and security are at stake. Everyone who works for a magazine is invested in the ongoing success of the venture.

What follows is a look not at the results of the redesign (which can be seen more fully at *www.jandos.com*) but at the process the in-house design team used to build consensus within the organization for a redesign and the direction it would take. Note that nowhere does it mention specific colors, typestyles, or other details of design. All of that, appropriately, came later. The points in the design brief may seem self-evident to seasoned magazine professionals, but they do the job of establishing a common understanding between a group of individuals of various talents and backgrounds, all of whom have their own ideas about what is important about editorial formats and page design.

The direction *Governing* eventually took is not the only way the magazine might have chosen to go, nor is it the inevitable outcome of this written understanding. Both the final design and this strategy came out of meetings with editors, designers, ad directors, and publisher, all working to figure out the magazine's needs—not just visual needs—and weaving it into a coherent strategy. I use footnotes to describe the considerations behind some of the statements in the brief.

Redesign Goals[1]

1. **Increase penetration among core readership groups.** *Governing*'s main advertisement for itself is itself. Whether mailed to prospective readers, seen on a colleague's desk, or passed along on the strength of a specific article, *Governing* should look immediate, essential, and fascinating.[2]
2. **Improve *Governing* as an advertising vehicle.** Create more front-of-book ad-placement opportunities, increase magazine length to make the front larger, increasing the number of preferred spots and reducing proximity conflicts. Update the magazine's appearance. Make *Governing* look more like a magazine and less like a journal.[3]
3. **Improve reader enthusiasm for the magazine.** Readers are spending slightly less time with *Governing* than they were a few years ago.[4] There's a general sense that the magazine often ends up at the bottom of readers' in-boxes. Create a design that makes the magazine's editorial virtues more obvious and accessible. The design should pull readers from spread to spread through more engaging presentation and improved flow.[5]

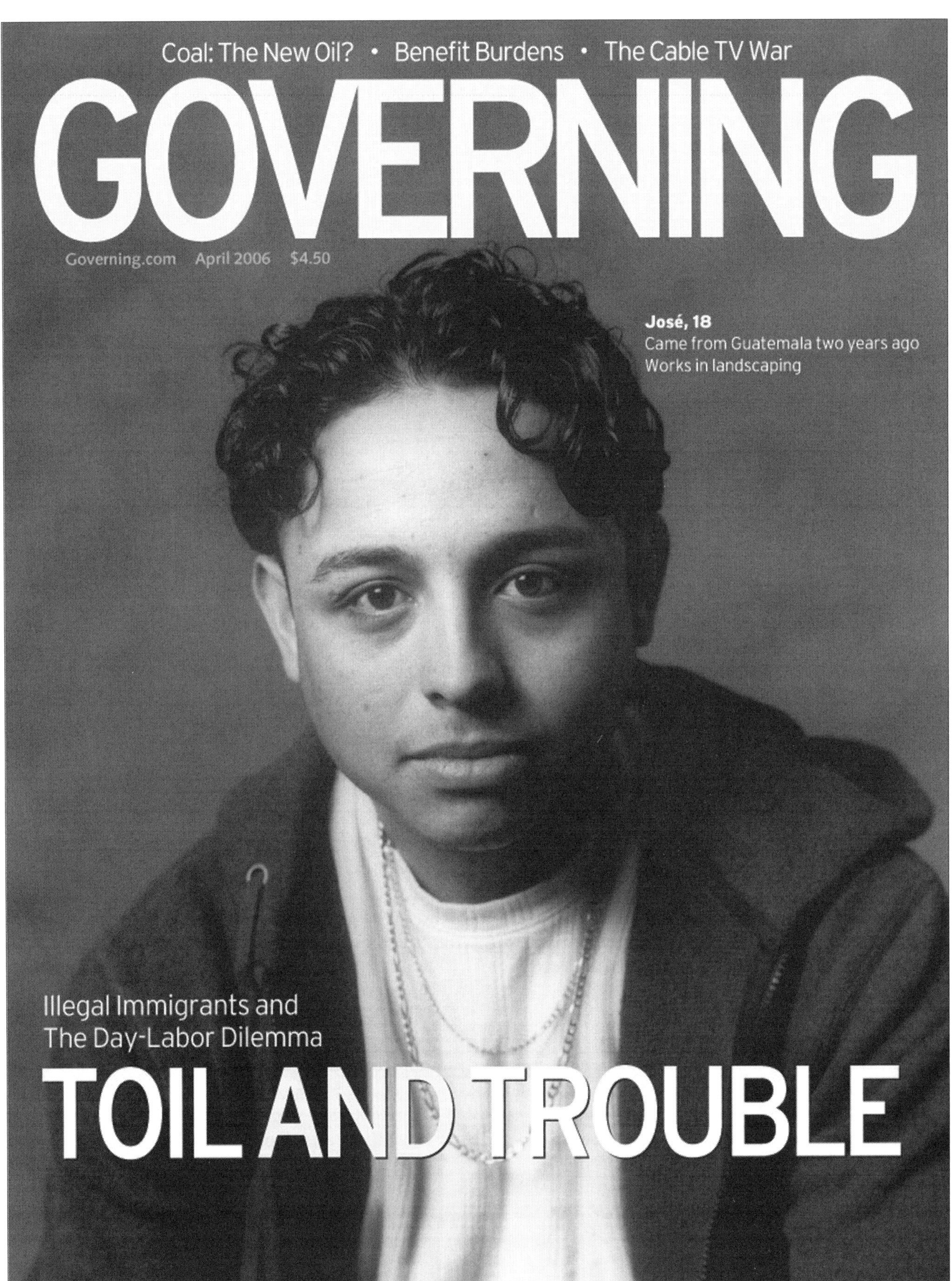
Coal: The New Oil? • Benefit Burdens • The Cable TV War
GOVERNING
Governing.com April 2006 $4.50
José, 18
Came from Guatemala two years ago
Works in landscaping
Illegal Immigrants and
The Day-Labor Dilemma
TOIL AND TROUBLE

After

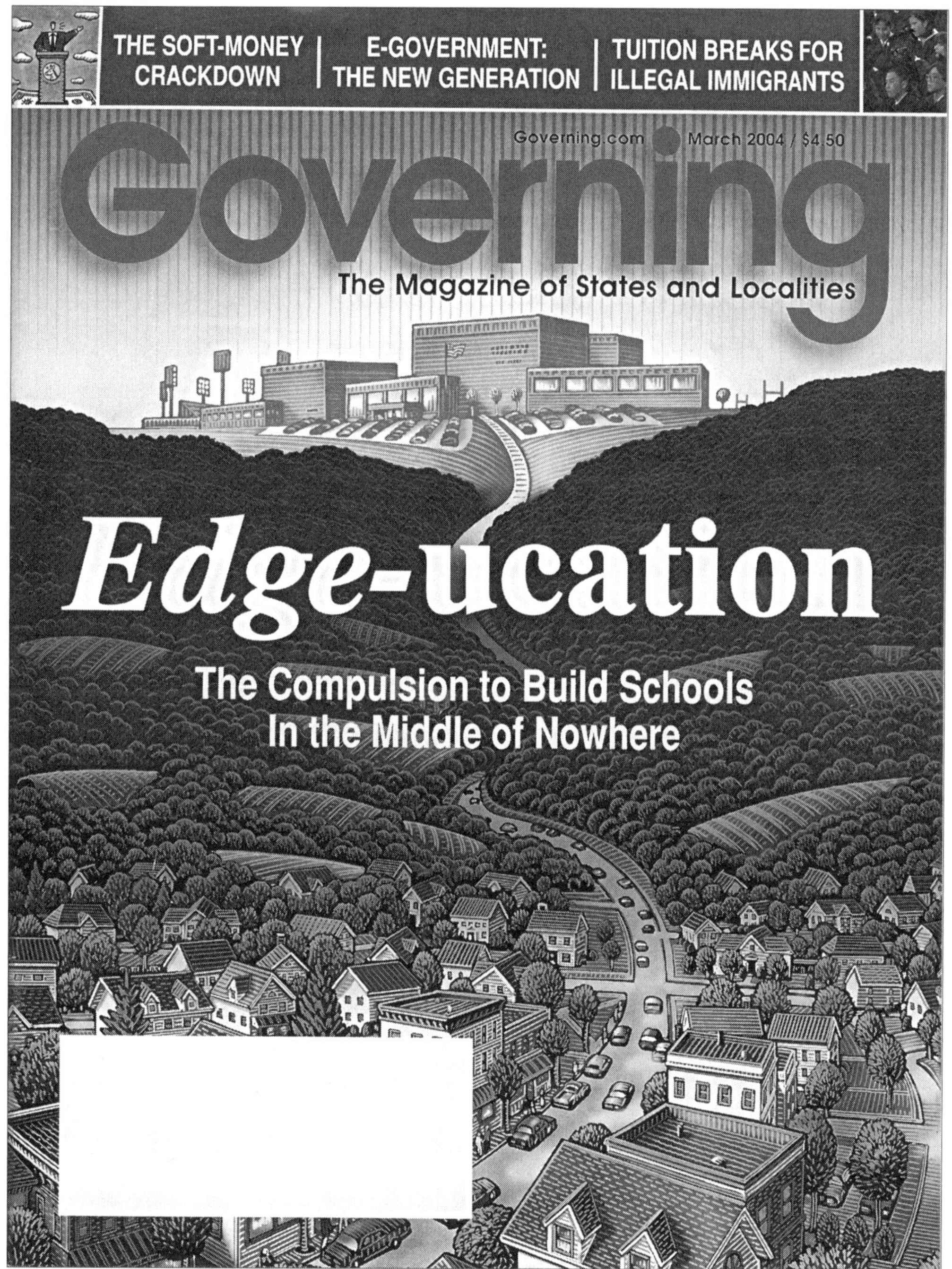

THE SOFT-MONEY CRACKDOWN
E-GOVERNMENT: THE NEW GENERATION
TUITION BREAKS FOR ILLEGAL IMMIGRANTS
Governing.com
March 2004 / $4.50
Governing
The Magazine of States and Localities
Edge-ucation
The Compulsion to Build Schools In the Middle of Nowhere

Before

4. **Add humor, increase liveliness.** These are goals best met outside the feature well, where short, humorous, and entertaining features can be more naturally incorporated.[6]
5. **Increase pride in presentation.**[7] Pride motivates editorial and sales staff alike. Excellent presentation improves perceived overall quality—for both contest judges[8] and readers.

An Initial Approach to Meeting Redesign Goals[9]

UPDATE THE TYPOGRAPHY AND SIGNAGE. *Governing*'s current design, though it had many virtues when introduced,[10] aged more quickly than it might have because it was so trendy. While the Web-influenced signage and early-seventies typography was enjoying a renaissance in the late nineties when the redesign was launched and while they do create a bold statement,

Observer

By Alan Greenblatt

A SMARTER DIG

Huge cost overruns are the rule on major public works projects. But they aren't inevitable.

Two massive public works projects were launched in Boston around 1990, each with a budget of about $6 billion. One of them, the "Big Dig" highway extravaganza, exceeded its projected costs by nearly $10 billion and has become a national symbol of sloppy government performance. But it's the other project that offers more useful lessons to public leaders elsewhere.

Many have forgotten, even in Massachusetts, that in 1990, Boston Harbor was so polluted that people had to dodge sludge if they wanted to swim there. The dirty harbor was a major embarrassment to Massachusetts Governor Michael Dukakis in his 1988 presidential campaign. Environmental lawsuits led to a federal judge taking responsibility for the cleanup effort, which has been run by the Massachusetts Water Resources Authority. By all accounts, the professional managers at MWRA got just about everything right—and are finishing the project early for one-third less than its original budget.

What made the cleanup run so much more smoothly than the Big Dig? In a word, oversight. There was, first of all, the role played by the late Judge David Mazzone, who stubbornly resisted demands to slow the project down from ratepayers who complained that it was forcing their water bills to soar. But the fact that local people were paying for the harbor cleanup—in contrast to the federal largesse that primarily funded the Big Dig—also had a positive impact. It generated a watchdog effect. Area officials and

GOVERNING SEPTEMBER 2006 **19**

The new front-of-book news section

they do so at the expense of editorial efficacy. Signage often overpowers the page. A new design should be simpler and call less attention to itself, allowing editorial content to shine. It should have a longer life than the current design because it should more easily allow for incremental modification and because the "look" of the magazine should be less dependent on standing art.[11]

REVITALIZE THE FRONT SECTION (COLUMNS). Readers see a page before they read it. While the contents of the magazine changes with every issue, page appearance often does not reflect the vitality of the writing because the pages look the same every month.[12] Content-driven illustration and the addition of deck heads would help make these pages visually exciting. I believe this can be accomplished within the current budget.[13]

MAKE THE TOC MORE FUNCTIONAL. Make the teaser copy more specific, and reduce clutter on the page both to improve readability and to reflect relative importance of content. Consider a two-page format,

Observer

citizens participated on boards that helped oversee MWRA's efforts. Several members of the independent board of directors served for a decade or more, lending stability and real institutional knowledge to the proceedings. It's one thing, after all, to pledge accountability, and something else to have people who actually demand it. The Big Dig lacked such a board, as well as the citizen advisory council that MWRA listens to.

For their part, MWRA managers rode herd over private contractors in a way that Big Dig officials didn't do. "At MWRA, there was a distinctive small group acting as the owner's team to whom the construction manager reported," says Doug MacDonald, a former head of the agency and now secretary of transportation in Washington State. On the Big Dig, he says, "it's not totally clear to whom the Bechtel corporation ever reported."

Taken in perspective, the Boston Harbor story isn't anything for government to get smug about. It was, after all, the failure of a public agency to budget properly for maintenance over many years that led to the sludge problem in the first place. Even now, ratepayers aren't crazy about meeting the costs of maintenance, so the nearly complete cleanup remains fragile.

The real lesson out of Boston Harbor isn't that public management is better or worse than private management on a mega-project. It's that public-private partnerships are delicate and need constant vigilance. Even in successful privatization efforts, oversight and competency on the government side remain a must.

FUCHSIA FUSS

"Girls' programs are often boys' programs painted pink."

Barry Krisberg, president of the National Council on Crime and Delinquency, releasing a study reporting that programs to help girls entering Florida's juvenile justice system are inadequate

Source: *St. Petersburg Times*

READ THEIR LIPS

Congress hates to raise taxes—unless it can force other levels of government to collect them.

No public official wants to be a tax agent for somebody else. That's one reason states and localities object to a new federal law that threatens to turn them into de facto instruments of the IRS. But it's not the only reason.

As the result of a provision in the tax package enacted by Congress this spring, state and local governments that spend more than $100 million annually must withhold 3 percent of their payments to vendors for goods and services, then send the proceeds along to Washington. There are many problems with this provision. For one thing, it violates the Unfunded Mandates Act passed by Congress in 1995 and designed to prevent Washington from making state and local governments perform duties the feds aren't willing to pay for.

There will indeed be extra costs to states and localities from the new tax provision. Contractors, who are lobbying for the provision's repeal, warn that they'll have to raise the prices they charge public agencies in order to maintain their cash flow. Three percent may not sound like much, but in some cases it represents more than a contractor's entire profit from a government job.

There also will be administrative and software costs, although no one knows what those will amount to. The provision was slipped into the bill just prior to passage, leaving no time for tweaking or even careful study. The law is vague about issues such as how governments should report withheld amounts either to the IRS or to vendors, how often payments must be sent to Washington and what penalties would apply in cases of late payment or inaccurate reporting. It's also unclear how governments can withhold 3 percent of everyday purchases made with credit cards. "If we buy a box of pencils, do we pay 97 percent of the bill and withhold 3?" wonders Tim Firestine, finance director of Montgomery County, Maryland.

For all the headaches, the provision won't even generate that much money. The feds will see a one-time acceleration of income, but revenues will drop off as vendors start receiving refunds from previous years' overpayments. The provision is expected to generate $6 billion in 2011, the first year it will take effect, but only about $200 million a year after that. In essence, it's an accounting trick.

What's more, the whole thing could be unconstitutional, in light of a 1997 Supreme Court decision, in the case of *Printz v. United States*, holding that Congress could not force states and localities to perform administrative tasks for the federal government. "The objection is not frivolous on its face because of the *Printz* case," says William Van Alstyne, a constitutional scholar at the William and Mary School of Law. "To put it bluntly, if the feds want their tax, let them go and collect it."

Still, Van Alstyne predicts, the provision will likely survive court scrutiny should a challenge be filed. In that case, the debate over the withholding provision won't do much to clarify the constitutional relations between Washington and lower levels of government. What it will do is further poison those relations.

SUDAN SQUEEZE

Disinvestment remains a powerful human-rights weapon—as long as it's done carefully.

Washington and the United Nations continue to ponder their options in response to the genocidal killings and ethnic cleansing in Darfur, the westernmost region of Sudan. But many state and local officials are already taking action. Their pension funds are selling billions of dollars' worth of shares in companies that do business with the Sudanese government.

It's the biggest divestment campaign since the protests over apartheid in South Africa some 20 years ago. "Having U.S. companies divest from Sudan will play a major role, because at the end of the day, money talks," says Kansas state Senator Donald Betts, who intends to introduce a divestment bill during next year's session. Seven states have passed bills or nonbinding resolutions, and legislation is pending in at least an equal number. In April, Providence, Rhode Island, became the first city to approve a divestment ordinance.

But policy makers must take care that in crafting their proposals they don't

OTIS WHITE'S URBAN NOTEBOOK

The Problem with Free Transit

As part of their efforts to reduce air pollution, **San Francisco** and its suburbs offer free transit rides when pollution spikes. Ridership on BART and the other transit systems has soared on those days, causing some leaders to wonder if transit ought to be free all the time. But the San Francisco experience also offers some cautions: Misbehavior on the transit systems also soars on free days. There was considerable mischief and some outright lawbreaking on the buses and trains on free-ride days. BART's police chief thinks the problems are so great that he wants the free rides to be limited in the future, perhaps to morning commute hours. Two teenage girls got into a fight at one station; one stabbed the other, who ended up in the hospital. Others played boomboxes on trains, ate and drank, and tossed litter everywhere. It wasn't all kids, though. There were reports of homeless people riding trains and buses to beat the heat, the *San Francisco Chronicle* said. All of which is to say that there's good reason to charge something for transit. People don't tend to abuse things for which they pay.

Fixing a Regional Organization

For the past three years, Northeast Ohio's latest economic development effort, Team NEO (including **Cleveland** and **Akron**), has talked big, tried many things and accomplished little. Since its inception, the organization has loudly announced big goals only to quietly abandon them, changed strategies frequently and turned over its executive team, the *Cleveland Plain Dealer* reported recently. Team NEO's problem is it's not really a regional economic development organization, it's a confederation of chambers of commerce. It gets a little money from local corporations, but much of its meager funding comes from area foundations. This is a recipe for failure. What Team NEO needs is for those who would benefit most from a regional approach to economic development—the corporations, big universities and major governments—to rewrite the organization's charter so Team NEO can go directly to them for funding and not deal with the chambers. That's how successful regional economic organizations do it: They get annual dues from members to pay the organization's overhead and mount occasional fund-raising campaigns to finance their economic development initiatives. The campaigns give these organizations their focus: The organizations promise to create a certain number of jobs by undertaking specific, detailed initiatives.

Peddling Public Policy

Selling voters on new ideas is a critical part of the mayor's job in **Seattle** because, like many West Coast cities, it has to take a lot of things to referendums, including fairly routine transportation improvements. Seattle's a pretty liberal place, so persuading voters to tax themselves for urban improvements isn't impossible. Still, it's hard to get people revved up about a bond issue to install pedestrian signals, resurface streets and replace street signs, as Mayor Greg Nickels is proposing for this year's fall elections. So, he sponsored a public contest. In June, the mayor asked voters to send him their nominations for the worst traffic problems in Seattle—the bumpiest roads, the most irksome delays, the most dangerous bike routes. From the nominations, he said, he would create a "Dirty Dozen" list that would receive "very high priority" for repair. Nickels' intent was to shine a light on the city's backlog of transportation needs, generate some publicity for his upcoming referendum and show voters how such things connected with their everyday lives. More than 700 people wrote or e-mailed with their peeves. Nickels unveiled his Dirty Dozen at a press conference and talked at length about the need to repair all of Seattle's transportation infrastructure.

Urban Notebook is updated daily at www.governing.com/notebook.htm

20 SEPTEMBER 2006 GOVERNING

GOVERNING SEPTEMBER 2006 21

The new front-of-book news section

GLIMPSES

Fowl Out

To many of the 25,000 residents of Key West, Florida, the age-old joke about chickens crossing the road is no laughing matter. For the past several years, local officials have struggled with what to do about some 2,000 wild fowl that roam the streets. In January, the city commission voted to hire a municipal chicken catcher.

Three years ago, in response to growing complaints from citizens about the noise, the excessive droppings, and the traffic disruptions, officials deemed the birds both a nuisance and a health hazard and called for their extermination.

An organization called Wildlife Rescue of the Florida Keys, however, proposed a chicken-adoption program in conjunction with the Suncoast Seabird Sanctuary near Clearwater to relocate the chickens throughout Florida. A city ordinance was subsequently passed prohibiting the harassment and killing of the chicks. "Here in Key West, there's a 50-50 split," says Janet Matheny, the rescue group's director. "People either love the chickens or hate them."

Despite the concentrated effort to reduce their numbers, "the chickens kept breeding faster than we could catch them" said Assistant City Manager John Jones. "It cost a lot of money paying public works and parks and recreation people overtime" to keep up with the rapidly reproducing fowl. With each hen laying as many as 15 to 20 eggs per month, the only thing that outpaced the chicken population was the number of complaints flooding city hall.

So in January, local barber Armando Parra, who has raised and bred chickens for decades, was hired to catch 900 chickens to the tune of $22 per bird. Parra's operation will be run "more scientifically" and systematically than previous chicken-catching efforts, Jones adds. The apprehended fowl will then be shipped to farms in Florida.

—*Lindsay Clayton*

Three Easy Steps

Matt Kane, a policy analyst with the Northeast-Midwest Institute, joking to states in his region about how to get more money out of the federal government:

"You need to ratchet up your poverty rate, drastically reduce incomes, and recruit old and sick people."

Read 'em and Reap

Library book-reading contests aren't just for children anymore. The public library in Wichita, Kansas, launched its first annual adult reading program in January, enticing older readers with monthly prize drawings and a chance at the grand prize: an overnight stay at a Wichita hotel.

Modeled after similar programs in Missouri and Illinois, the goal of "Read Your Way Across the U.S.A." is not only to encourage adults to read more books but also to promote the exploration of a variety of works from around the country.

Participants "visit" five different regions—the Northwest, Southwest, Midwest, the South and New England—by choosing fiction or nonfiction in which the region is the subject, the setting, or the home of the author. They are eligible to enter the monthly prize drawings for each novel read (local businesses have donated gift certificates ranging from free oil changes to museum passes), and once they finish works from all five regions, they may contend for the grand prize.

"The theme requires adults to do some thinking about what they read," says Julie Linneman, the programming and outreach coordinator for Wichita's public libraries. "We're hoping they will step out of their niche and try other things. And we're hoping people who haven't been in a library for a while might say 'Hey, this sounds like fun.'"

Oh yes, unabridged audio books count, too.

—*Brad Amburn*

16 GOVERNING March 2004 Governing.com

Cheaters By the Dozen

In the San Francisco Bay area, law-breaking motorists have to worry not only about red-light cameras taking pictures of their illegal behavior but also about fellow drivers doing the same. A pair of local commuters has set up a Web site to display digital photographs of scofflaws driving solo in car pool lanes or violating other traffic and parking laws.

Sean McIntyre, who shoots photos and helps maintain the site, www.carpoolcheats.org, says the project was inspired by the experience of being tailgated at high speeds by a driver who didn't belong in the car pool lane to begin with. "That's why we did it originally, to vent our own frustration," he says.

When McIntyre and his partner spot cheaters, they pull into another lane to take pictures of the driver and the car's license plate. McIntyre adds that it helps "to relieve the boredom" during a 100-mile commute from California's Central Valley to San Jose. But he says he's received lots of e-mail messages from people who are supportive of the idea of embarrassing violators in hopes of changing their behavior.

It's not a technique the authorities are likely to embrace, however. Mike Wright, a California Highway Patrol spokesman, says that cheating in car pool or HOV lanes is inevitable and that studies have shown there aren't enough violators to reduce the effectiveness of the lanes.

A bigger danger, he says, is the possibility that McIntyre and his buddy might provoke a violent incident. One driver, whom the Web site calls the "Carpool Cheater Poster Boy," flipped them the bird and threw a ceramic mug at their car. "We want to curtail any type of confrontational activity on the highways," Wright says.

—*Alan Greenblatt*

Dead Heat II

Michael Carney and Bill Davignon thought they had experienced the ultimate election cliffhanger in 2001. Their race for a seat in the Niagara County, New York, legislature was so close that it was thrown to the courts, eventually taking 38 days to decide. When Davignon, the Democrat, pulled through with a one-vote victory (1,675 to 1,674), Republicans lost control of the legislature.

But a rematch this past November has resulted in the rare case of a sequel living up to the original. Davignon and Carney faced off again for the same seat, and although Davignon was ahead by 32 votes on election night, various challenges and absentee ballots subsequently whittled the tally down to a tie at 1,470 votes each.

The election, still in appeals, has taken so long to decide that the new members of the county legislature have already been sworn in. Meanwhile, Davignon has kept his seat. If he loses his appeal and the election remains a tie, Carney will be appointed to the seat, thanks to a new law clarifying ties passed by the county legislature (now firmly back under Republican control).

The appeal process has taken some strange turns, including a challenge to Carney's own ballot. Carney, who filed an affidavit ballot because he recently moved, forgot to circle his gender, rendering the ballot incomplete. In the end, the ballot was allowed.

For Davignon, the lesson of the two elections is clear. "Every vote counts," he says. "It's just that simple." —*Anya Sostek*

The Cousin Conundrum

State laws on marriage between cousins

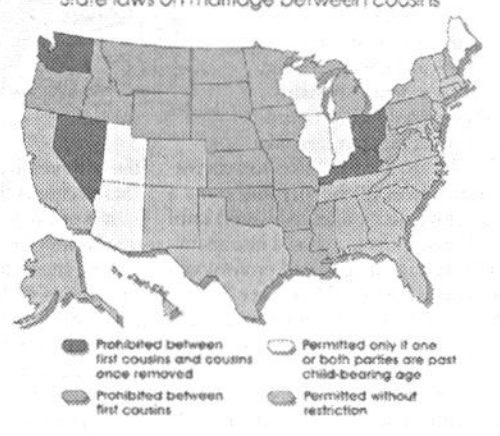

March 2004 GOVERNING 17

Old news section

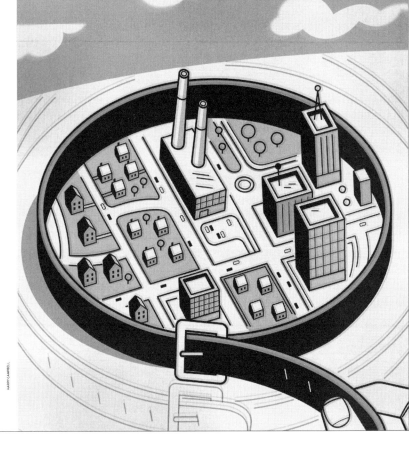

Smart Decline

In 40 years, Youngstown has lost more than half its population. Those people aren't coming back. But shrinking doesn't have to mean dying. By Christopher Swope

Anthony Kobak has borrowed the mayor's Ford Taurus for a spin around Youngstown, but as he steers the sedan down a pitted asphalt road, he wishes he'd borrowed a Jeep instead. Driving comes pretty close to off-roading in this part of Youngstown's east side, where the surroundings are mostly fallow lots and a few scattered homes. Kobak stops at one street that is little more than a dirt path into the woods. But it is a city-maintained road all the same, with water, sewer and power lines. "We're just 10 minutes from downtown, but you can see it's very rural," says Kobak, who is Youngstown's chief planner. He points out the window toward a lone deteriorating house in a field. "Those are chicken coops over there. You can see the cages."

This part of Youngstown is called Sharon Line—the name, Kobak explains, came from a street car route that used to run through the area. Back in the 1950s, this place was expected to develop into a bustling urban neighborhood. The steel mills were still roaring, and with 170,000 residents, Youngstown was Ohio's seventh-largest city and the 57th most populous in the United States. Planners believed that the east side would soak up continuing growth and prosperity. What in fact happened was quite the opposite. Not only did suburbanization suck the life out of city neighborhoods, as happened in much of America, but in the 1970s, the steel mills closed and population went into a free-fall. Quite suddenly, Youngstown's growth problem had turned into an abandoned-property problem. In Sharon Line, new houses simply weren't needed anymore. The area remained an odd country enclave tucked inside a fast-declining city.

Now, Kobak and other Youngstown officials have come around to a drastically different vision for Sharon Line. No longer are they holding out for a miracle growth spurt. Rather, they're embracing the radical idea of gradually turning this place back to nature. Roads and infrastructure may be taken out of service. Some properties could be converted to wetlands. Kobak calls this way of thinking "going from gray to green," and it's not just at work in Sharon Line. In

HARRY CAMPBELL

46 NOVEMBER 2006 GOVERNING

Feature opening spread, new

which would provide not only a better opportunity to advertise content but also an extra premium front-of-the-book ad position.[14]

IMPROVE EDITORIAL FLOW. Currently the longest "Briefs" item (the "Mega-Glimpse") seems disassociated from the section. Putting it first will result in better integration and start the "Briefs" section with a bang. Consider putting most of the columns after "Glimpses" so readers are pulled in by shorter, small-commitment items. Make the feature well more distinct, less like the columns. Consider how to handle "Business of Government," possibly integrating some of its contents into other sections. Give some sections—"BuisGov," "Glimpses"—a right-hand start, which more clearly signals the beginning of a new section. Consider incorporating "Second Glance" items into the news sections, and return "Players" to the back page or possibly move one of the other front columns to the back page. Consider breaking up "Glimpses" to create more front-of-book ad positions.[15]

BUILD BREATHING ROOM INTO THE FEATURE WELL. *Governing* places a five-page limit on features because editors don't want to overwhelm or turn off readers with too much text. This is a good instinct, but I believe that the policy has had the reverse of the intended effect. Few readers count pages before deciding to read an article. And because relatively lengthy features—sometimes as long as four thousand words—are shoehorned into small holes, the immediate visual effect is the appearance of a big reading commitment and there is less space for the sorts of points of entry that help pull a reader through an article. Looking at *Government Executive* is instructive. The feature average there is twenty-five hundred words in a six-page hole. As a result, the initial spread functions as an advertisement for the story, and space on subsequent pages is used to pull the reader through with value-adding graphics, display text, and images. Because younger readers in particular expect graphically engaging pages, I believe this change is the single most important thing we can do to ensure that *Governing* is picked up by the next generation of state and local employees.[16]

DEVELOP NEW WAYS TO PRESENT INFORMATION. *Governing* tends to rely on a relatively limited number of ways to present information: text, pie charts, fever/bar charts, and maps. Different means of presenting information—word tables, lists, Q&As, top-

E-Gov's New Gear

Governors and mayors learn to love the give and take of governing interactively.

BY CHRISTOPHER SWOPE

As groundbreaking ceremonies go, Martin O'Malley's event atop a bridge in Baltimore last August began in typical fashion. The mayor, reading from prepared remarks, celebrated the upcoming restoration of the 70-year-old steel-arch bridge. But then the event took an unusual turn: O'Malley, who had not yet seen the proposed design for the bridge, unveiled an illustration for the cameras and winced at its lollipop look and red color.

The design had been picked long before O'Malley took office, but now that painting was about to begin, the mayor desperately wanted the color changed. He knew better than to get into a fight about taste, so he put the matter up to a public vote on the city's Web site. For a week in October, citizens could pick between two schematics of the bridge: the original version with the arch bathed in rusty red or a new rendering with the bridge painted a bright Kelly green, which happened to be O'Malley's choice. More than 5,000 votes came in, but green lost.

To be sure, Baltimore's bridge poll wasn't exactly a bold transformational moment for democracy. Still, it was one small step toward something that could rightly be called interactive government. Most e-government services today amount to little more than paper processes reconfigured for the Internet. A Web poll, on the other hand, gives citizens a new outlet for influencing decision making. It is the sort of high-minded idea technologists have been promoting for years, but which states, cities and counties have been slow, even reluctant, to put into action.

More and more, however, they're trying out new modes of interactivity, channeling public participation both over the Internet and in face-to-face high-tech town hall meetings. It's not just small choices over paint color that are at stake but big decisions about how to spend billion-dollar budgets. "We're moving from e-government to e-democracy," says Beth Simone Noveck, a professor at New York Law School. "The first generation of technology delivered revenue-generating services such as licensing and permitting. Now we're talking about tools that give citizens greater voice in the process."

These flashy new tools—from government simulation games to remote-control clickers—can give state and local officials a quick, if not perfect, read on public opinion. They're also geared toward eliciting more focused thoughts from citizens—input that can sometimes be more useful to decision makers. They can improve upon public hearings that, especially at the local level, too often dissolve into shouting matches among the handful of concerned citizens who bother to show up. The tools serve not only the public but also the political motives of officeholders such as O'Malley who like to remind voters that they're listening to what the public is saying.

TAKING IT TO THE PEOPLE

Governments are cautious about moving toward interactive government and with fair reason. It's not yet clear how technology may alter the relationship between citizens and the people who govern them, or whether the new dynamic will necessarily be any better than the present one. Plus, some of the new methods for gauging public opinion simply aren't foolproof. In Baltimore's bridge poll, for example, nothing could stop people from voting more than once. Nor could any city official verify that the people voting were actually citizens of Baltimore. "There's a danger in assuming that information you get from a Web-based or e-mail solicitation represents the whole community," says Sharon Dawes, director of the Center for Technology in Government in Albany, New York. "It's a good way to get information, but that needs to be supplemented with more traditional ways of getting public opinion."

Baltimore officials were aware of the shortcomings, but didn't they see them as a barrier. In order to vote, people had to provide an e-mail address. Duplicates were thrown out. Yet nothing could stop someone with two or more e-mail addresses from voting multiple times. "It wasn't ironclad," admits city webmaster Frank Perrelli. "But it was good enough to give us an indication of where people stood. If someone felt strongly enough that they had to vote five times, then God bless 'em. We weren't out to win."

Moreover, there are unseen opportunities in the two-way process. Baltimore's interactive approach, for instance, takes advantage of e-mail to glean more focused feedback from certain constituents. O'Malley, who has been e-mailing weekly newsletters to local business and community leaders, recently began attaching surveys asking for reactions on particular issues. For example, after the mayor heard about Richard Florida's well-known book, *The Rise of the Creative Class*, he asked subscribers for their thoughts on how to encourage arts and culture in Baltimore. About 50 people responded with thoughtful suggestions, ranging from buying paint and easels for artists to rehabbing some old buildings into an "Artists Row." By any measure, the responses were more focused and useful than the typical batch of unsolicited e-mail. Now, Perrelli is conducting an e-mail survey to see if people are finding what they're looking for on Baltimore's Web site. "There's no way to govern efficiently if you don't have a daily dose of feedback from folks," Perrelli says.

An increasingly popular way to gauge public opinion is through the use of simulation games. For example, when Maine Governor John Baldacci took office last year and immediately faced a $1 billion budget deficit, he asked his information technology staff to develop a budget-balancing game for citizens to play on the state's Web site. What they came up with was not only a tool for interactivity but also for civic education. And for government geeks, it was even a little fun.

On one side of the screen, players saw a list of the programs Maine spends money on. On the other side, they saw taxes and other sources of state revenue. In the middle was the exact amount of the deficit: $1,078,556,945. As players cut expenses or raised taxes, the deficit number adjusted until it withered down to zero. Then by clicking "send," a player could fire off the mix of budget choices, along with an e-mail, to Baldacci, who was still drafting his own budget plan at the time.

Mixing It Up

Top 10 in a sampling of large cities using participatory technologies, such as online surveys and conversation forums:

Seattle
San Francisco
Indianapolis
Charlotte
Denver
Portland, Ore.
Phoenix
San Jose
Boston
New York

Source: Municipality eGovernment Assessment Project, Public Sphere Information Group, August 2003

Pick the color scheme

'Color it red,' Baltimore voters told Mayor Martin O'Malley when he asked for opinions about painting a bridge.

More than 10,000 people played the game, although only 1,200 actually sent in their proposals. If the number of responses was a bit disappointing, however, the quality of the feedback was more fine-tuned than usual. That's because the budget game forced these citizens to consider something that most people miss when they complain about taxing and spending: context. For his part, Baldacci has said he found the public's suggestions useful. It's also safe to say, since the Democratic governor had already pledged not to raise taxes, that he filtered the feedback through his own biases. In his budget address to the legislature last year, Baldacci neglected to mention the advice of citizens who thought raising taxes preferable to cutting programs. "I have gone through these messages," he said. "The ideas on consolidation, restructuring and making cuts were very thoughtful."

PLAYING BY THE RULES

If constituents aren't generally engaged in the budget process, then the nebulous world of agency rulemaking is even more impenetrable. Issuing rules and regulations is an important part of what states do, but the process is an insider's game played mostly by lobbyists and lawyers representing affected industries. Virginia is trying to open up the game to a wider public by bringing the rulemaking process online and making it more interactive.

The "regulatory town hall," as this effort is known, has been developing in stages since 1999. The first step was simply to put all the paper online, so agencies now post all of their rules, supporting documents and public comments on proposed rules on the Web at www.townhall.state.va.us. The next step is directing information to pertinent parties. People can sign up to receive an e-mail telling them whenever regulatory activity is occurring on an issue they're interested in.

The third step is to improve and widen the public's engagement in the issues. Virginia wants the public-comment process itself to be more engaging so that more people are involved and the rules are written to accommodate a wide range of concerns. "The ultimate goal is to increase the quality of the rules, as well as to increase the perception of the

40 GOVERNING March 2004 Governing.com March 2004 GOVERNING 41

Feature opening spread, old

ten lists, big quotes, and so forth—are cheap and easily enliven pages, and readers respond well to them.

REDISTRIBUTE THE ART BUDGET. *Governing*'s art budget could be used more effectively. We often get disappointing illustration results despite relatively generous budgets, and pay more for stock imagery than we would for commissioned art that would more specifically fit our needs. I would suggest that (making an exception for long-standing contributors) we reduce our pay rate[17]—particularly for spots used outside the feature well—and purchase more commissioned art, while reducing the total number of illustrations and photographs. In short, we should aim for fewer, higher-quality pieces—and give art and photographs more space so that our investment in illustration pays off.[18]

Footnotes

1. As for many redesigns, it was not certain when this brief was presented that a redesign would happen. There is always an argument—often legitimate—to postpone. This first section is essentially a sales pitch for going ahead.

2. Promotion is an issue for most magazines. Like many business-to-business (or, as in our case, business-to-government) titles, *Governing* uses a Web site, trade shows, seminars, and the administration of a governing award to promote itself. But as a controlled-circulation magazine (in other words, free to the readers whom advertisers would like to reach), *Governing* mostly needed to make readers desire the magazine enough to request it. It was always a fine magazine, but its look had become dated. It was important that the magazine look like it was a good enough to want.

3. Advertisers as a rule prefer their ads to be placed toward the front of a magazine, on the theory that more people see early pages. These first two sections were designed to get the magazine's business side on board and to suggest that there was a downside to postponement.

4. This fact came from a readership survey, something almost all magazines undertake on an annual or biannual basis. As designer, I was chiefly concerned that the sheer density of *Governing* (lots of text, with little room for art, headlines, or space) would make it difficult to implement a successful redesign. By describing the magazine as journal-like and citing the lesser amount of time readers were spending, I was starting to lay the groundwork for a more generous editorial hole.

5. Pre-redesign, the publication was quite cluttered, borrowing the busy Web-page aesthetic that was popular a few years before. My contention was that a simplified signage system would help readers focus more on text.

6. Over the course of the redesign, *Governing* actually became more serious, as the section of amusing tidbits, "Glimpses," was replaced by the more news-driven and longer "Observer." This decision felt right.

7. While it's best to avoid discussions of "what looks good"—taste is never a winnable argument—it is also fruitless to pretend that looking good does not come with benefits.

8. Like many magazines, *Governing* participates in various journalism and design contests. Just as, studies show, handsome people get higher-paying jobs—though, of course, not necessarily because they are handsome—handsome magazines win more prizes—though, again, not necessarily because they look better.

9. This section starts the heart of the redesign plan. Note that nowhere does it get bogged down by aesthetic considerations. Instead, it uses general-enough terms so as not to slow the discussion down nor throw a lot of design-speak at colleagues who are less invested in the visual end. The goal of this section is to start to build an agreement about what sort of steps will accomplish the previously outlined goals.

10. I could have stated my objections to the current design more strongly, but it would have been a mistake. First, the people I was working with had shepherded the previous format—best not start off with insults. Second, designers, myself included, see editorial format as more important than editors do. My objective was to sound serious (historical context helps this) but not zealous.

11. It was better to suggest that a new design could feature written content better. This reassured my colleagues that my priorities were in the right place—*Governing* is a serious magazine—as well as aligned with my personal beliefs about the principal function of editorial design.

12. The publisher's column always ran the same photograph of its author every month, the editor's column ran a realistic watercolor of its author, "Urban Notebook" ran a cartoonish picture of its author, and "Potomac Chronicle" ran an antique painting of the U.S. Capitol under construction. All this meant that the front of the book was somewhat disjointed, but more important, nearly anywhere an issue fell open, there was no visual difference between it and any other issue. The front of the book looked predictable month to month, rather than lively.

13. And we did (at least that first year), though it wasn't always easy. My main priority was more pages. I didn't want to make the new design prohibitively expensive.

14. A two-page contents page was the most cherished goal of the (then-) new advertising director. I had no strong feelings about the issue, although it aligned with my goal of more space. Putting a two-page contents page in front of the current overstuffed book would have been like "putting a two-story foyer on a shotgun shack," I suggested. Hey—humor never hurts.

15. A bit of a dump, this paragraph is intended to get a lot of the nuts and bolts of what I had been thinking about into the plan.

16. Design has a strategic voice to bring to the table, and that's really what this paragraph is about; there was a difference between what the magazine was trying to do and how it was likely perceived, particularly by younger readers. *Government Executive* was a good comparison because, though not a competitor, it fulfills largely the same function for federal employees that *Governing* fulfills for state, municipal, and county employees.

17. To any illustrators or photographers who may be reading this: Yes, I am Satan. Having gotten that off my chest, in *Governing*'s case I stand by this suggestion. *Governing* was spending nearly half its monthly art budget on its cover. The results were *Newsweek*-budget covers wrapping a more austere inside. The subsequent rejiggering of the budget has allowed the magazine to treat all visual contributors more fairly. In addition, the magazine has boosted its art budget annually since that first year.

18. At the end of the meeting in which this was presented, the publisher asked me if design could really do all that. I answered him honestly: No, it can't. However, *Governing* was and continues to be a superbly written and edited magazine, often ahead of other news sources on issues affecting state and local government. To improve the magazine at that time, the design was low-hanging fruit.

Edward Leida

GREG LINDSAY

15

Edward Leida has been responsible for the look and feel of Fairchild Publications' portfolio of glossies and trade publications for more than decade. As the company's group design director, Leida has set the tone and templates for the company's flagships, Women's Wear Daily *and* W, *the current reincarnation of* Details, *and an endless stream of marketing material, prototypes, and* Cookie, *an upscale parenting magazine. It wasn't Leida's idea to have Bruce Weber and other brand-name fashion designers shoot elephants wearing Chanel for* W*—that was his collaborator, Fairchild's creative director, Dennis Freedman. And it wasn't Leida who collected back-to-back National Magazine Awards for the design of* Details*—that would be the magazine's design director, Rockwell Harwood. But Leida is the one who meshes Freedman's envelope-pushing visual ideas with* W*'s typography, and he's also the one who laid the groundwork for* Details' *pair of Ellies. He's the invisible man of magazine design, even though he's one of its best practitioners.*

What's on your desk right this second?

Something close and dear to me. I'm doing sort of a soft redesign of *W*. There was no mandate or request for it from [Fairchild chairman] Patrick [McCarthy] or anyone else. It was something I sort of initiated myself. It wasn't a selfish thing—the magazine just sort of looked like it needed a boost or a little bit of a freshening. So I commissioned a new slab-serif font to replace ours. I saw so much of it being used by the half-dozen magazines knocking us off that I thought it was time to have something that was a little more personal for ourselves. It's sort of a preemptive thing. I'm not one to wait around for someone to say "God this looks tired" or maybe sales start lagging or whatever it is that often contributes to the mandate to change the magazine. The alterations sort of happen while I'm working on the [feature] well with Dennis [Freedman] simultaneously. Whatever downtime there is I use to reshape it . . . so in between I'm fitting it in with a little work at home.

How does your relationship with Dennis work, exactly? The two of you have an unusually close relationship as far as design directors and creative directors go. And how do the two of you work with Patrick McCarthy?

Patrick knows that our decision making has never been flippant or selfish in any way. I think we are strategic-thinking people, Dennis and myself, and we are of two minds: business and creativity. We lean towards the creative side, but we genuinely believe that creativity is an integral part of a successful business—especially in our industry.

Dennis and I have worked together for twenty years. For any work relationship, first you must establish a mutual respect. You build on that foundation. Dennis is brilliant in choosing talent to photograph for *W*. And he recognizes what I am able to do with those images. Together we share in the experience. There are edits that Dennis does that I am ecstatic about, and some I am not crazy about. I voice my opinions and he voices his about design. We spend a lot of time together laying out stories and bouncing ideas off each other, so it's a very open exchange. We sit down with [photographer] Mario Sorrenti and edit a story with him—it's not like he just sends a messenger to drop it off. He literally sits here and we work on it. It's very organic and very much about mutual respect. It really is sort of this "garage" mentality. The business side really is secondary, but the images we want to run that allow us to be "artistic" are built into the DNA of the magazine. So when you establish that, it just feeds on itself, and it's easy.

When you're that personally involved with a magazine, how do you avoid stepping on the toes of the magazine's design staff? And how do you propagate your ideas across Fairchild's magazines while taking your designers' thoughts and ideas into consideration at the same time?

They are aware of anything I'm involved with that is going to affect them. We work in an open environment, and all of the pages I'm working on are being printed out in our own art department, so they see them. I debrief them, basically, and tell them, "I think it's time to make some changes and I want you to meet the typographers." I just show them pages and text and galleys.

So they are involved, but they are also busy putting the book out. But a lot of the design decisions are really made by me. I generate them on my own, and I really believe often they need to come from one mind. I also play devil's advocate where I'll show people things and I have them look and I'll ask them what they think. So there's an open exchange that way, but the initial process is just maintaining focus and cohesiveness in a singular experience and mindset. The way I have to do that, given the nature of the way we work here and it being so noisy, is to just strap on my headphones and sort of tune out.

How do you juggle all of the projects that come your way? Besides *W*, you're working on internal projects, marketing materials, prototypes, etc. What have you done for *Cookie*, just to choose one—did you take the lead in deciding what a luxury parenting magazine should look like?

Well, I was involved in developing some marketing materials for *Cookie*. In that case—and this stems from the general philosophy of this company—we don't want it to look or feel like any of the other parenting magazines. Fairchild has always been seen as doing something clearly different in its approach, with an underpinning of quality—a little less commercial. Not that we aren't commercial, but we don't try and take every product and wrap it in the consumer clichés that everyone is used to. The Fairchild philosophy has been to create "really good stuff" and make it appeal to a very select audience, which I think is the same thing that was done at *Vitals*.

It makes me think of when James Truman wanted to start his art magazine. He wanted to start it outside of the Condé Nast offices, and I think he wanted to do that because it creates this "garage" mentality where it isn't all about the sales, the marketing, and all the infrastructure behind it to promote it and blow it out. It's really about getting down to what you want to say, and making it the best thing it can possibly be. And if you love it and it's a magazine you can genuinely love, then the success will come. That's where great things happen. Patrick is a great editor and allows that to happen, but he's not crazy and isn't going to shoot himself in the foot.

Where do you start when approaching a new project? I know you're a type guy—I've seen you identify fonts at a single glance.

I am a type guy. I'm not a type geek. Typically, what I begin with is text. I'm not even sure right away what

I am going to use, but I always just plunk down a galley of text. I have a blank page and I just put a column of text down it. I was having a conversation with a friend, trying to explain what type was, and I asked, "Do you know DeKooning, the painter? He always had this blank canvas and he would draw one line. After that, the rest would come." It's sort of the same with me. I take a piece of body copy, and I put it on a blank piece of paper, and I look at it. I don't really know what the process is, but it evolves into something.

I tend to be one that questions most of the things I do, and rethink them maybe too much. But I keep doing a series of experiments. You'll find around my desk, reams and reams of printouts of sometimes just body copy, or body copy with a headline, and that's how I do it.

What can you possibly see in a single block of text?

I'm looking to get excited. This sounds clichéd, but I'm always looking for some weird contrast when all the elements merge and the lights come on. There will be something about the text and the headline that immediately creates this little flicker or weird contrast where I say, "Oh, that's the way to go." I may find that it's the wrong direction, but I'll start by pursuing that.

Because Fairchild magazines aren't generally expected to sell a lot of copies on the newsstand, you have the luxury of concentrating on typography and a sort of quiet elegance. Could you do a celebrity weekly if you had to? Where would you start? Or do you think that formula—neon fonts and ugly paparazzi photographs—is going to burn itself out?

I think a lot of that approach comes from the need to be the loudest screaming magazine vehicle out there, and everybody is competing to be it. Who initially started this and which art director said, "Let's use Day-Glo green here because it will scream like hell," I don't know. But I'm saddened by the fact that it happened. It's a blessing and a curse. The very freedom that allowed it to emerge was new and great, but it screwed things up for the rest of us. It's just one of many things that is on the cliché list of what a consumer magazine is supposed to be. You're supposed to have raunchy cover lines, Day-Glo colors, and everything is sans serif, and on and on. It's this weird language that I'm completely familiar with, and it wouldn't take a whole lot for me to know how to execute it. If we were going to do it, I think I'd find some subversive way of using it and still make it elegant.

So where are you looking for inspiration at this point? Are there any magazines out there that genuinely excite you these days?

I am such a classicist and traditionalist, but I've been having this struggle recently because I am also a modernist. Sometimes I feel like I'm being split in two. Honestly, I haven't been looking at a lot of magazines. I've gone to the newsstand, and nothing is really turning me on. Either you have a whole barrage of vehicles trying to be modern, which I call the "flatliner" magazine in which everything is sans serif and nothing makes your heart race. You're in sort of a mild coma, and that's "cool." The other is sort of the traditional and classic look. And then you have some of the hipster magazines with a convergence of the two. They are using traditional fonts, and I don't know if this is by default because they aren't commissioning their own font, but I respect the art directors that are using them. But overall I can't say that there is any one magazine that is doing anything for me.

I've become interested in homogenization. It's interesting how globalization is creating homogenization and how it's affecting design. I was recently at an architecture symposium at the architect's league. People were talking about globalization. I found myself sketching a globe. The way I visualize homogenization is by picturing anything from the radius corners on an iPod to the Frank Gehry [Guggenheim Bilbao] Museum to the way serif typefaces have become a little bulkier and a little less super thick or thin. The same thing is happening in architecture and industrial design. The edges have been ground down—they've literally become rounded. That is something that interests me a lot more, rather than literally looking at magazines.

So what are you on the lookout for when scouting for new talent? Someone who thinks in terms of sharp edges, I would imagine.

They are of two schools. They might be staunch type freaks I can immediately recognize. And at the other extreme is the younger and more naïve recent graduate who, yes, is a possible future type geek.

But I'm very attracted to someone who has some fine art tendencies. Someone who draws and is maybe a little messy. Someone who is clearly a little different than I am when it comes to designs, but who is more like I was when I was in school—interested in both the fine arts and the graphic arts. They may not have tremendous typographic skills, but something interesting is going on with their drawing skills. I call those types of people "dangerous," because when they finally master the typographic skills and are able to merge them with a fine-art talent, they will be very dangerous. They can reach into their bag of tricks and pull something out that maybe I couldn't.

And then the pupil becomes the master? What's the skill set and career path that's led you to what is quite possibly the most powerful job in magazine design?

I originally studied industrial design. I took one semester of that, saw guys running around with calculators and slide rules attached to their hips, and I was out of there in a heartbeat. I graduated and I starting doing work for a small boutique-ish ad agency, but I was always interested in architecture and I always wanted to work for this design firm in Manhattan called Whitehouse & Katz. I got that job and got involved in some very interesting corporate identity work.

Then, in 1985 this job at Fairchild came up. *W* was a newspaper at the time and they were looking to redesign it. My experience in really focusing on type prompted the design director to try to hire me. He moved quickly, but I put it off initially. I was scared of going into the magazine business because I knew nothing about it. I came from a design office that was pristine with immaculate cubicles. Then I went to Fairchild—where they still had rotary phones and it was an open environment with people yelling across the room to each other.

I don't think there is a distinct "Eddie Leida look" today. I really try to do what suits the editor, and what suits the magazine best. And I owe that to my education at Whitehouse & Katz. It was developing corporate identities that led me to create specialized identities for each magazine.

I think people take themselves much too seriously in a lot of these businesses and I don't. I really believe in craft and I am really focused when I am here. But we do laugh and we do have fun.

16

Rich Niche?

SCOTT CRAWFORD

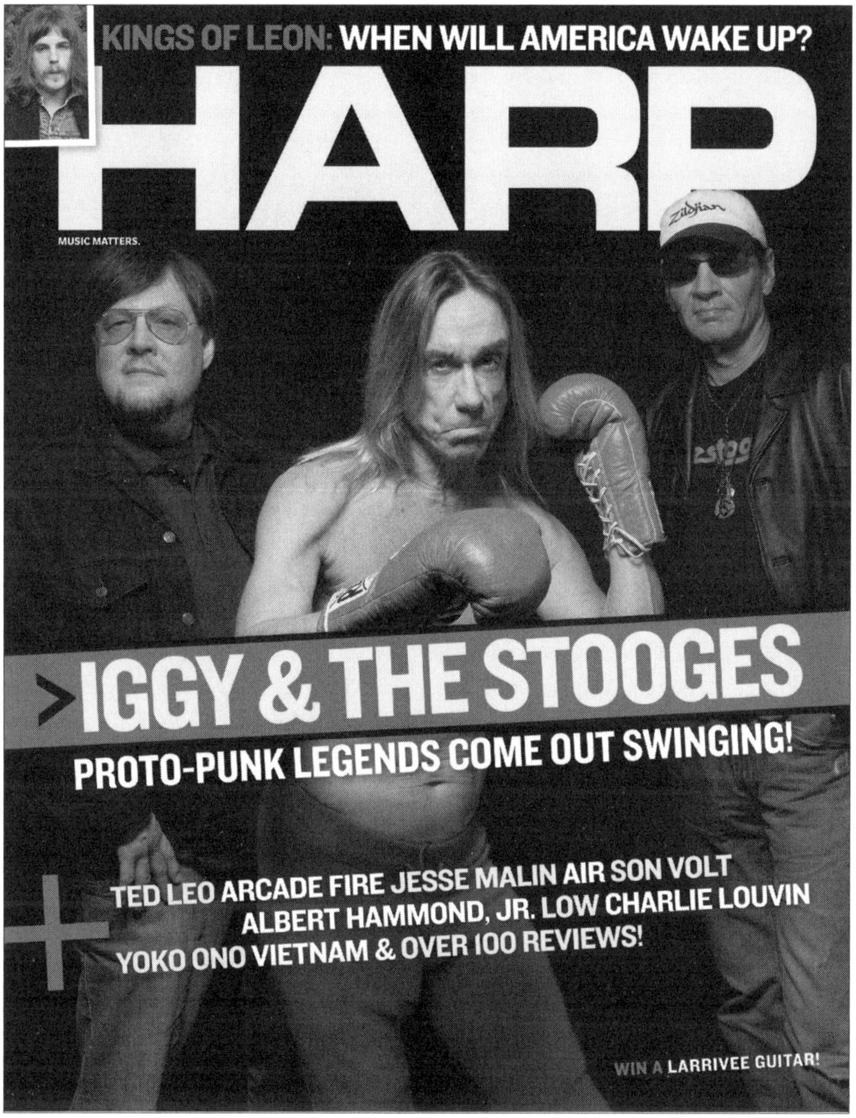

2007

After years as a freelance magazine designer (I've worked for Primedia, the Sci-Fi Channel, and others) I started to get an itch to do something new—to start over, to run my own idea up the flagpole and see who salutes it. In the spring of 2001, that idea became *Harp*, a magazine obsessed with alt-country and alt-rock (and all the alts in between). Having worked for several niche magazines over the years—and contributing to several launches—I had some knowledge of what was involved. And I'd also published several music zines when I was a kid. I wanted to try to make a magazine succeed on a larger scale.

Music is, and was not, underserved by glossies. At the time I launched *Harp*, you could find big boys *Rolling Stone*, *Spin*, and *Blender*, and a host of smaller, more specialized titles. A lot of people might look at the sea of musician portraits staring back from newsstand shelves and assume there wasn't room for one more. I had to find a void and fill it. I wish I could say that I did six months of market analysis, but the truth is that the hole I found was the magazine I wanted.

When I went to buy my monthly fill of music mags, I found myself buying titles for specific genre coverage—*No Depression* for my roots and alt-country fix, *Magnet* for indie rock, England's *Wire* and *Mojo* for their eclectic coverage and mammoth CD review sections. I read them all, but they all added up to a lot of money, they each had lots of fluff that wasn't interesting to me, and none of them, by themselves, covered everything I wanted. I didn't think I was the only one out there with such broad tastes. Why not have a magazine that covered the best of all these kinds of music? Naïve? Maybe. But in my mind I thought I could Americanize a title like *Mojo*—that is, shorten the bible-length features and offer more information on the up-and-coming artists that were flying well below the radar.

I never went after investment for the start-up—I decided (with the permission of my incredibly supportive wife) to finance it myself and let it grow organically with a modest initial circulation (under 10,000 copies per month). I'd give myself eighteen months to make *Harp* a success. If not, I reasoned, I would have at least tried, and as a consolation I'd have some nice, albeit expensive, portfolio pieces to show the employer I would need in a hurry after it crashed. I'm not much for spreadsheets and PowerPoint presentations, but I'd learned a few things about bare-bones marketing over the years. I knew I had to try to create some interest in a title destined for a jaded and crowded industry. I designed and sent out postcards with a mocked-up cover to all of the record labels and PR firms I could find, announcing *Harp*'s impending launch. I also had a Web site designed with basic information on the magazine including an editorial mission statement, mock cover, and ad rates.

The mailing garnered some response, but it didn't save me from countless days in my basement cold-calling potential advertisers. I also spent more time than I imagined possible recruiting freelance photographers and writers, schooling myself on distribution, printing options, mailing, and circulation. In the beginning I was a one-man church and state—the ad man and the editor. That was a combination I was never entirely comfortable with—not because of any pressure from advertisers to trade ads for coverage, but because it might create the perception that I would. Believe me, there are countless mags out there that trade favors as a matter of business. It wasn't something that I even wanted to be seen as taking part in and to this day have never succumbed to.

I decided on the former guitarist for both Rank and File and for Nuns Alejandro Escovedo for the first cover. Chosen because of his history in both the roots-rock and early punk-rock scenes and his stellar new CD, Escovedo seemed like the perfect choice. At the time, many fiends and writers suggested Ryan Adams for the cover—he was reaching the apex of his popularity—and in hindsight, it probably would've made more of a splash, but credibility was paramount to me.

Visually, I knew I wanted original photography and a bold, yet classic template to set *Harp* apart. The majority of readers wouldn't consist of the 'tween set or that coveted eighteen-to-twenty-four demographic since most of what we would cover would appeal (I hoped) to an older, less musically fickle (i.e., over twenty-five) audience. My color palette—earth tones—and typography was also designed to appeal to more mature and sophisticated tastes. The body type alternated between san-serif Din Alternate and serif Vendetta Medium. Both were modern and yet easy to read. *No Depression* relied heavily on an antiquated, Letraset look that I didn't think served their topic very well. Bold graphics, strong photos, and contemporary type would give the bands and personalities we would cover a frame that enhanced their cultural significance.

I divided the magazine into three sections: "Reverb," consisting of news bits, short Q&As, and so forth; "Features," where I insisted on at least four long features of at least two thousand words; and "Rants & Faves," consisting of CD, DVD, and book reviews. Pretty standard format for magazines—but at the time *Blender* and *Spin* were the only music magazines with front-of-the-book entry points.

Editorially, I wanted writers with a sense of history, irreverence, and the ability to get snarky if the subject warranted it. I wanted *Harp* to be edgy, fearless, and credible to its readers. In a marketplace with so many similar titles, publishing anything less ends up reading like a record store ad. There are times when I've felt we haven't been edgy or fearless enough, but I do think we've cultivated a reputation for tell-it-like-it-is journalism.

Roughly five months in the making, the first issue of *Harp* hit the newsstands in September 2001. It was a low-key launch, and not just because of what else was hitting the fans at the time. No champagne or press conferences, just a sixty-four-page color glossy in limited distribution to the major chains like Barnes & Noble and Borders. The buyer at the late Tower Records dismissed *Harp* though: "I'm not going to carry your title because I don't know what it is." He was referring to its title and the lack of clever teasers on the

Reverb NEWS & NOTEWORTHY

EVERY LITTLE THING SHE DOES

Is this writer obsessed with Eleni Mandell? We think so…

We could go on and on (and on) about Eleni Mandell's sweet, dusky voice and sublime, noirish songs or her side projects the Grabs and the Living Sisters. But rather than gush yet again, we'll let her tell you her favorite things about herself.

DANCING IN MY LIVING ROOM WITH MY FRIENDS
I was having weekly dinner/dance parties over the summer [and] I had a really intense one for my birthday. I danced the entire party and actually got injured from dancing for five hours. Straight. But it was really, really fun. I made the most perfect dance party mix. Echo and the Bunnymen, Adam and the Ants, Boston—any great hit song I could remember, I put on there.

SEWING
I've become an avid—I don't wanna say seamstress, 'cause I'm not that good. But I wanna get really good at it. I made a dress for my birthday dance party that I thought was really cool: navy blue velvet with a white satin petal collar. Every time I have something to do, I make something to wear for it. I just played at CMJ and I wore a dress that I made.

EATING REALLY GOOD FOOD
I had a really great appetizer when I was in New York—escargot and mussels with wild mushrooms over creamy polenta. I really like all kinds of food. I love a great cheeseburger. I love really good steak. I think a lot about food. Probably a little too much.

LISTENING TO CHARLIE WADHAMS
We kind of…have a relationship [laughs]. He's an incredible singer and songwriter. He's self-taught, so he doesn't really write the same I-IV-V chord progressions. His songs are really romantic—they're kind of short little romantic pieces. And he has a really creamy voice. Really sweet.

SINGING
When everything comes together, when I feel like I'm doing the best I can do, I'm singing a song that I think is good—even if I didn't write it…the stars align. There's this sort of indescribable connection with the audience where I feel like they're enjoying it and they get it. It's really sublime.

THE LIVING SISTERS
Is a group I have with Inara George and Becky Stark. We sing harmonies and wear matching outfits. Sometimes we have birds in our hair and crazy glitter disco dresses, but we sing kind of old-fashioned songs with really pretty harmonies. There's something about harmonies that I just love. They resonate in my body or something. I know that sounds really corny. RANDY HARWARD

Kink Flamingo

How to survive a Date with John Waters

IF JOHN WATERS WAS AFTER YOUR HONEYBUNS, wouldn't you like to know the plan of attack? Evidently he's a sportin' guy because he's laying it all out on *A Date with John Waters* (New Line). The compilation's 14 songs, says Waters, are sequenced "in the order if I was trying to seduce you, and had you over to my house."

Date starts with Patience and Prudence's "Tonight You Belong to Me"— Waters' first record—which he shoplifted. The eclectic 14-track compilation runs through tracks by Elton Motello (the power-queer-pop New Wave gem "Jet Boy Jet Girl"), Ike and Tina Turner ("All I Can Do Is Cry") and Clarence "Frogman" Henry ("Ain't Got No Home"). It also includes contributions by Waters' favorite actresses: Mink Stole croons "Sometimes I Wish I Had a Gun" from her never-released album and Edith Massey does her rare gem "Big Girls Don't Cry."

If you fail to glean romance from some of those tracks, remember this is John Waters. His films—*Pink Flamingos, Female Trouble* and *Pecker*, for example—betray his penchant for kink. That may be why he'll let you know when to expect The Move: to see that divine blend of terror and pleasure in your eyes.

"'(Night Time Is) The Right Time' is when I actually get laid in the album," he says. "Right when Margie Hendricks comes in and starts singing. She has the greatest, most alarming voice and the *dirtiest* sound." RANDY HARWARD

38 HARPMAGAZINE.C

Front news page, 2007

cover. My rationale at the time was that anyone who might buy the magazine would know who the artist was already, and goddamn it, I'm a designer, I wasn't going to clutter up my covers with tons of hyperbole and type. I was thinking way too small—a byproduct of having published fanzines—and not seeing the bigger picture: Newsstands are crowded and you have a finite amount of time to make an impression before people move on. It's a lesson I've never forgotten. By the third issue, that same buyer had requested full distribution at all of Tower's brick-and-mortar locations.

Why name the magazine *Harp*? I was struck by the word's multiple meanings. In addition to harps, mouth harps, and blues harps, "harping" on something is talking at length about it. I wanted the magazine to be known for meaty editorial. Ultimately, if you're successful at branding yourself, the title becomes meaningless, but it was a question I found myself answering a lot in the beginning.

That first year was full of hurdles to be sure, but it ultimately led to a partnership with another music magazine (and former employer of mine), *JazzTimes*, an established and profitable niche music magazine. It's a partnership that's enabled *Harp* to more than quadruple its initial circulation, double its page count, and more than triple its average number of ad pages. We're now sold in over fifteen countries with subscribers in South Africa, Lithuania, China, Brazil, and countless other places I'd never be able to find on a map. With the partnership came the use of *JT*'s staff of more than fifteen people and its office space (goodbye musty basement!). I'm no longer the lone wolf multitasking until the wee hours; I now have much of the help I so desperately needed in the early days with a full-time managing editor and several sales reps. Even so, our editorial staff is skeletal, but we still get *Harp* out on time eight times a year. It's amazing when I look at the mastheads of larger magazines and see how many folks it takes to put together an issue. The magazine industry's dirtiest little secret is that it doesn't take an inflated staff to put together a quality publication.

Our covers have evolved and at times become more provocative. But I haven't found a formula for making hot sellers. One month, I think I've done the most amazing cover ever but the sales are mediocre. The next issue is off the charts with a cover that's only OK. Sometimes I know why—a controversial or polarizing artist moves issues. Once I hired Danny Clinch to photograph perennial bad boy Ryan Adams and it remains one of my favorite covers. I'd come up with a concept that I thought would knit to a great coverline, for which I needed Adams to pose Christlike on a cross. Adams wouldn't do it (apparently it crossed some kind of spiritual line with him), but Clinch noticed a collection of crosses in Ryan's apartment and was able to get a shot of him tenderly cradling a bunch of them. It worked with my original title: "Ryan Adams: Saint or Sinner?"

I've also done a number of gatefold covers over the years that always sell well. For 2006, we assembled thirteen musicians on the cover for an article entitled "Rock of Ages: Artists and Their Spiritual Counterparts." In the photograph we linked younger artists with their musical influences by having them pose next to one another. Artists on that cover included REM's Michael Stipe with Conor Oberst, Sonic Youth's Thurston Moore with Television's Tom Verlaine, Towers of London with the recently reunited NY Dolls. Despite their success on the newsstand, I do these only once a year due to the headaches that come with planning each one. Logistically, getting that many people together on the same day in the same place is no easy task. And of course, the amount of politics involved is incredible. All of the publicists and managers want

Feature opening spread, 2007

their artist to be on the main flap. And no one wants to think that his or her artist needs to share a cover with another artist to sell a magazine. It's equal parts cajoling, planning, and marketing. In the end I think it's worth it because it gives readers (and advertisers) something to look forward to year after year.

In the beginning, I assigned too many wonky articles about songwriters' or producers' techniques or studio gear. But I didn't want *Harp* to become a magazine for industry insiders. Now, I'm trying to focus more on the personalities and motivations of the artists and I think we've become a better read because of it. I'm always trying to think up new ways of approaching a story rather than the standard Q&A format. One that I like in particular is called "Joyrides." We photograph an artist with his or her car and ask questions like, "What's the most memorable thing that's happened in your backseat?" and, "What's in your CD player right now?" Unfortunately, I've never really been that satisfied with the execution of the photography. There aren't that many photographers who can pull off the guy-and-his-car shot in a fresh way. The artists *Harp* covers, I should add, have rides a few dozen steps down from the $200,000 Bentley rapper Pimp C drives—there's very little bling in the section.

The look of the magazine has certainly evolved over the past six years, although it retains my basic emphasis on a clean and bold design approach. We still use Vendetta for our body text, while Stone has recently become the sans we use for sidebars and reviews. The somber earth tones have given way to a palette of bright primary colors. They're trendy, but they've created a livelier book overall.

With an ego like mine, change isn't always easy. However, if I've learned one thing in this business it's that you have to be willing to adapt to whatever may be thrown in front of you. We've expanded our online presence—we now offer every piece we've ever published, daily updates, and Web exclusive content. The Internet has changed the way people read and relate to magazines and has become an integral part of our marketing. Some people have suggested that the print version of magazines will someday serve simply as branding—with the Web site acting as our reader's main source of information. Truthfully, I hope that day never comes because the Web just doesn't excite me as much as print does.

Five years have passed quickly. Other music magazines have launched (and some have failed) since *Harp* began. Some titles covering the same terrain have borrowed liberally from our design and editorial approach, and as hard as it might be to swallow, I have had to find creative ways of staying one step ahead of the competition. Doing this magazine for a living means there's never a dull moment—there's always a new challenge to overcome, fires to extinguish, and Jiffy packs with CDs to open. The day those things become dull to me is the day I walk away.

2005

Redesigning Your Magazine In-House? A Few Reasons to Think Twice

17

RON REASON

Imagine a conversation like the following:

PUBLISHER TO ART DIRECTOR (AD): "I think it's time to consider a redesign for the magazine, and I want you to work on it."

AD: "OK, when will it debut?"

PUBLISHER: "End of January."

AD: "But it's already November."

PUBLISHER: "I know, I thought it would be good to give you several months to work on it, since I know you are busy with your regular job."

AD: "Well, I am, but we also have my assistant starting maternity leave soon, several major holidays, huge issues preceding those holidays, and a sixty-page supplement you've asked me to design! And our free-lancer budget has been cut."

PUBLISHER: "I know you do your best work under pressure."

AD: "Will we have new features? New content? Are we reorganizing?"

PUBLISHER: "Well, I haven't thought too much about that. I thought we'd take a look at your proto-types and go from there for those answers."

AD: "Well, what kind of look are you asking for? Do you want something dramatically different?"

PUBLISHER: "Something that will wake up the market. But not too much. Still, make me stop at the newsstand and take notice! But remember, I've never liked italics, and the editor doesn't like that dark red we tried out three years ago. . . ."

Redesigning a magazine can be a simple task, or a daunting one. It's simple if all you do is take your current templates and switch to a new typeface or tweak a color here or there. But much more than that done hurriedly or by unskilled hands may end up looking like an ill-fitting and out-of-season dress. A full-fledged redesign—complete with new typography, navigational systems, a color palette, story structures, perhaps a dramatic new logo—is a pretty tall order.

For many reasons—institutional pride, a tight timetable, or a limited budget—it's tempting to redesign in-house. But the go-it-alone approach has a number of potential downsides which are described below.

Loss of Staff Time and Energy

Prototyping, project maintenance, analysis, presentation, press tests, technical testing, and committee work are all significant commitments that can take months in a typical redesign. Where's the time gonna come from? Some publications are shocked to learn how the hours add up. The cost of taking an art director off line for the required period can be enormous: It means additional work for junior designers, lack of support for writers and editors, and perhaps temporary labor costs.

If the erosion of the current format is the motivation for redesign, consider the irony: If your art director hasn't been able to maintain and enforce a consistent design up to this point, he or she may be so strapped that a redesign would be an insurmountable burden.

On too many occasions, consultants have been brought in to shore things up only after the loss of many hours of staff talent that otherwise could have been devoted to the current product. Add up the salary costs of days, weeks, or even months of lost staff time that may result from ineffective prototyping, and you can see that in the long run, bringing in a qualified outsider with experience in redesign project management may be the more cost-effective solution.

Many editors and publishers find it helpful to look at the cost of consultants this way: Equate their professional fee to the cost of hiring a qualified art director or designer with this expertise for a limited period of time (say, two to five months). Tally up the goals of the project, assess the skills required for the job, and ask how much this change is worth to the magazine. You're creating a new corporate identity for your publication in the form of a look that should last several years. It's not a small thing.

Overly Devout Adherence to the Past

Do you want a dramatically fresh new look? Innovative structures for stories, charts, or listings? It may be hard to get something truly innovative out of the staff. They are entrenched in the current fonts, grid, color palette, and editing styles for forty hours or more each week.

A production editor or art director is also much more likely to be bullied by a publisher who "hates italics." Of course italic type is not always going to be suited for a logo or for a main headline font, but for the occasional headline, deck, or infographic chatter, it (or any other device on the "I don't like" list) may be just the right touch. An outsider has the benefit of not having heard these lectures delivered by supervisors. Because the consultant never received the memo prohibiting the use of purple, he or she can look at editorial needs without the institution's collected baggage.

Overly Devout Adherence to Institutional Publishing Missions

As with the ghost of design edicts past, a strict adherence to the "spirit" of the place may also limit what can be done during an in-house redesign. Even if a "project goals" statement is put in writing, the staff may be unintentionally committed to the traditional look of the publication. The familiar is comfortable. In-house designs can be timid, both in terms of design and content.

Consumers of all media are bombarded with a wide array of visual motifs and editing styles. Even if you put out a local publication in a conservative market, your readers can handle change—in fact, they often seek it out and embrace it. The Web has liberated print design. Readers are used to seeing so-called conservative content packaged in bold ways. Conversely, innovative content is sometimes presented meekly. An outsider can help find an effective new voice among the myriad options. A breath of fresh air has side benefits—it can reawaken, excite, and motivate staff.

Tunnel Vision Related to the Look and Flow of Print

A print art director or editor may not have skills that translate to the Web and other new-media ventures. Skill and success in print does not guarantee the knowledge to integrate print and Web in a redesign. Do you need new devices (drop-in promotional boxes or links) to encourage traffic to the Web site? Once these devices are designed, who will train writers and editors to use them? How will work flow and technologies be revised to make it all happen? An outsider with a bird's-eye view and experience with other progressive clients can more easily facilitate training and implementation because he or she has done it before. The results of an internal redesign—even one performed by a cross-departmental team—can be limited by walls, turf battles, cubicle rot, and other issues.

The Trap of Internal Politics

Does your art director get along famously with everyone, from reporters to editors to salespeople? Is he pals with the marketing/promotions department and the publisher? If so, terrific. If not—and often there's another key player who doesn't see eye to eye with the art director—there could be problems. While not all outsiders are a great fit with everyone on your team, a consultant is at least starting with a clean slate. A history of animosity can poison an internal redesign before it starts.

A key question to ask when interviewing consultants and checking up on their references is how they interacted with previous internal teams. What special skills do they bring to the table that allow them to communicate quickly and creatively with strangers, and what skills allow them to negotiate across departments? The consultant will be a collaborator, mediator, and diplomat—working to develop a look that is just right for your publication. It's important that he or she really click with the staff, and not just the graphics staff but also the copydesk, pressroom, marketing department, and boardroom.

Inadequate Skills

Your art director may be quite skilled at putting out your weekly or monthly publication; working with the word people; assigning, editing, and coaching freelancers; and communicating with production. But those skills may not be enough to pilot you through a redesign.

Consider some of the following concerns: Can the art director create a complex project timetable with tasks and assignments? Does she have the authority and confidence to delegate? How are her communication skills? Will she keep everyone in the loop? Is she diplomatic when dealing with touchy situations, but forceful when you need to move forward quickly? Does she make solid decisions? Does she understand multimedia and branding issues (particularly if she inherited the design you are currently working with)? Is she aware of advanced techniques with color, architecture, white space, or special photo effects like soft drop shadows (if this is something that interests you)? Does she have an eye for cutting-edge typography and know how to select new fonts and combine them into something cohesive and functional yet unique? Does she have the time and skill to produce a clear, easy-to-understand design style guide, or at least usable templates and style sheets? Does she have the journalistic sensibility you may need to produce prototypes that are fundamentally better from a content standpoint, rather than just aesthetically interesting?

That last one is a particularly important consideration when looking outside: Ask yourself whether your magazine or newsroom needs a consultant who is trained and experienced as a journalist, as a designer/art director, or both. Even some top consultants may not bring strength in both these areas to the table.

Does This Mean that No One Can Redesign In-House?

Of course not. Many magazines have gone it alone and done just fine. But it pays to be sure of the decision to keep the design in-house before you get started. In general, in-house redesigns work better when there is a consensus on the needs of the publication. If you know you have a cold, go ahead and take an aspirin. If all you know is you're sick, get a doctor.

SECTION 6

Brand versus Greatness

Some magazines are formulaic, even cynical, whereas others are consistently interesting, finding the universal in their subjects so that even readers who are indifferent to their specific topics can find something of interest.

But beyond the merely good, a few publications in their brief heydays have managed to rise above the rest, to find the most exciting stories to tell—and to tell them in new ways. Some have caught the winds of cultural change and become revolutionary newspapers of sorts, at the center of a shift in the zeitgeist. The three magazines discussed in this section—*Esquire* in the sixties, *Spy* in the eighties, and *Wired* in the nineties—have much in common. *Wired* and *Spy* were new ventures at the time they caught fire. *Esquire* was a venerable but foundering title under new editorial management. All were independently owned, all were daring in subject matter, and all had, at least in some ways, a design that was just as groundbreaking as the topics they covered. It's a small group, but to these it would be possible to add others—the *New Yorker* in the twenties and again in the fifties and sixties, *Rolling Stone* in the late sixties and early seventies, and a few more. There are also a number of magazines that don't quite belong in the group—magazines that for reasons of timing, topic, or geography never quite had the same impact: *Wigwag*, *Nest*, and the seventies version of *Chicago* magazine, to name three.

It is impossible to separate any of these magazines from their eras. That they captured their times so well is part of what makes the old issues of continuing interest. All succeeded in making the reader feel like an insider—at the center of what was hot and important. That feeling (along with a little added time travel) is still available in the yellowing pages of any of them.

Esquire Magazine in the Sixties 18

AN INTERVIEW WITH GEORGE LOIS

Launched in the 1930s, Esquire, *a once-prosperous magazine for men, had faded when Harold Hayes was promoted to editor in 1961. Realizing he needed outside help to create effective covers, Hayes turned to ad man and graphic designer George Lois to crystallize each issue's content on the cover. Lois might have improved any magazine, but* Esquire *under Hayes was not just any magazine.* Esquire *caught the tumultuous political spirit and cultural shifts of the 1960s as early and as well as any mainstream publication. Lois's covers survive as wry comments on that era.*

Can you tell me a bit about how you started with *Esquire*?

I was never an art director at *Esquire*. I had left Doyle Dane Bernbach to start my own ad agency in 1960—Papert Koenig Lois. A year or so after that, *Esquire* editor Harold Hayes called me up, introduced himself, and said he'd love to have lunch. . . . I knew the magazine. It wasn't doing great, but it was well edited. When I met Hayes, he had just been made the supreme editor [after coediting the magazine]. . . . He wanted some tips on how to do better covers, and that's what he asked me.

I said, "Well. . . . Maybe. How do you do them today?"

He said, "We all . . ."

"What do you mean 'you all'? Who's 'all'?"

"Well, there's like six editors, four people in the art department—about twelve people, we all discuss the most important story and what the cover should be, and then we all go away for a couple of days, and everyone comes back and we all have ideas."

I said, "Oh my god, group grope, that's horrible! That's what you do when you assign a story? You decide on Norman Mailer and then you have twelve people tell him how to write it? What you do is get one person. Obviously you don't feel there's anybody on your staff who's capable of doing great covers—but if there is, leave him alone and let him do it on his own. Or go outside, find an art director who's got terrific talent, who understands the culture, politics, who's literate. . . ."

I started to give him some names of people.

He said, "George, can you do me a favor?" I said, "Yeah."

"Could you do one cover so I know what you're talking about?"

I said, "All right, one cover. When's your next issue coming out?"

He said, "Four days. I'll give you the one after that."

I said, "No, give me the one that has the deadline in four days—what's in it?"

He said, "Two pages on Sonny Liston, a couple on Floyd Patterson. . . ."

I said, "So you mean it's coming out a week or two before the championship fight? That's all I want to know."

We finished lunch, I went back to the office, and I called up a photographer I was working with at the time, Harold Krieger, and I said, "Hey, Harold, I want to do a cover for *Esquire*. I want to get a guy who's built like Floyd Patterson—I want to shoot it at St. Nicholas Arena. . . . I want an empty arena, everyone's gone, and he's left for dead. He got knocked out—his handlers have left him, the refs left him, he's all alone. It's a metaphor for what happens when you lose: Everyone abandons you."

A couple of days later I told Hayes I was finished—done. I had sent the cover over. He called me and said, "I never saw anything like this in my life." I said, "Yeah, thank god."

"You're actually calling the fight?" I said, "Yeah."

"How do you know you're right?"

I said, "I know I'm right. I mean, that's the one thing I'm sure of."

He said, "If you're right, it's amazing, and if you're wrong, it's embarrassing." I said I wasn't wrong.

I found out later that when Hayes showed the cover to everyone at the magazine, they thought he was crazy. The publisher [Arnold Gingrich] refused to run it. Hayes made an ultimatum: Either you run it or I leave. I found this out a year later—Harold never told me what his problems were. He did all the fighting.

The issue came out a couple months later and the magazine got lambasted by the press—the sports press went crazy. Patterson was something like a ten-to-one favorite. Nobody was giving Liston a chance because Patterson was faster, terrific left hook, blah, blah, blah. All the time I knew he was going to get killed.

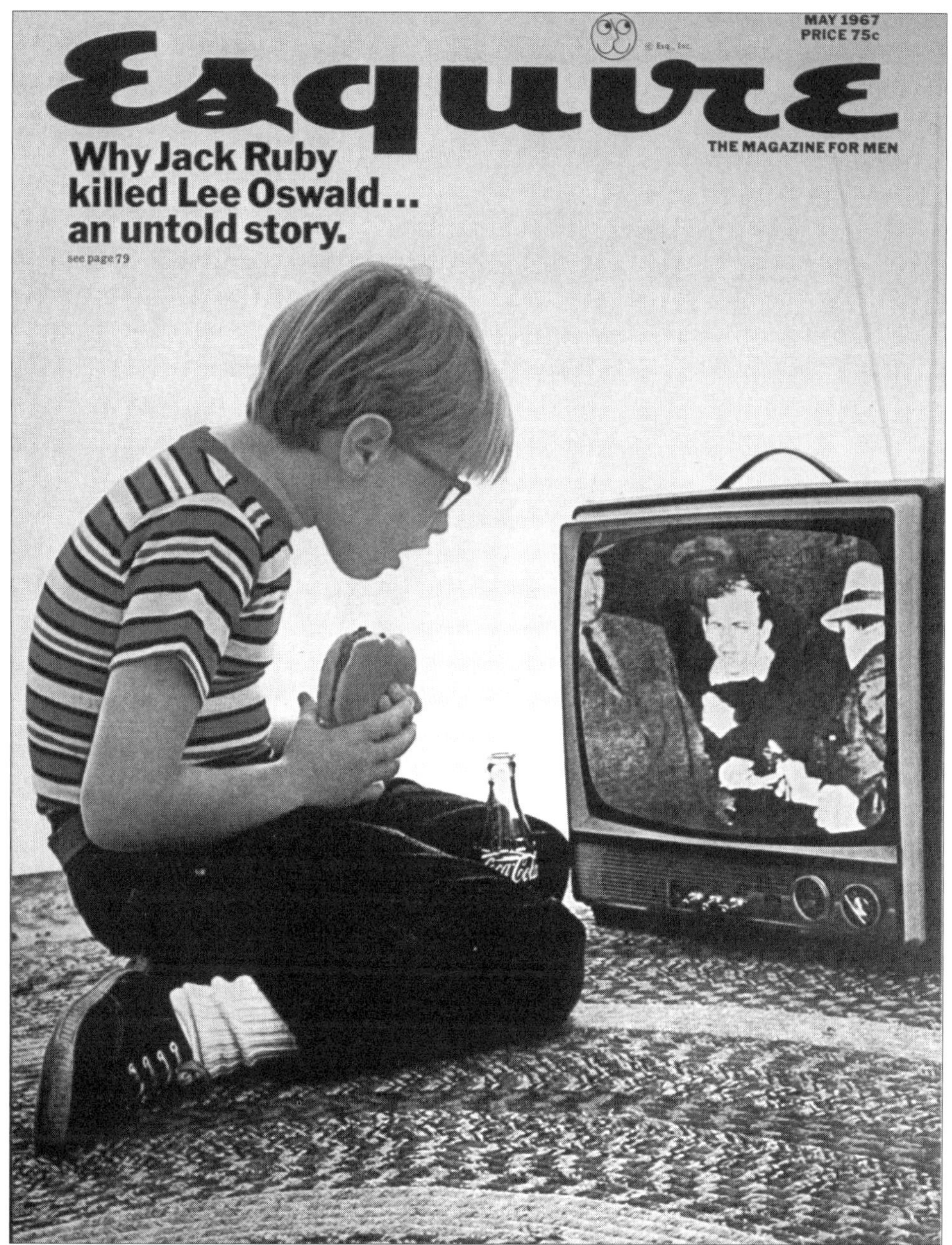

1967

Liston knocked him out in the first round. I think he knocked him down four times—just destroyed him. It got tremendous publicity. They took the issue back to press and sold something like an extra three hundred thousand copies on the newsstand. So boy, wham—look what a cover can do.

I did them for the next eight, nine years. Every four or five issues they got into trouble with advertisers, because we did some really controversial covers. But, in succeeding months, they'd pick up more than enough to make up for it.

The covers were fun to do, but they were only fun because I didn't have to argue with anyone. I don't know if Hayes loved every one, but he always said he did, which was not what any editor today would do. Sometimes, I had to do a lot of convincing to get people to pose for me, but the hard part—getting [the covers] to go over—Harold did that.

I told him I'd try to make every cover witty, make it have bite, but I'd only get him into trouble a few times a year. When I did Sonny Liston posing as Santa, I said, "You're going to get into big trouble." He said,

"Yeah." I did Sonny as Santa Claus. This was in the middle of real racial problems in America—Ali said the last thing anybody would want to see coming down the chimney was that black motherfucker. . . .

Those covers nailed down not only the times but what kind of magazine *Esquire* was. It was a great magazine before I did the covers, but what happened is, when I did the covers, people started to notice and talk about it.

But without Harold, nothing would have happened—not one cover would have run.

When you look at magazines like *Esquire*—publications that really capture the spirit of their time—they tend to have both strong content and strong design, as if traditional ways of storytelling and visual storytelling are inadequate.

Vanity Fair is a great magazine. When you get it, there's seven or eight articles you have to read. But then you see Brad Pitt on the cover. That's not the magazine. Sure, there's an article in there about him and they try to make it interesting, but how interesting can you make it? It's sycophantic. What's Jane Morris gonna

1965

tell you, and who gives a shit? Who cares what Tom Cruise and those people think? The cover doesn't represent the magazine—it represents the ding-dong celebrity-driven culture. I see articles in *Vanity Fair* and think, oh, wow, what a cover that could have been.

Do you think that in the sixties, *Esquire*'s editorial quality was reflected in the inside design as well?

Inside? No, I don't think the inside art direction was very good. Here and there . . . but I think inside art direction today is much better. It was kind of timid inside. . . . I wished I could have designed the whole thing, but I had an ad agency. . . . Jesus Christ, that's not the kind of project you can take on with one hand in your pocket. But with one hand in my pocket and working passionately, I can come up with a great idea for a cover. . . .

In the sixties, *Esquire* was much more text-heavy, which may have created limited options for the in-house design staff.

Oh yeah, but that was one of the great things about it. *Esquire* always was a reader's magazine, and it wasn't little sound bites. Today, you open to a spread and you don't know what to look at first. You look at *New York* magazine—well art-directed, but so busy you get a headache. There's no such thing as white space any more. Editors think readers want to see a lot of stuff. They don't want to see a lot of stuff—they want to see something great.

I'd like to talk about how the Big Idea approach to advertising—which you helped pioneer—connected to your covers. It's conventional wisdom in magazine circles these days that the cover is an advertising rather than an editorial page. When I tell my students about the Big Idea movement, I generally say it's characterized by the interdependence of words and pictures, a sense of humor, a strong visual, and probably a softer sell.

It's funny about the Big Idea. When I was at DDB working for Bill Bernbach . . . I'd say to Bill, "You need two mnemonics—you need a visual mnemonic and a verbal mnemonic." And if you have both of them in an ad—you see a visual and remember a line that focuses what the product's all about—it's better than one single great idea. It's "I want my MTV." I got Mick Jagger to pick up the phone and say, "I want my MTV." That says it all. I always tried to come up with a visual that drove a slogan. In advertising, you need a great visual, but when you have a slogan along with the visual, it's a winner.

But that wasn't the situation doing covers. Once in a while I did a cover that required words. When I read the John Sacks story about a company in Vietnam and some GI said, "Oh my god, we killed a little girl," those words, without an image, became the cover. This was early in the war when nobody was complaining about it. There couldn't have been a stronger cover in the world, because it seemed so crazy. The reaction was "You're saying GIs are hurting people?" Yeah, when you're put in harm's way, shit happens. I was in Korea—I know.

But with most of my covers—Patterson dead in the ring, Andy Warhol drowning in a can of soup—those are visual. They were quick, witty ideas, and they said all they needed to say visually. Covers need an economy—not of thought but of communication. The image can be dependent on the reader's knowledge—my cover of Nixon being made-up worked because everyone knew he lost the debate with Kennedy because of his five-o'clock shadow—but it needs an economy of explanation. That doesn't mean you don't think about it.

Readers don't think about covers now, because magazines have Nicole Kidman on the cover. That's the assignment, case closed. That's not an assignment—that's ridiculous. The way you solve it is you get a terrific photographer, and he does bullshit. Annie Liebovitz takes a picture of someone with a thumb up his ass. Who cares? We have so many terrific photographers now—when you go to the newsstand there are five or six really good photographers who have taken a picture of a celebrity that month—they're competing with each other. But what are you competing about? There's nothing to think about.

I thought of your covers as linking words and pictures, but looking at them now, I see you're right. The words are pushing the concept, but they are not necessary.

Most times, you don't need the words. For Muhammad Ali as St. Sebastian, I have a very small line at the bottom—"The Passion of Muhammad Ali"—but you don't need it. Everybody got it. When he became a Muslim, everyone was "Ah, screw you—another reason to hate a black guy." Then he came out against the war and they took his title away—he couldn't work, and they lambasted him. The draft board went back, reviewed his status, and drafted him. Nixon, it later came out, said he wanted to put that black son of a bitch in jail—he used those words. And so I'm looking at it and saying, Jesus, he's a martyr. So I did the cover. That's what the magazine was about. And yeah, I thought that, too. I wouldn't have done that cover unless I believed in it, but at the same time, we helped push the culture.

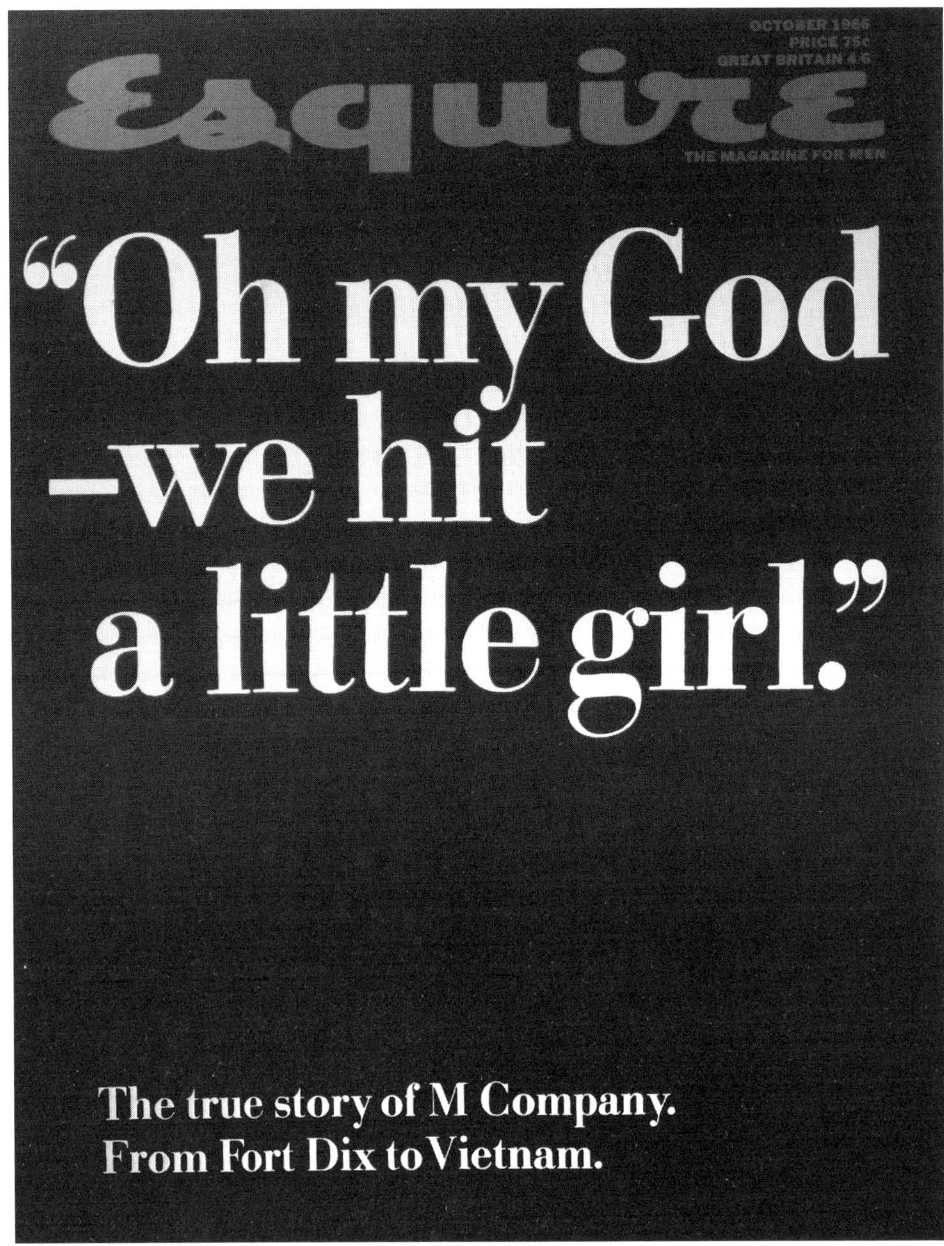
OCTOBER 1966
PRICE 75¢
GREAT BRITAIN 4/6
Esquire
THE MAGAZINE FOR MEN
"Oh my God
–we hit
a little girl."
The true story of M Company.
From Fort Dix to Vietnam.

1966

Magazines below the top tier—when you look at the small political magazines or business-to-business publications, you see a lot of covers that are, in some sense, trying to do what you did, but they're using stock art, or they're doing stuff that doesn't require any cultural knowledge for the reader to get them.

They're using stock art, they're using Photoshop, they put heads on bodies—they think that's what it's about. They all know what the tools can do, but they're not using them intelligently. It reminds me of the old *Spy* covers—there were some good *Spy* covers, but most of them were too complicated. I tried to do covers that provided a punch in the mouth—they didn't need to be negative. I shot Ed Sullivan with a Beatles wig and a shit-eating grin on his face a month after he had the band on his show. Everyone thought he was the biggest stiff in the world, but he was saying, "You think I'm not with the culture, you think I'm not hip—I just had the Beatles." It was a joyous image.

I've read interviews with both *Esquire*'s current editor and recently departed art director, and both of them

MAY 1969
PRICE $1
Esquire
THE MAGAZINE FOR MEN
The final decline and total collapse of the American avant-garde.
See page 142
Campbell's
CONDENSED
TOMATO
SOUP

1969

said something like "Oh, yes, everyone talks about Harold Hayes and those George Lois covers, but they didn't sell."

The only reason I got away with those covers is because they were selling. . . . Circulation grew from five hundred thousand to two million while I was doing covers for Hayes. Hayes was obnoxious to the management, too—that's why at a certain point they tried to kick him upstairs, give him the publisher's job. He came to my office—he said, "George, could I come talk to you." I knew something was going on. He said they wanted him to be the publisher. I completely misunderstood. I said, "Publisher . . . you got to take guys to lunch and kiss their ass, and besides who has time to be the editor when you're the publisher?" He said, "No, you don't understand. They want me to be just the publisher." A couple of weeks later he was out completely.

It took a year, but the magazine went back down to five hundred thousand circulation. It was almost an immediate dip—next month down, month after that down again. Readers knew it was a different magazine.

You quit shortly thereafter?

Immediately. Hayes said, "George, you got to do me a favor. You got to keep doing the covers." I didn't want to, but I agreed to try one.

I got the articles, I didn't tell them what I was doing, and I sent it—and I got a call: "We love the cover." I was shocked.

"Now could you come over and talk about it? There are some things we want to change." I said, "Come on . . . go fuck yourself." And that was that. Harold and I laughed about it for about an hour on the phone.

Did they run it? Did they change it without you?

Oh no, no. They threw it away and didn't even pay me for photography. I had to pay the photographer myself.

Do you think covers like yours would sell today?

Absolutely. . . . [T]oday you have this field—this montage of the faces of celebrities. One cover is just like another—full of faces and blurbs. If you took any cover I did back then, or a cover I would do today, and put it in the middle, it would leap out—even more than it did back in those days. If you have the right idea at the right time, it's unbeatable. A lot of my covers had celebrities, but I used them in a way that didn't look stupid. . . .

A lot of people have flirted with me. They ask me to come in and tell them about my ideas—they have six people who all will think about it. I don't think so! I'm not going to do group grope. A cover needs just one mind or two minds doing things their way.

Spy Magazine

19

AN INTERVIEW WITH KURT ANDERSEN, COFOUNDER OF *SPY* MAGAZINE

Kurt Andersen and Graydon Carter founded Spy *in 1986 and served as the magazine's coeditors until 1989. Andersen continued on as editor until 1991. While* Spy *was only briefly profitable, it was revolutionary in content and design—its hip, smarmy journalistic style and various graphic techniques have permeated the magazine mainstream. The magazine folded in 1993.*

Jack Shafer, media critic for *Slate,* wrote that it would be impossible to revive *Spy* today—too many magazines have appropriated the *Spy* attitude and bits of its vocabulary. *Spy* was short-lived, but it casts a long shadow over magazine publishing. What do you think are the most important or notable legacies of *Spy*?

I think Jack is right. In addition to the proliferation of *Spy*'s "memes" in print, the *Spy*-ishness on the Web is so ubiquitous as to make a central locus like *Spy* ever more impossible. Among the legacies, things we did that weren't so common back then, are "point of view" in journalism; irony and/or satire as a mode of journalistic and social and political discourse; topical intellectual analysis that isn't dry or earnest; regular and even relentless blog-style reporting on powerful private institutions (such as, in *Spy*'s case, the *New York Times* and Hollywood's Creative Artists Agency); funny sidebars and funny charts of all kinds; and various graphic gestures.

Could you tell me a bit about your editorial objectives when *Spy* was launched? Did you see *Spy* as a magazine that would be of interest mostly to New Yorkers? Did you see it as falling within a tradition?

We definitely thought of it as a New York magazine—it said "The New York Monthly" on the cover for the first two or three years. We saw ourselves in the traditions of the early *New Yorker* and the *American Mercury*, and *Esquire* in the sixties and early seventies, with a sprinkling of *Mad* and Britain's *Private Eye*. I had written for magazines for ten years when we started *Spy*, but never edited anything; my co-founding editor, Graydon Carter, had published a small literary magazine in Canada.

The process of creating *Spy* wasn't particularly systematic, and while lots of ideas were rejected, its basic nature and form were pretty clear and unchanging from early on. The drafts of an editorial prospectus we wrote in January 1985 are what the magazine turned out to be when it launched in October 1986. Particular certain ideas we or our colleagues had as we went along, and which we developed—the "Separated at Birth" feature, for instance, and our column covering the *New York Times*—ultimately had a disproportionate impact in defining the magazine for people, and the magazine evolved in various ways (as a result of being able to afford more ambitious journalism and art direction and of trying to keep ourselves interested and our readers surprised).

As you say, *Spy* took on some big issues with its brand of reporting, but it also took on some very small issues. For one of the articles I remember, the magazine once sent tiny bogus refund checks to various New York celebrities, reporting on just how small an amount they would regard as worth depositing. It also skewered people like Ved Mehta. No doubt he deserved it, but then so did a lot of others. I would guess that articles like these were critical to the magazine's relationship with its readers.

Our mission and motto from the start was "Smart Fun Funny Fearless," and that pretty much defined what we were trying to do. We wanted to do smart, fun, funny, fearless things that we (and people like us) would be entertained by, and that nobody else had done or was doing. Often those things required us to be resolutely non-"serious" and unfair and unbalanced. Although on a case-by-case basis we also constantly drew lines about what we wouldn't do, whom we wouldn't rag on, what we wouldn't say, and so on.

Do you think independence is necessary to creating a great magazine?

Independence allowed us to put out exactly the magazine we wanted to—which is an enabler of greatness, I think.

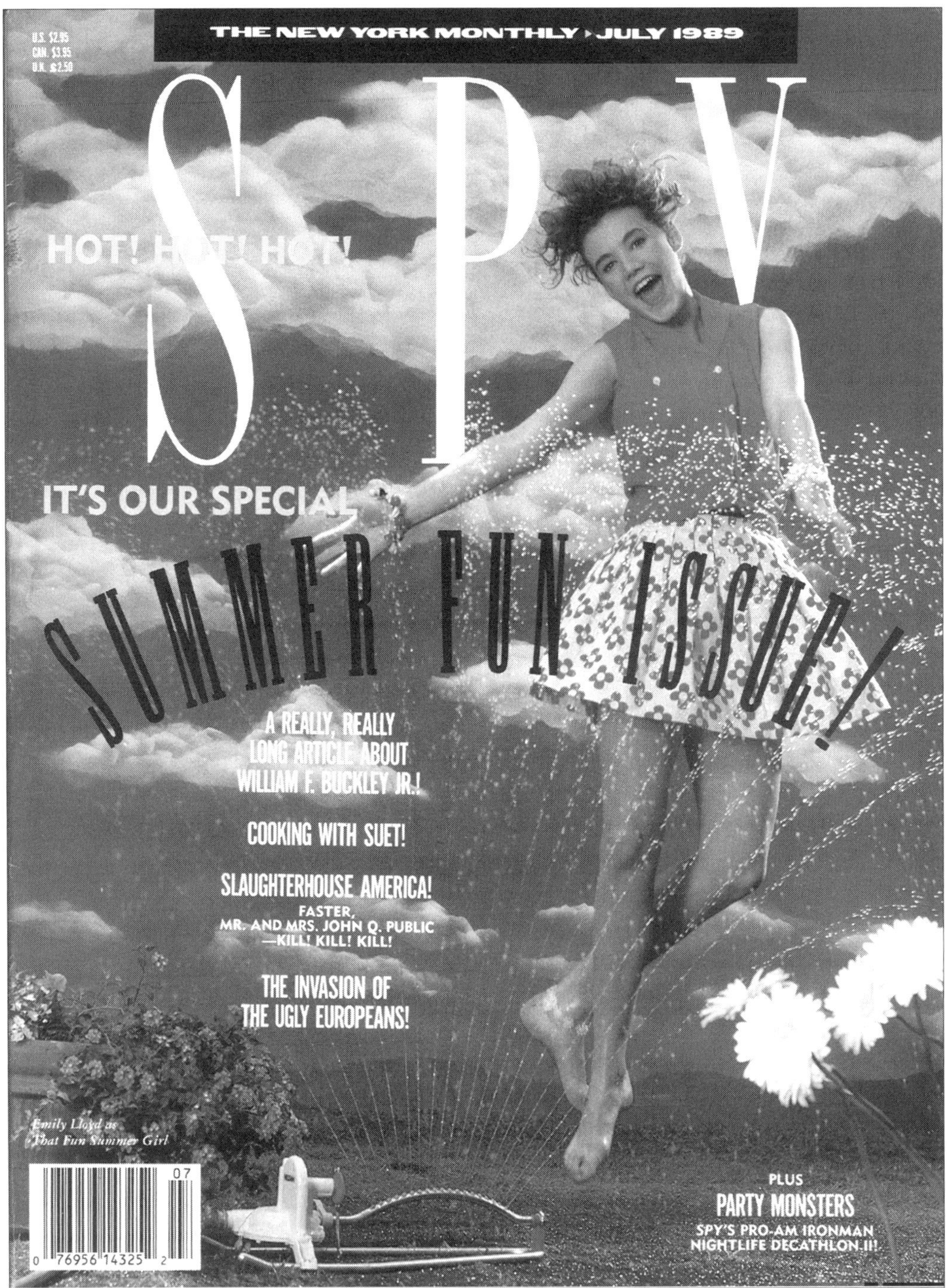

THE NEW YORK MONTHLY ▸ JULY 1989
U.S. $2.95
CAN. $3.95
U.K. £2.50
SPY
HOT! HOT! HOT!
IT'S OUR SPECIAL
SUMMER FUN ISSUE!
A REALLY, REALLY LONG ARTICLE ABOUT WILLIAM F. BUCKLEY JR.!
COOKING WITH SUET!
SLAUGHTERHOUSE AMERICA!
FASTER, MR. AND MRS. JOHN Q. PUBLIC —KILL! KILL! KILL!
THE INVASION OF THE UGLY EUROPEANS!
Emily Lloyd as That Fun Summer Girl
PLUS
PARTY MONSTERS
SPY'S PRO-AM IRONMAN NIGHTLIFE DECATHLON II!
0 76956 14325 2
07

1989

***Spy*'s design was also quite groundbreaking for its time. I remember multiple parallel tracks of text in the front section and articles that flowed in unexpected ways. There were also, of course, the now-ubiquitous disembodied heads and info-graphics such as integration of art and text for elaborate visual storytelling. Did the design emerge directly from editorial goals, or did you go about trying to create something unexpected graphically? How important was it to have designers who bought into the *Spy* vision (if in fact, they did)?**

It was crucial that our designers bought into the *Spy* vision so that they then could help us invent what that meant in art-direction terms. The design emerged from an interest in type and playing with various graphic conventions, lack of money, and the particular whimsies and tastes of our designers and Graydon and me.

Spy was hugely labor-intensive in all ways, including as a designed artifact. And we, the editors, worked constantly and closely with our art directors to create it.

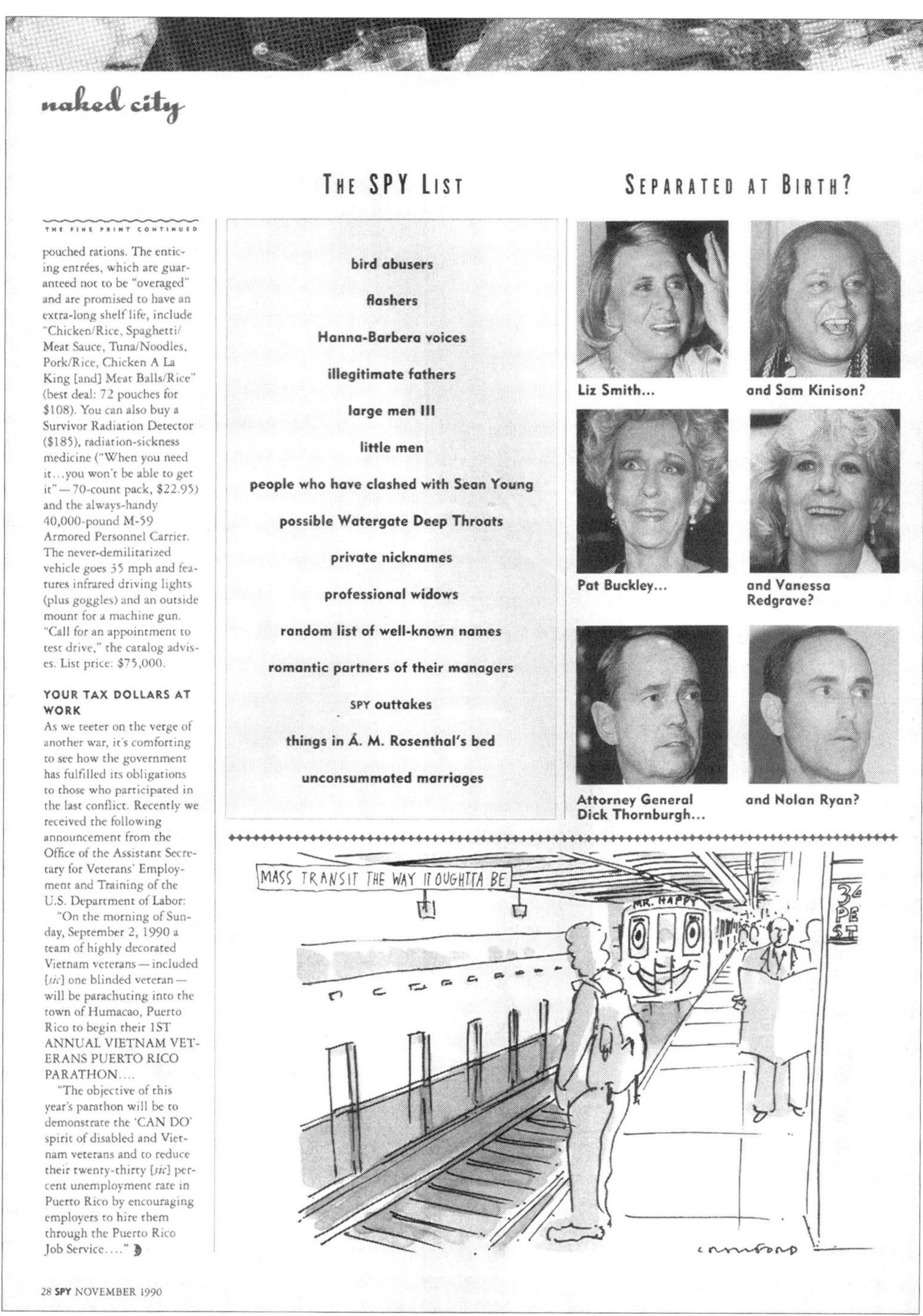

naked city

THE FINE PRINT CONTINUED

pouched rations. The enticing entrées, which are guaranteed not to be "overaged" and are promised to have an extra-long shelf life, include "Chicken/Rice, Spaghetti/Meat Sauce, Tuna/Noodles, Pork/Rice, Chicken A La King [and] Meat Balls/Rice" (best deal: 72 pouches for $108). You can also buy a Survivor Radiation Detector ($185), radiation-sickness medicine ("When you need it...you won't be able to get it" — 70-count pack, $22.95) and the always-handy 40,000-pound M-59 Armored Personnel Carrier. The never-demilitarized vehicle goes 35 mph and features infrared driving lights (plus goggles) and an outside mount for a machine gun. "Call for an appointment to test drive," the catalog advises. List price: $75,000.

YOUR TAX DOLLARS AT WORK

As we teeter on the verge of another war, it's comforting to see how the government has fulfilled its obligations to those who participated in the last conflict. Recently we received the following announcement from the Office of the Assistant Secretary for Veterans' Employment and Training of the U.S. Department of Labor:

"On the morning of Sunday, September 2, 1990 a team of highly decorated Vietnam veterans — included [*sic*] one blinded veteran — will be parachuting into the town of Humacao, Puerto Rico to begin their 1ST ANNUAL VIETNAM VETERANS PUERTO RICO PARATHON....

"The objective of this year's parathon will be to demonstrate the 'CAN DO' spirit of disabled and Vietnam veterans and to reduce their twenty-thirty [*sic*] percent unemployment rate in Puerto Rico by encouraging employers to hire them through the Puerto Rico Job Service...."

THE SPY LIST

bird abusers

flashers

Hanna-Barbera voices

illegitimate fathers

large men III

little men

people who have clashed with Sean Young

possible Watergate Deep Throats

private nicknames

professional widows

random list of well-known names

romantic partners of their managers

SPY outtakes

things in A. M. Rosenthal's bed

unconsummated marriages

SEPARATED AT BIRTH?

Liz Smith...

and Sam Kinison?

Pat Buckley...

and Vanessa Redgrave?

Attorney General Dick Thornburgh...

and Nolan Ryan?

28 SPY NOVEMBER 1990

Naked City, 1990

While it's been long enough that I no longer remember the day-to-day of putting out *Spy*, I've been fortunate at *Spy* and afterward to work with smart designers who care about words and ideas and who read—who care about that stuff as much as I do, about the way things look. With *Spy* especially we were always trying to see what we could make ink on paper do that other magazines weren't doing—to push the edge of the design and physical-production envelope, as the cliché goes. And with designers I always try, with rare and very particular exceptions, not to prescribe any particular solution, but rather to be as suggestive as I can about the kind of result I want and then hopefully await their realization of my inchoate visions in a form much better than I, a nondesigner, could ever hope to achieve.

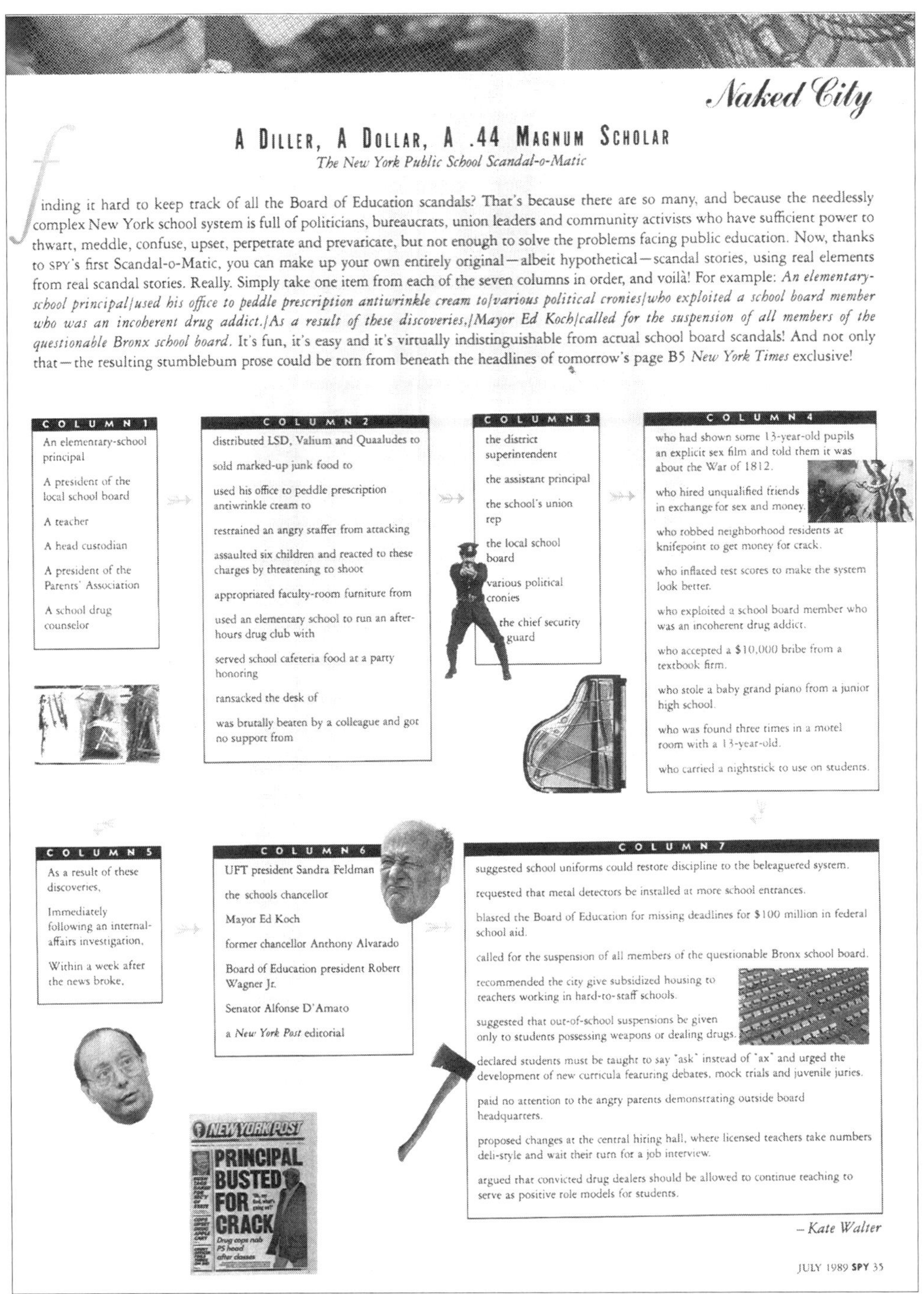

Naked City

A Diller, A Dollar, A .44 Magnum Scholar

The New York Public School Scandal-o-Matic

Finding it hard to keep track of all the Board of Education scandals? That's because there are so many, and because the needlessly complex New York school system is full of politicians, bureaucrats, union leaders and community activists who have sufficient power to thwart, meddle, confuse, upset, perpetrate and prevaricate, but not enough to solve the problems facing public education. Now, thanks to SPY's first Scandal-o-Matic, you can make up your own entirely original—albeit hypothetical—scandal stories, using real elements from real scandal stories. Really. Simply take one item from each of the seven columns in order, and voilà! For example: *An elementary-school principal/used his office to peddle prescription antiwrinkle cream to/various political cronies/who exploited a school board member who was an incoherent drug addict./As a result of these discoveries,/Mayor Ed Koch/called for the suspension of all members of the questionable Bronx school board.* It's fun, it's easy and it's virtually indistinguishable from actual school board scandals! And not only that—the resulting stumblebum prose could be torn from beneath the headlines of tomorrow's page B5 *New York Times* exclusive!

COLUMN 1

An elementary-school principal

A president of the local school board

A teacher

A head custodian

A president of the Parents' Association

A school drug counselor

COLUMN 2

distributed LSD, Valium and Quaaludes to

sold marked-up junk food to

used his office to peddle prescription antiwrinkle cream to

restrained an angry staffer from attacking

assaulted six children and reacted to these charges by threatening to shoot

appropriated faculty-room furniture from

used an elementary school to run an after-hours drug club with

served school cafeteria food at a party honoring

ransacked the desk of

was brutally beaten by a colleague and got no support from

COLUMN 3

the district superintendent

the assistant principal

the school's union rep

the local school board

various political cronies

the chief security guard

COLUMN 4

who had shown some 13-year-old pupils an explicit sex film and told them it was about the War of 1812.

who hired unqualified friends in exchange for sex and money.

who robbed neighborhood residents at knifepoint to get money for crack.

who inflated test scores to make the system look better.

who exploited a school board member who was an incoherent drug addict.

who accepted a $10,000 bribe from a textbook firm.

who stole a baby grand piano from a junior high school.

who was found three times in a motel room with a 13-year-old.

who carried a nightstick to use on students.

COLUMN 5

As a result of these discoveries,

Immediately following an internal-affairs investigation,

Within a week after the news broke,

COLUMN 6

UFT president Sandra Feldman

the schools chancellor

Mayor Ed Koch

former chancellor Anthony Alvarado

Board of Education president Robert Wagner Jr.

Senator Alfonse D'Amato

a *New York Post* editorial

COLUMN 7

suggested school uniforms could restore discipline to the beleaguered system.

requested that metal detectors be installed at more school entrances.

blasted the Board of Education for missing deadlines for $100 million in federal school aid.

called for the suspension of all members of the questionable Bronx school board.

recommended the city give subsidized housing to teachers working in hard-to-staff schools.

suggested that out-of-school suspensions be given only to students possessing weapons or dealing drugs.

declared students must be taught to say "ask" instead of "ax" and urged the development of new curricula featuring debates, mock trials and juvenile juries.

paid no attention to the angry parents demonstrating outside board headquarters.

proposed changes at the central hiring hall, where licensed teachers take numbers deli-style and wait their turn for a job interview.

argued that convicted drug dealers should be allowed to continue teaching to serve as positive role models for students.

–Kate Walter

JULY 1989 SPY 35

Naked City, 1989

When do you think *Spy* peaked?

Depends what you mean by that. With something so fundamentally novel and odd, there's inevitably an early "peak" when it can no longer be novel or odd, because it's been around for a while and has influence—and by that measure, I suppose it was about three years in, late 1989. Which corresponded to when we became profitable—just before the 1990 recession began and we reverted to unprofitability. But circulation continued to increase 1990 to 1992, and during that period we kept doing remarkable, new, singular things editorially.

I think we did quite good work even after Graydon's departure. *Spy*'s uniqueness was combining tough-minded, truth-telling journalism with a comic,

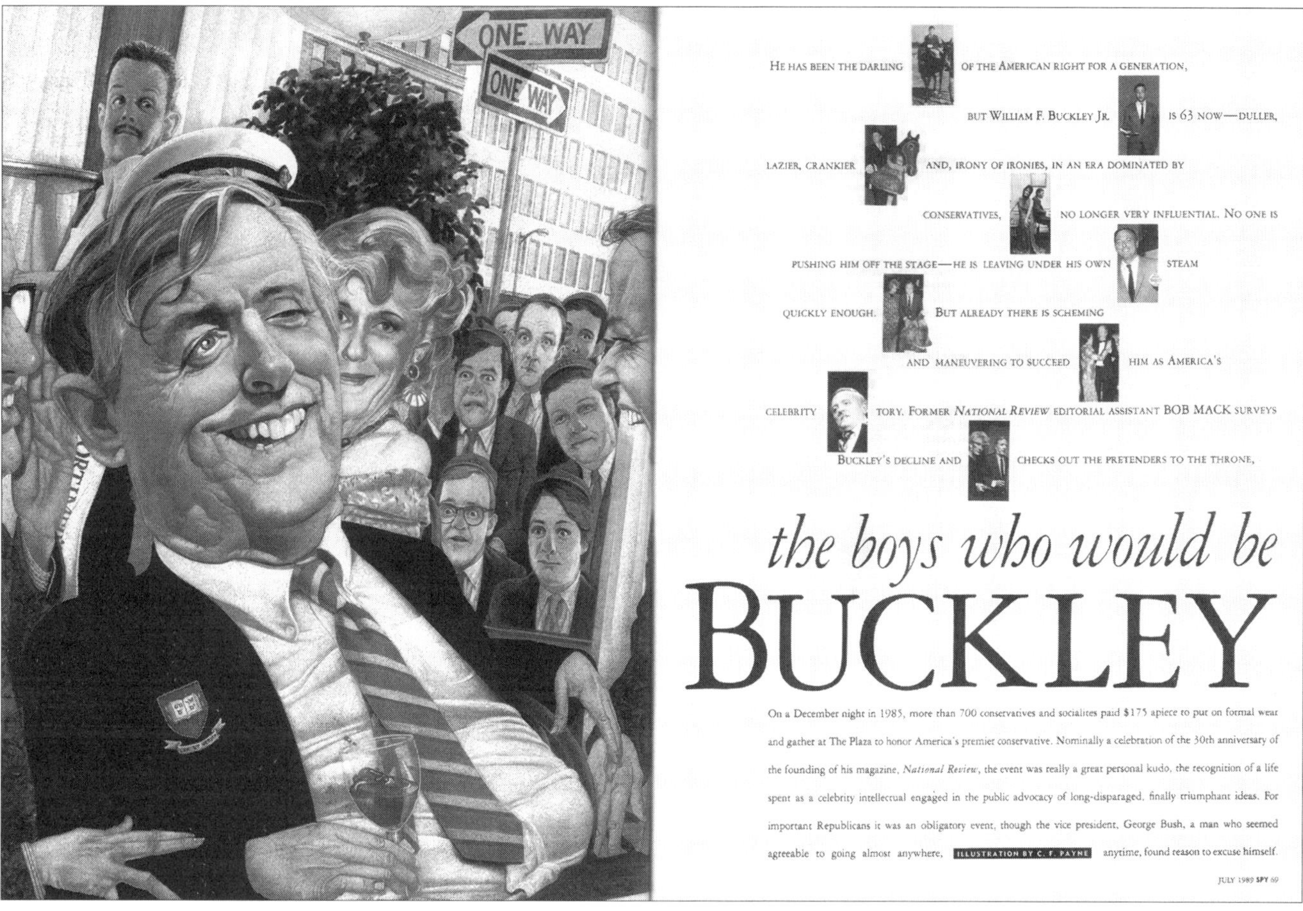

He has been the darling of the American right for a generation, but William F. Buckley Jr. is 63 now—duller, lazier, crankier and, irony of ironies, in an era dominated by conservatives, no longer very influential. No one is pushing him off the stage—he is leaving under his own steam quickly enough. But already there is scheming and maneuvering to succeed him as America's celebrity tory. Former *National Review* editorial assistant BOB MACK surveys Buckley's decline and checks out the pretenders to the throne,

the boys who would be

BUCKLEY

On a December night in 1985, more than 700 conservatives and socialites paid $175 apiece to put on formal wear and gather at The Plaza to honor America's premier conservative. Nominally a celebration of the 30th anniversary of the founding of his magazine, *National Review*, the event was really a great personal kudo, the recognition of a life spent as a celebrity intellectual engaged in the public advocacy of long-disparaged, finally triumphant ideas. For important Republicans it was an obligatory event, though the vice president, George Bush, a man who seemed agreeable to going almost anywhere, ILLUSTRATION BY C. F. PAYNE anytime, found reason to excuse himself.

JULY 1989 SPY 69

Feature opening spread, 1989

mischievous sensibility. We continued doing mainly that hybrid for the eighteen months after he left—such as the "1000 Reasons Not to Vote for George Bush" package and accompanying investigation of Bush Sr.'s possible sexual dalliances—but also did some spectacular pure journalism—such as the investigation of a Palm Beach society murder that directly resulted in the murderer's indictment and conviction—and pure comedy—such as a *New York Times* parody that we managed to distribute on the floor of the Democratic National Convention in August 1992.

What did you think of *Spy* after you left?

I guess my basic take/conclusion is that *Spy*, or any magazine like it, is very, very difficult to do well, and requires all kinds of luck. And I do think a brilliant, wise, committed, deep-pocketed owner (like, say, the *New Yorker* had) could have kept *Spy* good longer. . . . I didn't much read it after I left.

The total independence we enjoyed for the first four-and-a-half years enabled us to invent the thing—it's during that invention period that such a non-second-guessed, editorially fearless approach was invaluable. There are obvious benefits the right rich, wise owner could've brought: an ability to withstand inevitable financial cycles (e.g., the advertising recession of 1990–1991) and a more solid, professional marketing/circulation foundation to grow the business.

A publication's history and internal culture often shape the form of the publication as much as who is currently working there. How would you compare *Spy's* culture to that at other magazines you have edited? Was there anything you were able to do at *New York*, for example, that you couldn't have done at *Spy*?

A general-interest weekly like *New York* is so different from a very specifically sensibility-driven monthly like *Spy* that it's an impossible apple-and-orange comparison. But I would say that I have never experienced a magazine culture that prized and insisted on labor-intensive excellence to the degree that *Spy*'s did.

Was it the 1990s that killed *Manhattan, inc.*, the best business magazine to come along in decades? Or was the culprit Clay Felker, the man of a thousand mastheads and precisely one great idea? From *Life* to the *New York Herald Tribune* to *New York*, from *Esquire* to the *Battery News* to the strange hybrid *M Inc.*, come along with us as we join the world's most famous editor on his

Voyage to the Bottom of the Newsstand

At first it seemed to be just another weeknight at Elaine's. The year was 1987, and the usual crowd was out in force. Frank Rich was at a front table with a couple of friends. The actor John Paul Henry was reenacting an obscure Civil War battle for the TV producer David Black and a gathering of writers and editors two tables back. Elsewhere along the middle wall, screenwriters, novelists, actors and real estate speculators discussed, in minute detail, the week's events—not the ongoing Iran-contra hearings, but the large advances Andrew Wylie was getting for his writers. But then the door swung open and

by Rachel Urquhart

Felker, circa his mid-1970s *New York* heyday, holding a phone to his ear while lifestyle article ideas gestate in his head

60 SPY NOVEMBER 1990

Feature opening spread, 1990

Is there anything important to know about *Spy* that you think its critics and fans have missed?

Capturing a generational wave, its singular nature while it lasted, and its ahead-of-the-curve influence (not just in its satirical/skeptical sensibility and graphics but in its intense editorial energy) are the basic things. And that we constantly drew lines for ourselves in terms of fairness and taste. Plus the fact that, maybe counterintuitively, such an enterprise was conducted with such a spirit of collective goodwill and mutual support internally. Also, my own personal belief that we are closer to the end of the Magazine Era (1850–2050?) than the beginning, and that *Spy* is an important (mannerist?) example of the Late Period—and as a corollary to that, that the absence of the Internet was a prerequisite for doing what we did as well and with as much impact as we managed.

By alluding to the demise of magazines, do you mean that what we think of as magazines will be delivered through electronic means, and the paper products will disappear, or do you mean that magazines will be eclipsed by different approaches to delivering information? To me it seems that as the Web has evolved it has certainly become more useful, but it has not gotten better at the sort of storytelling and text-and-image integration that magazines do well. Indeed, many of the newest multimedia capabilities take the Web further away from magazine-style journalism.

I mean that Internet delivery of a lot of information and images has and will continue to moot a lot of ink-and-paper magazines. And that long-form magazine journalistic storytelling of three thousand to ten thousand words doesn't seem well-suited to online reading. And maybe most of all I mean that the highly circumscribed nature of traditional magazines—a walled garden of one or two hundred pages, all carefully architected and arranged—is essential to their beings, and that "magazines" online, both because they don't exist on paper and (maybe even more) because they are linked (for better and worse) to a vast sea of other magazines and newspapers and blogs and whatevers, are fundamentally very different organisms.

This interview was conducted via e-mail.

Wired Magazine in the Nineties **20**

AN INTERVIEW WITH JOHN PLUNKETT

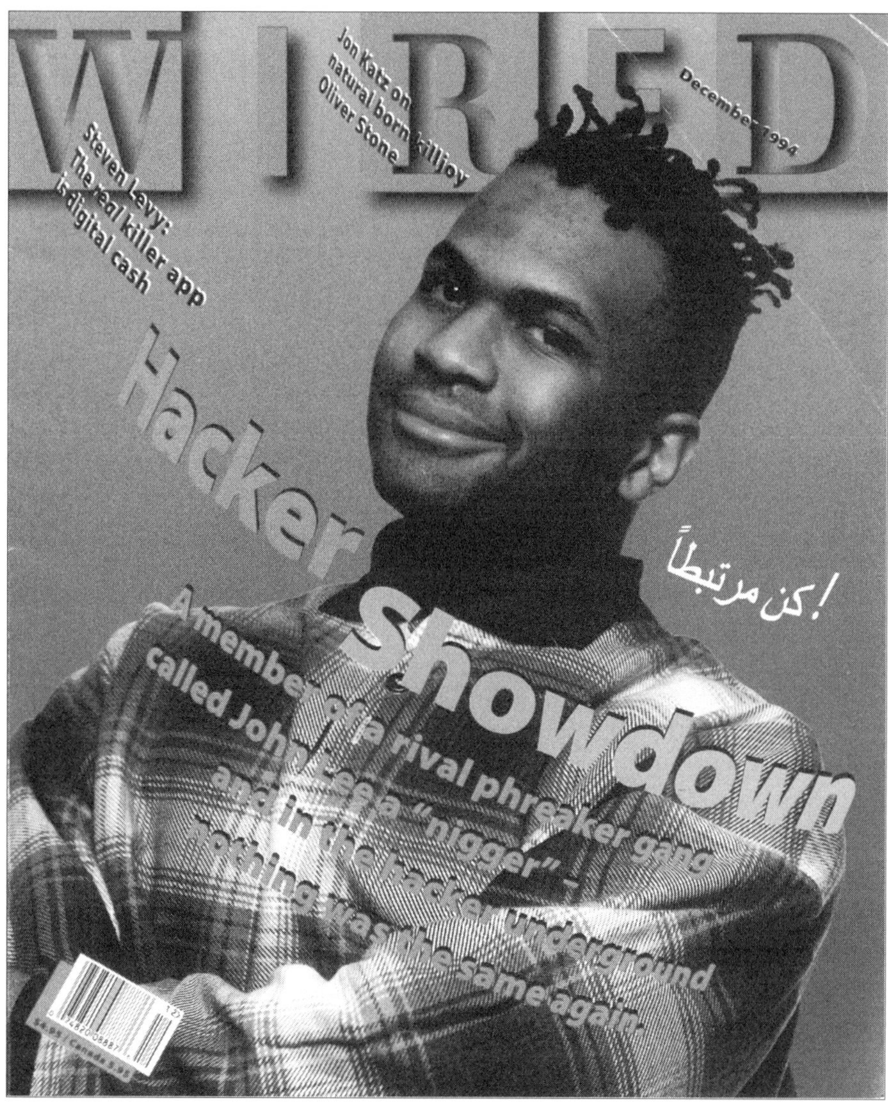

1994

John Plunkett designed Wired *magazine with his wife, Barbara Kuhr, for the first six years of its existence. While magazines that reported on advances in technology and software were common when* Wired *was founded in 1992, it was the only publication that looked at technology as a cultural force.* Wired *held that berth until the magazine was purchased by Condé Nast in 1998.*

Can you tell me a bit about the very early days, and your first association with [*Wired* founder] Louis Rossetto?

Well, it goes back to before there was a *Wired*. Louis Rossetto [who started the magazine with his wife, Jane Metcalf] and I met in Paris in around 1984. Louis was the editor of an investment newsletter that I designed, so we became pals. I don't think I had a professional interest in magazines then, but we were both magazine junkies and we brought magazines back from the newsstand for each other to critique. We were also complaining that there wasn't a great magazine like *Esquire*, *Rolling Stone*, or some of the others that merged visual and verbal ideas so seamlessly. *Wired* was very much Louis's idea. And the creation of it was very much what went on between him and myself.

Even back in the Paris days, Louis would say we should start a magazine, but it was nothing I ever took seriously. He went on to Amsterdam and started editing a trade magazine [*Electric Word*] about language technology—this was '86, '87, and it was about trying to create voice-recognition software. It was very esoteric, but it introduced Louis to this whole range of people around the globe who were doing all these interesting things with technology. So he came up with the idea for *Wired*, and he called me—at the time my wife, Barbara [Kuhr], and I were working in New York—and he told me he came up with an idea for a magazine about computers. Although I was using a computer, it didn't sound exciting to me. He said, "You don't understand. Computers are going to be the rock and roll of the nineties," and I said, "You're right—I don't understand." So it was really Louis's brainchild, as well as his persistence in finding somebody on the planet to provide funding. He played the role of the ringmaster, bringing in people like [managing editor] Kevin Kelly [who had been at *Whole Earth News*]. So you have to give a lot of credit to Louis for *Wired*. But Barbara and I do think we had a lot to do with making it real and making it successful through our design tools.

Barbara and I did a prototype in 1991 in our studio in New York—it was very small, maybe twelve pages—that began to give a sense of the look and feel for what *Wired* would become later. Then Louis and Jane took that prototype and walked around the Earth for almost two years looking for any magazine publisher who was willing to finance it—they never [found one]. But it was either at the second or third TED [Technology, Entertainment, Design] conference where we tackled Nicholas [Negroponte, of MIT's Media Lab], who understood the idea and was interested. He found seed money from Charlie Jackson of Silicon Valley, and that gave us what we needed to launch a trial issue in the fall of '92. *Wired* was really very hand-to-mouth for the next year or so, trying to keep publishing. It was interesting because I think from the start people assumed—because it was on the newsstand and because it was unusual-looking—that we had some massive budget or something, but we couldn't have been more broke if we tried.

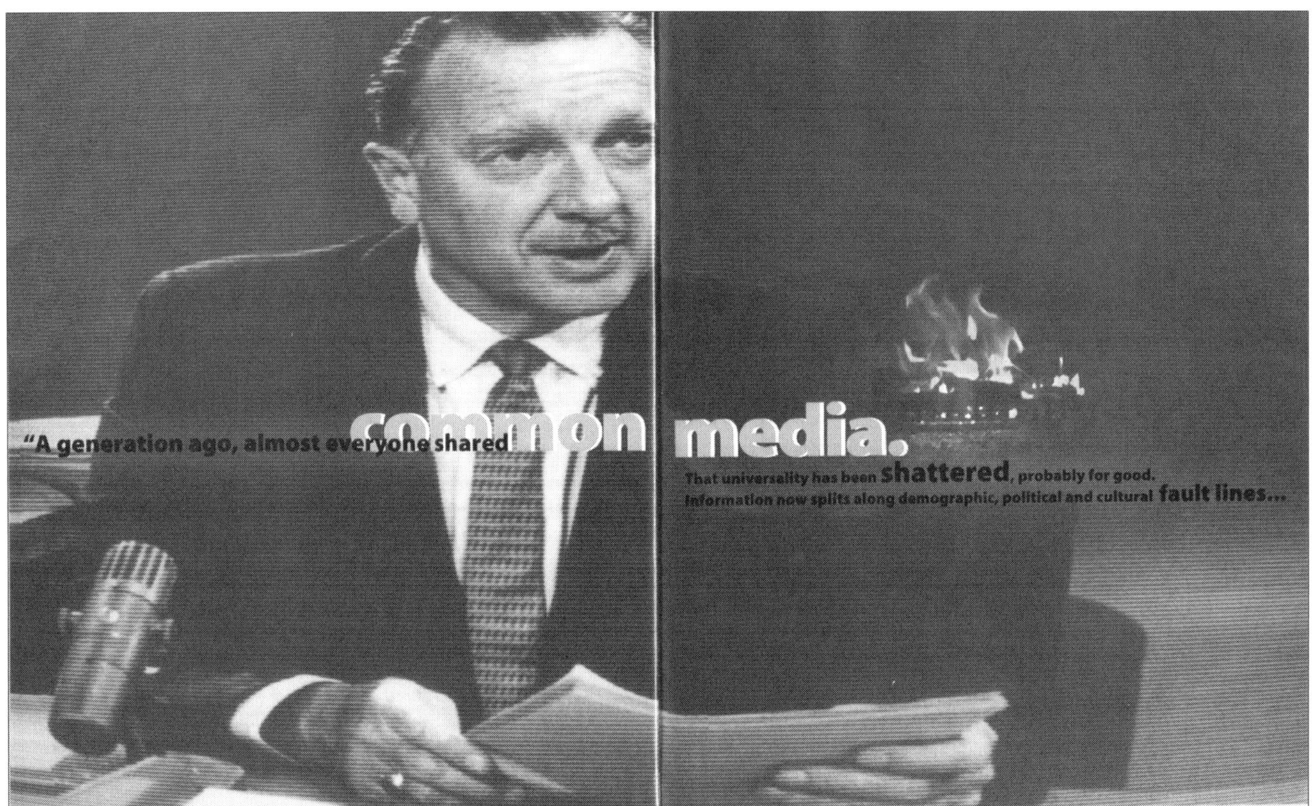

Wired *typically ran a quote from a feature story as part of a multipage collage*

Looking at *Wired* today, you might guess—though it would be incorrect—that those early layered pages and the frenetic colors were an attempt to capture the RGB colors and motion of the Internet. But that was before the Internet was really there. What do you think were some of the factors that influenced *Wired*'s design?

There were three different design problems with *Wired*. The first one is the one readers were familiar with and the one you're asking about. When we launched *Wired*, there was such a thing, in a way, as the Internet, but it was invisible to most everybody unless you were at a college or working for the government, because Mosaic [the first Web browser] didn't come along until 1994 or so. What we were aware of was the notion of electronic technology—almost in a way Marshall McLuhan was talking about it in the sixties—that people would be communicating digitally, but we had no sense of what that might look or feel like. So most of the decisions that Barbara and I made were in trying to envision a future that didn't exist yet, and trying to use the old medium of print to represent a new medium that was on its way. That really led us to fluorescent inks and to the visually complex layered design approach that we used on some pages that had to do with envisioning many messages being delivered simultaneously and trying to contrast that with the traditional linear feed of the three-column print formula. It was trying to say there's an electronic medium coming, but in the meantime you have to read about it in print. So that's what people could see.

The other two things were not visible, but the second-most-important thing to us was that we did not have a $40 million launch budget or anything remotely like that—I think we produced the first issue with seed money of about $250,000, which probably got us through commissioning the editorial and paying for the paper but did not pay for the printing. Anyway, we had no money to promote *Wired*—I didn't know the *Spy* guys, but I would guess they were in a similar boat. Because we had no money for promotion, we had to gain the attention of the media world and the advertising world. So part of our thinking was to draw attention to ourselves. If you think of a magazine as packaging [our unusual design was a way to] draw attention to [our]self on the newsstand.

The third issue about design: Louis had this idea that the magazine should be a higher-quality product than other magazines, and Louis was adamant about selling it for $5 rather than the $2 or $3 that I think magazines were then. So another question became: How do you make a higher-quality magazine that is more like a book than a magazine, and how do you do it when you have no money?

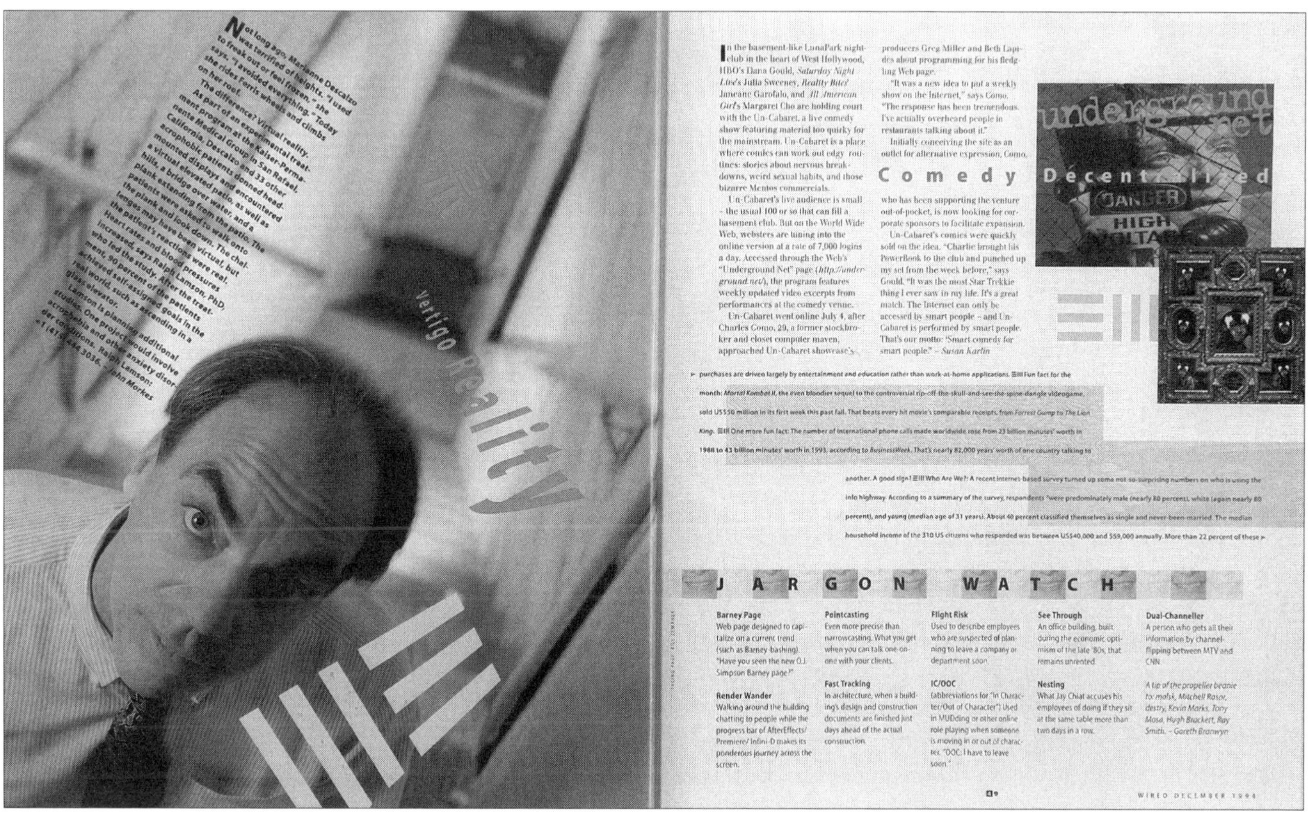
Vertigo Reality

Not long ago, Marianne Descalzo was terrified of heights. "I used to freak out or feel frozen," she says. "I avoided everything." Today she rides Ferris wheels and climbs on her roof.

The difference? Virtual reality.

As part of an experimental treatment program at the Kaiser-Permanente Medical Group in San Rafael, California, Descalzo and 33 other acrophobic patients donned head-mounted displays and encountered a virtual elevated patio, as well as hills, a bridge over water, and a plank extending from the patio. The patients were asked to walk onto the plank and look down. The challenges may have been virtual, but the patient's reactions were real. Heart rates and blood pressures increased, says Ralph Lamson, PhD, who led the study. After the treatment, 90 percent of the patients achieved self-assigned goals in the real world, such as ascending in a glass elevator.

Lamson is planning additional studies. One project would involve acrophobia and other anxiety disorder conditions. Ralph Lamson: +1 (415) 444 3036. – John Morkes

In the basement-like LunaPark nightclub in the heart of West Hollywood, HBO's Dana Gould, *Saturday Night Live*'s Julia Sweeney, *Reality Bites*' Janeane Garofalo, and *All American Girl*'s Margaret Cho are holding court with the Un-Cabaret, a live comedy show featuring material too quirky for the mainstream. Un-Cabaret is a place where comics can work out edgy routines: stories about nervous breakdowns, weird sexual habits, and those bizarre Mentos commercials.

Un-Cabaret's live audience is small – the usual 100 or so that can fill a basement club. But on the World Wide Web, websters are tuning into the online version at a rate of 7,000 logins a day. Accessed through the Web's "Underground Net" page (*http://underground.net/*), the program features weekly updated video excerpts from performances at the comedy venue.

Un-Cabaret went online July 4, after Charles Como, 29, a former stockbroker and closet computer maven, approached Un-Cabaret showcase's producers Greg Miller and Beth Lapides about programming for his fledgling Web page.

"It was a new idea to put a weekly show on the Internet," says Como. "The response has been tremendous. I've actually overheard people in restaurants talking about it."

Initially conceiving the site as an outlet for alternative expression, Como,

Comedy

who has been supporting the venture out-of-pocket, is now looking for corporate sponsors to facilitate expansion.

Un-Cabaret's comics were quickly sold on the idea. "Charlie brought his PowerBook to the club and punched up my set from the week before," says Gould. "It was the most Star Trekkie thing I ever saw in my life. It's a great match. The Internet can only be accessed by smart people – and Un-Cabaret is performed by smart people. That's our motto: 'Smart comedy for smart people.'" – *Susan Karlin*

► purchases are driven largely by entertainment and education rather than work-at-home applications. Fun fact for the month: *Mortal Kombat II*, the even bloodier sequel to the controversial rip-off-the-skull-and-see-the-spine-dangle videogame, sold US$50 million in its first week this past fall. That beats every hit movie's comparable receipts, from *Forrest Gump* to *The Lion King*. One more fun fact: The number of international phone calls made worldwide rose from 23 billion minutes' worth in 1988 to 43 billion minutes' worth in 1993, according to *BusinessWeek*. That's nearly 82,000 years' worth of one country talking to another. A good sign! Who Are We?: A recent Internet-based survey turned up some not-so-surprising numbers on who is using the info highway. According to a summary of the survey, respondents "were predominately male (nearly 80 percent), white (again nearly 80 percent), and young (median age of 31 years). About 40 percent classified themselves as single and never-been-married. The median household income of the 310 US citizens who responded was between US$40,000 and $59,000 annually. More than 22 percent of these ►

J A R G O N   W A T C H

Barney Page
Web page designed to capitalize on a current trend (such as Barney-bashing). "Have you seen the new O.J. Simpson Barney page?"

Render Wander
Walking around the building chatting to people while the progress bar of AfterEffects/Premiere/Infini-D makes its ponderous journey across the screen.

Pointcasting
Even more precise than narrowcasting. What you get when you can talk one-on-one with your clients.

Fast Tracking
In architecture, when a building's design and construction documents are finished just days ahead of the actual construction.

Flight Risk
Used to describe employees who are suspected of planning to leave a company or department soon.

IC/OOC
(abbreviations for "In Character/Out of Character") Used in MUDding or other online role playing when someone is moving in or out of character. "OOC: I have to leave soon."

See Through
An office building, built during the economic optimism of the late '80s, that remains unrented.

Nesting
What Jay Chiat accuses his employees of doing if they sit at the same table more than two days in a row.

Dual-Channeller
A person who gets all their information by channel-flipping between MTV and CNN.

A tip of the propeller beanie to: molsk, Mitchell Rasor, destry, Kevin Marks, Tony Mosa, Hugh Brackett, Ray Smith. – Gareth Branwyn

9

WIRED DECEMBER 1994

"Electric Word," Wired's *front news section*

We were also very interested in to what degree we could use electronic prepress. High-quality printing and digital work flow was where my experience in corporate design came in handy. Because of my work with Pentagram, I had done a lot of early work with electronic prepress and a lot of six-color printing for annual reports and so on, and I happened to be good friends with a fellow named Bill Sherman, who ran Danbury Printing and Litho outside of New York City, in Danbury, Connecticut. In the late eighties, they had bought a six-color Heidelberg half-web press, but by 1992, when we were talking to them, there was a real dip in the economy in New York, and Danbury had nothing to print on that press. So Bill and I—we made a handshake deal with him that they would do the printing and prepress for *Wired* for their overhead or a bit more, maybe, and it would give them something to print on their fancy new Heidelberg. Now, the other neat thing about Danbury is that they were one of the first printers—maybe the first—to use a Sytex electronic prepress system. They were ideally suited for us technically, and just by luck in timing we could afford to print with them. All of that was invisible to most readers, but I don't think *Wired* would have been *Wired* without that particular combination. And I think it had a lot to do with gaining the attention of the media and advertising worlds. You would look at the magazine and assume we had deep pockets to do what we wanted, when in fact it was the opposite.

Looking at *Wired*'s design legacy today, I think one of its lasting influences—it was first, or among the first magazines, to go short and tight with their front section. Most people were writing five-hundred-word pieces in their news sections, but *Wired* was doing that collagelike section up front with one-hundred-word or fifty-word pieces and various nonlinear approaches to storytelling. Now all of those are pretty standard. Can you tell me how that section came about?

Wired was not the first to write short. As I said, Louis and I were both magazine junkies, and Louis had a big hand in the structure of the magazine from beginning to end. Louis was an editor who had a very big knowledge of, and interest in, design, and I was a designer who was interested in writing and content, so we really went back and forth as to which hat either one of us was wearing. But as for those sections in the front of the book, certain business magazines were using that format at the time. Off the top of my head, I would say *Fortune* and *BusinessWeek* were using that format, which also has a lot to do with creating ad pockets in the front. *Vanity Fair* was another magazine that was of interest to us, and I should say part of the interest in doing that up front is we very much wanted to have an unbroken feature well. I don't think that's any longer the case with *Wired*, but we wanted our feature well to havc a beginning and an end and a rhythm to it—both visually and in terms of content. We really pushed that idea, even though our ad salespeople were aghast at it.

The collage section—"Electronic Word" [after Rossetto's earlier magazine]—I think what we were trying there was [to] report on what's happening now. It was our late-closing section, even though it was visually complex. There was a gossipy column that ran through it—horizontally kind of under and over other short articles—and one thing in our mind regarding that was the early *Spy*. They had a feature called "The Fine Print"—it was six- or seven-point type, you really had to want to read it, but if you did, it gave you the feeling of being in on a secret. Our version was written by [managing editor] John Battelle [who later founded *Industry Standard*], and it was probably the last thing that would close for the magazine, and we would just plaster it horizontally across that whole section.

It's funny, there was a period of time when people would complain that *Wired* was hard to read, blah, blah, blah, and that always struck me as kind of funny, because in any issue of *Wired* there were maybe half a dozen pages that were really complex like "EW," and the rest of it was a fairly traditional typographic presentation. But those [unusual] pages would really stick in people's minds. I think probably those intro quotes that we did in the front of the magazine [during the first years *Wired* ran a lavishly illustrated pull quote over several pages before the table of contents] combined with "Electric Word," for good or bad, gave *Wired* the rap of being "that hard-to-read magazine."

Well, even in the feature well, it had a lot of type on brightly colored backgrounds, which you usually don't see in more conservative publications.

That's true, and I have to admit that sometimes we tried a color that appeared great on screen and then we discovered how wrong we were when we were on press, so we created a few travesties that were pretty embarrassing. But we tried to learn from our mistakes. . . . [W]e did an article once, a wonderful piece of fiction, a long story that we printed in black type on blue, and you literally couldn't—or at least didn't want to—read it, and that was just terrible. People were screaming at Louis about that, and he would say, "If we don't fail once a month, we're not doing our job."

Yes, it's great when you're working for an editor with that attitude, who recognizes that if you try new things some of them are going to be goose eggs.

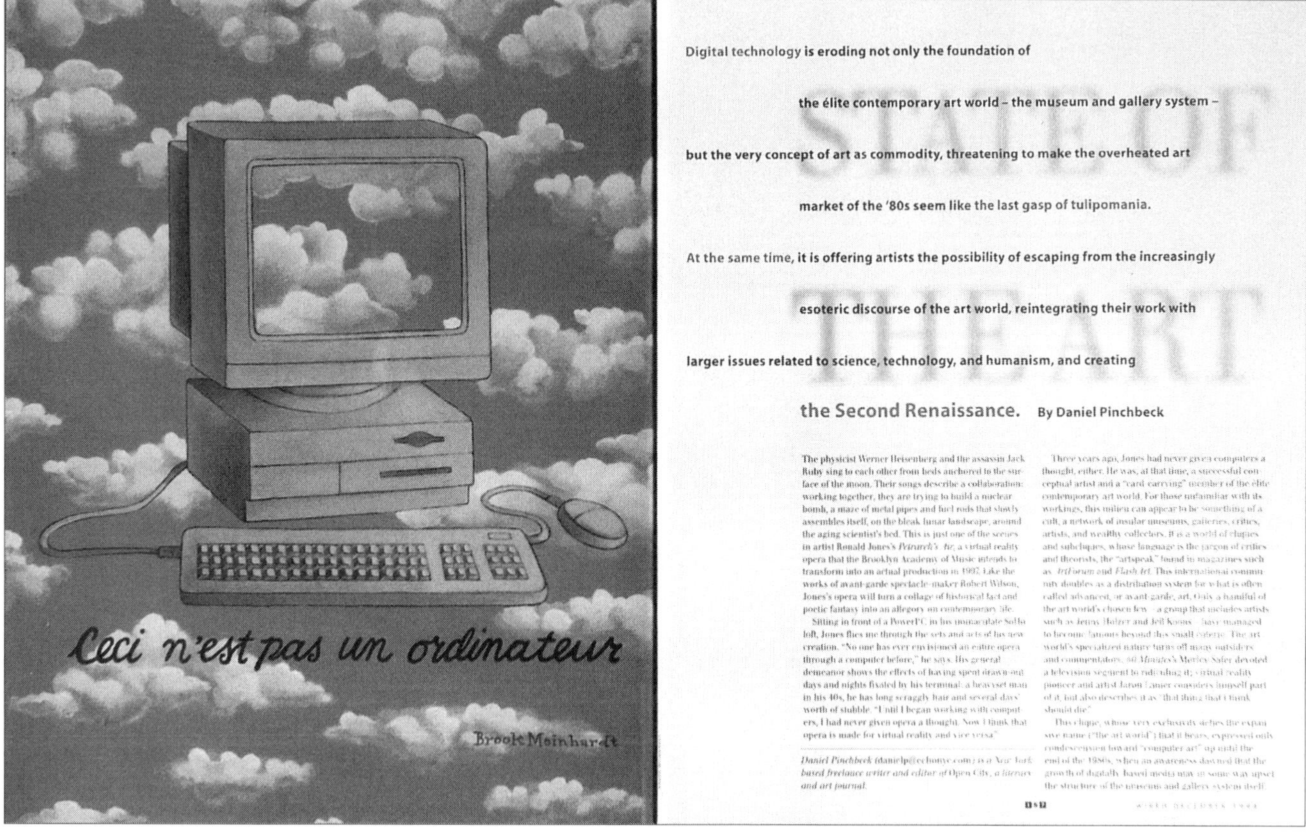

STATE OF THE ART

Digital technology is eroding not only the foundation of the élite contemporary art world – the museum and gallery system – but the very concept of art as commodity, threatening to make the overheated art market of the '80s seem like the last gasp of tulipomania. At the same time, it is offering artists the possibility of escaping from the increasingly esoteric discourse of the art world, reintegrating their work with larger issues related to science, technology, and humanism, and creating the Second Renaissance. By Daniel Pinchbeck

The physicist Werner Heisenberg and the assassin Jack Ruby sing to each other from beds anchored to the surface of the moon. Their songs describe a collaboration: working together, they are trying to build a nuclear bomb, a maze of metal pipes and fuel rods that slowly assembles itself, on the bleak lunar landscape, around the aging scientist's bed. This is just one of the scenes in artist Ronald Jones's *Petrarch's Air*, a virtual reality opera that the Brooklyn Academy of Music intends to transform into an actual production in 1997. Like the works of avant-garde spectacle-maker Robert Wilson, Jones's opera will turn a collage of historical fact and poetic fantasy into an allegory on contemporary life.

Sitting in front of a PowerPC in his immaculate SoHo loft, Jones flies me through the sets and acts of his new creation. "No one has ever envisioned an entire opera through a computer before," he says. His general demeanor shows the effects of having spent drawn-out days and nights fixated by his terminal: a heavyset man in his 40s, he has long scraggly hair and several days' worth of stubble. "Until I began working with computers, I had never given opera a thought. Now I think that opera is made for virtual reality and vice versa."

Daniel Pinchbeck (danielp@echonyc.com) is a New York-based freelance writer and editor of Open City, *a literary and art journal.*

Three years ago, Jones had never given computers a thought, either. He was, at that time, a successful conceptual artist and a "card-carrying" member of the elite contemporary art world. For those unfamiliar with its workings, this milieu can appear to be something of a cult, a network of insular museums, galleries, critics, artists, and wealthy collectors. It is a world of cliques and subcliques, whose language is the jargon of critics and theorists, the "artspeak" found in magazines such as *Artforum* and *Flash Art*. This international community doubles as a distribution system for what is often called advanced, or avant-garde, art. Only a handful of the art world's chosen few – a group that includes artists such as Jenny Holzer and Jeff Koons – have managed to become famous beyond this small coterie. The art world's specialized nature turns off many outsiders and commentators; *60 Minutes*'s Morley Safer devoted a television segment to ridiculing it; virtual reality pioneer and artist Jaron Lanier considers himself part of it, but also describes it as "that thing that I think should die."

This clique, whose very exclusivity belies the expansive name ("the art world") that it bears, expressed only condescension toward "computer art" up until the end of the 1980s, when an awareness dawned that the growth of digitally based media may in some way upset the structure of the museum and gallery system itself.

WIRED DECEMBER 1994

Feature opening spread, 1994

When *Wired* was beginning and no one knew if it was going to be a success or not, in a way there was a lot less pressure on us. It was much more about having fun and experimenting. But as it became more successful, and there were more people in the building, I think people became worried about it. I think we started out with a great attitude—almost a naiveté and a sense of humor about it—and over time we became more worried and serious. It's interesting. As I look back at the content, the first year I see a lot of humor in the magazine, and after that it's hard to find a joke in there.

That reminds me: As I was looking through my old *Wired*s, I came across the black-and-white issue, which looked almost like a photocopy of a typical *Wired*. It was really surprising and unexpected for a newsstand magazine to try something like that, but once you got over the shock, it was also really in keeping with the *Wired* aesthetic.

That was for our first anniversary. We had it in our mind that we wanted to do something special every year for our anniversary. We kept kicking the question: What could we do to surprise people? I think we did that each month given the context of the last three, four, five issues, and once a year we tried to push that even further. The first time we tried that, I'd be hard-pressed to say whether it was Louis or I who came up with the black-and-white issue—we may have come up with it simultaneously—but once we came up with it, I immediately thought, in terms of the cover, of the Beatles and the White Album, and I said we should do a blank cover. Everybody was sort of freaked out by that, with the exception of Louis. Often he and I were the only ones in the room who thought half of what *Wired* did was a good idea. But we did it and at least at that time it ended up being our biggest-selling issue. It really caught people's attention.

What do you think of *Wired* these days, if you're still reading it?

Oh lord, I think editorially it just went to hell for a few years there after Condé Nast bought it. The editor that came in after Louis—I don't know that she ever had a vision for what *Wired* could be, I know she had a vision for what it had been, and that it shouldn't be that any more. So I would say she was more interested in dismantling both the content and the visual language that Louis and I had built. I wasn't too thrilled with

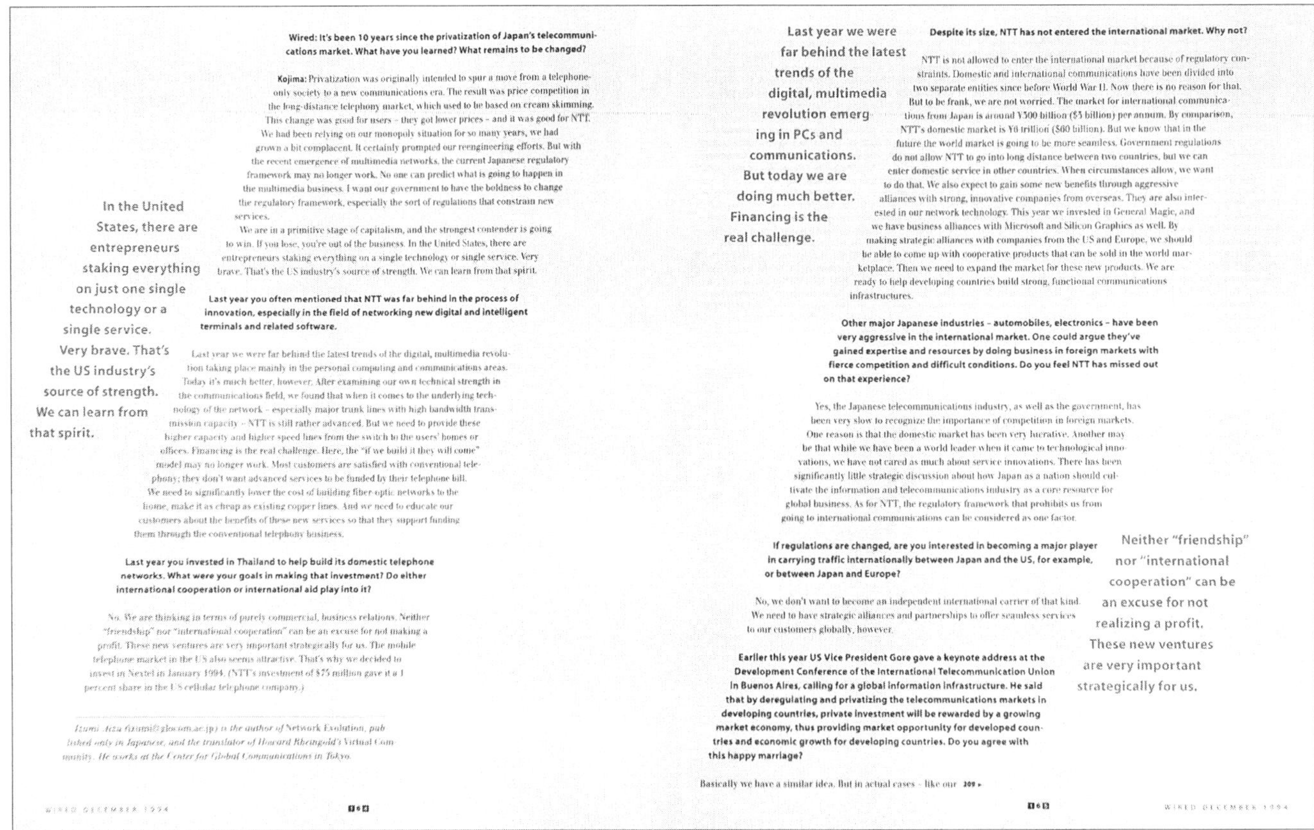

Wired: It's been 10 years since the privatization of Japan's telecommunications market. What have you learned? What remains to be changed?

Kojima: Privatization was originally intended to spur a move from a telephone-only society to a new communications era. The result was price competition in the long-distance telephony market, which used to be based on cream skimming. This change was good for users – they got lower prices – and it was good for NTT. We had been relying on our monopoly situation for so many years, we had grown a bit complacent. It certainly prompted our reengineering efforts. But with the recent emergence of multimedia networks, the current Japanese regulatory framework may no longer work. No one can predict what is going to happen in the multimedia business. I want our government to have the boldness to change the regulatory framework, especially the sort of regulations that constrain new services.

We are in a primitive stage of capitalism, and the strongest contender is going to win. If you lose, you're out of the business. In the United States, there are entrepreneurs staking everything on a single technology or single service. Very brave. That's the US industry's source of strength. We can learn from that spirit.

In the United States, there are entrepreneurs staking everything on just one single technology or a single service. Very brave. That's the US industry's source of strength. We can learn from that spirit.

Last year you often mentioned that NTT was far behind in the process of innovation, especially in the field of networking new digital and intelligent terminals and related software.

Last year we were far behind the latest trends of the digital, multimedia revolution taking place mainly in the personal computing and communications areas. Today it's much better, however. After examining our own technical strength in the communications field, we found that when it comes to the underlying technology of the network – especially major trunk lines with high bandwidth transmission capacity – NTT is still rather advanced. But we need to provide these higher capacity and higher speed lines from the switch to the users' homes or offices. Financing is the real challenge. Here, the "if we build it they will come" model may no longer work. Most customers are satisfied with conventional telephony; they don't want advanced services to be funded by their telephone bill. We need to significantly lower the cost of building fiber-optic networks to the home, make it as cheap as existing copper lines. And we need to educate our customers about the benefits of these new services so that they support funding them through the conventional telephony business.

Last year you invested in Thailand to help build its domestic telephone networks. What were your goals in making that investment? Do either international cooperation or international aid play into it?

No. We are thinking in terms of purely commercial, business relations. Neither "friendship" nor "international cooperation" can be an excuse for not making a profit. These new ventures are very important strategically for us. The mobile telephone market in the US also seems attractive. That's why we decided to invest in Nextel in January 1994. (NTT's investment of $75 million gave it a 1 percent share in the US cellular telephone company.)

Izumi Aizu (izumi@glocom.ac.jp) is the author of Network Evolution, *published only in Japanese, and the translator of Howard Rheingold's* Virtual Community. *He works at the Center for Global Communications in Tokyo.*

WIRED DECEMBER 1994

Last year we were far behind the latest trends of the digital, multimedia revolution emerging in PCs and communications. But today we are doing much better. Financing is the real challenge.

Despite its size, NTT has not entered the international market. Why not?

NTT is not allowed to enter the international market because of regulatory constraints. Domestic and international communications have been divided into two separate entities since before World War II. Now there is no reason for that. But to be frank, we are not worried. The market for international communications from Japan is around ¥500 billion ($5 billion) per annum. By comparison, NTT's domestic market is ¥6 trillion ($60 billion). But we know that in the future the world market is going to be more seamless. Government regulations do not allow NTT to go into long distance between two countries, but we can enter domestic service in other countries. When circumstances allow, we want to do that. We also expect to gain some new benefits through aggressive alliances with strong, innovative companies from overseas. They are also interested in our network technology. This year we invested in General Magic, and we have business alliances with Microsoft and Silicon Graphics as well. By making strategic alliances with companies from the US and Europe, we should be able to come up with cooperative products that can be sold in the world marketplace. Then we need to expand the market for these new products. We are ready to help developing countries build strong, functional communications infrastructures.

Other major Japanese industries – automobiles, electronics – have been very aggressive in the international market. One could argue they've gained expertise and resources by doing business in foreign markets with fierce competition and difficult conditions. Do you feel NTT has missed out on that experience?

Yes, the Japanese telecommunications industry, as well as the government, has been very slow to recognize the importance of competition in foreign markets. One reason is that the domestic market has been very lucrative. Another may be that while we have been a world leader when it came to technological innovations, we have not cared as much about service innovations. There has been significantly little strategic discussion about how Japan as a nation should cultivate the information and telecommunications industry as a core resource for global business. As for NTT, the regulatory framework that prohibits us from going to international communications can be considered as one factor.

If regulations are changed, are you interested in becoming a major player in carrying traffic internationally between Japan and the US, for example, or between Japan and Europe?

No, we don't want to become an independent international carrier of that kind. We need to have strategic alliances and partnerships to offer seamless services to our customers globally, however.

Neither "friendship" nor "international cooperation" can be an excuse for not realizing a profit. These new ventures are very important strategically for us.

Earlier this year US Vice President Gore gave a keynote address at the Development Conference of the International Telecommunication Union in Buenos Aires, calling for a global information infrastructure. He said that by deregulating and privatizing the telecommunications markets in developing countries, private investment will be rewarded by a growing market economy, thus providing market opportunity for developed countries and economic growth for developing countries. Do you agree with this happy marriage?

Basically we have a similar idea. But in actual cases – like our 209 ▸

WIRED DECEMBER 1994

Feature pages, 1994

that period of *Wired*, I kind of gave up on it. I think Chris Anderson, the current editor, has been great for taking *Wired* back to its roots editorially.

I wish the design of *Wired*, and especially the photographs, were a lot more interesting. I think it's become a good magazine from a contents standpoint, but visually it's often less interesting than *Newsweek*. It's become a very conservative visual product.

After Condé Nast came in, it seemed as if *Wired* quickly turned into a business magazine. I don't know if that was the allure of the Internet boom or whether it was the result of a new editorial strategy.

I wasn't there, but I'm sure they were chasing all those business dollars that were flowing—we sold it in '98, so they had two years before the Internet started to go to hell, so I'm sure that had something to do with it. My memory of the magazine at that time, our initial edition of *Wired* was maybe a bit more than a hundred pages. Under Condé Nast it became a phone book for a while—three hundred to four hundred pages, with an insane number of ads, but then the ad boom disappeared when the dot-com crash happened.

It was interesting for me to work at a magazine after doing corporate publications because at Pentagram, we would agonize for hours if not days over a typographical decision. At *Wired*, I realized after a while that the things I spent two weeks doing at a corporate studio, I would do in two hours or maybe two minutes on a magazine. The other thing with the corporate design world is you're always working on a finished product—it would have a start and a finish, and then you're done with it. At a magazine, it took me a while—in fact I think it took a lot of us a while—to realize that you're never done with it, and you're always late. I would like to think it really improved my ability to solve a design problem, because you have to solve them quickly and then move on. Periodicals tend to loosen up a designer in a good way.

You never did another magazine.

No, not yet anyway. People have talked to me and I've thought about it, but to tell the truth, *Wired* was so all-consuming—and maybe I would feel differently if *Wired* had just been the magazine, but once the Web site came along, we decided we could not ignore the Internet. So we went from being a magazine that reported on technology to being a company that tried to invent technology. . . . [F]or the launch issue, there were twelve of us. A year later, for the magazine there were fifty of us, and at the end of the second year we had maybe one hundred and fifty people, but then the Web hit and we went from one hundred and fifty people to three hundred people, and half of them were involved in trying to invent a publishing medium that didn't exist yet. None of us saw it coming, but we actually ended up with this 24/7 lifestyle that *Wired* was writing about—we actually were living it, and not necessarily because we wanted to. For Barbara and me, it was really eight years where we rarely had a day off and usually did work sixty to eighty hours a week.

Our home and office is and was in Park City, Utah, so every three or four days we were getting on an airplane to *Wired*'s San Francisco office or somewhere, and then there was this awful period of time when we had foreign editions in the U.K. and Japan, so for a while I was orbiting the Earth trying to help these foreign editions. Even for workaholic designers like my wife and me, it was the ultimate burnout. Gosh, I don't know what it would take to get me to do a magazine.

I think *Wired* also kind of spoiled me because it was such a magazine about ideas that I really got hooked on that aspect of it. To do another magazine—I'd want it to be something that could have the kind of impact that *Wired* did, and maybe that just comes along once in a while. We all think back to the wonderful covers that George Lois did for *Esquire*, and I bet he thinks back to those, too. It's not that often that you get an editor and a designer that see eye to eye and are willing to take a chance and enjoy it while it lasts.

SECTION 7

After the Launch

Successful redesigns accomplish any of a number of things: sprucing up tired pages, implementing substantive changes to a publication's approach, and making a splash with readers and advertisers. But for a magazine's staff, a redesign is not a thing you see—it is a tool you use. It's there to facilitate the business of magazine making—storytelling in all its various forms. Between redesigns, editors and art directors come and go, new features are introduced, and old features are eliminated. The format must somehow accommodate all of the clamoring voices of the institution and the people who work there.

This section looks at designs in use. Every redesign looks like a winner before the launch, but nearly all of them require adjustments small and large. Experiments fizzle, readers make valid complaints (readers nearly always make some complaints . . .), life goes on.

A design is not judged a failure because it has to adapt; it is the mark of a good design that it can adapt. A good design is based on visual ideas interesting enough to accommodate the vicissitudes of publishing in the real world.

Home Erotic

21

STEVEN HELLER

EVERY GENERATION PRODUCES A MAGAZINE THAT defines the age, and a "lifestyle book" called *Wallpaper** ("*The stuff that surrounds you") has found a snug berth as the magazine of the late nineties. *Wallpaper** projects an au courant attitude and proffers a distinctive air, much of which comes through the magazine's stylish typography and photography. From the moment the British magazine (now published by Time Warner) arrived in the United States in late 1996, the buzz in publishing circles was that it would capture the demographic of an ostensibly white, upwardly mobile, twentyish-to-thirtyish, post–Gen X audience whose primary interests are (according to a cover line) "interiors* entertaining* travel." And true to this promise, *Wallpaper** has delivered the goods through a plethora of catalog-style flacktoids (aka advertorials) and easily scannable features about hip habitats and daring destinations. Likewise, as a touchstone—indeed, as the next stylistic wave—of contemporary editorial design, *Wallpaper** has earned plaudits from design juries and proudly announces on every cover the receipt of the Society of Publication Designers' Gold Medal for Overall Design '97. "The format is lively and original," one juror told me. "I'm just so pleased it's not another *RayGun* clone."

Given the excessive mimicry of David Carson's designs, it is refreshing to find a magazine that is a tad reactionary—where type is used as type, not as an abstract pattern. While many magazines slavishly follow the youth culture code of illegibility and dis-

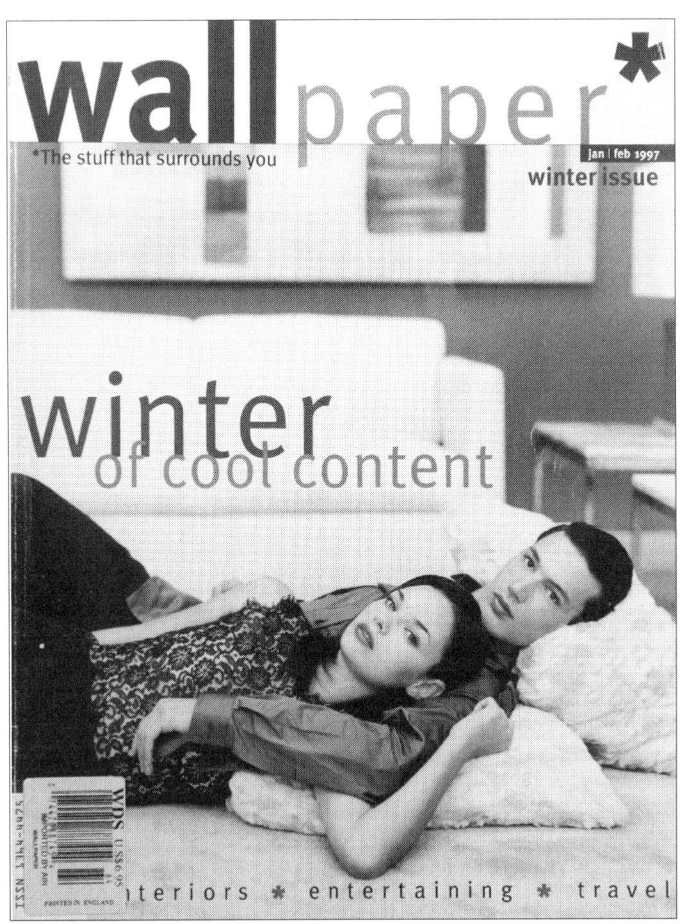

Wallpaper*, *1997*

torted layouts, Wallpaper* has turned away from this early nineties style, offering instead a kind of late modernist sensibility with bold, crisp Gothic type framed by generous white space and skillfully styled tongue-in-cheek photography. And there's never more than one piece of overlapping type in each issue's headlines. Just consider the implications of that.

Unlike the designers at various contemporary monkey-see-monkey-do magazines, *Wallpaper**'s art director, Herbert Winkler, has not apparently downloaded a template off the Internet in a vain attempt to simulate multimedia. In fact, he has assiduously avoided the "end of print" aesthetics of chaotic design, instead following magazines' traditional pacing, with their highs and lows modulated to keep the reader moving sequentially through the feature wells. Maintaining the semblance of an editorial well is an achievement in itself, as ads increasingly encroach upon this territory in many magazines.

But for all its virtues, *Wallpaper**'s format has limitations. The magazine is divided into several thematic sections, and although it has editorial wells to accommodate them, it also runs many single editorial pages facing ad pages. Wherever text and images are balanced, these pages are easily distinguishable from the ads, but usually the editorial pages are so colorfully visual that, save for an identifying kicker (e.g., "In House," "The Space," or "The Event"), the editorial and ads blur the line of church and state.

*Wallpaper**'s format, although unified by its close-fit sans-serif typography, is dominated by choppy, incohesive pagination, a seemingly avoidable flaw. The catalog nature of many single pages—with as many as six boxes, each containing a picture of merchandise—has become so accepted in magazines that one easily forgets that it encourages bad design. In *Wallpaper**'s case, this design includes variously colored, overlapping one-point-rule boxes with tight-fitting type, resulting in a cluttered mosaic. Now don't get me wrong—each is perfectly readable, but on the whole, the page is little better in quality than *Pennysaver*.

Each thematic section also is introduced by a single-page "billboard" announcing the stories therein. Although this concept is designed to aid navigation and prevent an abrupt switch from ad to editorial, the billboards in fact take on the appearance of ads, and in a magazine so fraught with them, this "solution" does not have the desired impact.

intelligence

Exmouth Cometh | **next decade's department store** | **Vespa scoots ahead** | Glasgow gets stacked ...

DISTURBANISMS

When a benefactor donated money to the Royal College of Art and gave them carte blanche to do what they wanted with it, Nigel Coates and Ben Evans of the RCA's architectural design department dreamt up Disturbanisms, a series of lectures by some of the world's most interesting and influential urban theorists. They began by drafting a wish-list of speakers they would most like to hear. One is Rem Koolhaas, slated for Feb. 3, the author of the coffee table crusher S,M,L,XL whose works in progress include the Universal Studio complex – tipped to be Hollywood's hippest corporate headquarters – and Seoul airport. The rest of the cast runs from French academic Marc Augé on 11 March to Princeton's Beatriz Colomina on 13 May. Winding up the series on 3 June will be Daniel Libeskind, architect of the Jewish Museum in Berlin and bane of the Save The V&A brigade. Add them together and expect Disturbanisms to deliver the most exciting lecture series for London's architecture junkies in years.

For free tickets, call the RCA architectural design department on 0171 590 4273.

expanding C-cups

Having revitalised the top end of St. John Street, **the team behind Crowbar Coffee are about to do the same for Exmouth Market in Clerkenwell. 'We've been around that neighbourhood for years and have always wondered why it hasn't taken off,' explains Sam Hardingham,** one-third of the team **behind Crowbar** (other partners are her architect husband **William McLean and Adam Sodowick.) Double the size of the St. John Street café, the new Crowbar dispenses the same Portuguese coffee and pastries but this time the patrons are likely to be editors at** [illegible] **and** *The Guardian*. '**This could really be the next great street** because there are so many **amazing people working and living around here,' says Hardingham. With** Crowbar blazing the trail, **a team of ex River Café and Eagle chefs looking to launch a new restaurant by early February and a host of retailers lined up behind them, Westbourne Grove's fifteen minutes might well be up.**

Crowbar Coffee, **55 Exmouth Market, London EC1.**

STRIP MALL

After a decade that saw many of America's most venerable department stores vanish from the retail landscape, it's not surprising that Bloomingdale's has just completed phase one of a major design initiative which it hopes will help bolster the chain's presence in America's more affluent suburbs. Having commissioned New York architecture firm Kohn Pedersen Fox (KPF) to come up with an alternative to the windowless masses of red brick that have become the standard blueprint for suburban department stores across the US, the firm has just launched three new stores directly targeted at the auto-obsessed Californian. Recognizing that they needed to 'break open the box,' KPF's stores for Bloomingdale's in Palo Alto, Century City and Sherman Oaks have been built with both transparency and visibility in mind. Where walls of concrete used to shroud merchandise, the KPF team have installed stretches of glass to draw in the odd pedestrian. And for commuters hurtling by in their BMW cabriolets, images will be projected onto perforated metal screens, enhancing the 'drive-by' shopping experience. Due to be rolled out nationally in America, the new design is likely to influence the suburban department store boom that's about to sweep Britain. In the meantime, legislators will be looking at ways to curb retailers from projecting scantily clad images of Amber at rush hour.

030 | wallpaper*

MOD OF TRANSPORT

If Wallpaper* had an annual design award, there's no question that our intelligence editors would hand the statuette to the brilliant team at Piaggio who unveiled a new and much-improved Vespa to the commuting masses late last year. With smooth lines that nod to both the past and the future, the new Vespas have started making conspicuous appearances at intersections up and down the country. Of course, our favourite is the ET4 (125 cc) in alabaster. To ensure the quickest commute to work contact Piaggio UK on 01689 898876.

full volume

When Waterstone's surfaced **in the early 80s, the idea of high-street bookshops selling tens of thousands of titles and staffed by people who loved reading as much as customers was hailed as an innovation. Now Waterstone's is innovating again.**

Last summer, it sent half a dozen branch managers on a whistle-stop tour of the world's best bookshops to dig up ideas on how to reconstruct Waterstone's for the late 90s, starting with the opening of its first book superstore in Glasgow later this year. With at least 150,000 titles spread across 25,000 square feet of a 19th-century building, the Glasgow store will be the biggest bookshop to open in Britain since the War, and the closest thing this side of the Atlantic to the Borders and Barnes & Nobles sprawling across the States.

Waterstone's is still tweaking final details, but the superstore is also likely to sell magazines, newspapers, computer software and art videos. There will be some sort of café – probably an espresso bar. It will open earlier and close later than other bookshops. If Waterstone's first book superstore goes well, it will look for sites in other cities.

wallpaper* | 031

One of several sections of briefs

the report

new yorkers

PLANET FLAT PACK

Up there with Saab, Volvo and Abba, Ikea is Sweden's most pervasive export, flogging cut-price sofas from Paris to Pasadena. **Nonie Niesewand** deconstructs its global appeal and finds that it's not the same furniture for all people

the germans

illustrated by Demetrios Psillos

052 | wallpaper*

wallpaper* | 053

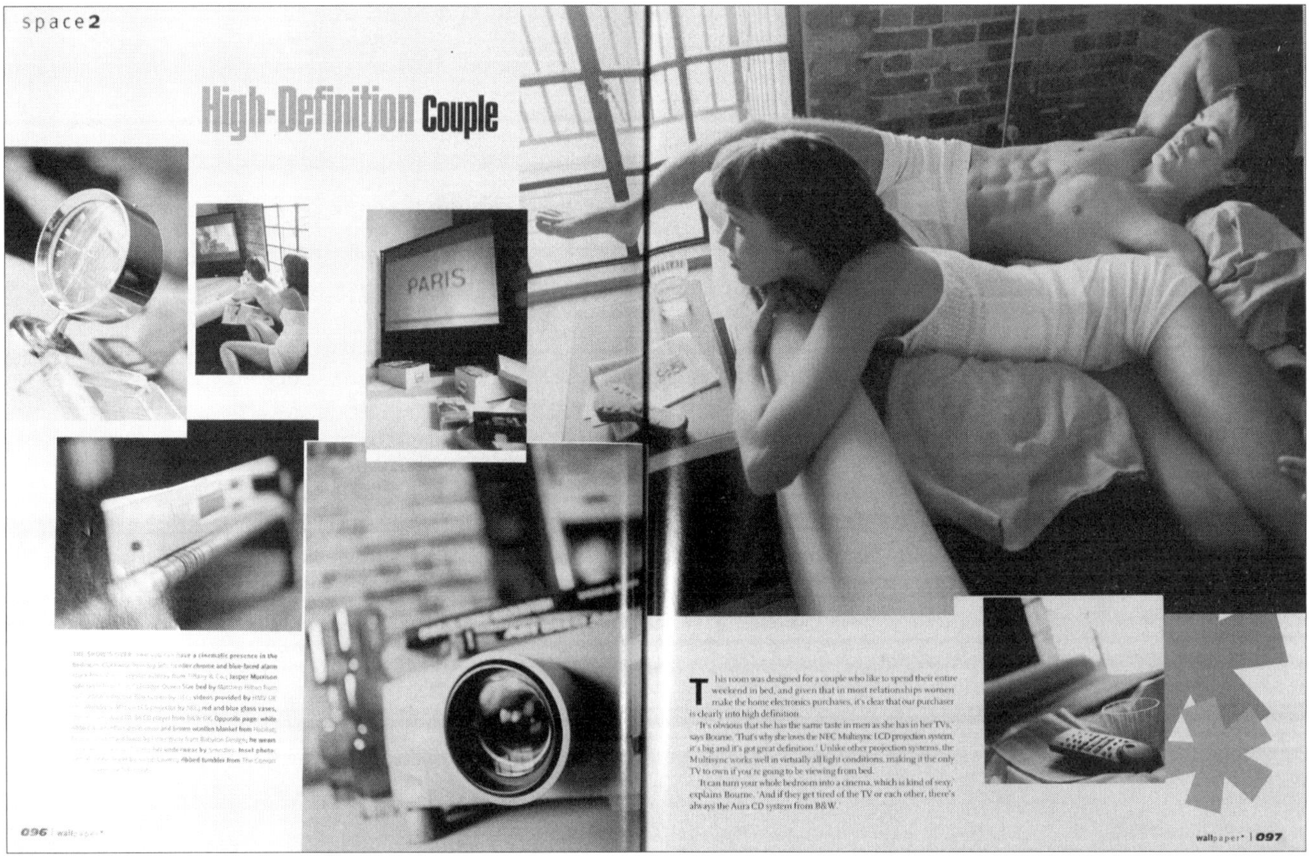

space2

High-Definition Couple

PARIS

This room was designed for a couple who like to spend their entire weekend in bed, and given that in most relationships women make the home electronics purchases, it's clear that our purchaser is clearly into high definition.

'It's obvious that she has the same taste in men as she has in her TVs,' says Bourne. 'That's why she loves the NEC Multisync LCD projection system, it's big and it's got great definition.' Unlike other projection systems, the Multisync works well in virtually all light conditions, making it the only TV to own if you're going to be viewing from bed.

'It can turn your whole bedroom into a cinema, which is kind of sexy,' explains Bourne. 'And if they get tired of the TV or each other, there's always the Aura CD system from B&W.'

096 | wallpaper*

wallpaper* | 097

Wallpaper* *features*

Despite its flaws, *Wallpaper**'s design is excellent. But for all its departures from accepted youth codes, it should be seen less as innovative and more as a synthesis of various magazine ideas from the sixties and seventies (including ideas from Hearst's late-sixties lifestyle book *Eye*, which combined psychedelia and modernism in a hybrid form).

Compared to a new upstart "shelter" book called *Nest* ("a quarterly magazine of interiors"), *Wallpaper** is fairly conventional. *Nest*, however, is radical without being absurd. In fact, *Nest*, art-directed by founding editor in chief Joseph Holtzman (with assistance from "design technician" Tom Beckham and typographer Michael Zöllner), is a perfectly readable yet remarkably unconventional portfolio of features. Granted, it lacks the cachet and circulation of *Wallpaper**, but it's still a slick, glossy, full-color newsstand magazine that attracts the same kind of advertising (if as yet not as much). From a design standpoint, it is much freer and more imaginative than any similar magazine in its class.

Nest avoids *Wallpaper**'s pitfall of editorial blurring with ads simply by not publishing a front-of-the-book section. Following a number of pages of uninterrupted classy ads, issue 2 leads off with a classically designed black-and-white page of introductory text, printed on translucent rice paper. The features are on glossy paper, printed mostly in color, modulated by some black-and-white imagery. And each feature is so uniquely designed that it does not reflect an overall standardized format. While this variety may seem disconcerting, the spreads fit together perfectly in the editorial flow. *Nest* does not permit advertising in its expansive editorial well, and if it did, these feature spreads might not hold up as a unified whole. But it takes some risk to design a section of posed full-color photographs depicting how female prisoners decorate their cells, with minimal accompanying text, followed by an odd feature on the full-page color advertisements of upholstery designer Hasi Hester, which look as if they came from an old trade magazine. Not every feature works, but there's magic in some of the juxtapositions. And *Nest*'s uniqueness is enhanced by its upper page corner, which is curved like that of a school notebook.

*Wallpaper** and *Nest* are two ends of a fascinating spectrum of contemporary magazine design. Both reject the early-nineties obsession with "deconstructed" typography—for one, by means of a return to tradition through synthesis of older ideas, and for the other, by an attempt to have fun by matching interesting content to unfettered design.

Left Wanting

22

Why do liberal magazines have such conservative design?

DAVID BARRINGER

I BELIEVE MAGAZINE DESIGN CAN EMBODY LIBERAL principles. I don't know how design might express underdog sympathies, cultural tolerance, and the expansion of individual rights. But I do have the impression that not a single liberal magazine is giving it a go. Why are liberal magazines so conservative?

Three reasons. Lack of money. The desire for stability. And design-phobia.

"No political magazine in America has ever made money because advertisers don't want to be in contentious magazines," says Milton Glaser, who worked on redesigns of the *Nation*. "It's important for these magazines to look frugal."

The humble look of liberal magazines—such as the *Progressive*, the *American Prospect*, *In These Times*, *Dissent*, and *Washington Monthly*, among others—presumably evokes ascetic intellectualism. Many political magazines are thin, printed on cheap paper, and obey a structure familiar to anyone who has marched through the *Marine Corps Gazette*: page after page of two-column layouts of dense, if not crammed, type and one or two inset photographs, typically of talking heads. Serious photojournalism is rarely featured. Controversial photographs are avoided and illustrations are restrained, if they exist at all. A Danish newspaper will take the heat for printing satirical cartoons, but an American political journal won't. Layouts are uniformly plodding, respecting rules more than the reader and loyalty to repetition more than legibility. The more you survey the design of these magazines, the more you imagine even the typesetters grinding their teeth. Writers may be taking stands on issues but the design has been told to take a seat. Liberal American editors must believe that even though stories look like frogs on the page, when kissed by the reader, they become princes in the mind. But a reader has to work up the appetite to kiss a frog.

Money is always a concern, of course, but it shouldn't be an excuse. Cheap paper may be a fact of life, but not even cheap paper deserves coarse design. A lack of money doesn't excuse lazy design any more than it would excuse lazy journalism. "Money doesn't always give you results," argues Mirko Ilic, who has illustrated covers for the *Village Voice* and, with Glaser, wrote the book *The Design of Dissent*. "A designer with ideas, passion, and very little money can do it." And there is a cost for insisting on posing in a shabby suit. "Many liberal magazines take transformative aspirations and render them lifeless," says Brian Awehali, editor of the low-budget, radical-left *Lip Magazine*.

In their defense, liberal magazines might be resisting change in order to express ideological commitment through design stability. "It's in the nature of ideological magazines to suggest constancy," says Glaser. "Magazines have specific historical references, and they serve their readership. The *Nation* is polemic, less elegant, with lower production values, and it has a sense of being noisy and aggressive. My struggles with redesigning the *Nation* through the years have always been with the prospect that anything that changes will be deeply resisted. Trends change, but they want to tell you that their ideologies don't."

Editors may not want to change their minds every week on political issues, but surely liberalism will survive if they at least try to support their arguments with fluent design, which might include photojournalism, incisive illustration, and intelligent typography. Framing liberal ideas within a stagnant structure, however, sends the wrong message, so that you sympathize with Ilic when he says, "There are no liberal magazines. Left-leaning media bend over backwards to please the center. I was born in Bosnia, and I know you can never please any extreme group, left or right, until you are 100 percent with them."

Editors may devalue design because they don't trust what they don't understand. Resistance to the benefits of good design may be due to their narrow understanding of design—in essence, a prejudice against the visual. Design-phobia clearly afflicts even the best editorial minds. The staff may have strong journalistic skills, but the art of magazine making—clarifying information, supporting stories visually—is not particularly valued. Ilic is blunt: "Change is hard, and in the meantime they are all crying out for change of government, of country, but they are not starting with themselves. People from inside the magazine are so bogged down

4 The Nation. *February 19, 2007*

COMMENT

The Nation.

EDITOR & PUBLISHER: Katrina vanden Heuvel

PRESIDENT: Teresa Stack

MANAGING EDITOR: Karen Rothmyer
LITERARY EDITOR: Adam Shatz
EXECUTIVE EDITOR: Betsy Reed
SENIOR EDITORS: Richard Lingeman (*on leave*), Roane Carey, Esther Kaplan
WEB EDITOR: Joan Connell
COPY EDITOR: Judith Long
ASSISTANT COPY EDITOR: Mark Sorkin
COPY ASSOCIATE: Lisa Vandepaer
ASSISTANT TO THE EDITOR: Peggy Suttle
ASSISTANT LITERARY EDITOR: Christine Smallwood
INTERNS: Molly Bennet, Michelle Chandra, Stephanie Condon (*Washington*), Michael Corcoran, Emily Douglas, Wes Enzinna, Rob Fischer, Elizabeth Schuster, Rebecca Tinkelman

WASHINGTON, DC: EDITOR: David Corn; CORRESPONDENT: John Nichols

NATIONAL AFFAIRS CORRESPONDENT: William Greider

COLUMNISTS: Eric Alterman, Alexander Cockburn, Naomi Klein (*on leave*), Katha Pollitt, Patricia J. Williams, Gary Younge

DEPARTMENTS: *Architecture*, Jane Holtz Kay; *Art*, Arthur C. Danto; *Corporations*, Robert Sherrill; *Defense*, Michael T. Klare; *Environment*, Mark Hertsgaard; *Films*, Stuart Klawans; *Legal Affairs*, David Cole; *Peace and Disarmament*, Jonathan Schell; *Poetry*, John Palattella; *United Nations*, Ian Williams; *Deadline Poet*, Calvin Trillin

CONTRIBUTING EDITORS: Kai Bird, Robert L. Borosage, Stephen F. Cohen, Marc Cooper, Mike Davis, Slavenka Drakulić, Robert Dreyfuss, Susan Faludi, Liza Featherstone, Thomas Ferguson, Doug Henwood, Max Holland, Molly Ivins, John Leonard, Michael Moore, Richard Pollak, Joel Rogers, Kirkpatrick Sale, Robert Scheer, Herman Schwartz, Bruce Shapiro, Ted Solotaroff, Edward Sorel, Gore Vidal, Jon Wiener, Amy Wilentz, Art Winslow

CONTRIBUTING WRITERS: Ari Berman (*Washington*), Lakshmi Chaudhry, Christopher Hayes, Bob Moser, Eyal Press, Scott Sherman

BUREAUS: *London*, Maria Margaronis and D.D. Guttenplan; *Southern Africa*, Mark Gevisser

EDITORIAL BOARD: Deepak Bhargava, Norman Birnbaum, Barbara Ehrenreich, Richard Falk, Frances FitzGerald, Eric Foner, Philip Green, Lani Guinier, Tom Hayden, Randall Kennedy, Tony Kushner, Elinor Langer, Deborah W. Meier, Toni Morrison, Victor Navasky, Pedro Antonio Noguera, Richard Parker, Michael Pertschuk, Elizabeth Pochoda, Marcus G. Raskin, Andrea Batista Schlesinger, David Weir, Roger Wilkins

ASSOCIATE PUBLISHER, SPECIAL PROJECTS/WEBSITE: Peter Rothberg
ASSOCIATE PUBLISHER, DEVELOPMENT/ASSOCIATES: Peggy Randall
VICE PRESIDENT, ADVERTISING: Ellen Bollinger
ADVERTISING MANAGER, SMALL DISPLAY, EVENTS, CLASSIFIED: Leigh Novog
VICE PRESIDENT, CIRCULATION: Arthur Stupar
CIRCULATION MANAGER: Michelle O'Keefe
CIRCULATION FULFILLMENT MANAGER: Miriam Camp
PRODUCTION DIRECTOR: Omar Rubio
TYPOGRAPHER/WEB PRODUCER: Sandy McCroskey
PRODUCTION MANAGER: Timothy Don
NATION ASSOCIATES MANAGER: Peter Fifield
PUBLICITY/SYNDICATION DIRECTOR: Mike Webb
EDUCATION/COMMUNICATIONS COORDINATOR: Habiba Alcindor
VICE PRESIDENT, WEB SITE AND TECHNOLOGY: Scott Klein
TECHNOLOGY COORDINATOR: Amirt K. Barksdale
WEB PRODUCER: Jason Das
CONTROLLER: Mary van Valkenburg
ASSISTANT TO VICTOR NAVASKY: Mary Taylor Schilling
DATA ENTRY/MAIL COORDINATOR: John Holtz
ASSISTANT TO THE PRESIDENT: Kathleen Thomas
BUSINESS ASSISTANT: Johange Wright

PUBLISHER EMERITUS: Victor Navasky

LETTERS TO THE EDITOR: E-mail to letters@thenation.com (300-word limit). Letters are subject to editing for reasons of space and clarity.
SUBMISSIONS: Queries only, no manuscripts. Go to www.thenation.com and click on "about," then "submissions" for a query form. Queries may be mailed to The Nation, 33 Irving Place, New York, NY 10003. SASE for poems.

The Nation (ISSN 0027-8378) is published weekly (except for the second week in January, and biweekly the third week of July through the second week of September) by The Nation Company, L.P. © 2007 in the U.S.A. by The Nation Company, L.P., 33 Irving Place, New York, NY 10003. (212) 209-5400. Washington Bureau: Suite 308, 110 Maryland Avenue N.E., Washington, DC 20002. (202) 546-2239. Periodicals postage paid at New York, NY, and at additional mailing offices. Subscription orders, changes of address and all subscription inquiries: The Nation, PO Box 55149, Boulder, CO 80322-5149, or call 1-800-333-8536. Publications Mail Agreement No. 40041477. Return undeliverable Canadian addresses to Circulation Dept. or DPGM, 4960-2 Walker Road, Windsor, ON N9A 6J3. **When ordering a subscription, please allow 4–6 weeks for receipt of your first issue and for all subscription transactions.** Basic annual subscription price: $52 for 47 issues. Back issues $4 prepaid ($6 foreign) from: The Nation, 33 Irving Place, New York, NY 10003. The Nation is available on microfilm from: University Microfilms, 300 North Zeeb Road, Ann Arbor, MI 48106. Member, Audit Bureau of Circulations. POSTMASTER: Send address changes to The Nation, PO Box 55149, Boulder, CO 80322-5149. Printed in U.S.A. on recycled paper.

www.thenation.com

Surge for Peace

What, realistically, can the antiwar movement accomplish right now? Tom Andrews, a former Congressman from Maine and national director of the Win Without War coalition, answers the question without hesitation: "We can stop this war."

For the first time since the Iraq War began, activists are optimistic—and getting serious about the political process. With Bush proposing an escalation and a Democratic Congress that owes its new majority, at least in part, to antiwar sentiment, everyone agrees that there has never been a better opportunity to end this tragic policy. Fresh from January 27's successful demonstration in Washington, the peace movement is now focusing all of its organizing energies on—and dedicating serious resources to—the people who truly have the power to stop the war: members of Congress.

At this writing, numerous resolutions are floating around the Hill, 800 peace activists working with United for Peace and Justice (UFPJ) are meeting with more than 270 Congressional representatives and MoveOn.org has called a Virtual March, in which constituents will flood Capitol Hill with 1 million calls against the war on February 1. MoveOn, Win Without War, the Service Employees International Union and other groups have launched Americans Against Escalation in Iraq, an $8 million–$10 million campaign that will organize constituents in twenty to twenty-five states to pressure fence-sitting legislators. The effort, explains Tom Matzzie, MoveOn.org Political Action's Washington director, is "very intense, modeled a lot on a presidential campaign." In another of this war's firsts, active members of the military have joined the fight. Says Jonathan Hutto, founder of the active-duty troops' group Appeal for Redress, which advocates a political rather than a military resolution of the Iraq War, politicians "don't usually hear from us. Soldiers are trained to be grunts. But now is the time."

The battle for public opinion on the Iraq War is over—not so much because of the antiwar movement's work but because the situation in Iraq has proved so disastrous. Many mainstream journalists, pundits and politicians now speak against the war as eloquently and convincingly as peace activists do. Only 17 percent of the American people agree with Bush's current escalation plan. The challenge is to translate that power into a change in policy. Until now, the antiwar forces have had fewer than five full-time Washington lobbyists. But much of the antiwar movement now agrees that there is no contradiction, or conflict, between chanting in the streets and lobbying in the halls of Congress. An impressive showing of demonstrators in DC (UFPJ says half a million) along with the thousands of smaller local protests over the past few weeks bolsters the lobbying effort, showing that peace activists are an impassioned constituency, while protests would be meaningless without additional pressure on politicians.

Success, however, is not assured. A tentative majority in Congress opposes the Bush policy, but there's a world of difference between supporting a nonbinding resolution and blocking

February 19, 2007 The Nation. 5

COMMENT

appropriations. That's why the effort to persuade Congress will require such a massive grassroots campaign. "If we had to vote right now on defunding the war," MoveOn's Matzzie said recently, "we would lose. We have to be very strategic and smart." He sighs. "I have nightmares about the gap between what we need to do and what we are doing. I lose sleep over this."

There are some within the peace movement who believe that Congressional Democrats will never agree to stop funding the war. They may be right. (As demonstrators assembled in Washington, Senator Hillary Clinton, in Iowa, dismissed the call to cut off funding as a "soundbite.") Given the Democrats' trepidation about appearing to cut off support for the troops, some antiwar strategists argue that the movement should shift the focus of its lobbying from defunding the war to funding a real plan for withdrawal.

It's worth thinking, too, about the broader mission of an antiwar movement. Author and blogger Rahul Mahajan, of UFPJ's steering committee (speaking for himself, not the organization), worries that unlike in the Vietnam era, today's peace movement has had little success in getting Americans to rethink the role of the United States in the world. He's right. The talking point among some Democrats is that while the United States has been so generous, those damned Iraqis have screwed up the war. That way of thinking isn't going help us avoid further misadventures in imperial arrogance. It's hardly reassuring to hear Iraq War opponents like Democratic presidential hopeful John Edwards say that for Iran, "we must keep all options on the table." Stopping the war in Iraq is important, but to truly make the world a safer place, we need to change the conversation.

LIZA FEATHERSTONE

Liza Featherstone is a Nation *contributing writer.*

Workers, Not Guests

Ten days before Christmas, the Woodfin Suites Hotel in Emeryville, California, suspended Luz Dominguez and twenty other housekeepers and maintenance workers. Managers announced they'd received a letter from Social Security saying the numbers they'd given when the workers were originally hired didn't match government records. The twenty-one workers have been making beds, washing toilets and vacuuming carpets there for years. Dominguez recalls, "Before, they sometimes told us they'd received a notice about our numbers not matching. We never had to do anything about it." What had changed?

In 2005 an Oakland-based worker advocacy group, the East Bay Alliance for a Sustainable Economy, convinced Emeryville voters to pass Measure C. The new ordinance established a $9 hourly minimum in the city's four hotels. Housekeepers required to clean more than 5,000 square feet in an eight-hour shift now have to be paid time and a half. "Before the law was passed, we cleaned sixteen suites, sometimes seventeen," says Marcela Melquiades, another fired housekeeper. The new law dropped that to around ten.

The four hotels—the Woodfin Suites, Sheraton Four Points, Marriott Courtyard and the Hilton Garden Inn—spent $115,610 to defeat the measure (but garnered only 1,051 no votes). When they lost, they tried to get an injunction to prevent it from taking effect and lost again. Workers began asking Woodfin to comply.

That's when the hotel suddenly demanded new Social Security numbers. "We felt defrauded," Dominguez says. "We'd worked really hard for them."

No-match letters have become a form of immigration enforcement increasingly favored by the Bush Administration. But they're often used, unions charge, to retaliate against workers when they stand up for themselves.

Such workplace enforcement cost the jobs of thousands of workers last year. In raids this past December at six Swift meatpacking plants (five of which had union contracts), the Immigration and Customs Enforcement (ICE) bureau detained 1,300 laborers. Many were deported. At other workplaces, like the Woodfin Suites, the Social Security Administration has been pressed into service.

In November about 1,000 meatpackers walked out of the huge Smithfield pork processing plant in Tar Heel, North Carolina, after the company fired sixty workers for Social Security discrepancies. Mark Lauritsen, a director at United Food and Commercial Workers (UFCW), says the government and the company were colluding to thwart the union's organizing ef-

BUSH'S 'LEGACY'

The White House PR machine keeps making noises about the Bush regime's "legacy." This "legacy" will not include any domestic legislation, since there is none to speak of—unless, perhaps, Bush signs a law declaring that the polar bear is an endangered species (so are ordinary Americans, but that's another story).

Surely, George W. ("I'm the decider") Bush will be remembered for one thing: the folly of his pre-emptive war in Iraq.

Here's his legacy:

One: The United States has lost the Iraq War. Bush has failed as Commander in Chief.

Two: The Bush regime has blood on its hands. It's responsible for at least 25,000 US casualties (killed and wounded).

Three: The United States has spent roughly $400 billion, and counting, to finance this lost cause.

Four: The United States is responsible for exacerbating sectarian war in Iraq and other nations, causing thousands of civilian deaths.

Five: The United States has been diminished in the United Nations and has tarnished its glory around the world.

All of the above prove that Bush has been the most dangerous President in American history.

HERBERT MITGANG

Herbert Mitgang, an author and former editorial writer for the New York Times, *is a fellow of the Society of American Historians.*

The Nation

fighting bureaucratic crap, they have no outside perspective. If liberal magazines cannot be revolutionary, then who?"

Editors of these magazines tend to come from other liberal organizations, some academic, some literary, and some journalistic, and with their backgrounds, they often distrust contemporary visual media, if not graphic design itself. "We have to be careful, those of us coming from the design community, because we have different values," warns Glaser. "But I disagree that these magazines are susceptible to one illness. Each is reflective of [a] single editor with an attitude."

While editorial personalities influence individual magazines, readers may still notice design trends among the magazines taken as a whole. Even a brief examination reveals that editors of liberal political magazines (possibly all political magazines) regard the real estate of the blank page as too valuable to surrender to what they consider "gratuitous" imagery. But what's gratuitous about photos of Abu Ghraib or the first Iraq war's so-called Highway of Death?

"*Life* magazine had the most profound political effect on my life," says James Petersen, former editor of "Playboy's Forum," an eight-page op-ed insert modeled on political magazines. "The evolution of man, the antiwar movement, the burning monk, the girl running in Vietnam, the police chief executing the Saigon prisoner: those photos are what move your conscience. That's what's missing from all these liberal magazines. I wanted to run, in the pages of *Playboy*, images from the Highway of Death during the first Iraq war, showing what America did to those people, but I was overruled. No one I know ran those pictures."

"Editors are nervous about the introduction of visual ideas. They are afraid that visuals misrepresent facts," explains Glaser.

"A picture of Abu Ghraib is worth more than ten thousand words," adds Ilic.

Reintroducing photojournalism was part of Rhonda Rubinstein's redesign of *Mother Jones* in 1999. "Up until then, *Mother Jones* was couched in nice, polite design. I wanted to make it more visible and relevant, appealing to the next generation's visual literacy."

8 FEBRUARY 12, 2007 ▶ THE NEW REPUBLIC

The Resolutionary War.

Get In Line

BY EVE FAIRBANKS

THE NEW REPUBLIC ▶ FEBRUARY 12, 2007 9

John McCain's hatchet man.

Smelly Nelly

BY CONOR CLARKE

The New Republic

LETTERS

Party pooper

State of emergency

In defense of Wal-Mart

Why we buy

Tilting at windmills

By Charles Peters

The best plan (your) money can buy (your Congressman)

Unspeakable

The new proletariat

La Causa

Karl, Grover, and Sharyl

"People in the $100,000 to $500,000 income range now see themselves as underprivileged."

6 January/February 2007

The Washington Monthly 7

The Washington Monthly

began working with the Department of Citywide Administrative Services (DCAS), which handled leasing for city agencies. No one was more determined to do the command center up big than DCAS Commissioner Bill Diamond, a wealthy real-estate heir and Republican financier who had spent much of his life in patronage positions. For virtually the entire 12 years of the Ronald Reagan and George H.W. Bush administrations, Diamond had held the politically pivotal position of regional administrator for the General Services Administration, which put him in charge of contracting and leasing in the Northeast.

In 1989, Diamond started contributing to Giuliani's campaign committees, hitting contribution limits more than once. By 2005, he and his two wives had given a total of $36,000 in donations to every political committee Giuliani has ever formed. The broker assigned by Diamond's agency to find space for the command center was a national firm with a tiny New York presence, CB Real Estate Group. On its board of directors were three Republican giants, including the former counsel to the Reagan-Bush campaign, Stanton Anderson, who'd gotten to know Giuliani when he worked for the Reagan administration. James Didion, CEO of CB Real Estate at the time, says, "There was a relationship with City Hall. But I don't know who was involved."

Hauer recalls that Diamond himself was quite enthusiastic about 7 WTC, which splendidly fit the bill of a high-profile building for a high-profile project. "He did everything he could to facilitate it." The Port Authority owned the land underneath all the Trade Center structures. But in the early 1980s, the authority had given developer Larry Silverstein a 99-year lease to build the 7 WTC tower. Slated as Silverstein's prize tenant was Drexel Burnham, an investment firm that had been one of Wall Street's giants. But in a bizarre turn of fate, Giuliani had turned his prosecutorial sights on Drexel, and when his case concluded, the indicted company was finished. So was its agreement to lease a new headquarters at 7 WTC, and Silverstein's biggest project soon began to look like his biggest blunder. But happily for Silverstein, nine federal agencies took space in the building during Diamond's tenure at the General Services Administration, agreeing to pay rents that were often an overpriced embarrassment. As much Silverstein space as the federal government leased, however, no one ever rented the 23rd floor, once planned as Drexel's trading floor, which remained vacant for a decade. Instead of Giuliani target Michael Milken reigning supreme on that floor, Giuliani himself would reign as commander in chief of a state-of-the-art command center.

Silverstein had given nary a dime to either of Giuliani's first two mayoral campaigns, spurning the candidate's courting of him in 1993. But by the time 7 WTC emerged as a possible command center site in 1996, their relationship had greatly improved. In October 1994, the developer began donating to Giuliani's committee, beginning with a meager $500. By November 1996, he, his wife, and his company had contributed $17,500—or nearly $5,000 over the legal limit (the excess was returned after a newspaper reported it). He also hosted a $1,000 per couple party for Giuliani aboard his yacht docked in the Hudson River in June 1996, collecting another $36,100 from his invited friends. When Giuliani, unable to run for re-election, formed a federal exploratory committee in 1998, Silverstein and an executive of his company gave another $3,000. That contribution was made at a party in Howard Rubenstein's Fifth Avenue home. Silverstein had long been one of the public relations czar's top clients, and power-broker Rubenstein confirmed a private breakfast attended by Silverstein and Giuliani at Gracie Mansion. In addition to Silverstein, two top executives of the construction company he was using to build the command center, Jay Koven and Jack Shafran, gave $4,000 at the party, bringing the Silverstein-connected total to at least $7,000. "Attendance was obligatory," recalls Shafran. "The invitation meant we were expected to give a contribution."

The timing couldn't have been queasier. Two weeks before the event, Silverstein had signed the lease for the command center. The day before, the budget office had rushed through approvals for $12.6 million, the initial renovation cost. Finally, in July 1999, just a month after the command center opened, Silverstein hosted another yacht fund-raiser for Giuliani, raising $100,000 for his prospective U.S. Senate race against Hillary Clinton.

The invisible combination of Bill Diamond's history with 7 WTC, and Larry Silverstein's intricate new relationship with the Giuliani administration, had resulted in a decision to locate the city's command center high above the one spot on American soil that had been the target of an attack by foreign terrorists.

The line of critics who have blasted the siting of the center includes the highest-ranking uniformed police official of the Giuliani era, Chief of the Department Lou Anemone, who says he was a fierce opponent when the decision was made. "I did a couple of memos against that site, citing the closeness to an intended target, the 23rd floor dangers and hazards," he said years later. "It was a joke. You don't want to confuse Giuliani with the facts, and his 'yes men' would agree with him. In terms of targets, the World Trade Center was No. 1. I guess you had to be there in 1993 to know how strongly we felt it was the wrong place."

Yet Sunny Mindel, the former mayoral press secretary who is now the spokeswoman for Guiliani's consulting firm, Giuliani Partners, suggests it's all hindsight. "At the time, given the type of emergencies that could beset a modern urban center, it seemed absolutely appropriate," she said in 2002. "No one could have predicted the events of September 11." In fact, Silverstein's property risk assessment report identified the scenario of an aircraft striking a tower as one of the "maximum foreseeable losses" just months before 9-11. A congressional inquiry after 9-11 cited numerous indicators that such attacks were a possible terrorist tactic, including one specific aircraft threat involving the World Trade Center.

The contention that no one could have predicted a terrorist return to the World Trade Center is particularly clueless. Says U.S. Attorney Mary Jo White, "I didn't think it made any sense to put the command center at 7 WTC, where it was in the zone of likely attack." Police Commissioner Ray Kelly, who formerly worked as a security consultant to the Port Authority, adds, "If Giuliani had any sense of the threat, he would have gotten out of the City Hall area. He put it right next to a target. It was just unwise." TAP

From the forthcoming book Grand Illusion *by* ***Wayne Barrett*** *and* **Dan Collins**. *© 2006 by Wayne Barrett and Dan Collins. Published by arrangement with HarperCollins Publishers. Anna Lenzer provided research assistance for the book.*

ARGUMENT

ILLUSION AND REALITY

The violence in the Middle East shows the negative consequences of the administration's contempt for engagement. But the tough talk has failed.

BY FLYNT LEVERETT

On the evening of September 11, 2001, I was one of a small group of State Department staffers called in to confer with Secretary of State Colin Powell and work through the night to produce a diplomatic strategy for assembling an international coalition to destroy Osama bin Laden's base in Afghanistan. Powell took this strategy to the White House on the morning of September 12, and it became the blueprint for marshaling international support for Operation Enduring Freedom, launched months later.

In the weeks following 9-11, my colleagues and I at State developed a comprehensive diplomatic strategy to support the war on terrorism. This strategy envisioned, beyond a military campaign in Afghanistan, a sustained global effort to "wrap up" bin Laden's operational networks and affiliates in the Middle East and elsewhere. Iraq would continue to be contained. As other state sponsors of terrorism like Iran and Syria came to the United States to offer assistance against al-Qaeda and the Taliban, that help would be accepted; this tactical cooperation would then be used as a platform for persuading these states to terminate their own involvement with anti-Israeli terrorist groups in return for a positive strategic relationship with Washington. The United States would also develop a credible plan for resolving the Israeli-Palestinian conflict.

In March 2003, the invasion of Iraq clearly committed America to a very different strategy, aimed at creating what President Bush described as a "new Middle East." The main elements of this alternative strategy were diametrically opposed to the strategy my colleagues and I had outlined a year and a half earlier. Now:

• Beyond Afghanistan, "rogue" regimes were to be uprooted, either by military force (as in Iraq) or through diplomatic isolation and political pressure (as the administration has tried with Iran and Syria). The United States would not offer "carrots" to such states to induce positive changes; diplomatic engagement would be limited to "sticks."

• Traditional "allies" like Egypt and Saudi Arabia were also to be fundamentally changed, through U.S.-mandated political transformation. Such transformation would bring a wider range of elites into these countries' decision making; these elites would be more focused on internal reform and grateful to the United States for their empowerment, which would improve the regional security environment.

• In White House meetings, I heard President Bush say confidently that democratization would even facilitate a settlement of the Israeli-Palestinian conflict by shaping a Palestinian leadership more focused on internal governance (i.e., providing services such as collecting garbage) and less "hung up" on final-status issues like territory, settlements, and Jerusalem.

Three and a half years after the invasion of Iraq and five years after 9-11, the outbreak of armed conflict between Israel and radical groups in the Palestinian territories and Lebanon has revealed how badly the president's chosen Middle East strategy has damaged the interests of the United States and its allies in the region. The current conflict—which comes alongside a growing likeli-

The American Prospect

Writing to America Luis J. Rodríguez

Ortega Returns

Daniel Ortega is back. So is Robert M. Gates.

In early November, Ortega, the former Sandinista president in the 1980s, again won the presidential elections in Nicaragua.

Also in early November, President Bush nominated Gates to replace Donald Rumsfeld as Secretary of Defense. The Senate overwhelmingly confirmed Gates in December, even though in 1984 he called for the bombing of Nicaragua in a memo to his boss, then-CIA Director William J. Casey.

Gates, who was CIA deputy director at the time, argued in the December 14, 1984, memo that Nicaragua was being controlled by the Soviet Union, possibly making Nicaragua another Cuba. "The United States will do everything in its power short of invasion to put that regime out," he wrote.

Apparently his suggestion of air strikes was considered too extreme even for Reagan.

I visited Nicaragua in the spring of 1983 and had a chance to meet Ortega, as well as other Sandinista leaders, including Tomás Borge, Rosario Murillo, and Ernesto Cardenal. I was part of a fact-finding group with another Chicano writer and friend, Manual "Manazar" Gamboa. The Nicaraguans welcomed us Chicanos. Borge, who had spent two years imprisoned under the Somoza regime, was particularly taken by Gamboa, who had spent seventeen years in California prisons such as San Quentin, Folsom, and Soledad, mostly due to a twenty-year heroin addiction. Gamboa, who had been

DARREN THOMPSON

clean for many years by then, became my mentor in facilitating writing workshops in prisons, barrio community centers, and juvenile facilities.

The Sandinistas soon opened up doors to various Nicaraguan communities, organizations, and even prisons that had been off limits to other writers. We traveled throughout the country—Managua, Estelí, León, Ocotal, Bluefields, and other areas. I spoke to imprisoned Miskito indigenous fighters. I interviewed children and adults taking part in a vast literacy campaign. I met with Sandinista men and women who fought, some with maimed limbs, against the U.S.-supported Somoza government, which the Sandinistas toppled in July of 1979. I spoke to anti-Sandinista businessmen as well as pro-Sandinista youth, to Marxist priests and amazing thirteen-year-old poets. I read poems in Barrio Sandino, a new housing development in the capital of Managua.

One day, four of us ventured into southern Honduras to locate the Contra camps, which at the time the Reagan Administration refused to say it was aiding. We traveled by jeep through rough terrain, across the Rio Coco. Finally, we located a camp and tried to get as close as possible to take photos. Then, much to our horror, we felt the tremors of an explosion not far from our jeep. Somehow the Contras spotted us. We jumped back into the jeep and tried to speed off back to Nicaragua. But I soon heard the whistling of another bomb, which fell right in front of our vehicle. We all placed our arms over our heads, as if this could possibly shield us.

After a long pause, we realized the bomb did not go off. The Sandinista soldier who was driving us stepped out of the jeep and walked toward the bomb. The rest of us followed. Embedded in the ground was a small winged round object—a dud. The soldier got a towel from the jeep and then pulled the bomb out. It was a U.S. government-issued ordnance.

We carefully placed the bomb onto the jeep, jumped back on, and drove safely across the border. We carried proof of U.S. involvement, what I thought was an important story for the media back home. Yet, it was difficult for me to get any major U.S. publication to accept this story. In time, the fact of U.S. involvement in funding and training the Contras became big news.

Now Ortega is back in office. Nicaragua is in an economic mess. U.S.-backed governments since Ortega was ousted in a 1990 election have only made things worse. As in other Latin American countries where people have elected leftist leaders, the people want answers to increased globalization, rising unemployment, and obscene national debts.

I welcome Ortega's return. I know he's not the same firebrand I heard speak at Sandinista rallies in the poorest sections of the country back in 1983. He's older, maybe wiser, but also compromised—as his alliances with former Contra members and rightwingers testify. But he is part of a growing and promising trend away from U.S. influence and IMF policies to more localized, popularized, and socially based strategies.

Something new and vital is emerging throughout the continent. Ortega is the sixth major left-of-center politician to take office or be reelected in a little more than a year. (The other five are the presidents of Bolivia, Brazil, Chile, Ecuador, and Venezuela). Although Ortega is Sandinista Lite these days, he is not that much different from most of the other recent victors who have complicated, often mediated, relationships to their office, the people, and the economy. They are all on a track of progressive change in their respective countries.

Meanwhile, Bush is rapidly losing ground in his Iraq War. Even Gates says the United States is not winning. But Bush is undeterred, cemented in delusions and the ideology of force. That is the same ideology Gates was acting upon when he advised bombing Nicaragua in the 1980s. It would not have worked then; it doesn't work now.

We need to end this ideologically led inanity. We were wrong to interfere in Nicaragua back in the 1980s. We are wrong to interfere in Iraq today. And we'd be wrong to interfere in what is going on today in Latin America.

It's time to learn that the practice of bombing, undermining, and impoverishing countries does not work and should be banished. Otherwise this practice, and this ideology of force, will become our legacy. ◆

Luis J. Rodríguez is the author, most recently, of "Music of the Mill: A Novel" and "My Nature Is Hunger: New & Selected Poems."

The best way to publish your book. Guaranteed.

Trafford can publish your book quickly, affordably, effectively and make it available Worldwide!

"The people at Trafford are top-notch professionals. They care about authors and I strongly recommend their service. After my book was completed, I received a publishing contract in South Korea and a movie contract with a company in the United Kingdom. There is even a play called *American Hiroshima* that is starting in London this year."

David Dionisi author of *American Hiroshima*

#1 Worldwide Distribution. Through Amazon.com, major chains and your local bookstore

Have control of the publishing process every step of the way!

Retain copyright forever and earn larger royalties

Sell paperback, color picture book, hardcover and eBook editions!

From manuscript to published book in under 6 weeks

100% Money Back Satisfaction Guarantee, No Questions Asked!

Finally, a different approach that has already made the dreams of more than 10,000 authors come true. Learn more about it in our FREE Publishing Guide.

For your **FREE** Publishing Guide,
visit our web site www.trafford.com/1872 *or* **call now**
1-888-232-4444 or 250-383-6864 **Promo Code** 1872
Hablamos español • Nous parlons français

Worldwide Distribution Through: amazon.com INGRAM libri.de BARNES & NOBLE

Trafford PUBLISHING

The Progressive

As for today's generation of upstart magazines, many of them deny the liberal label. "I take 'liberal' as an insult," says Awehali. "*Lip* is not in that category." Awehali is in good (and venerable) company, as even art director Stacey D. Clarkson says, "We at *Harper's* don't consider ourselves a 'liberal magazine' but, rather, a vehicle for critical thought and fine writing." And Jason Kucsma, founding copublisher of [the now suspended] *Clamor*, concurs: "I don't consider *Clamor* to be a liberal magazine. I consider it to be a radical leftist magazine that appeals to a wide range of left-leaning individuals, from academic liberals to direct-action activists."

Today's activist magazines are less concerned with the great American liberal experiment than with expressing an anticorporate critique and satisfying a civic-minded, not necessarily political, youth culture. But they take design seriously. "I grew up reading the *Nation*, the *Progressive*, and *Z Magazine*, and I was disappointed," says Kucsma. "I was disappointed by their utter lack of attention to creating something that is even remotely visually engaging. I wanted to work on a magazine that was politically radical and aesthetically engaging."

Timid political art. Stale design. The money excuse. The market dynamic, in which political speech is toned down for a presumably thin-skinned public. Artistic cowardice masquerading as commercial sensibility. These are the charges, but what is the role of design and art in political magazines? Is it to perpetuate a template? To signify stability?

There are always excuses for the status quo, and while they might rationalize, they don't really justify. If editors took design seriously (and deferred to the designer's expertise), then why shouldn't the magazine's design embody liberalism's principles? That is: change, progress, growth.

"Design is order, economy, teaching people beauty, creating individuals," says Ilic. "Good design is subversive. And because it's subversive, good design is left wing."

The design of a political magazine could put form in service of content, and if the content is liberal or progressive, then the design (over the life of the magazine) could express in some measure, liberal ideals and principles. Most political magazines refuse to allow that design can be more than Photoshop tricks and weird fonts. They deny, by virtue of their bland design, that

Commentary

Fog Watch

Bush's Alleged Democracy Goal in Iraq

By Edward S. Herman

Liberation and democracy came late as an alleged major goal of the Bush administration in its invasion-occupation of Iraq. Despite this lateness, and a vast array of reasons and evidence that at best only a nominal or "Arab façade"-democracy was on the Bush agenda, to a remarkable degree the mainstream U.S. media, pundits—including many liberal pundits—as well as the UN and other members of the "international community" quickly accepted the notion of a democratic aim. This, of course, has served the Bush administration well, transforming a major act of aggression and violation of the UN Charter, and a brutal, destructive, exploitative, and illegal occupation, into a pursuit of noble ends, including "stability"—which the invasion-occupation destroyed—as a supposed means to democracy.

This dubious acceptance of a creditable objective was an important feature of the media's and establishment intellectuals' treatment of the Vietnam War almost a half century back. The U.S. aims at that time were always treated as benevolent: repelling "aggression," protecting "South Vietnam," and helping to give the southern Vietnamese the right to "self-determination." The evidence that the National Liberation Front (NLF) had mass support whereas the U.S.-imposed client government had very little, that "South Vietnam" was an artificial U.S. creation, and that most of the fighting and killing by the United States was of South Vietnamese in the southern part of Vietnam, that "self-determination" was precisely what the United States was fighting against, and that only the United States was the external aggressor, never caused the media to challenge the claimed noble ends (or to identify this as a case of U.S. aggression).

The client government of the southern part of Vietnam was a classic puppet. U.S. General Maxwell Taylor pointed out in internal communications that we could replace a recalcitrant or ineffective leader with another of our choice whenever deemed desirable. In its later years this government was manned by U.S.-selected former mercenaries of the earlier French colonial regime who openly acknowledged their inability to compete with the NLF on a purely political basis. But the word puppet was never applied to this government by the mainstream media any more than they would use the word aggression to describe their own government's role.

Things have not improved since the Vietnam War years. The United States fought then to maintain a client government and dependency in the southern part of Vietnam. The Bush administration aimed similarly to depose Saddam Hussein and put in his place a client government and dependency in Iraq. Of course we sponsored elections in Iraq and gave Iraq its "sovereignty" in 2004, but we sponsored elections in Vietnam in 1966 and 1967, and "South Vietnam" had been declared sovereign by its U.S. sponsor in 1954, and anybody capable of making an independent assessment would have been aware that the sovereignty was purely nominal. Also that the elections were "demonstration elections" designed to prove something to the U.S. public rather than free elections that gave the locals a real choice. Iraq's election was held under a military occupation and in the midst of a counterinsurgency war that was provoking a simultaneous civil war so that, like the Vietnam elections, it was compromised in advance.

George Bush himself pointed out the incompatibility of a military occupation with an honest election. With reference to Lebanon, Bush stated that France as well as the United States, "said loud and clear to Syria, you get your troops and your secret services out of Lebanon so that good democracy has a chance to flourish." The U.S. occupation of Iraq has been far more extensive, intrusive, transformational, and violent than that of Syria in Lebanon, but the patriotic double standard applies here and is unchallenged in the U.S. mainstream. Our troops, secret services, control of finances, and imposed structural and legal changes in the occupied country do not threaten "good democracy." This is strictly a triumph of ideology and state-supportive propaganda.

The ease with which the democracy objective has been institutionalized as the Bush goal in Iraq is truly striking. My favorite illustration is Michael Ignatieff's lengthy article "Who Are Americans To Think That Freedom is Theirs To Spread?" in the *New York Times Magazine* of June 26, 2005. In this article, Ignatieff lauds Bush for putting his presidency on the line in the interest of liberation/democracy ("risked his presidency on the premise that Jefferson might be right"). Ignatieff is on target in saying that Bush risked his presidency in his invasion and subsequent lengthy pursuit of some kind of victory in Iraq, but it is obvious that he did this for reasons other than democracy promotion—such as power projection, control of oil, helping Israel, the pleasure of beating up a virtually disarmed state. Furthermore, after

8 Z MAGAZINE FEBRUARY 2007

Commentary

getting into the quagmire. Bush may have really put his presidency on the line because of a vain, weak incompetent's unwillingness to admit a mistake and accept a defeat.

How does Ignatieff know that Bush's motive was simply the love of democracy? He does not present one fact or argument in support of the alleged democracy objective beyond Bush's proclamation that this is so. There is admittedly a "gap between his words and...performance" and "the democratic turn in American foreign policy has been recent." No structural or any other analysis with content is offered to supplement Bush's word, but Ignatieff is convinced. This is news analysis worthy of *Pravda* at its worst, but it is put forward in the *New York Times*, and by a person who had been selected by the editors as a magazine "regular" and frequent contributor to the opinion page (Ignatieff's byline has appeared in the *New York Times* 33 times since 1988, including 9 book reviews, 6 op-ed columns, and 18 magazine articles, according to a Nexus database search).

Another important liberal spokesperson for the notion that Bush was pursuing democracy has been George Packer, who like Ignatieff writes often for the *New York Times*, is a regular in the *New Yorker* and published a book on Iraq policy in 2005, *The Assassins' Gate: America in Iraq*. Like Ignatieff, Packer rests his case exclusively on Bush's word: "No one should doubt that he and his surviving senior advisers believe in what they call the 'forward strategy of freedom,' even if they've had to talk themselves into it.... Bush wants democratization to be his legacy. So when his critics, here and abroad, claim that his rhetoric merely provides cynical cover for an American power grab, they misjudge his sincerity and tend to sound like defenders of the status quo" (*New Yorker*, January 7, 2005). Given that he doesn't offer an iota of evidence for this claim or tell us how he measures "sincerity" or stop to analyze what Bush might mean by "democracy" and what kind might satisfy his new dedication, Packer tends to sound like a gullible apologist and willing executioner for "an American power grab."

Like Ignatieff, Packer doesn't discuss any structural factors or anything else affecting U.S. foreign policy and he is even more obscurantist that Ignatieff, who at least mentions that historically the United States has often supported tyrannies and that the turn to "democracy promotion" has been recent—Packer ignores both the power structure and history. He repeatedly asserts that this is a "war of ideas," with freedom versus tyranny the issue, again without the slightest attempt to examine whether material interests might be the driving force with ideas providing the cover. He never tries to explain why the war of ideas doesn't extend to policy toward Saudi Arabia, Kuwait, Egypt, Pakistan, Turkmenistan, Uzbekistan, and Israel, and why with ideas so decisive these countries can be exempted from democracy promotion, while "democracy" is aggressively promoted in Iraq and the Ukraine. It's odd that Bush should literally invade Iraq and threaten to invade Iran to "promote democracy," but in cases like Saudi Arabia, Kuwait, and Egypt not only doesn't he invade, but he actually provides economic aid and/or military protection to undemocratic regimes.

There is also the question of reconciliation of democracy promotion abroad with Bush's steady erosion of democracy at home. In his book *The Fight Is For Democracy* Packer acknowledges that under increasing business domination and pressure democracy is "atrophying" in the United States itself, but he fails to address the problem of consistency and the challenge this atrophying poses to the sincere and passionate desire of Bush to promote democracy abroad. Could his desired legacy be democracy abroad and authoritarianism at home?

As regards Iraq, what if the Iraqi people reject us and, in fact, want us out badly enough to develop a formidable resistance to the occupation? Packer never addresses this question directly, but the whole tone of his work suggests that it is acceptable to impose a regime on a

Z MAGAZINE FEBRUARY 2007 9

Z Magazine

good design can contribute to meaning. They deny, by virtue of their stagnant design, that design can convey a message of strength and growth. Their resistance to accepting design as a valuable tool in their progressive mission suggests that political magazines are in essence conservative: that is, resistant to progress and resistant to the idea that form should be taken seriously. If the magazine merely preaches to its choir, then its mission is not so much a liberal one as a tribal one. It devolves into an insular community newsletter, defying the very principles—expansive tolerance and respect for all individuals in this country—it purports to espouse. The whole idea of a liberal magazine in this context becomes frustratingly paradoxical—the sober, timid, dense, inflexible design turns off readers who share their ideals—not because these readers are young, but because they're tech savvy, design literate, and ad aware. Even readers of political magazines can stand in front of a newstand and see the stark differences for themselves.

Readers deserve to be challenged, not tasked with "deja view." Of course, some people only trust the familiar. Perhaps a conservative resistance to change is an expression of the American style of governance, the balance of powers keeping political change behind the curve of culture. The job of the liberal magazine may be to mark a symbolic place, to mimic a community without asking its readers to incur the cost of participating in one.

But liberal design could yet invigorate a liberal magazine. Directed evolution, rather than stagnation or revolution, could shape the magazine's identity over time, like a personality or a government, working for political change while grudgingly admitting to a change in themselves. Maybe I've composed a mission statement for a magazine that doesn't yet exist. In the meantime, liberal political magazines champion conservatism by design.

In Defense of Shoppers

23

MARGARET LITTMAN

For more than two years I've written the weekly "10 Things To Do This Weekend" column for the Web site for *Crain's Chicago Business*. Each item starts off with a verb, emphasizing the "do" part of the thing. I try to mix it up, highlighting all the active things one can do in Chicago, from canoeing down the Chicago River to rollerblading along Lake Michigan. As much as I strive for diversity, there's one verb that shows up week after week, regardless of season: "Shop."

While other countries (France and Italy come to mind) are known for being shoppers' paradises, only in America does shopping qualify as a sport, a verb, a pastime that requires loads of how-to advice. Traditional fashion and shelter magazines are aspirational, often showing goods that aren't affordable, or even available, to the general public. Women's magazines and others, like the celeb-obsessed *InStyle*, offer page after page of things that real people can buy, wear, and integrate into their homes.

Such advice cannot be provided by short mentions in entertainment columns like my "10 Things" text. Enter the shopping magazine, the how-to guide for those who are idea-challenged when it comes to where to find the best handbags, home decor, and chocolate-dipped honeycomb.

When *Lucky* magazine arrived on newsstands and in mailboxes in late 2000, there was much hand-wringing. Some felt this Condé Nast publication resembled a catalog more than a magazine—hence the snide moniker "magalog"—with high production values and a wealth of options. Not to mention little sticky notes enclosed so that you could flag all those things that suddenly became your heart's desire because you saw them in the glossy pages. Wasn't this just a yuppie version of the boatload of catalogs most women receive in their mailboxes each year?

No, this little magazine (not so little, in fact, with 1,005 pages of advertising in 2002, a 37 percent increase over its first year, according to *Advertising Age*) didn't look like traditional journalism: There were no narrative features, and sidebars and boxes were designed to look like notes one would write to oneself, such as a thumbtack holding up fashion favorites of painter Jenna Gribbon. Photo captions took on an above-average importance, with more details on the goods depicted, as well as how much they cost and where they can be found. Until *Lucky*, most magazines relegated such details to a back page, littered with small type. But like shopping itself, reading a shopper is an inherently interactive experience. The pages invite readers to explore the nooks and crannies of one choc-a-bloc layout after another or to rip color chips off the pages to accompany them on a buying expedition.

Lucky unleashed a slew of competitors, as well as additional creative gift guides and shopping sections in more traditional magazines, including *Newsweek*. Other *Lucky* spawn included the now-defunct short-lived *Cargo*, Condé Nast's answer to a *Lucky* for men, and Hearst's *Shop, Etc.*

As a journalist with a master's degree specifically in magazines, I was conflicted. Nowhere in the pages of *Lucky* were the eight-thousand-word opinion pieces we were taught to write but had few places to sell. And I'm not much of a consumer for consumption's sake. (My Visa credit card is wrapped with a list of eight questions from the folks behind Buy Nothing Day.) But as I started to look deeper, I saw that these magazines met many of the criteria of a "good" magazine. They had a cohesive voice that was easily discernible from that of their competitors. They answered questions their readers have that are not answered elsewhere, such as how to set up a guest room if you're really hesitant to have folks share your living quarters. And, really, how were their pages of editorial designed to complement said advertising different from those in the women's magazines? As many as 80 percent of brides say they choose their wedding gown based on a picture in a magazine. It's hard even for a professional to discern when those pictures are advertising and when they're editorial. Sure, the focus was on shorter blocks of copy, but was that a significant difference from *Real Simple*, *InStyle*, or even *Maxim*? Women's magazines like *Glamour* mastered the "one dress, four ways to wear it" story long before *Lucky*.

Despite the on-paper legitimacy, I still felt guilty about one of my favorite new magazines, *Domino*, the shopping magazine for those who crave wallpaper more than wallets and chandeliers more than shoes. I loved

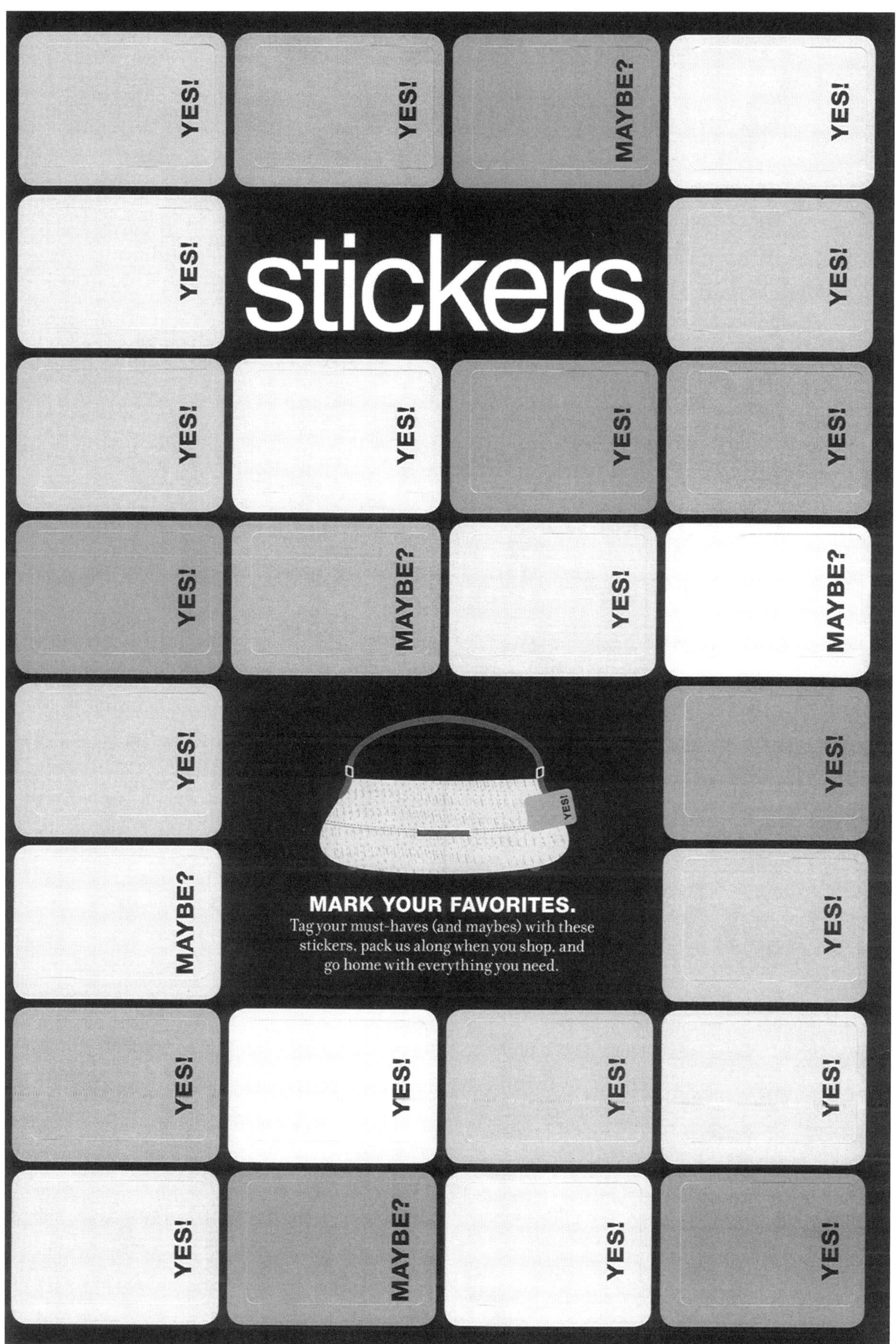
YES!
YES!
MAYBE?
YES!
YES!
stickers
YES!
YES!
YES!
YES!
YES!
YES!
MAYBE?
YES!
MAYBE?
YES!
YES!
YES!
MARK YOUR FAVORITES.
Tag your must-haves (and maybes) with these stickers, pack us along when you shop, and go home with everything you need.
MAYBE?
YES!
YES!
YES!
YES!
YES!
YES!
MAYBE?
YES!
YES!

LUCKY EDITOR'S PICKS
what I want NOW!
"I love how black-and-white florals are playful and sharp all at once."
This slinky cami gathers and drapes in exactly the right places
SILK-BLEND "MINNI" TOP $225, Jill Stuart 212-343-2300
BELTED RAYON-BLEND TOP, $69, BEBE.COM. WOOL-BLEND SKIRT, $59, ANN TAYLOR LOFT, 800-DIAL-ANN FOR LOCATIONS
Meredith Kahn Rollins
executive editor
A gorgeously full shape constructed of the softest silk
SILK TWILL SKIRT $79, WD NY 212-395-9309 FOR STORES
The most relaxed cut—and it's so cute with a big belt
Very astronaut's wife: The funnel neck on this is really striking
COTTON-BLEND JACKET $118, ECI New York. Mark Shale, Chicago 312-440-0720
"WORK" FLATS $245, Delman. Dewey, Venice, CA 310-392-2974
Just a brilliant way to make skinny jeans look properly ladylike
Such a bold and ingeniously substantial shoulder bag
CANVAS HOBO BAG $695, Stella McCartney. Select Nordstrom 800-695-8000
SILK DRESS $450, 3.1 Phillip Lim NET-A-PORTER.COM
SUSAN PITTARD. HAIR: JEN LEONARD FOR ULTRA HAIR SALON. MAKEUP: DANIEL MARTIN FOR LANCÔME AT CA MANAGEMENT. STILL LIFES: LUCKY DIGITAL STUDIO
LUCKY 34
WWW.LUCKYMAG.COM

Lucky

stepping into cluttered, comfortable homes—often tiny New York apartments—in the pages of *Domino* and seeing stuff that I covet. I purchased a wedding gift for a friend thanks to the cover of a summer issue (a limited edition silkscreen poster that reads, "For Like Ever"). I felt simultaneously flattered and hopelessly pedestrian when the color scheme of my office showed up in *Domino*'s palette.

Despite the fact that I write for (and read) more "serious" arts magazines such as *Arts & Antiques*, I cited *Domino*'s article on collecting art multiples as some of the best consumer art writing I had seen all year. Still, I felt like I should hide *my* issues of *Domino* like the journalism porn they are before I had peers over for drinks.

BEAUTY

MEDIUM/OLIVE SKIN

FOR A LUMINOUS/SATIN FINISH | FOR A SEMI-MATTE/MATTE FINISH

	FOR A LUMINOUS/SATIN FINISH		FOR A SEMI-MATTE/MATTE FINISH	
DRY	**Cover Girl Advanced Radiance Age-Defying Liquid Makeup in soft honey, $9.99;** Duane Reade and other drugstores.	**Revlon Age Defying Makeup with Botafirm for Dry Skin in rich tan, $13.99;** Rite Aid and other drugstores.	**Black Opal True Color Cream-to-Powder Foundation SPF 8 in heavenly honey, $9.95;** Longs and other drugstores.	**Giorgio Armani Designer Foundation in shade 9, $65;** Nordstrom, 800-723-2889, or giorgioarmanibeauty.com.
NORMAL/COMBO	**Shiseido Lifting Foundation in natural deep ivory, $40;** Barneys, 888-822-7639, or Nordstrom, 800-723-2889.	**L'Oréal High Intensity Pigments Flawless Liquid Makeup in sepia, $13;** Walgreens and other drugstores.	**Neutrogena Healthy Skin Liquid Makeup in spiced almond, $11.75;** CVS and other drugstores or ulta.com.	**Nars Balance Foundation in sedona, $40;** Barneys, 888-822-7639, or narscosmetics.com.
OILY	**Flirt Act Natural Light and Sheer Foundation in bronze splash, $12;** Kohl's, 866-887-8884, or kohls.com.	**Napoleon Perdis Minimal Makeup in look 4, $40;** Saks, 877-551-7257, or napoleonperdis.com.	**Make Up For Ever Mat Velvet Oil-Free Foundation SPF 20 in no. 3, $37;** Make Up For Ever, 877-757-5175, or sephora.com.	**Estée Lauder Double Wear Stay-in-Place Makeup SPF 10 in bronze, $32.50;** Saks, 877-551-7257, or esteelauder.com.

COOL / WARM

SHOPPING KEY: NEW ITEM · THE LINE'S MOST POPULAR SHADE FOR MEDIUM/OLIVE SKIN · MAKEUP ARTIST FAVORITE · STAFF FAVORITE

! Base with benefits: 75% of women look for foundation that won't cause breakouts, and 44% want formulas with anti-aging properties.*

WHO REALLY NEEDS...A FOUNDATION BRUSH?

Women using lightweight liquid or loose-powder formulas. For the former, a nylon-bristled brush—we like **Jane Iredale Foundation Brush, $35.80** (*near right;* 800-762-1132 or janeiredaledirect.com)—will best spread the liquid. Natural-hair brushes, such as **Chanel #16 Foundation Brush, $36** (*far right;* Saks, 877-551-7257, or chanel.com), are better at evenly distributing loose powders, makeup artist Maulawizada says. As for other tools, he recommends sponges for highly pigmented foundations (thicker liquids, matte-coverage mousses and sticks), and suggests dampening the sponge before working foundation into it and then pressing it into skin. Fingers are fine with tinted moisturizers and sticks: Place a dot of color on each cheek and blend outward, applying to the T-zone last to keep it as sheer as possible.

Shop, Etc.

My hidden stash of *Dominos* (along with *ReadyMade* and my *Rejuvenation* catalogs) started taunting me when I was asked to edit 2006 *Chicago Shops*, *Chicago* magazine's annual shopping magazine. Could I helm a publication in a genre about which I had been known to be embarrassed? I had written for the magazine in the past, but didn't think about how the pieces I wrote fit into the larger whole. As the editor, I realized that while what *Shops* was doing may look like a listing of goods that competed only with a classified section, what we were doing was creating the ultimate service magazine. We helped people know where to go to find what they need and whether or not they'll be able to park and pay with a credit card when they get there.

Readers wanted to know that there were quirky shoe boutiques and tea houses on the South Side. I took pride in hiring writers to search out what was unique about those neighborhoods, so that locals could have options other than those touted in the tourist and travel magazines. While those who shop as sport may already know every place in town that carries Skip Hop diaper bags, those who are childless and need the "it" baby gift of the month don't. And they don't want to spend hours searching like a recreational shopper. A quick flip through a shopping magazine tells them where to go. Why does that seem less legitimate than the travel magazine that recommends a spa in Barcelona or a women's magazine that offers five tips for reducing the risk of gum disease?

These magazines are different than the "we think these shoes are pretty, buy them" attitude, which is what everyone—including myself—assumed a shopping magazine would be. Instead, they offer an egalitarian approach to shopping. A recent issue of *Lucky* featured a $1,595 Michael Kors dress just a few pages away from a $25 number from Forever 21. Few traditional fashion mags offer such diversity.

In addition, the shopping magazines are designed to be easily cross-referenced, with easy-to-find things (with or without the sticky tabs). They have an empowering "you can do this" vibe, whether it refers to overhauling a wardrobe or repainting a bedroom. Because they have so many pages to fill and are trying to highlight looks not on the pages of other mags, the shop-

home

Foods & Gifts

Consuming Pleasures

The answer to the unique gift question? Edibles
by Judy Sutton Taylor

FOOD MAKES A GREAT GIFT FOR JUST ABOUT ANY OCCASION— particularly if the recipient's willing to share. New homes, new babies, or just because you're feeling generous—no matter what's happening, everyone's gotta eat, right? And with homegrown purveyors of world-class cuisine and our own celebrity chefs, Chicago's a perfect place to indulge culinary cravings.

FOR THE HEDONIST Dazzle even the most finicky foodies with **Pastoral**'s lavish "Connoisseur" basket, overspilling with indulgences, including five-year aged Dutch gouda, Neal's Yard Montgomery's cheddar, Coach Farm triple-cream goat cheese, Basque Ossau-Iraty cheese, roasted figs, Marcona almonds, pecorino-stuffed sundried tomato rolls, a pound of Molinari salametti, Australian Yarra Valley crackers, and a bottle of rare Paso Robles's 2003 Garretson Mourvedre wine. For dessert, they've added Coco Rouge chocolate truffles and a bottle of 2002 Peter Lehmann Botrytis Semillon, plus—for your reading as well as eating pleasure—a copy of *Zingerman's Guide to Good Eating*. $250 at Pastoral, 2945 N. Broadway, 773-472-4781, www.pastoralartisan.com.

FOR THE SERIOUS SWEET TOOTH **Translucent Chocolates**'s tier of eye candy features individual boxes of chocolate-covered apricots, praline pecans mixed with cashews, English toffee caramel balls, white dark chocolate-covered pistachios mixed with milk chocolate toffee pistachios, metallic blue-coated dark chocolate-covered almonds, and white chocolate-covered sunflower seeds with metallic silver- and gold-coated almonds. $88 at Fly Bird, 719 Lake St., Oak Park, 708-383-3330; www.fly-bird.net.

FOR HOUSEWARMINGS New pantries need the Ethnic Chicago Deluxe Gift Box holding ten spice blends representing Chicago neighborhoods, from Back of the Yards Garlic Pepper Butchers' Rub to Lake Shore Drive Seasoning. $39.95 at **The Spice House,** 1512 N. Wells St., 312-274-0378; or 1941 Central St., Evanston, 847-328-3711; www.thespicehouse.com.

FOR HEALTHY TYPES **Seedling Fruit**'s sampler gift contains a rotating bounty of seasonal and diet-minded goodies, usually including two jars of fruit preserves, four varieties of dried fruit, four packages of chocolate-covered dried fruit, and a handy OXO kitchen tool. $45 at Seedling Fruit, 6717 111th Ave., South Haven, Michigan. www.seedlingfruit.com.

FOR NEW PARENTS Weary new moms and dads will get sustenance from baker Siobhan Straka's goodies, which can come stylishly grouped in an antique bowl. Expect three one-pound bags of her housemade granola, a pound of coffee, P.B. Loco peanut butter, Funky Chunky pretzels, a six-pack of either biscotti or shortbread, three bars or brownies, one rattle-shaped shortbread cookie and—just to show you're thinking of everyone—a bag of homemade dog treats. $130 at **Grazer's Gourmet,** 5333 N. Lincoln Ave., 773-561-5600; www.justgraze.com.

36 CHICAGO SHOPS 2006

2006 CHICAGO SHOPS 37

Chicago Shops

pers give young fashion designers a chance—other than scoring a slot on *Project Runway*—to show their stuff to a national audience.

Even as the shoppers have evolved—after two years on the stands, *Lucky* began showing celebs on its covers instead of everyday consumers—they remain devoted to the shopping credo of retailer Marshall Field: "Give the Lady What She Wants."

With attention spans getting ever shorter and savings rates continuing to decline, what the lady wants is a magazine like *Lucky*. The format may change—shopping podcasts and content delivered to your cell phone based on your proximity to a store is just around the corner. But advice about shopping, whether it is *Field and Stream* offering tips on the best hunting and fishing equipment or *Lucky* helping you find an outfit to wear should you want to get lucky, is here to stay.

After all, Americans shop, therefore, we are.

Bored at 40,000 Feet

24

GREG LINDSAY

I SPENT SEPTEMBER LITERALLY LIVING IN AIRPORTS. I was on assignment in "Airworld"—the limbo on the far side of the metal detectors—and during what was essentially a three-week layover, I toe-touched a dozen cities from Los Angeles to Singapore (the long way around), flew twenty-six thousand miles, and once spent eighteen consecutive hours in the air. But it wasn't until a few weeks ago, after I had missed my American Airlines flight to San Francisco and had to fly standby in a middle seat, with no live satellite television, no movies, and definitely no Wi-Fi to keep me occupied, that I bothered to crack the spine on an in-flight magazine.

It wasn't that I had failed to notice them during my three weeks in the air. On the contrary, I had dutifully swiped copies from every airline and schlepped them around the world—United's *Hemispheres*, *Delta Sky*, *American Way*, Southwest's *Spirit*, Frontier's *Wild Blue Yonder*, British Airways' *High Life*, and even Singapore Airlines' *Silver Kris*.

Your standard-issue in-flight magazine is an exercise in licensing. Editing, production, and ad sales are farmed out by the airlines to one of a handful of custom publishers who edit, produce, and sell ads for the magazines in exchange for the lion's share of the revenues. In exchange, the airlines receive a royalty fee and a cut of the profits. It's a mutually beneficial relationship that flies in the face of the airline industry's otherwise bleak financial picture. Pace Communications, for example, is solidly profitable even though two of its largest clients—United and Delta—are in Chapter 11, while a third (U.S. Airways) only recently emerged. American Airlines, meanwhile, is one of the few that produces its own magazines in-house. Its four-title stable, which includes *American Way*, *Spirit*, and separate first-class and Spanish-language titles, has been more steadily profitable since 9/11 than the airline itself.

In an effort to get the word out that his own magazines were flying high, even if United and Delta weren't, Pace's chief marketing and sales officer Craig Waller tracked me down. "We have the very unique distinction of being the publisher for three bankrupt airlines," he joked at the time. "We're a very underappreciated sector of the media. When you're in Europe, you'll see that the magazines there are much more upscale. There's the same commitment to editorial excellence here, but if you talk to anyone who doesn't travel, or a twenty-four-year-old media planner, there's nothing to read. We had a meeting with someone at [the advertising agency] Mindshare not long ago, and she was surprised to learn we weren't just recycling editorial from other magazines. The reality is, we make a huge effort." As proof, he offered the example of *Delta Sky*, which relaunched this fall with a fresh look by Robert Priest (the David Childs of magazine design) and a splashy party at MoMA that would have made any Condé Nast publisher proud.

Speaking of Condé, the median household income of Pace's readership is $106,731 according to MRI, a touch higher than *Condé Nast Traveler*'s $101,102, the highest of any mainstream magazine. Add that stat to Pace's combined readership of seven million per month (a figure calculated with the help of the dark art of pass around) and it's no wonder that ad pages in *Hemispheres*, *Attaché*, and *Sky* were up 30.8 percent, 24 percent, and 12.2 percent, respectively, through October 2005. *American Way*'s ad pages have risen 17.7 percent and Southwest's *Spirit*'s 26.8 percent. And these gains are on top of double-digit percentage increases last year.

And yet, despite that resolutely rosy outlook—*the planes are full, the passengers are rich, and we're everywhere*—my gut feeling is the opposite after my time in "Airworld." Perusing these magazines at home only confirmed it: They're on the brink of a long fall back into irrelevance and possible extinction if they don't stop coasting and overhaul themselves right now.

Easy to Ignore

How did I manage to avoid them altogether for three weeks? It wasn't hard when I had twenty-four channels of live satellite TV in my seatback on both JetBlue and Song, plus even more elaborate diversions when flying abroad—an actual bar in Virgin's Upper Class, or the Mandarin Chinese language instruction available through Singapore Airlines' entertainment system. I never accepted Frontier's invitation to sample its own in-flight TV, nor did I have the opportunity to Web surf with Lufthansa's and SAS's on-board Wi-Fi. And when the FAA inevitably relaxes rules on cell phone use during flight, it may become impossible to even concentrate on a magazine.

The fracturing of media consciousness that took decades down on the ground will happen in the air within another five to ten years. That should be enough time for advertisers seeking the road-warrior demographic to investigate the airlines' and airports' own efforts to steal a slice of the advertising pie. Those include everything from tray-table ads on U.S. Airways flights (courtesy of Sky Media) to competing magazines like *Washington Flyer*, a city title sponsored by the airport authority of Washington, D.C. for travelers passing through the city's Ronald Reagan and Dulles airports.

Collectively they suffer from the same genetic deficiency that killed a generation of giant-circulation, general-interest titles like *Life* and that afflicts *Reader's Digest* and *TV Guide* today, which is to say that they are sans edge in an era that prizes knowingness and snarkiness above all.

A quick tour of the latest issues produces the following: *American Way*'s cover subject, B-lister actress Mariska Hargitay, walks the interviewer through her very favorite places in Manhattan as part of the magazine's usual conceit (although with different cities each time). What did she choose? You know . . . Nobu. Babbo. The SoHo Grand. Barneys. The usual.

Over at *Hemispheres*, there's a pair of features ripped straight from the headlines of *Food & Wine*—a lament against Robert Parker, the emperor of wine, and an anointing of America's best new chefs. At *Attaché*, there's an excursion to the Yucatan, a golf column, and a shorter piece on great pizza. And in *Delta Sky*—which now looks gorgeous—there are stories on Atlanta's up-and-coming neighborhoods, writing children's books, grizzly bears, margarita recipes . . . and about a million other disconnected pieces strung together in the name of general interest.

The problem with these stories and their presence in the mix isn't that they are bad, but that they are *safe*. They're the same stories on sale at the airport's newsstand, and in most cases, they suffer by comparison. I blame the clients—the airlines—for this, because if there's one thing they're obsessed with, it's safety. But it's up to the publishers to give their readers—the passengers—a better reason to read their magazine than simply being there.

Experiment, Experiment, Experiment

You may compete with satellite TV, but you're not being sold on newsstands and you don't need celebrities on the cover. My favorite in-flight magazine is *Carlos*, created for Virgin Atlantic's Upper Class passengers by the British custom publisher John Brown Citrus Publishing. *Carlos* is more of a quarterly curio than a typical magazine with an FOB (front of the book), feature well, and back of the book.

It's pamphlet sized, printed between cardboard covers, and illustrated entirely with pencil drawings, and the subject matter matters only to the media-savvy "jetrosexuals" that populate Upper Class (at least in Virgin's imagination.) One of the copies I begged Virgin for two years ago had an illustrated Kate Moss on the cover and contained an extended meditation on the personal style that launched a thousand knockoffs at Topshop and H&M. Other features in that issue included a piece on digital music piracy and a vintage Tom Wolfe profile of Phil Spector from the sixties. *Carlos* neither looks nor reads like any magazine you'd find in a seatback or on a newsstand, which is how it manages to distract its media-savvy audience from the on-board bar just long enough to peek at the full-color inserts for Marc Jacobs, Paul Smith, and Mulberry.

The general rules of magazine making don't necessarily apply at forty thousand feet. If we're starting from the assumption that these educated, affluent readers are trapped in aluminum tubes with hours at their disposal, why not make in-flight magazines the final preserve for long-form journalism, publishing the same sort of megafeatures as the *New York Times Magazine*'s recent retelling of last December's tsunami?

Considering the lower cost structures and surging profits, there should be plenty of cash on hand to lure A-list writers into the magazines, thus raising their profiles (by republishing these stories on their Web sites) and inspiring every other freelancer out there to bring their A-games when fulfilling assignments. If there's one thing that's hurt the reputation of in-flight magazines, it's the perception that no one is reading them, or at least no one the writers know. (I had the same feeling when—full disclosure—I wrote a piece for another one of John Brown's magazines earlier this year.)

Or why not try the reverse—a magazine filled with nothing but news readers can use, with the centerpieces being stories in which everything—airfare, hotel, skiing lessons, and so forth—is bookable at a click on the magazine's Web site. It's published by an airline, after all. Where's the integration? Where's the added value? Give me something more than what I can find on the newsstand . . . or on TV.

Remember the Ladies

Women read these magazines, too. The advertising should reflect that. The road warrior cliché—the middle-aged guy's guy predisposed toward Dockers,

Samsonite, whiskey, and a fine cigar—is true . . . up to a point. The audience research firm Arbitron released a study last year confirming that the seventeen million or so frequent flyers in America are three times more likely to make $100,000 a year than the general population, that they skew about 60-40 male, and that they comprise 60 percent of all advertising impressions in "Airworld."

So it should be no surprise that ad sales staffs have locked in on this demographic, to the annoyance of the seven million women plying their trades in the sky. I met up with one such road warrior, Jennifer Moody, at O'Hare. When she isn't jetting all over the country as cofounder of her own consulting business, she's the moderator of the "Women Travelers" forum on the online frequent-flyer community FlyerTalk. Over drinks at the Red Carpet Club, Moody expressed her irritation at the publishers' obsession.

She once discovered a job posting on American Airlines' site for an editor at *American Way*. The posting described the magazine's readers as "upper-middle-class affluent *males* in their forties," she said. "Apparently they've made some determination that these are their readers. Not that I even flip through it. It gets boring looking at ads for matchmaking services, cigars, and condos in Miami."

She forgot to mention the steakhouse chains, mail-order dress shirts, and gadgets of every persuasion. But she's right to be annoyed, and—are you listening, publishers?—*she owns her own business*. Isn't she someone worth pursuing? The ads say just as much about your magazine as the editorial does.

To his credit, Pace's Craig Waller already seems to get all of this. He pitched JetBlue on a magazine and was shown the writing on the wall when the airline turned him down. He knows *Carlos* well, having published magazines for BA, Virgin Express, and another low-fare carrier during his publishing career in the U.K. And he's doing his best to win more upscale advertisers for his titles.

"Why is it," he asks rhetorically, "if we have the readers with the highest incomes out there, that we have a bunch of direct-response ads in the magazine? We're only just embarking on a concerted campaign to fix that now." He added, "I think we need to be innovative, and I don't think this generation is print adverse. In-flight Wi-Fi is going to be held back by the costs, and print, for the time being, is the delivery vehicle of choice."

But for how much longer? You'll know the answer yourself the next time you fly.

SECTION 8

Structure and Subject

A lot of what's involved in redesigning a magazine is strategic—finding a visual voice to match the editorial voice. But, in another sense, a magazine is very much a physical object, made of specific sections—pieces and parts that must function together as surely as gears in a machine. Each of the pieces has to do its job, and the whole has to work together.

Every design, every budget, every editorial approach, every topic imposes limitations and possibilities on the form the magazine's pages will ultimately take. When those boundaries are not respected, problems arise. Perhaps the designer imagined an art-intensive format for a low-budget magazine and the pages end up looking sparse. Perhaps editorial staffers are unable to keep themselves to intended word lengths and text is spilling out of its space. Perhaps the organization of pages suffers because there are no rules for the placement of advertising, or perhaps there simply aren't enough ads. The shelves are full of publications that unwittingly exhibit a disconnect between the magazine as it was imagined and the magazine as it exists on a month-to-month basis.

The mechanics of editorial design, what to do when you lift the hood and start fiddling with the engine, is perhaps the most time-consuming part of magazine redesign—time spent away from colleagues at the sketch pad or computer. Its importance should not be forgotten, as the brand and voice of the publication is manifest in the physical and visual decisions the designer makes.

Briefs

25

JANDOS ROTHSTEIN

FOR MANY READERS, THE HEART OF A MAGAZINE is not in the middle—the well, filled with long features—it's at the edges. Busy readers are drawn to the FOB (front of the book), which typically contains shorter items such as columns, reviews, letters pages, and one or more sections of brief items, as well as more utilitarian material—the table of contents and masthead.

The most important part of the FOB is unquestionably the "briefs"—essentially a little newspaper within a magazine. Briefs pages often have a newspapery layout, with multiple unrelated items on each page, but to different effect. Unlike broadsheet newspaper pages, which can hold several in-depth articles (or, in the case of a section front, the beginnings of multiple stories that jump to later pages), magazine briefs pages carry text in demitasse portions. These pages are most suited toward light, breezy, or even humorous articles. They are loved because they are grazable, offering a lot of information (or yuks) in quick-reading spoonfuls, and because, despite the diminutive size of the text and pictures, they are highly visual.

Most magazines have a second section of short items in the back of the book (BOB), following the feature well, although others have eliminated the BOB (traditionally more briefs, columns, and reviews), choosing instead to front-load shorter items.

The explosion in briefs sections has occurred over the past fifteen years. The so-called lad magazines that have come to prominence in that time—*Maxim*, *FHM*, and so forth—are, in fact, little more than a long, snarky briefs section with a few naughty photos added for good measure. But nearly every magazine has seen its briefs section grow in size, the number of items per page increase, the amount of art in the briefs section increase, and the average word count per item decrease. These changes have been across the board. Issues-oriented *Mother Jones* had four pages of briefs in 1982, five in 1992, and seven in 2006. *Wired* had eighteen pages of briefs in 1997 and twenty-nine in 2006.

Briefs sections tend to be more time-consuming to edit and design than feature stories. Multiple items require a boatload of ideas, reporting, and fact-checking to fill. Most briefs sections impose strict word lengths (articles are rarely jumped), so tight and careful editing is essential. They can be a frustrating puzzle just to fit together, but designers are required to look beyond the mechanical challenges and find ways to offer graphic variety and visual surprises over what can be thirty pages or more of itsy items.

Briefs pages also require more rounds of page revisions than features, both because changes to one piece may affect other elements on the page and because many of these sections rely on alternative story forms, or ASFs (see chapter 29)—word tables, maps, timelines, stand-alone pull quotes, and charts. ASFs often depend on surprising juxtapositions and the visualization of nonspatial relationships. To pull off, they require substantial production time—particularly in cases where data serve as art on the page—and careful editing for clarity and accuracy.

Before Beginning

Like all magazine design structures, briefs pages emerge from the editorial goals for the section being developed. The designer should, at a minimum, be able to answer the following questions before undertaking a new design for a briefs section. The tricky part, particularly at magazines with fewer resources, is making sure the answers are realistic. A redesign is an aspirational exercise in addition to a practical one. Briefs are a particular danger spot—editors are likely to aspire to more than they can realistically achieve in production.

Is the primary purpose of the briefs section to entertain or inform?

All magazines aspire to do both, but knowing which is most important helps determine the visual tone the section will have and how important words and pictures will each be. Newsy sections like *Mother Jones*'s tend to have longer pieces; entertaining sections like *Wired*'s are more visual and graphic.

How long will articles be allowed to run? Will the section have to accommodate jumps?

Jumps are often deadly on news pages—they can lead to gray zones and are out of sync with the goal of creating a quick read. However, some publications treat their news section as a dumping ground for articles too short or trivial to run elsewhere. These publications require a design with lots of flexibility.

Will there be regular branded items?

Most briefs pages, even if they have relatively long articles, also accommodate shorter, branded items. *Wired* does "Jargon Watch," which lists and defines new slang; *Time* does "Verbatim," a collection of quotes, and "Numbers," a look at the week's news through statistics. These regular features can be the designer's friend; they help give pages within the news section a distinct personality. Pages can be built around these "destination features" if they are so planned from the beginning, but branded items should not be tacked on as an afterthought. Ideally, they should always appear on the same page within briefs.

Does the real text support stated editorial objectives?

It's important to design a prototype news section with real text and art that is at least a fair representation of what the finished section will contain. Some publications hope to achieve an exciting, layered, information-rich look but do not have the resources to support the amount of reporting required to achieve it. A frank evaluation of what is editorially possible before the section goes "live" is in everyone's best interest. This is often a time when the designer has to show serious backbone—who knows, they may even be thanked for it later.

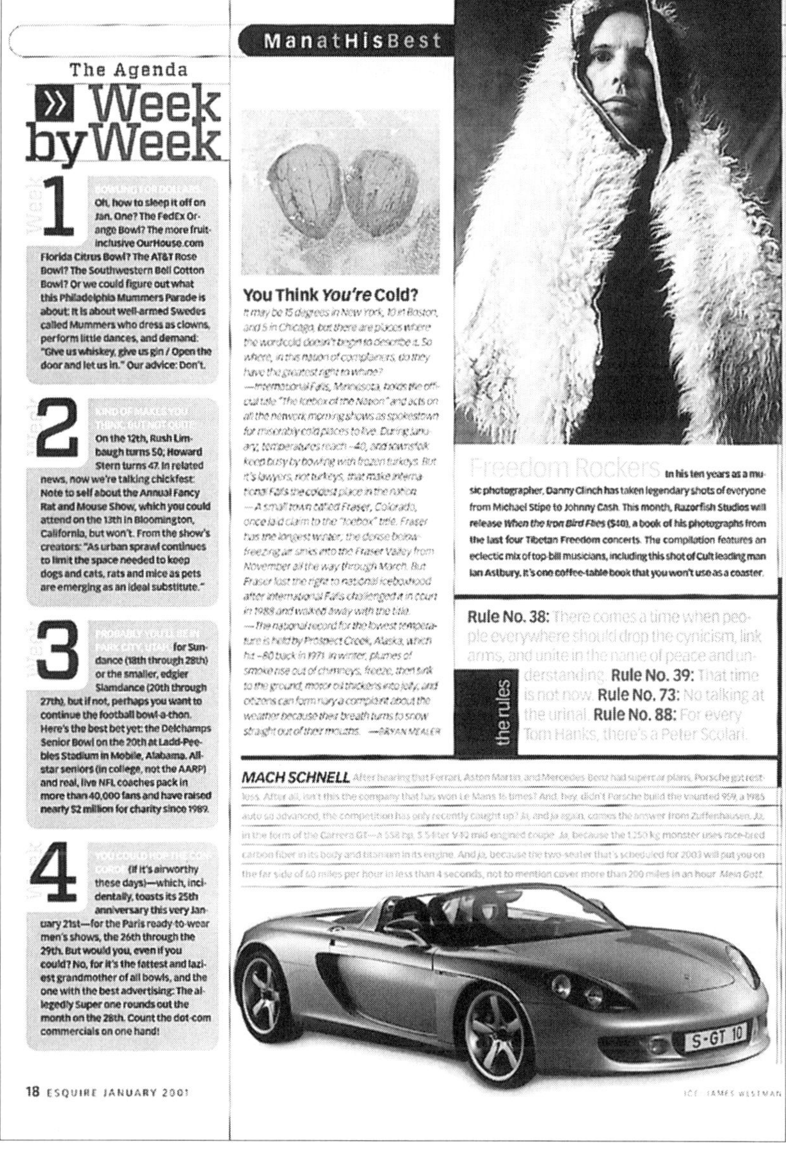

The Agenda

» Week by Week

Week 1

Oh, how to sleep it off on Jan. One? The FedEx Orange Bowl? The more fruit-inclusive OurHouse.com Florida Citrus Bowl? The AT&T Rose Bowl? The Southwestern Bell Cotton Bowl? Or we could figure out what this Philadelphia Mummers Parade is about: It is about well-armed Swedes called Mummers who dress as clowns, perform little dances, and demand: "Give us whiskey, give us gin / Open the door and let us in." Our advice: Don't.

Week 2

On the 12th, Rush Limbaugh turns 50; Howard Stern turns 47. In related news, now we're talking chickfest: Note to self about the Annual Fancy Rat and Mouse Show, which you could attend on the 13th in Bloomington, California, but won't. From the show's creators: "As urban sprawl continues to limit the space needed to keep dogs and cats, rats and mice as pets are emerging as an ideal substitute."

Week 3

for Sundance (18th through 28th) or the smaller, edgier Slamdance (20th through 27th), but if not, perhaps you want to continue the football bowl-a-thon. Here's the best bet yet: the Delchamps Senior Bowl on the 20th at Ladd-Peebles Stadium in Mobile, Alabama. All-star seniors (in college, not the AARP) and real, live NFL coaches pack in more than 40,000 fans and have raised nearly $2 million for charity since 1989.

Week 4

(if it's airworthy these days)—which, incidentally, toasts its 25th anniversary this very January 21st—for the Paris ready-to-wear men's shows, the 26th through the 29th. But would you, even if you could? No, for it's the fattest and laziest grandmother of all bowls, and the one with the best advertising: The allegedly Super one rounds out the month on the 28th. Count the dot-com commercials on one hand!

18 ESQUIRE JANUARY 2001

ManatHisBest

You Think *You're* Cold?

It may be 15 degrees in New York, 10 in Boston, and 5 in Chicago, but there are places where the word cold doesn't begin to describe it. So where, in this nation of complainers, do they have the greatest right to whine?

—International Falls, Minnesota, holds the official title "The Icebox of the Nation" and acts on all the network morning shows as spokestown for miserably cold places to live. During January, temperatures reach −40, and townsfolk keep busy by bowling with frozen turkeys. But it's lawyers, not turkeys, that make International Falls the coldest place in the nation.

—A small town called Fraser, Colorado, once laid claim to the "Icebox" title. Fraser has the longest winter; the dense below-freezing air sinks into the Fraser Valley from November all the way through March. But Fraser lost the right to national iceboxhood after International Falls challenged it in court in 1988 and walked away with the title.

—The national record for the lowest temperature is held by Prospect Creek, Alaska, which hit −80 back in 1971. In winter, plumes of smoke rise out of chimneys, freeze, then sink to the ground, motor oil thickens into jelly, and citizens can form nary a complaint about the weather because their breath turns to snow straight out of their mouths. —BRYAN MEALER

Freedom Rockers In his ten years as a music photographer, Danny Clinch has taken legendary shots of everyone from Michael Stipe to Johnny Cash. This month, Razorfish Studios will release *When the Iron Bird Flies* ($40), a book of his photographs from the last four Tibetan Freedom concerts. The compilation features an eclectic mix of top-bill musicians, including this shot of Cult leading man Ian Astbury. It's one coffee-table book that you won't use as a coaster.

the rules

Rule No. 38: There comes a time when people everywhere should drop the cynicism, link arms, and unite in the name of peace and understanding. **Rule No. 39:** That time is not now. **Rule No. 73:** No talking at the urinal. **Rule No. 88:** For every Tom Hanks, there's a Peter Scolari.

MACH SCHNELL After hearing that Ferrari, Aston Martin, and Mercedes-Benz had supercar plans, Porsche got restless. After all, isn't this the company that has won Le Mans 16 times? And, hey, didn't Porsche build the vaunted 959, a 1985 auto so advanced, the competition has only recently caught up? Ja, and ja again, comes the answer from Zuffenhausen. Ja, in the form of the Carrera GT—a 558 hp, 5.5-liter V-10 mid-engined coupe. Ja, because the 1,250 kg monster uses race-bred carbon fiber in its body and titanium in its engine. And ja, because the two-seater that's scheduled for 2003 will put you on the far side of 60 miles per hour in less than 4 seconds, not to mention cover more than 200 miles in an hour. *Mein Gott.*

S-GT 10

Esquire, *2001*

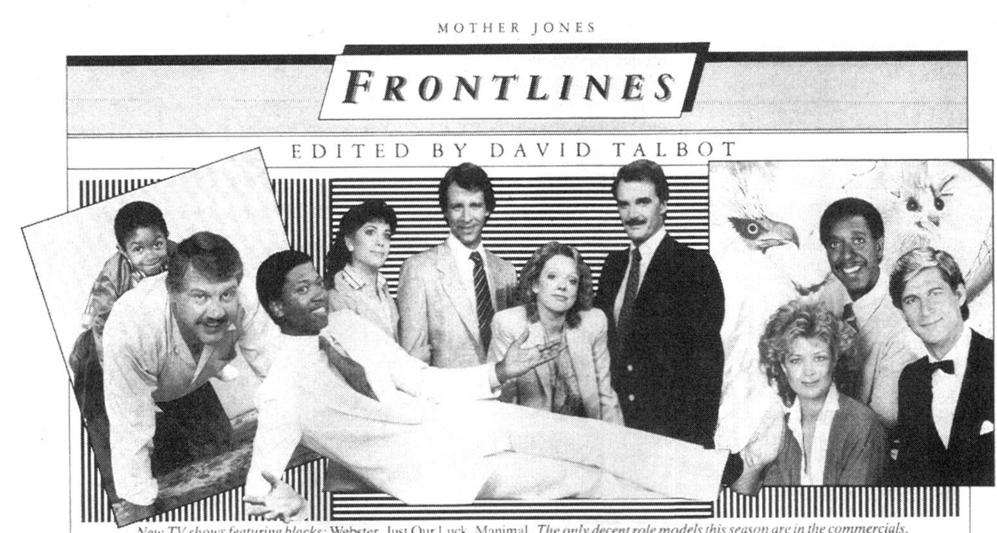

MOTHER JONES

FRONTLINES

EDITED BY DAVID TALBOT

New TV shows featuring blacks: Webster, Just Our Luck, Manimal. *The only decent role models this season are in the commercials.*

From Amos 'n' Andy To Shabu And Mr. T

How long, oh, Lord, how long? Years after everyone thought blacks had been permanently freed to play decent television roles by enlightened producer Norman Lear, network TV has taken several giant steps backward. As in Washington, affirmative action no longer seems operative in Hollywood. A *Mother Jones* survey of the fall TV lineup now sedating millions of Americans—and driving legions of others into the arms of cable—found that of the 200-plus new characters, a mere six are played by black actors. Among the black characters dreamed up by TV-town are a modern-day genie who amiably serves his white master (ABC's *Just Our Luck*) and yet another cuddly little black boy adopted by white parents (ABC's *Webster*).

One reason why the TV industry retains such a daffy and distorted view of black life is that blacks have been unable to break into the ranks of TV writers in sufficient numbers. Half of the new shows with black characters began the fall season without any black writers on staff. When a committee of black writers within the Writers Guild created a fuss, several blacks were given freelance writing assignments—but only one was awarded a staff position.

By any standard, the most repulsive of the new shows has to be *Just Our Luck*, featuring Shabu, the black genie, who conjures up money, vacations and women for his white master. The ABC sitcom has elicited howls of protest from civil rights groups, including the NAACP, which has called for the show's removal. "It's an embarrassing and degrading portrayal of a black male in the '80s," says Willis Edwards, president of the Beverly Hills-Hollywood NAACP. ABC has pitted the show against NBC's *The A Team*, featuring black muscleman Mr. T, in an apparent effort to win over those viewers who prefer their blacks as buffoons.

Meanwhile, far from the Hollywood minstrel show, Rep. Mickey Leland (D.-Texas) was holding hearings on the plight of minorities in the TV industry. "They were held to remind the industry that there are considerations that are going to have to be met before Mickey and others will even talk about [TV industry] deregulation," says Mark Holcomb, Leland's press secretary. "In order to change the situation, we need minorities in front of and behind the camera, and most of all, we need to encourage minority ownership of telecommunications properties."

Television activist Arnold Torres, executive director of the League of United Latin American Citizens, was among those who testified before Leland's subcommittee. Torres made it clear that the situation for President Reagan's favorite minority group was no better than it was for blacks in Hollywood. Among the six new Hispanic TV characters is a baseball team mascot and another who dies in the series' fifth episode. When *Mother Jones* called NBC to find out whether *The Yellow Rose*, a new television series set in West Texas, featured any minority roles, a network spokesperson cheerfully replied, "Sure. Edward Albert plays Quisto, a half-breed—his mother is supposed to be an Indian, I think."

—*Kathryn Olney*

New German Resistance

In Germany, the past cannot be easily erased. It's preserved in the building fragments left standing as unintentional war memorials and it's alive in the urgent voices of disarmament activists. "The American people don't understand the terrible gravity of the Cruise and Pershing missile deployment," says a young West Berlin actor who has temporarily abandoned his career to do full-time peace work. "It's like 1932 all over again: we're on the brink of war. With the new Euromissiles in place, missiles that can reach the Soviet Union in less than ten minutes, it's just a matter of time before a computer error sets off a nuclear holocaust."

Scores of actors, painters, writers and musicians are involved in the West German disarmament movement. Their determined efforts bring to mind an earlier period of intense politicization, when many German artists fought against the rise of fascism. "That generation of artists

—Continued on next page

DECEMBER 1983
6

Mother Jones, *1983*

Will the news section have an art budget?

It's difficult to build an engaging section month after month with handouts and stock art—as is proved monthly by the many magazines that try. Some editors believe—perhaps rightly—that their budgetary priority should be the feature well, but because news sections tend to be what's looked at first, they often make the first and most lasting impression. Without at least some investment in the front of the book, that first impression will be a bad one. It's possible to design an attractive and engaging news section around a few strong illustrations or photographs. But, as with the text, the briefs prototype must be designed based on a realistic assessment of what will be possible on a monthly basis.

voices develop into characters and then I know that I am pregnant with a story. I write stories precisely when I can step into several antagonistic claims, diverse moral stances, conflicting emotional positions. There is an old Hasidic tale about a rabbi who is called upon to judge two conflicting claims to the same goat. He decrees that both claimants are right. Later, at home, his wife says that this is impossible: how can both be right when they claim the same goat? The rabbi reflects for a moment and says, "You know, dear wife, you are right, too." Well, sometimes I am that rabbi.

In the end, you pick up your pen and start writing, working like an old-fashioned watchmaker, with a magnifying glass in your eye and a pair of tweezers between your fingers; holding and inspecting an adjective against the light, changing a faulty adverb, tightening a loose verb, reshaping a worn-out idiom. This is the time when what you are feeling inside you is far from political righteousness. Rather it is a strange blend of rage and compassion, of intimacy with your characters mingled with utter detachment. Like icy fire. And you write. You write not as someone struggling for peace but more like someone who begets peace and feels eager to share it with the readers; and you write with a simple ethical imperative: Try to understand. Forgive some. And forget nothing.

By Mark O'Donnell. From Tang, a Los Angeles magazine. Vertigo Park and Other Tall Tales, a collection of O'Donnell's writings and drawings, will be published this month by Alfred A. Knopf.

[Video Script]

A WEST BANK SETTLER'S NIGHTMARE

From a transcript of Danger: Autonomy, *an eighteen-minute film produced last year by the Committee for the Struggle to Annul the Autonomy Program, a group of Jewish settlers on the West Bank. The film, which is being distributed on videotape to Israelis and to Jewish organizations in the United States, was produced by Elyakim Ha'etzni, a former member of the Israeli Knesset. Ha'etzni has said that he made the film to warn Israelis of the dangers of granting Palestinians autonomy in the occupied territories; Israeli Prime Minister Yitzhak Rabin has outlawed new Jewish settlements in the occupied territories, and has proposed extending to Palestinians limited authority over their own affairs, beginning later this year. Translated from the Hebrew by Rachel Persico.*

ANNOUNCER *[over aerial shot of West Bank]*: Judea and Samaria—names that evoke the scent of history. The view from these mountains is stupendous, a moving vista during peacetime—but this region is also a security zone of supreme strategic importance.

Seventeen years ago, Yitzhak Rabin, who was then prime minister, authorized a settlement here in the village of Ariel for security purposes. Back in those days, Zionist political settlement was not considered objectionable. But these days, Ariel, like the other settler communities, is anxiously anticipating the coming Palestinian autonomy. Elections, which will be termed free but will be clearly controlled by the terrorist establishment, will promote P.L.O. personnel to positions of control in the territory.

[Shot of Israeli flag being lowered.]

SUBTITLE *[over actor playing Israeli officer]*: April 26, 1996. Two and a half years into the autonomy.

ISRAELI OFFICER: Ever since the establishment of the autonomy, our forces have been pretty limited. We are authorized to intervene if there is an Arab pogrom against one of the Jewish communities around here, but we don't get involved with stone-throwing incidents like we used to. As a rule we stay here in the camp.

[Shot of radio dial.]

VOICE OF RADIO ANNOUNCER: *[in Arabic]* This is the Voice of Palestine, broadcasting from Ramallah [on the West Bank]. *[in Hebrew]* Here is the news in Hebrew: The president of Palestine, Mr. Yasser Arafat, today will be broadcasting his first talk to the Palestinian nation, encompassing the entire territory of Palestine from the river to the sea. This is to be his first speech from the liberated land, and the excitement in the streets is enormous.

[Shot of Jewish settler sitting in a candlelit room, speaking to the camera.]

SUBTITLE: June 5, 1996.

SETTLER: We haven't had any electricity now for three days. That's not too bad, really—sometimes we get cut off for a whole week. This sort of thing has been going on ever since we were hooked up to the Hebron Power Company.

Here, have some mineral water. Don't think we've become snobs; it's simply that the tap water is undrinkable. You get diarrhea and throw up. *[raises glass]* L'chaim!

When you call the authorities, you get some clerk who pretends she doesn't speak Hebrew, so you have to speak English. Me, an Israeli, talking to the power company in English! *[He holds up a postage stamp with Arafat's portrait on it.]* And if I want to send a letter I have to lick Arafat's ass!

[Shot of Palestinian flags gradually covering a map of Israel.]

RADIO ANNOUNCER: This is the voice of Israel from Jerusalem. A spokesman from the Israeli Defense Forces reports that a Katiusha rocket fired from the Palestinian territory hit an army reserve post inside the Green Line [which separates Israel from the occupied territories]. One soldier was critically wounded.

[The actor who played the settler, now out of character, faces the camera.]

ACTOR: The nightmare you have just witnessed is not yet a reality. But this devastation will be prevented only if tens of thousands of Jews defiantly settle in Ye'sha [the territories]. These thousands, who would rather go to prison than betray the ideals of their homeland, will stop the catastrophe with their bodies.

SUBTITLE: We are running out of time. The train of autonomy has left the station. If we don't want to be run over, we've got to stop it now!

[Report]

REVOLUTION NUMBER SEVEN

From "Trial Board Findings and Decision in the Matter of [Police] Corporal Brian Yinger," a report issued last October by Ronald F. Deziel, the Dearborn, Michigan, chief of police.

Proceedings

On October 23, 1992, a Trial Board was conducted for the purpose of hearing charges brought against Corporal Brian Yinger. Corporal Yinger was charged with violation of Section 17 of the

[Handbook]

COVERING THE BALKANS UNDER FIRE

From "Journalists' Advisory on the Former Yugoslavia: How to Survive and Still Get the Story," a booklet distributed last November by the Committee to Protect Journalists (CPJ), in New York City. CPJ published the advisory "because of the unprecedented casualty rate among journalists covering the war in what used to be Yugoslavia"; to date, at least twenty-seven journalists have been killed in the conflict.

• Don't go out alone. Travel by road in groups, with at least two cars in case one breaks down. Keep track of escape routes.

• Rent a four-wheel-drive vehicle that can go off-road, but get one that doesn't look like a military jeep. One CBS correspondent recommends renting a white vehicle because "someone who wants to take a potshot at you might think you're U.N., and not shoot."

• Think about your license plates. You don't want to cross troop lines with the wrong plates. Hungarian, Slovenian, and Austrian plates are currently favored among reporters as neutral. Bear in mind, however, that the insurance on a car rented in Austria or Hungary may not cover damage incurred over the border.

• Should you mark your car with TV or PRESS? In most places these days, press labels seem to draw more fire than they prevent. A journalist in Belgrade suggests that PRESS probably is a good idea but that TV probably isn't, because television is seen as more powerful and is the main propaganda weapon of all sides.

• Don't ride in the backseat of a two-door car. It's hard to get out quickly. Even in the front seat, if it's really dangerous and you're not in an armored car, keep the doors ajar so that you can dive out. Keep the windows open so that you can hear what's happening outside.

• Watch your lights, especially at night. Be careful with flashes; don't shine flashlights; cover all camera lights. Drape dark cloth over your head if you're shooting a video camera so that no one can see the dim blue glow of the viewfinder leaking from around your eye. Cameraman Sebastian Rich of ITN almost took a sniper's bullet while shooting from a window at night. It hit the window frame and sprayed glass into his face.

18 HARPER'S MAGAZINE / FEBRUARY 1993

READINGS 19

Harper's, *1993*

Will the news section accommodate fractional (partial-page) ads?

Small advertisements can be a kiss of death on news pages. Very short stories are easily overwhelmed by ads that would seem small and inoffensive in another context. Some magazines keep ads out of their feature well as a matter of policy. In fact, the last few pages of a feature story—when the reader is hooked and happily reading along—are the best place to put smaller ads. Magazines that lard news pages with fractionals are demonstrating a disconnect between what is most important to readers and what is most important to editors.

Raising these questions and concerns before beginning a redesign accomplishes several goals: It gives the designer a realistic sense of what the priorities for the section are; it reveals roadblocks to creating a successful section early in the process; and it encourages editors and publishers to consider their own views about what the briefs section should be. The first meeting about the briefs section should not establish lines that the designer will not cross, but an informed designer will start with a better understanding of where the news section likely can and can't be taken. As always, designers should not ask questions if they don't want to know the answers. Color schemes, typefaces, and other specific visual issues are best discussed, if at all, after the first prototype(s) and in a context of what will accomplish editorial goals, not what pleases personal tastes. A designer can lead a magazine to a better approach through dialogue and the creation of a compelling prototype.

Building the Briefs

Briefs pages generally follow one of a few standard structures. There is variety within each, and, in practice, many magazines mix and match, resulting in some pages that are more image-driven and others that are type-dependent.

LAYERED. A risotto requires the adding of more and more liquid to cooking rice until each grain is nearly bursting. So it is with the "layered look," which adds more and more small elements to a page until it virtually can't hold any more. *Esquire* has stepped back from this approach, but this example from 2001, which holds eight separate stories, shows just how compelling

In the Modern World

NorCal Mod / By Pierluigi Serraino / Chronicle Books / $35 / www.chroniclebooks.com / When recalling the works of architectural photographer Julius Shulman, one usually imagines a Pierre Koenig Case Study House set in the arid hills of Southern California. Many people don't know Shulman and his contemporaries had just as many important modernist examples in Northern California to chronicle in the 1940s, '50s, and '60s. Pierluigi Serraino investigates the overlooked region, and in addition to collecting a dense archive of images and information about the influential people and projects involved, discusses why the L.A. area garnered more attention.

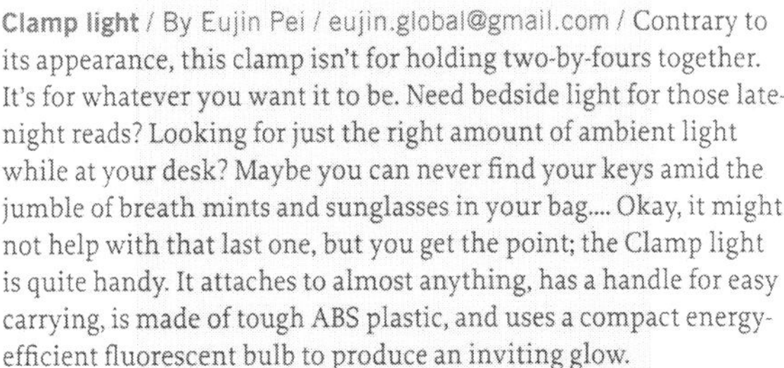

Clamp light / By Eujin Pei / eujin.global@gmail.com / Contrary to its appearance, this clamp isn't for holding two-by-fours together. It's for whatever you want it to be. Need bedside light for those late-night reads? Looking for just the right amount of ambient light while at your desk? Maybe you can never find your keys amid the jumble of breath mints and sunglasses in your bag.... Okay, it might not help with that last one, but you get the point; the Clamp light is quite handy. It attaches to almost anything, has a handle for easy carrying, is made of tough ABS plastic, and uses a compact energy-efficient fluorescent bulb to produce an inviting glow.

Flytip rug / By Committee for the Rug Company / www.therugcompany.info / Aside from being attractive hodgepodges of everyday imagery, these colorful and eclectic rugs will make your living room look more orderly than it really is—discarded clothes and errant soda cans will blend right in with the design. Committee founders Clare Page and Harry Richardson have a style as varied as their body of work, having designed furniture, lighting, textiles, wallpaper, and interiors.

60 Dwell Dec/Jan 2007

Dwell, *2007*

an overstuffed page can be. The designer hewed closely to a twelve-column grid, and editorial staff wrote to tightly proscribed length to achieve the sense of order and balance.

NEWSY. Newsy sections look and read like newspaper pages because, editorially, they are trying to accomplish news goals. The articles tend to be longer—they may even jump—and they succeed in putting a lot of text into a small area. Despite their relative unattractiveness, newsy pages are time-consuming; it is a challenge to get fewer, longer stories to interact effectively. And, if there are jumps, even minor changes in text length in a single story can affect two or three other stories.

LINEAR. A linear layout, in which one story flows into the next in a continuous stream of text, represents probably the most efficient and attractive way to design a text-heavy section. It allows the production designer to treat all stories in the chain as a single big story—but

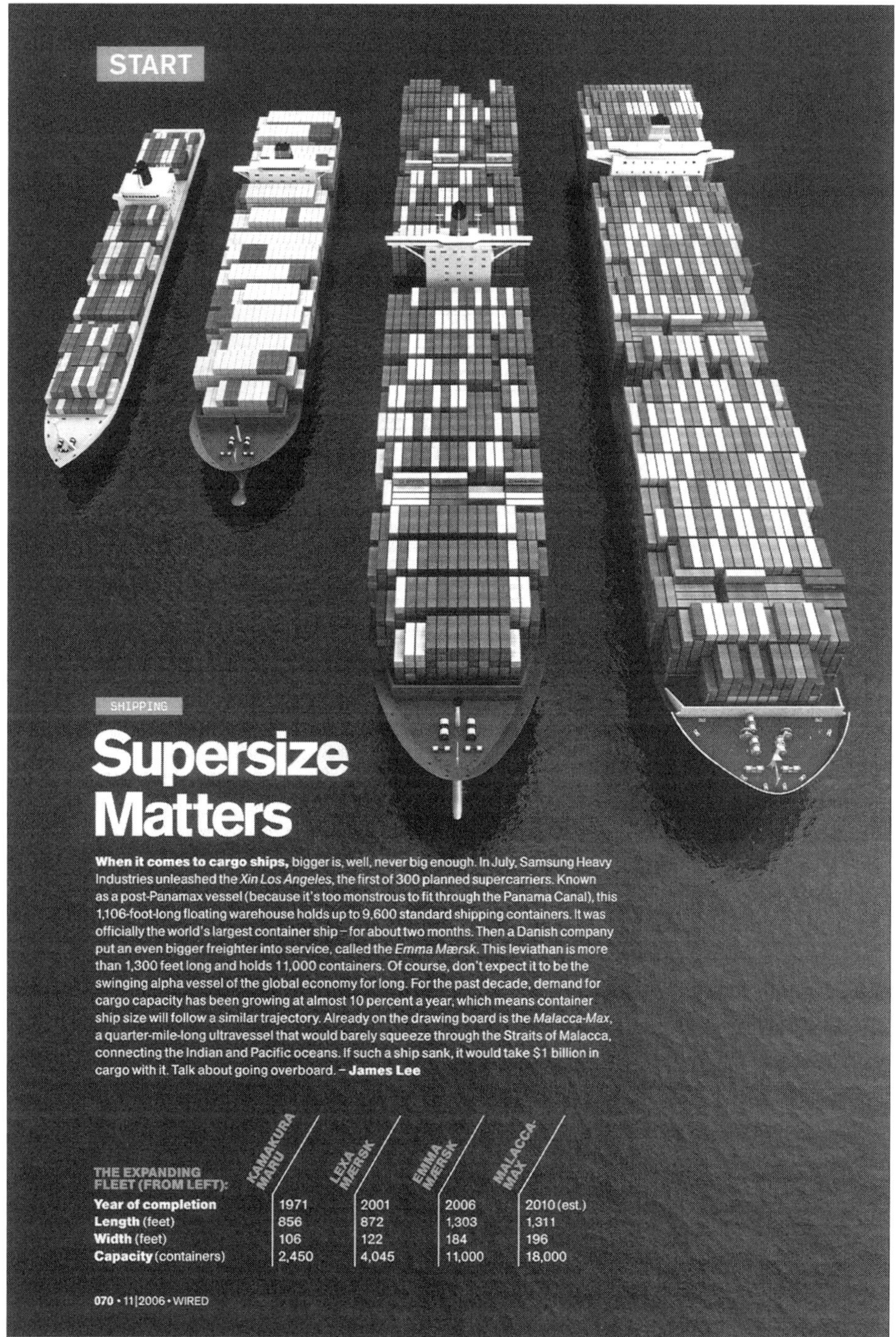

START

SHIPPING

Supersize Matters

When it comes to cargo ships, bigger is, well, never big enough. In July, Samsung Heavy Industries unleashed the *Xin Los Angeles*, the first of 300 planned supercarriers. Known as a post-Panamax vessel (because it's too monstrous to fit through the Panama Canal), this 1,106-foot-long floating warehouse holds up to 9,600 standard shipping containers. It was officially the world's largest container ship – for about two months. Then a Danish company put an even bigger freighter into service, called the *Emma Mærsk*. This leviathan is more than 1,300 feet long and holds 11,000 containers. Of course, don't expect it to be the swinging alpha vessel of the global economy for long. For the past decade, demand for cargo capacity has been growing at almost 10 percent a year, which means container ship size will follow a similar trajectory. Already on the drawing board is the *Malacca-Max*, a quarter-mile-long ultravessel that would barely squeeze through the Straits of Malacca, connecting the Indian and Pacific oceans. If such a ship sank, it would take $1 billion in cargo with it. Talk about going overboard. – **James Lee**

THE EXPANDING FLEET (FROM LEFT):	KAMAKURA MARU	LEXA MÆRSK	EMMA MÆRSK	MALACCA-MAX
Year of completion	1971	2001	2006	2010 (est.)
Length (feet)	856	872	1,303	1,311
Width (feet)	106	122	184	196
Capacity (containers)	2,450	4,045	11,000	18,000

070 • 11|2006 • WIRED

Wired, *2006*

with a few wrinkles. Headlines cannot break across columns, so art must be inserted or items reordered to achieve an attractive flow. Linear layouts also demand a significant investment in art, or at least the inclusion of visually compelling freestanding destination items within the section. Without these additions, linear sections can (and often do) become visually drab.

COLLAGE. Collage layouts use art and text as equal partners, with more art per item than newsy or linear layouts. It is usually best to separate items with white space rather than architectural elements so that different items stay distinct. While collage pages most often use a grid, for organization they rely on balancing the two or three separate items per page and on putting text and image in proximity to each other.

ART-DRIVEN. An art-driven layout can make for a very luxurious-feeling briefs section. Such an approach is characterized by one-item-per-page layouts. In

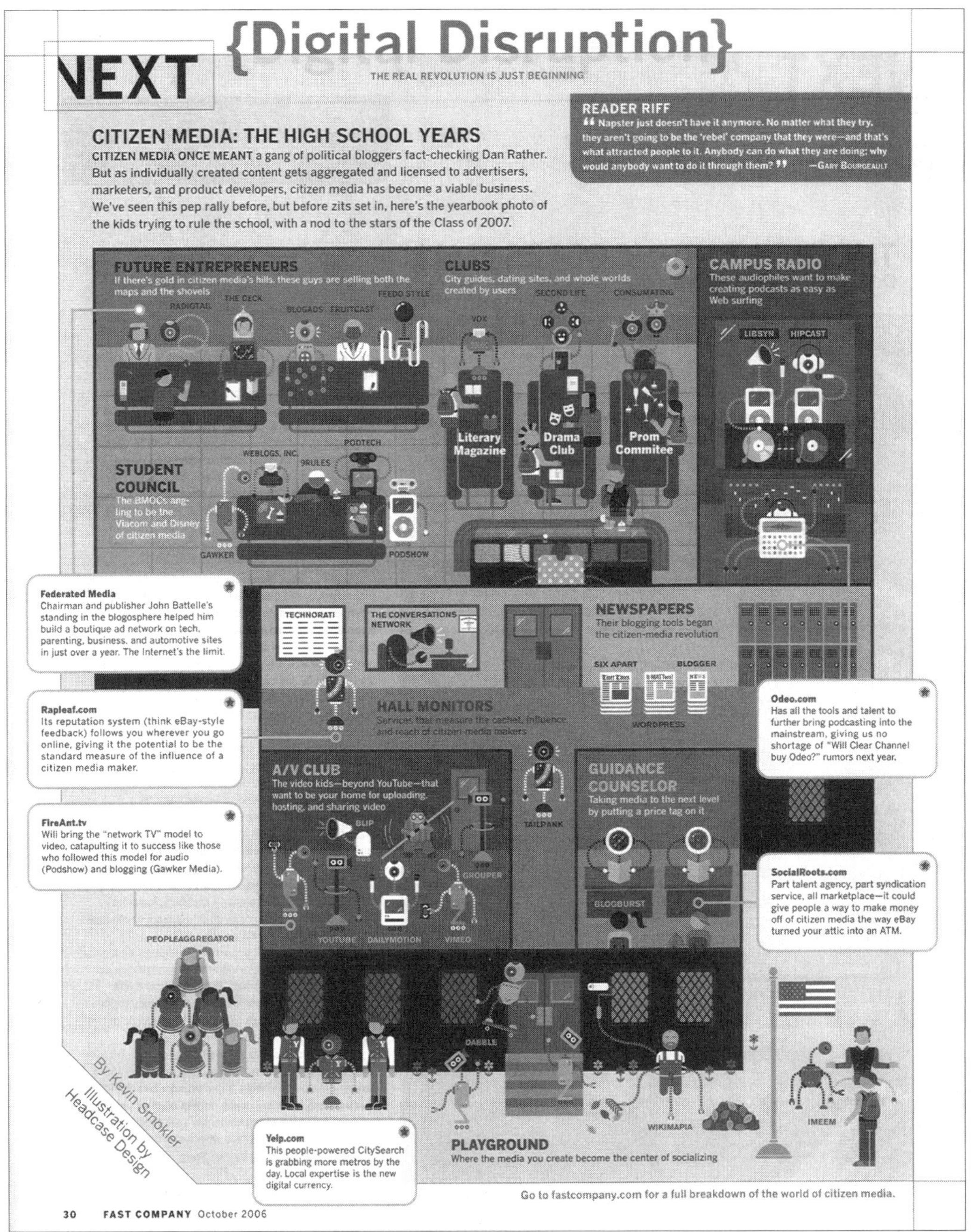
NEXT

{Digital Disruption}

THE REAL REVOLUTION IS JUST BEGINNING

READER RIFF

“Napster just doesn't have it anymore. No matter what they try, they aren't going to be the 'rebel' company that they were—and that's what attracted people to it. Anybody can do what they are doing; why would anybody want to do it through them?” —Gary Bourgeault

CITIZEN MEDIA: THE HIGH SCHOOL YEARS

CITIZEN MEDIA ONCE MEANT a gang of political bloggers fact-checking Dan Rather. But as individually created content gets aggregated and licensed to advertisers, marketers, and product developers, citizen media has become a viable business. We've seen this pep rally before, but before zits set in, here's the yearbook photo of the kids trying to rule the school, with a nod to the stars of the Class of 2007.

FUTURE ENTREPRENEURS
If there's gold in citizen media's hills, these guys are selling both the maps and the shovels
RADIOTAIL
THE DECK
BLOGADS
FRUITCAST
FEEDO STYLE

CLUBS
City guides, dating sites, and whole worlds created by users
VOX
SECOND LIFE
CONSUMATING
Literary Magazine
Drama Club
Prom Commitee

CAMPUS RADIO
These audiophiles want to make creating podcasts as easy as Web surfing
LIBSYN
HIPCAST

STUDENT COUNCIL
The BMOCs angling to be the Viacom and Disney of citizen media
WEBLOGS, INC.
9RULES
PODTECH
GAWKER
PODSHOW

Federated Media
Chairman and publisher John Battelle's standing in the blogosphere helped him build a boutique ad network on tech, parenting, business, and automotive sites in just over a year. The Internet's the limit.

TECHNORATI
THE CONVERSATIONS NETWORK

NEWSPAPERS
Their blogging tools began the citizen-media revolution
SIX APART
BLOGGER
WORDPRESS

HALL MONITORS
Services that measure the cachet, influence, and reach of citizen-media makers

Rapleaf.com
Its reputation system (think eBay-style feedback) follows you wherever you go online, giving it the potential to be the standard measure of the influence of a citizen media maker.

Odeo.com
Has all the tools and talent to further bring podcasting into the mainstream, giving us no shortage of "Will Clear Channel buy Odeo?" rumors next year.

A/V CLUB
The video kids—beyond YouTube—that want to be your home for uploading, hosting, and sharing video
BLIP
GROUPER
YOUTUBE
DAILYMOTION
VIMEO

TAILRANK

GUIDANCE COUNSELOR
Taking media to the next level by putting a price tag on it
BLOGBURST

FireAnt.tv
Will bring the "network TV" model to video, catapulting it to success like those who followed this model for audio (Podshow) and blogging (Gawker Media).

SocialRoots.com
Part talent agency, part syndication service, all marketplace—it could give people a way to make money off of citizen media the way eBay turned your attic into an ATM.

PEOPLEAGGREGATOR
DABBLE
WIKIMAPIA
IMEEM

By Kevin Smokler
Illustration by Headcase Design

Yelp.com
This people-powered CitySearch is grabbing more metros by the day. Local expertise is the new digital currency.

PLAYGROUND
Where the media you create become the center of socializing

Go to fastcompany.com for a full breakdown of the world of citizen media.

30 FAST COMPANY October 2006

Fast Company, *2006*

art-driven sections, text is largely ancillary, but they can be a challenge for the designer who must still build graphic variety into the section through page arrangement. Many magazine staffs incorporate one or more art-driven pages into their briefs sections because they add visual impact to a section otherwise dominated by small items.

ALTERNATIVE STORY FORM. Alternative Story Forms (ASFs)—in which information is presented in the form of a graphic, map, chart, or table—have taken over magazines and newspapers in the past few years, particularly in briefs sections (a few briefs sections even rely exclusively on ASFs). ASFs are time-consuming and hard to do well. (Pie and bar charts can be automated, but offer little that isn't conveyed more efficiently in text form—they're also visually boring.) A commitment to ASFs can tempt editors to select stories based on suitability to an alternative format rather than merit, but at their best, ASFs do quickly what narrative writing does slowly or not all. They can be visual and intellectual "toys," inviting the reader to explore them rather than merely read them.

Swinging on a Shoestring

26

HANA JUNG

IT WASN'T GOING TO BE THIS WAY. WHEN I GRADuated from a BA design program just over a year ago, I thought I would, like most of my friends who graduated with me, spend a few years in a junior position at some design firm or ad agency before moving up to a fancier title and fatter salary. Those first lean years would come with some consolations, however. When you're a freshman designer, mistakes don't cost that much because nobody expects that much from you.

Instead, as design director of *Northern Virginia Magazine*, an upstart regional monthly, I have the job I was hoping, with luck, to get five or ten years from now. I'm glad to be here, but I've had to create my own Rome, and quickly. At twenty-three (now twenty-four), I've carried the weight of our magazine's uncertain future on my shoulders for its first few months, careful not to let my publisher and the rest of the staff down.

I've missed out on a lot of mentoring. This was never so embarrassingly apparent than when I coordinated my first formal photo shoot. It was with Miss Virginia 2006, Adriana Sgarlata, who was the cover model for our "Top Salons" issue. A tony local salon agreed to do her hair and makeup in exchange for the publicity—that's how we roll here: lots of trades and deals.

Looking at those photos now, I can't believe how well they turned out. The trouble with paying the lowest rates in town and working with volunteers is that, in the absence of money, both the photographer and the stylist were concerned with getting what they wanted out of the shoot, which wasn't the same thing. The photographer was clearly trying to plump his portfolio as he marched poor Miss Virginia to four different locations for photographs that I wouldn't have room for. The stylist wanted her work to come off as perfect, not mussed in a whirlwind trip around the state. Both thought their discounted involvement entitled them to run the shoot. The needs of the magazine seemed to have been forgotten. I've learned that I have to be a leader in these situations—spell out exactly what is expected to all parties and how the day is going to go. We all look good, or none of us does. Instead, I heard complaints from the photographer and the stylist for two weeks afterward. Miss Virginia, at least, was the perfect lady.

People skills aren't just for the phone. I'm grateful to be working with both of my current designers because we share high expectations and strong commitment. For a while I had a designer—hired to create advertising and to maintain the restaurant guide—who didn't carry his weight. He might have been fine at an established magazine, but startups require staff willing to put in more and get back less. It didn't help that he was older than me and clearly resented reporting to a kid. He tried to work around me, going with his work directly to the publisher, who, after a while, started sending him back to me. We ended up arguing a lot, which, along with his short (by our standards) days, was harming design department morale. I had a few long heart-to-hearts with him, which was hard for me, as I found it difficult not taking his attitude personally. Eventually even the publisher, who tries to keep his hands out of department issues, was complaining about his work. Although I can urge, I cannot force my will on those who demonstrate little commitment. I have learned that hiring is about the person as much as the portfolio.

Despite challenges like these, I'm still here. Why: Talent? Risk-taking? Trust? A mix maybe. I owe my deepest gratitude to Sang Yang, my publisher, who saw my potential and "took a gamble" as he puts it. He knew I lacked experience but trusted that my talent, still fresh and malleable, could be shaped into something stronger. I had a little time to build that trust before the magazine came along. He first hired me as the solo designer of a free advertorial circular with a print run of three hundred thousand, which he had published for five years before launching the magazine. I had only been around for two months when he decided to change directions in favor of the glossy we now publish.

One of the biggest challenges for me has been finding my place within the hierarchy of the magazine—supervising staff designers and freelancers as well as becoming a part of the management team. Design school teaches design, but does little to help students with those soft skills, especially the ability to convey

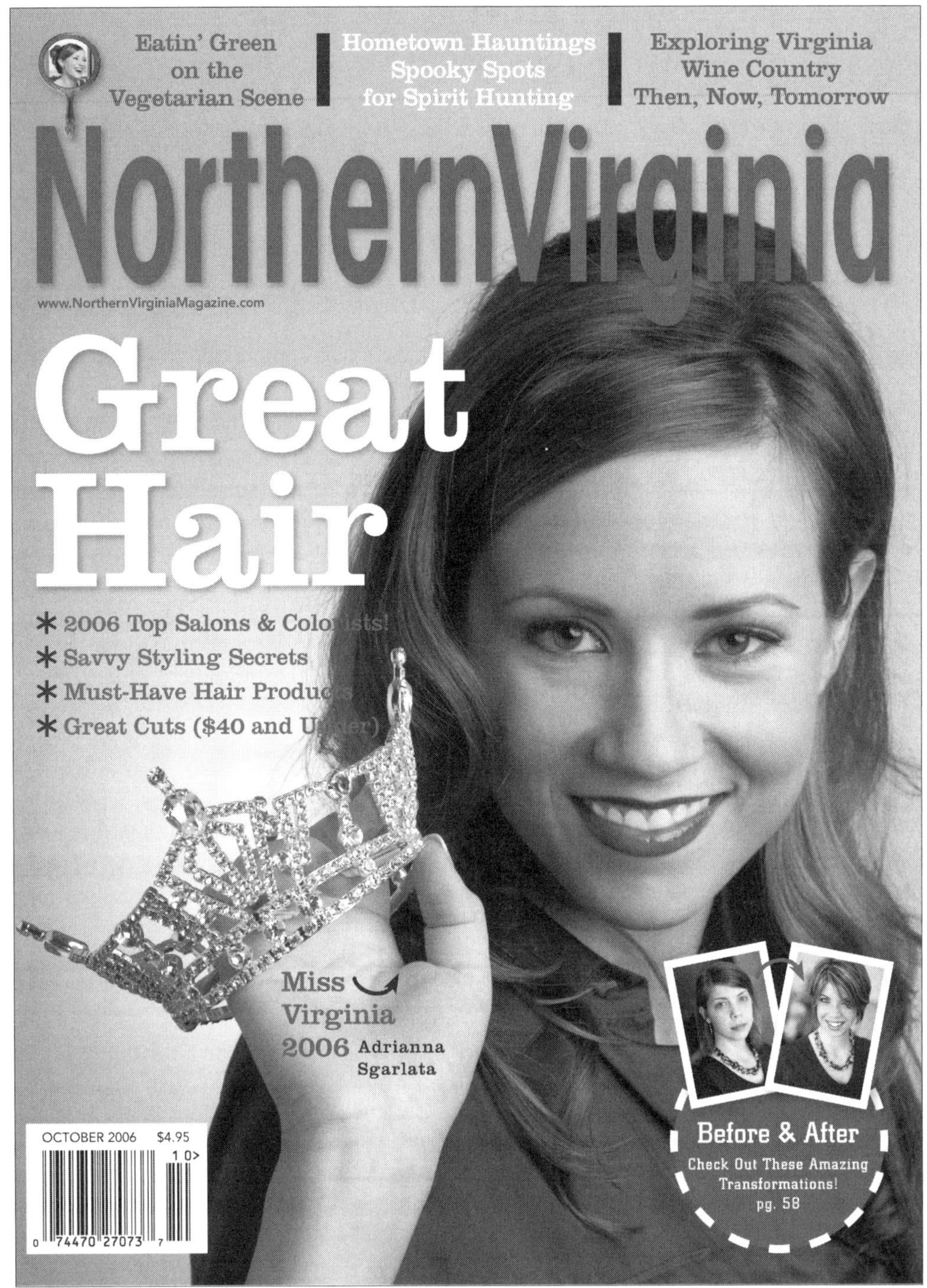

2006

visual ideas in language that makes sense to word people, and to find compromises that don't, when printed, look like compromises. I also ask with every layout whether I am upgrading or downgrading our reputation with the design choices we have made.

Working with the designers in my department, my role has grown into a hybrid of counselor and supervisor. It is important that my designers enjoy and are proud of what they do—they could be somewhere else. We are individual yet parallel thinkers who share the same goals but may approach each design problem differently. My design team is smart and can sense how much consistency means to my vision. I like to unify the design of our magazine through the use of templates, typefaces, and small graphic elements. I've recently redesigned our front of the book section

By Kathy Witt

Retirement Is Just a Transition and Old Talents Can Mean New Business

During the Cold War in the 1980s, Alexandria resident Joe Egerton frequently made runs to the airport in Washington, D.C., to pick up Russian translators. Although his charges were often concerned about being tailed by the KGB, Egerton was neither FBI nor CIA. Rather, he was the executive vice president of Hemisphere Publishing Corporation, a company he co-founded in 1974 that published books and journals in the fields of health sciences, psychology and engineering, as well as technical reference books.

Born in 1938 in Youngstown, Ohio, the 68-year-old Egerton had been raised and educated in Bowie, Maryland. He had worked his way through the University of Maryland, an art major, in the late 1950s and early 1960s but, impatient to begin his career, dropped out in 1962. Scripta Technica, a company that translated Russian and Japanese scientific journals for the American market, hired Egerton as a production manager.

Book publishing was a job at which the soon-to-be entrepreneur excelled. In 1985, Egerton sold Hemisphere Publishing Corporation to Harper and Row Publishers in New York City, remaining with the company until 1987 when he took early retirement at age 49. Retirement,

www.NorthernVirginiaMagazine.com | 89

2006

(FOB), "Events and Restaurant Guide," to keep up with modern trends and to decrease production time. Though these sections stay true to the integrity of a template, I've created multiple versions to accommodate larger or smaller images and word counts. I allow the most freedom for features, limiting only type choice to our signature fonts. This way, the design of our magazine is unified but also offers visual variety. I like to discuss concepts with designers before the pages are laid out, especially with major features, so that my expectations are known ahead of time. I've learned that establishing goals at the beginning of the process works better than criticizing at the end. I listen to staff ideas first and then help refine them. When I assign features to my designers, we discuss type and the number of illustrations (which I assign) that they will have.

When we have disagreements, I usually give my designers a chance to develop their ideas. When I redesigned our FOB and the back of the magazine (BOB), one of my priorities was to keep our events sections consistent with our restaurant guide. My designer, Daidra, thought that the small articles within the restaurant guide needed more flexibility, so I gave her the go-ahead to create a mock-up. Her layout had merit but wasn't built on our template. She changed the background color to white and added decorative graphic elements like colored circles and text boxes. Although I could not approve her work, her approach showed me that my initial layouts were too conservative. We incorporated several of her ideas—text wraparounds and silhouetted images—into the final, which will add visual variety. That's the difference between being a designer and a design director. Designers are free to innovate, but when you're in charge, your outlook is colored by the necessity of maintaining the brand and keeping the schedule. The designers in my department are not mini-me's—we need each other.

My goal for the years ahead is to close the gap between what I can imagine and what I can implement. Because of our tight deadlines and small staff, I find that our covers do not receive proper attention. The week our magazine is due to the printer is always disorderly because I am trying to finish the magazine and design the cover simultaneously. As a result, we've

DINING REVIEWS
VINO
COCKTAIL CORNER
CHEW ON THIS
RESTAURANT GUIDE

RELISH

Pop that Rocks

DRY Soda Delivers Mouthwatering Refreshment

Tired of feeling "left out" during dinner outings while pregnant (wine was a no-no, sparkling water lacked pizzazz), epicurean entrepreneur Sharelle Klaus came up with DRY Soda—a gourmet cooler for those bored with high fructose corn syrup-bearing fare.

Each "culinary soda" boasts a bare-bones blend of carbonated water, cane sugar, all-natural ingredients and phosphoric acid. DRY currently produces four wild flavors, including: rhubarb (a refreshingly tart entry inspired by Klaus' grandma's summer pies), lavender (subtle flavor tickles the back of your throat), kumquat (a symphony of bright citrus notes) and lemongrass (pleasant spice makes this feel like a more mature ginger ale).

Klaus claims her alterna-beverages are already a big hit with West Coast foodies and cocktail mixologists. "People are so excited about what we're doing," she says, adding that she already has two more "cutting-edge" flavors in the pipeline for 2007 and is mulling seasonal offerings.

Single-flavor 12-packs or sampler multi-packs are available at www.drysoda.com for $25 plus shipping. A DRY soda spokeswoman says the company is hoping to secure East Coast distributors by early 2007, adding that a handful of D.C. restaurants have expressed interest in the off-beat thirst quenchers.

www.NorthernVirginiaMagazine.com | 121

Newsbriefs, 2006

rarely been able to coordinate and execute formal photo shoots, relying instead on stock art and typographical solutions. We have to do better.

Budget and scheduling concerns have not stopped me from finding talented artists. While I'm a long way from being able to hire Annie Leibovitz, every posting I've placed has yielded several dozen interested local freelancers who are like me—young, hungry recent graduates more interested in clips than cash. I hope we all make the big time together. I look for versatility in my contributors—something a lot of younger talent doesn't yet have—but I've been given a break, and I want to share that opportunity. Although working with a low budget is a challenge, I stretch my bottom dollar by using stock images for some stories. And what my art budget lacks, my team's typographical skills can, to some extent, compensate for. September's "Home" article, "Cool Designs," was flat on art but high on design. Eunice, one of our designers, had the daunting task of working with mediocre builder-supplied images. She made the best choices she could and then took inspiration for page composition, color scheme, and type choice from each picture; the photos and the design both looked better as a result.

Budget is a challenge in other ways. Unlike more established magazines, our deadlines are only suggestions. Our ad pages fluctuate until the very end as advertisers come in—we don't say no, as we need the money—and drop out. But it's a hardship for the design department who must accommodate this instability. Revisions are common. We've learned to design for the tightest possible layout and expand later on if needed. That way we don't face the heartbreak of shrinking a beloved photo down from a page to a few inches. The editorial team also helps out. I request cuts when I can't find another route to take.

My team and I have gotten used to fifty-hour-plus workweeks as we put out a 164-page monthly with a design staff of three. We gobble down our lunch at our computers and stay late. Our dedication doesn't go without recognition: the designers (all women) are rewarded with a day at the spa now and again and rotating comp days once a month. I realize that we can't maintain—we must grow. However, I do ask myself how much is too much. We are relaunching our Web site early next year—a major renovation—which we hope will have the quality of much larger regional magazines' sites. We have a few months before our first print deadline of the new year to concept the site while the editorial team figures out the content, all the while planning our issues. It's a struggle to get it all done.

I once saw a job posting for a magazine designer that specified the ability to hold up the editorial wall. I giggled because now I know exactly what that means. At times, the editorial department is very set on how an article should be packaged. I discourage discussions of visual concept and layout between the editorial and design teams in favor of tone and goals. I do, however, always listen to writers' and editors' suggestions because they sometimes have value even if I choose not to use them—no one understands a story better than its writer. I also work closely with managing editor Karen Chaffraix, but at *Northern Virginia* it's clear that we manage separate departments. Unlike many magazines in which the design director reports to the editor, I report to the publisher, which gives me a freedom many more experienced design directors don't have. Sang knows that design has the potential to make or break the magazine. Through a year of proving myself, the editors have come to trust my instincts, and they know that I won't let them leap over the wall.

As I look back on my first year at *Northern Virginia*, even the brutal first half, I can't help but smile—I'm lucky to be here and proud that we've been successful. I'm in the middle of it—the little girl with a shiny red cape and a tight, itchy leotard, longing to be Super Girl. I can't fly, but I can design a magazine I'm proud of.

A Brief Introduction to the Use of Grids in Magazine Design

27

JANDOS ROTHSTEIN

MOST MAGAZINES AND NEWSPAPERS ARE DESIGNED on a grid—a prearranged guide that defines margins, the number and width of columns, and, in some cases, horizontal positions for placing advertisements and modules of information. Why do editorial designers use a grid? It's tempting to blame Gutenberg. He invented a technology that facilitated grid-based design. The chase, or rectangular frame that held hand-set type in place, the blocks of "furniture" used to fill that frame out, and the square bodies upon which letters were cast depended on structure and precision to stay in place under a press. However, the grid long predates the invention of movable type.

Gutenberg's series of inventions was used to imitate handwritten models. With few exceptions, scribes, who could put letters in any size anywhere on a page with as much facility as a designer with a Mac DuoCore running the latest version of the Creative Suite, instead opted for regularity, standardization, and predictability—one layout was usually used for the entirety of an ancient scroll or medieval codex.

If regularity had been an artifact of mechanization, it could now, presumably, be abandoned, because modern tools permit infinite flexibility. The truth is that readers take comfort in standardization and familiarity. Structure also aids function—predictability allows the reader to read rather than decode each layout as she comes to it.

If the grid serves readers, it has also survived because it is an invaluable production tool for medieval scribe and modern magazine designer alike. It is possible to design spectacular pages—particularly feature spreads—without a grid. But a regular column structure frees the designer to focus on the substantive goal of storytelling rather than structural or interface issues. The grid is an excellent tool for two common tasks: the organization of information composed of lots of separate small components, and the organization of information composed of a few large components and white space.

Grid Basics

Grid structure can vary throughout the course of a magazine, as long as it does so in a logical way. Generally, short articles can tolerate a narrow column width, which is why front-of-the-book (FOB) sections such as letters and briefs are often put on a four-column grid, whereas feature stories and columns are more likely put on a two- or three-column grid. Margins, however, must be consistent throughout.

The designer need not put an element against all four margins on every page, but if an element is in proximity to the margin, it must snap to it. Otherwise, the result is content that seems to float around the magazine like a balloon, never quite anchored to anything. This minor unpredictability can make reading unpleasant or even stressful. It can also subtly undermine the authority of the words. If the layout is lackadaisical, can you expect better from the text? Generally, designers should apply the "if it's close, it must be exact" rule to all grid guidelines.

The more columns the underlying grid has, the more design flexibility is built into the structure, because more columns give more standardized ways to divide the page. Following a one-column grid requires that all columns of text and pictures be the same width. A two-column grid allows images to take up half the width of the page or the whole page. A three-column grid allows an image to take the width of one-third, two-thirds, or the entire page.

The designer may occasionally decide to "break" the grid—for example, by allowing pictures to cut into a column. This can be an effective technique if used sparingly, but breaking the grid requires care. The skinny columns of type that result from text wrapping around a picture can be unattractive and unpleasant to read—resulting in too many or incorrect hyphenations at the end of lines (bad breaks) and "rivers and gullies" (several lines with unattractively large gaps between words in a justified line).

Gutters

In addition to columns, most grids provide space, called gutters or alleys, between the columns. Most publications use one pica (approximately one-sixth of an inch) for this gap, in part because most software defaults to that width and in part because a pica is the minimum reasonable distance between columns—closer than that

Clockwise from top left: A boxlike addition clad in recycled corrugated glass marks the Pittsburgh Glass Center, which reuses a 1920s car dealership. The building is heated in part by recovering waste heat from glass processing. Lights for the gallery space adjust to its occupancy level. Windows that operate like garage doors air the space in warm weather.

which preserved historic buildings excel.

"I appreciate the LEED people," says Kevin Gannon, a principal with DGGP Architecture. "They need to have a fair standard. But standardized testing won't work for every condition." In designing the Pittsburgh Glass Center, Gannon began with a sympathetic client who embraced the values of the rating system and was able to score a preliminary rating of gold, thanks in part to rehabilitating an older building. The Glass Center occupies a former car dealership from the 1920s that presses up to the sidewalk line amid a mixture of storefronts, houses, and parking lots on busy Penn Avenue, the border of Pittsburgh's Bloomfield and Garfield neighborhoods. The project is adaptive use, not pure preservation. One of its most distinctive features is a long box sheathed in salvaged corrugated glass that projects from one side of the second floor. Operable garage-door-type windows give the upstairs space an almost outdoor feel in good weather, especially welcome amid the heat from glass-making.

Gannon hoped to get more LEED credits for that and other innovative features, including a mechanical system that captures waste heat from the furnaces. "It would be nice if LEED could recognize the uniqueness of certain things," he says, and others agree. Architect Rob Pfaffmann points out that the program was originally developed for new commercial office buildings. "The Building Council was going for the low-hanging fruit, for big buildings and consumers of energy," he says. Old buildings, with numerous unknown existing conditions, tend to be much more complex.

As executive director of the Green Building Alliance of Pittsburgh, Rebecca Flora has helped gain LEED certification for many buildings here. One of the nation's first such certified professionals, she is on the board of USGBC, in which position she advocates updating the LEED code and making it more preservation-friendly. "Some of these [criticisms] are based on, for the first couple of years, using a system that was still in development," she says. Improvements are occurring—updates like LEED-EB for existing buildings, one of a growing number of specialized program divisions. "People just aren't necessarily aware of them yet." Topics such as life-cycle cost analysis and more elaborate evaluations for existing buildings are part of a new rating system being developed.

PITTSBURGH HAS MORE LEED-RATED BUILDINGS THAN ANY other city in the country, says the Green Building Alliance, which tries to maintain the distinction. Underlying that feat is support from the Heinz Foundation, where Teresa Heinz Kerry has insisted that all of the projects it aids follow green principles. Meanwhile, groups like Sustainable Pittsburgh promote green values in local and regional planning, and several neighborhood organizations embrace similar values in community redevelopment. Pittsburgh also boasts Carnegie Mellon University's Center for Building Performance and Diagnostics, recognized worldwide for its studies of mechanical systems and related areas of air flow, energy usage, and daylighting, all crucial components of sustainable design.

On the preservation side, the Pittsburgh History and Landmarks Foundation (PHLF) is by far the leading local force, and has been for decades. It earned an international reputation for its commonsense activism against the aggressive urban renewal projects of the 1960s. Its successful renovation of the moribund Pittsburgh and Lake Erie Railroad buildings into Station Square in the 1970s was a case study in creative preservation and the highly effective use of development funds. Although the complex was sold in the 1990s, the organization is as active as ever, promoting sensitive development along with its extensive programs of education, architectural surveys, grants, loans, and publications. Other local organizations, including Preservation Pittsburgh and the Young Preservationists Association, work in support of PHLF and sometimes in counterpoint to it.

Jane Werner, executive director of the Children's Museum of Pittsburgh, oversaw a remarkable expansion of her organization's facilities, synthesizing adaptive use, modern design, and green building. To further an institution that was outgrowing its home in a gemlike Renaissance revival dome—the former post office on Pittsburgh's North Side—Werner drew in people and even an extra building from next door. The Buhl Planetarium, a quirky and endearing Machine Age temple of astronomy, had sat unused and decaying for some 10 years. "We recognized that we lived next to this extraordinary building," she commented, "but it was just going to fall apart if nobody used it."

She organized a national design competition informed by a series of local charrettes, then directed participants to embrace green principles and reuse the old planetarium. As a result, the Buhl is now revived, with both museum exhibits and office space for affiliated organizations. A new three-story wing by Koning Eizenberg Architecture joins the old post office to the Buhl with refreshingly humane modernism. The new-old complex has won an American Institute of Architects Honor Award and a LEED silver rating, the largest museum to do so. A long roster of features—including recycled structural steel, low-energy mechanical systems, organic flooring materials, and nonvolatile paints, as well as recycling in its ongoing operations—contributed to the rating.

Werner sees sustainable architecture and adaptive use as morally necessary. "Both are about the kind of world we will leave to our children," she says. Instilling these priorities as values, not viewing them as just bargains or fads, will be crucial if the future is to be as ecologically sound as much of the past is turning out to be.

Preservation and green architecture will play an important role at the National Trust's annual conference that starts in late October, particularly at a forum called the National Summit on Greening of Historic Properties, which will focus on the future of this complex but rich marriage of ambitions. Led by PHLF and the Green Building Alliance, the summit is intended to reinforce areas of mutual interest and to resolve "issues that are somewhat frustrating," according to Ellis Schmidlapp, one of the organizers. Rebecca Flora anticipates "a daylong summit roundtable with solutions-oriented discussion ... followed by a town meeting" to present guidelines and case studies. The forum should inspire dialogue between preservationists and greens, two camps that have a few members who have been "fanatical, but not willing to debate," says Jean Carroon. "I'd love to see the Trust put both sides together."

Charles L. Rosenblum is a Pittsburgh writer who specializes in architecture and planning.

40 PRESERVATION September/October 2006

September/October 2006 PRESERVATION 41

Despite the simplicity of the two-column grid, this spread from Preservation *magazine offers a dynamic layout and a range of sizes for photographs without "breaking" the format.*

and columns feel claustrophobic. A wider gutter can often make a publication feel airier and more open without a large sacrifice in usable space; compare *Harper's*, which has an elegant two-pica gutter, to *Entertainment Weekly*, which uses the standard one pica. Some designers prefer a graph-paper-like square-block grid without gutters, but these are not suited to periodical design.

Grid Elements

After a number of years in which clean, uncluttered layouts were the rule, a number of magazines are becoming increasingly ornate. Custom Oxford rules—parallel lines of uniform width—and Scotch rules—parallel lines of contrasting widths—along with boxes and textures are again becoming part of page architecture. While these decorative flourishes hark back (at least most recently) to the sixties and seventies, in modern layouts they do not have quite the same visual effect. Contemporary pages that combine information-dense layouts and decoration seem at once daunting and inviting. The clutter promises substantive content, and various decorative doodads can make pages look lush. They can, however, also clutter up pages without a payoff in information. Also, they offer the practical disadvantage of putting a lot of little elements on a page that may need to be fussed over during page production. Designers who use them must carefully plan the grid for their incorporation. Extra rules, boxes, and frames reduce usable text and image space.

Modular Design

All grids provide a vertical column structure. A number of magazines and most newspapers also divide their pages into regular horizontal increments. For newspapers, the resulting modules have the twin production advantages of accommodating standard ad sizes and providing vertical placements for editorial matter. Aesthetically, modules provide the same pleasing regularity and order down the page as columns provide across the page.

The Twelve-Column Grid

Most magazine designers, knowingly or not, use a twelve-column grid. Of course, a standard-size page is never laid out with twelve actual columns—the result

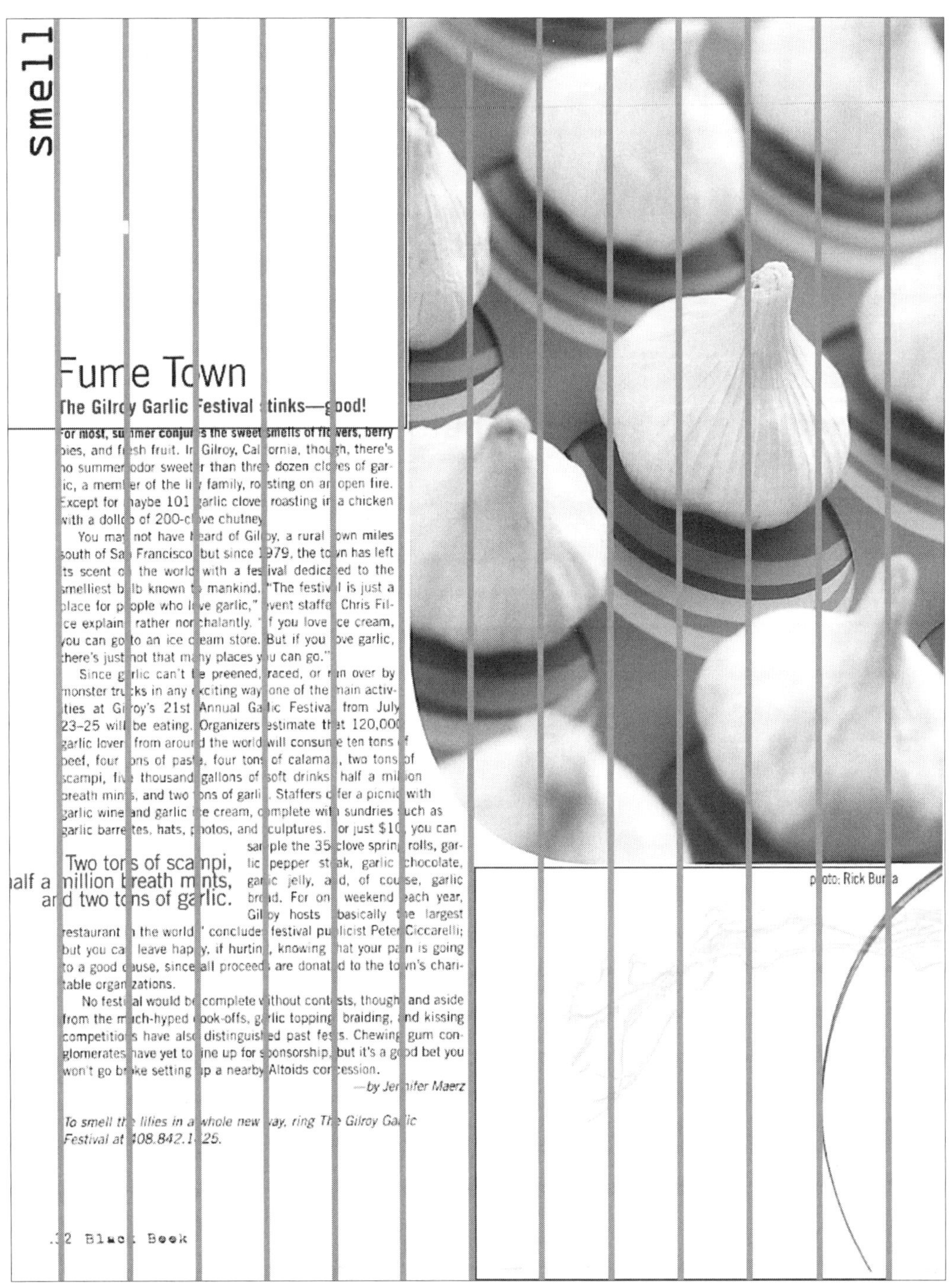

smell

Fume Town

The Gilroy Garlic Festival stinks—good!

For most, summer conjures the sweet smells of flowers, berry pies, and fresh fruit. In Gilroy, California, though, there's no summer odor sweeter than three dozen cloves of garlic, a member of the lily family, roasting on an open fire. Except for maybe 101 garlic cloves roasting in a chicken with a dollop of 200-clove chutney.

You may not have heard of Gilroy, a rural town miles south of San Francisco, but since 1979, the town has left its scent on the world with a festival dedicated to the smelliest bulb known to mankind. "The festival is just a place for people who love garlic," event staffer Chris Filice explains rather nonchalantly. "If you love ice cream, you can go to an ice cream store. But if you love garlic, there's just not that many places you can go."

Since garlic can't be preened, raced, or run over by monster trucks in any exciting way, one of the main activities at Gilroy's 21st Annual Garlic Festival from July 23–25 will be eating. Organizers estimate that 120,000 garlic lovers from around the world will consume ten tons of beef, four tons of pasta, four tons of calamari, two tons of scampi, five thousand gallons of soft drinks, half a million breath mints, and two tons of garlic. Staffers offer a picnic with garlic wine and garlic ice cream, complete with sundries such as garlic barrettes, hats, photos, and sculptures. For just $10, you can sample the 35-clove spring rolls, garlic pepper steak, garlic chocolate, garlic jelly, and, of course, garlic bread. For one weekend each year, Gilroy hosts "basically the largest restaurant in the world," concludes festival publicist Peter Ciccarelli; "but you can leave happy, if hurting, knowing that your pain is going to a good cause, since all proceeds are donated to the town's charitable organizations."

Two tons of scampi, half a million breath mints, and two tons of garlic.

No festival would be complete without contests, though, and aside from the much-hyped cook-offs, garlic topping, braiding, and kissing competitions have also distinguished past fests. Chewing gum conglomerates have yet to line up for sponsorship, but it's a good bet you won't go broke setting up a nearby Altoids concession.

—*by Jennifer Maerz*

To smell the lilies in a whole new way, ring The Gilroy Garlic Festival at 408.842.1625.

photo: Rick Burda

152 Black Book

This page from Black Book *reveals the use of a twelve-column grid and horizontal organizational lines to balance white space, image, and text. Even the curve of the photograph and the gray ring respect the guides. Despite its simplicity, it's a dynamic page.*

would be unreadable. But, at its most basic, a twelve-column grid provides twelve units from which the designer can derive most standard magazine layouts. Six units plus six units renders a two-column layout, three-unit columns provide a four-column layout, and four-unit columns provide a three-column layout. These can sometimes be mixed on the same page—it's not uncommon to see a sidebar use a different grid structure than the main story.

One of the strengths of the twelve-column grid comes from its use to organize space in open layouts. Using this grid might allow the expansion of gutters to

thenotebook

COPYCATS

Hot Exposé!

How local TV news recycles its sexiest stories.

On February 24, viewers of a San Diego news broadcast were told to be prepared for a disturbing report. A website, the KGTV anchor said, was promoting illicit sex in public bathrooms on local college campuses. What followed were close-ups of a computer screen with listings of San Diego locations where men can find anonymous gay sex. Next came footage described by KGTV's reporter as depicting "a sex act involving several men"—only their legs were visible—shot with a hidden camera in a San Diego State University bathroom.

Over the next few months, viewers in at least ten other cities—including New York, Miami, and Houston—saw strikingly similar reports on their local broadcasts. Though some stations refrained from showing men engaged in sex, and some staked out parks instead of bathrooms, all of the stories told viewers about the website and mentioned local cruising venues. Where did the stations get the idea for their stories? Had it come from police? Citizen complaints? Not exactly. Most of the TV stations used a source they are turning to again and again: newscasts from other cities.

"I really feel it's a good thing to share story ideas," says reporter Chris Heinbaugh of Seattle's KOMO-TV, which served as ground zero for this report. (The rash of copycats was first publicized by the Gay & Lesbian Alliance Against Defamation.) Heinbaugh chatted up the story with friends and former colleagues in four cities; word of mouth carried it the rest of the way. The story's built-in tip sheet, the website, supplied exact locations in each city—down to specific public bathroom stalls—and decoded the signals men use to set up encounters.

This story is just the latest to make the rounds of local stations. Others with high pass-along value include the on-line seduction exposé, in which reporters sign on to Internet chat rooms claiming to be minors to see if any men propose meeting for a sexual encounter. Some have—and have been caught on camera by stations in Miami, Phoenix, and Portland, Oregon. Another favorite is exposing emergency medical technicians with criminal histories; four stations—in Ohio, Arizona, and Washington—have done that story since May 1997.

"If it works in one place, it often works in another," says Detroit reporter Mike Wendland, whose TV station, WDIV, aired its own version of a report that's appeared in at least three other cities and on ABC's *PrimeTime Live*: testing hotel rooms to see if they were dirty (they were). Reporters often find ideas at the annual Investigative Reporters and Editors conference, where they show tapes of their stories to colleagues to be critiqued—and, inevitably, knocked off.

"As long as you don't have something that's incredibly exclusive, it's great to be able to share it with people, and then have them throw you a bone sometime," says Brian Collister, a reporter at KTBC-TV in Austin. This cooperation, he says, has "sprung up as a result of the pressure on us to put on stories. It helps us crank out stuff."

What viewers are rarely told is that an investigative report touted by their local station may be a knockoff. "People think, 'This is something that my local reporter thought up for me,'" says Phyllis Kaniss, who teaches at the University of Pennsylvania's Annenberg School for Communication. "They think their local news is the diner down the street. They're not expecting McDonald's." —*Jennifer Greenstein*

A videotaped scene of three men in a public bathroom, as broadcast by KGTV in San Diego.

NETWORK CLUTTER IN PRIME TIME

Except on ABC, TV clutter—defined as non-programming content like commercials and network promotions—dipped slightly in prime time last year, according to the annual Television Commercial Monitoring Report of the American Association of Advertising Agencies and the Association of National Advertisers, Inc. This graph shows the number of non-programming minutes per prime-time hour on the four broadcast networks.

BRILL'S CONTENT JULY/AUGUST 1998

24

CONNECTIONS

FUN, FEARLESS FAMILY MEMBER

Don't tell *Cosmopolitan* it's not a family magazine. In the March installment of a monthly feature called "Fun, Fearless Females" that usually recognizes achievers like the Spice Girls and 1998's Miss America, *Cosmo* saluted Kim Myers Robertson for being one of only a handful of female photographers ever to shoot for *Sports Illustrated*'s swimsuit issue. It also cooed that she is the mother of "a picture-perfect 1 ½-year-old-daughter, Drue." The feature never mentions husbands, but this time the editors might have reconsidered: Kim Myers Robertson is married to Donald Robertson, *Cosmo*'s creative director.

"I don't think that our readers could care less who she's married to," says editor in chief Bonnie Fuller. "It would never have occurred to me to make a point of saying that she's married to our creative director." (Frank Bennack, president of parent Hearst Corporation, did not return phone calls.) It apparently occurred to someone on her staff, though. "I think it was in there at one point," says Donald Robertson, who can't recall exactly what the story said about him or who changed it. "I guess it got cut."

While the story touted Kim Myers Robertson's success in the "highly competitive, male-dominated world of fashion photography," it left out something else: she is one of *Cosmopolitan*'s favorite freelance photographers (her work has appeared in at least 12 of the last 15 issues). "It doesn't say that?" asks Fuller. "If it doesn't say that, then that was definitely cut for space, because it did say that she shot for *Cosmo* frequently." —*Jennifer Greenstein*

Cosmopolitan's March item about "Fun, Fearless Female" Kim Myers Robertson

Bookmarks

Editors' Web Picks

We asked the editors of two leading music and entertainment magazines to tell us their favorite places on the Web. *VIBE*'s Danyel Smith says she likes to "jump on for a quick ride" whenever she has a spare moment. *SPIN*'s Michael Hirschorn logs on two or three times daily for "quick scans of my favorite webzines." —*Michael Kodish*

Danyel Smith
Editor in chief, VIBE

→**Internet Travel Network** (www.itn.net), web travel agency and magazine.

→**gURL** (www.gurl.com), a humorous feminist webzine aimed at young women.

→**Fast Company** (www.fastcompany.com), the new, hip business monthly's website.

Michael Hirschorn
Editor in chief, SPIN

→**The Hollywood Stock Exchange** (www.hsx.com), a fantasy stock exchange where you invest in movies and actors rather than corporations.

→**TheStreet.com** (www.thestreet.com), James Cramer's financial news and advice site.

→**Salon magazine** (www.salon1999.com), the literary and current events web magazine.

CORBIS-BETTMANN (SIMON & SCHUSTER)

LOOKING BACK

FROM THE ARCHIVES OF *FORTUNE* MAGAZINE

"One highly important factor in the Simon & Schuster success revolves around the personalities of the partners. Simon, the salesman, is nervous, high-strung, with a certain suggestion of perpetual adolescence; Schuster, the man who has the bulk of the ideas, was born old. Both are Jews; one comes from a family of extremely modest circumstances. Both possess an enormous urge for self-improvement which is typically Jewish—and typical also of the heroes of all stories beginning with poor-but-honest parents. Still another racial trait that shines out strongly in both Simon and Schuster is a vast autistic emotionalism which can well up from within at a relatively weak stimulus from without. In 1926, with a black year behind them, these two qualities of the partners suddenly made them rich and, in their world, famous."
—*Fortune*, January 1934

Lincoln Schuster (left) and Richard Simon, founders of Simon & Schuster.

The late Brill's Content *used a ten-column grid in their news section. Each text column is three units; the extra tenth column is used to hold captions and art. Its placement—either as a "wing" (or extra-large outside margin) or as an extra-large gutter—allows for the introduction of white space on otherwise dense pages.*

one-twelfth of the page, or precise placement of pull quotes or sidebars, or integration of white space in a pleasing ratio to other elements on the page. I tend to think of a grid as similar to the beat in music—the twelve-column grid provides a rhythmic structure to support an orderly page, but it also allows freedom to improvise.

Asymmetrical Grids

Some designers prefer asymmetrical grids because they encourage dynamic page layouts. A common choice is the seven-column grid, which permits a three-column layout (two units for each column) with an extra unit for a "wing"—a skinny column for marginalia or white space. The extra unit can be placed on either side of the page or between columns. The ten-column grid is similar to the seven-column grid, with three, three-unit columns and a one-column wing. It is usually used on larger-than-standard-sized pages; the wing of a ten-column grid would be too skinny to be useful for all but the tiniest text on an $8\frac{1}{2} \times 11$ sheet.

Irregular Grids

A few designers use irregular grids, which replace the structured cadences of a sonata with the syncopated rhythm of ragtime. Irregular grids require extra effort. All layout programs offer plenty of flexibility for basic grid creation, but irregular structures must be created in a drawing program or on paper. Used well, these oddball grids provide what I imagine you might get if you put David Carson on Ritalin: a slightly more structured and consistent free-for-all. Nontraditional grids are rarely used for periodicals because they increase production time and are not suited to linear storytelling.

Designing without a Grid

Speaking of David Carson, it's possible to design a magazine without a grid at all. His best pages in *Beach Culture* shimmered, even as they seemed antithetical to normal magazine design goals—many critics perceived the articles as ancillary to the visual statement. Even if a designer finds a magazine willing to entertain the gridless approach, such an undertaking is not to be tackled lightly. Grids help establish a "family resemblance" between pages—the grid relieves part of the burden of making different parts of the magazine look as if they belong together. Without a grid, every photograph, every illustration, every word of type must work extra hard to communicate the publication's personality.

For this reason, most gridless publications have been in the hands of a single designer with a single vision. To return to the music analogy: The beat of the grid (and style sheets) keeps everyone in time. Gridless design is closer to freeform jazz. It's possible—just—for it to be music and not noise.

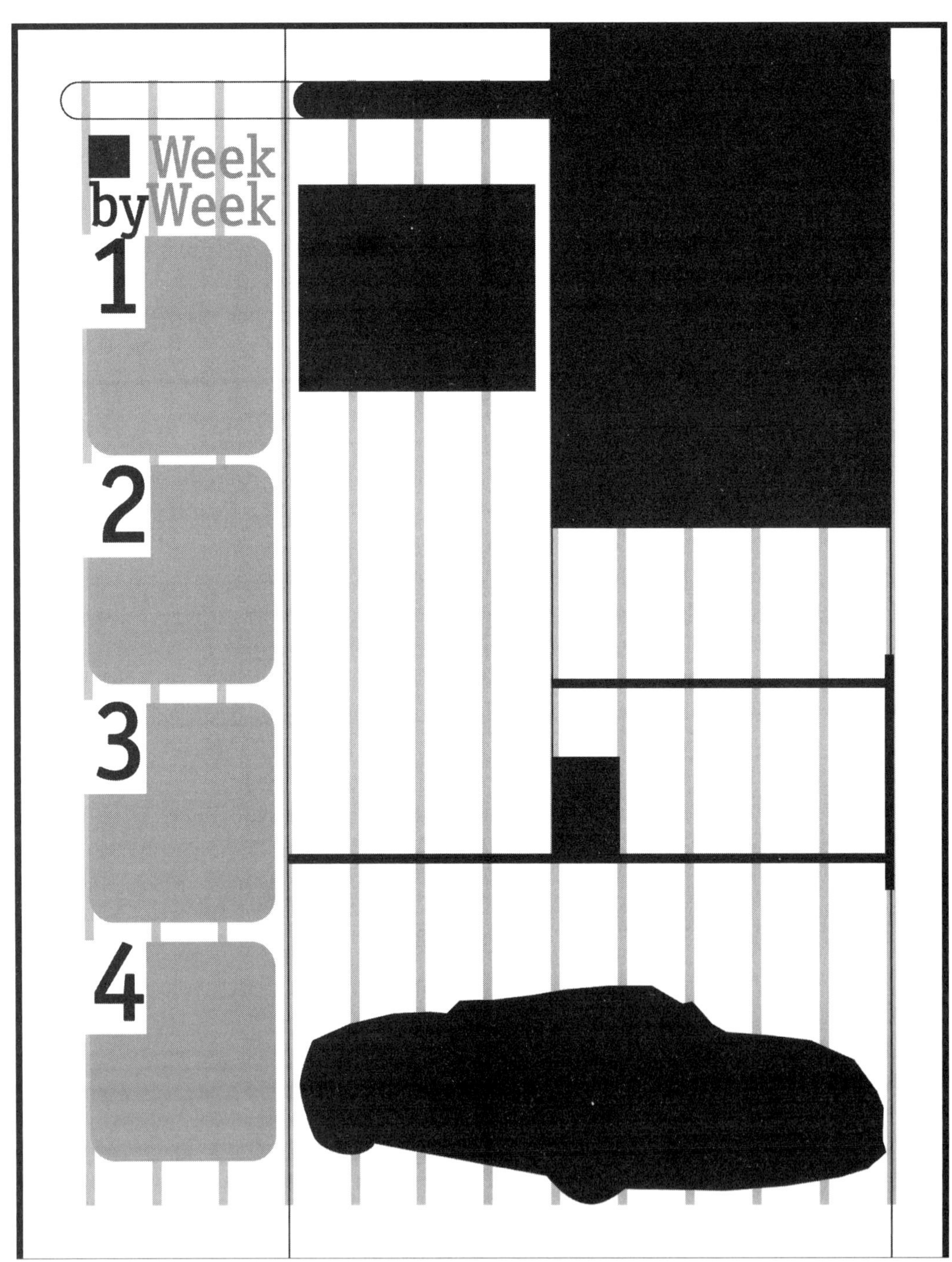

This FOB page from Esquire Magazine *(see page 134) hews closely to a twelve-column grid to accommodate eight separate stories on a single 8.25 × 10.45 page. Even though every column is a different width, they have a proportional and pleasing relationship to each other across the page. The leftmost column uses three units, the middle column uses four units, and the right column uses five units, adding up to twelve. The designer respected the grid in myriad small ways.*

Using the Grid to Structure Layered Pages

Just as twelve-column and other highly flexible grids are invaluable for incorporating white space into an open layout, they are also useful for structuring very dense, information-rich pages as exist in a typical magazine news section. When one article flows into the next—as they do in the "Talk of the Town" section of the *New Yorker*, for example—almost any grid will do. Pages that seek to put a lot of different elements on a page need a newspaper-style multicolumn grid. For a standard-size magazine, that often means four or more columns.

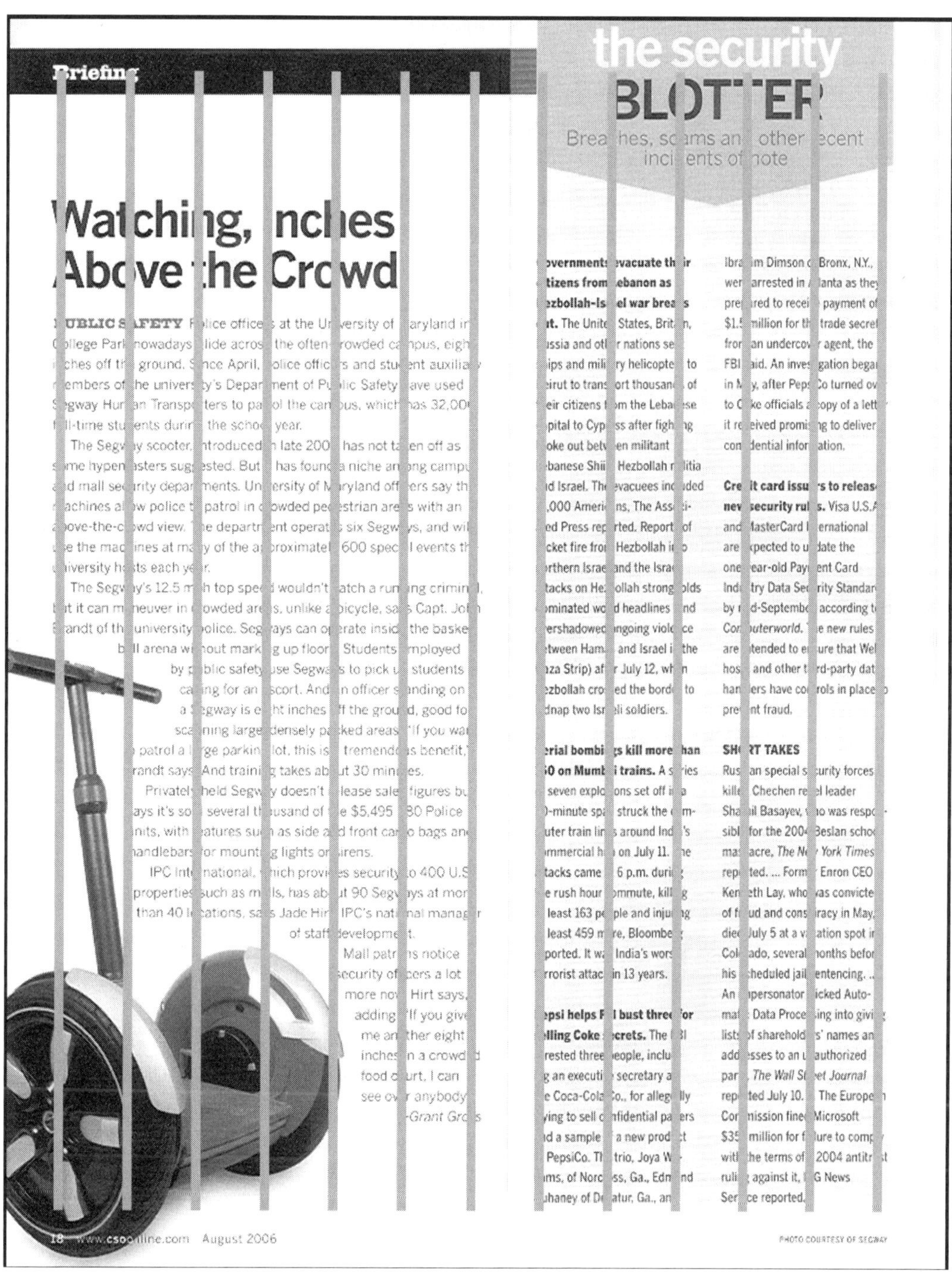

CSO's FOB page is also using a twelve-column grid, but to a different effect than Esquire's. *Unlike* Esquire's *friendly clutter, the* CSO *page feels open and airy even though there are five separate short articles.*

A Last Word

While grids are a valuable production tool, they do not come with papal infallibility. There are times when, perhaps due to an oddly shaped or overly long headline or another element, the grid hinders rather than helps a solution. On these occasions, judgment should dictate that visual considerations must win. However, if judgment overrides the grid with too much frequency, odds are that the problem is with the specific grid in use. On such occasions, the grid must be changed to reflect the needs of the publication. Grid-based organization is inviting to readers, increases production efficiency, and improves the perceived authority of the text. These benefits should not be lost to too many ad-hoc modifications.

This essay seeks only to introduce the topic of grids, a subject about which books have been written. More information can be found in *Grid: A Modular System for the Design and Production of Newspapers, Magazines, and Books*, by Allen Hurlburt, and *Grid Systems: Principles of Organizing Type*, by Kimberly Elam.

Pacing

28

JANDOS ROTHSTEIN

MUCH HAS BEEN WRITTEN ABOUT THE WAY GRIDS are used to structure magazine pages. While consistent margins and a logical column structure help pages look rational in and of themselves, and consistent over the course of the magazine, the cohesion of a publication can still be undermined by a poorly considered or missing "temporal" structure. In other words, a magazine or newspaper must continue to make visual sense over the period of time you read it. Unlike grid structure, which can be divined by anyone with a straightedge and a pencil, the overarching structure of the magazine—why articles appear where they do—is less immediately apparent, at least consciously. Nevertheless, readers are dependent on it to happily navigate most publications.

It is true that many magazine readers are skimmers—they skip around, read from back to front, or open the magazine at random. Nevertheless, even they look to the macro structure of the magazine to tell them where they are in the "book" and to help them find the sort of material they are looking for. Feedback from the physical object helps—one knows roughly where one is because the stack of pages on one side is fatter. But without structure, this feedback would be close to useless. It's possible for most readers to look at a spread from a well-designed magazine and know roughly where they are in terms of location and content. Visual feedback, the result of good structural planning, reinforces physical feedback.

Because pacing is so important, those undertaking a redesign or a launch ignore it at their peril. This may mean that the redesigner is advocating editorial changes—the creation or destruction of sections, the rearrangement or reshaping of the publication—a process that can be fraught, particularly when working with an editor who is excited about getting a feature into a publication that doesn't have an appropriate place to put it. Nevertheless, these sorts of considerations are arguably more important than type choice or a color palette in creating a positive user experience. The structure of a publication affects both content and design. In a healthy process, both editors and designers will bring insights to this area.

There are many ways to structure a publication. However, two are dominant—what I refer to as "Bell Curve," and "Inverted Pyramid." Designers need not feel shame in relying on them; they provide a preloaded framework of familiarity that new readers can use to navigate a publication they have never seen before, they help a publication feel organized and inviting, and when combined with a rational page grid and signage system, they constitute the most important elements of magazine design.

Super symmetry is a mathematical field that, among other things, explores how local phenomena repeat on a grander scale. A tiny stretch of beach—the way the water interacts with ounces of sand over a few inches—is likely a good approximation in miniature of how millions of gallons of water interact with tons of sand over the course of the whole beach. Looking at the beach from the air, one may not be aware of the myriad small forces that went into shaping it, but they nevertheless have had their effect. Most publications use a pacing that emerges—intentionally or not—from the unseen but pervasive expository structure the publication uses.

Magazine Structure

Most magazine articles follow a literary style of writing. An article, no matter how long, starts with a lead—an anecdote or bold statement meant to intrigue the reader and pull him or her into the body of the article. The lead is followed by the meat of the article—one or more arguments sustained over what may be thousands of words. Finally the article reaches its conclusion—perhaps a summary, speculation about what will happen next, or another anecdote. If you were to graph the informational value of every paragraph in a typical piece of literary journalism, you'd get something very much like a bell curve: less information at the front and back, with the substantive material in the middle. If you assigned an entertainment value to each paragraph you might well get the reverse—the article starts and ends with a bang.

Magazines as a whole tend to mimic the structure of literary journalism. Most tend to concentrate small, more entertaining, but also more trivial items in the front and the back, and concentrate longer items in a "feature well" in the middle. The front of a magazine tends to have a contents page, brief news items, letters, and personality-driven columns. It may also contain an editor's or publisher's note, various special features such as brief personality profiles, a photo essay, and a contributors' page. The back of a magazine tends to have reviews of arts or technology, more columns, a news section (usually more sharply focused and possibly longer than the front news sections), a "gadgets" column, and feature jumps, although these days many magazines try to avoid jumps. It's common for magazines to put a humorous one-page column opposite the inside back cover, otherwise known as Cover 3.

In some sense, this classic layout evolved in consideration of advertising interests. Advertisers tend to prefer being near the front of the book. The creation of lots of one- and two-page features "far forward" allows for a predictable number of logical places for ads. While there's nothing inherent in short features that aids ad placement (often the reverse is true) slots opposite these short items are doubly desirable to advertisers because of content. Ads for high-tech products will often appear in a "gadgets" section. Often advertisers will request placement next to popular columns. Reviews provide a logical editorial environment for advertisements for the class of product—books, music, skin-care products, technology, or what have you—that is being reviewed.

Occasionally, the imperative to create "far forward" ad placements drives editorial form. Two-, three-, and even four-page tables of contents are designed with ad positions in mind. Most readers would prefer to see all their choices on a single page, and most editors would rather devote that space to another article. Another example of a created ad placement is the contributors' page. Readers (if they care) would generally prefer to see author's biographies with the article. The *New York Times Book Review* faced a substantial number of complaints when it moved reviewer biographies to a dedicated page in 2004. To the publication's credit, it abolished the page and returned bios to their previous position with reviews. *Create* magazine "solves" this problem of whether to serve readers or advertisers in a unique if not entirely admirable way: It runs the same bios twice—once on a contributors' page and once with articles.

These days, most magazines are sent in their entirety to press at one time. However, such was not always the case. Magazines longer than thirty-two pages are printed in "signatures"—gathers of pages that in the case of stapled or saddle-stitched magazines are wrapped around each other, and in the case of perfect-bound magazines are stacked in a row. When magazine signatures were sent on separate schedules, processing the outer, or the front and back, signature last allowed for more timely pieces in the front and back. However, logical flow is the main reason most magazines use a bell structure.

Newspapers

The super-symmetry analogy also applies to newspapers, although the form newspapers take is different because classic newspaper expository writing is a different form of journalism. While many newspaper articles employ a more literary style these days, classically reporters were taught to put the essential information—the who, what, where, and why—into the first paragraph. As the article progressed, the value of the information gradually diminished. This "inverted pyramid" form of writing, which assumed that most readers do not complete most articles, assured that wherever the grazer stopped, he or she would not miss out on information more important (at least in the judgment of the newspaper) than what he had so far read.

Newspaper sections also follow a flow based on the inverted pyramid. The front page of the front section holds the most important information. Articles become, as a rule, increasingly less important or more remote from the reader's presumed interest as the pages are turned. Similarly, business, sports, and special weekly sections, which have less news value than the front section (although any may be read first), are tucked inside. And each of them follows the same inverted-pyramid format. When special-interest articles are judged extremely important (the local sports team makes the playoffs, Enron goes bust), these stories are moved from the sports and business sections to the front page of the front section, or, rarely, to the inside of the front section. (A special section cover is considered more prominent than a front-section inside page.)

Readers (and editors, for that matter) are in the habit of describing publications based on paper quality and size: If it's printed on newsprint and is bigger than 8½ × 11, it's a newspaper. If it's printed on glossy and is 11 × 17 or smaller, it's a magazine. In fact, the way a publication is paced is a much better guide than paper choice to the nature of the publication. The *Week* and *CQ Weekly*, despite their diminutive size and high-quality paper, are newspapers—they follow newspaper conventions in reporting and pacing. Most alternative newsweeklies (such as the *Village Voice*, the *San Francisco Bay Guardian*, and the *Chicago Reader*), despite the cheap paper and news-driven reporting, are magazines. Bell-curve pacing and literary-style writing peg them as such.

Other Ways to Structure a Publication

The bell curve and inverted pyramid are by far the most common structures. However, some publications employ other approaches, most often because they do not use the range of story lengths—very short to very long—that conventional publications do.

Lad Magazines

The lad magazines—*Maxim*, *FHM*, *Co-Ed*, and so forth—take a form resembling the bell-curve structure, but they are not really conventional magazines because there is no in-depth reporting. With few exceptions, "long articles" are really collections of related short articles or are short pieces stretched out over several pages through the use of a photo essay. Lad magazines tend to resemble stretched-out front-of-the-book sections from more conventional publications. They can be extremely entertaining, though they offer little substance.

As a rule, women's magazines and traditional men's magazines have not abandoned long-form (or at least longish-form) journalism, so do not follow lad format, although there are exceptions. Shoppers like *Lucky* are structurally similar to *Maxim*.

Freight Train

Many literary and academic journals now follow a structure closer to consumer-magazine-style bell curves. However, some start with little more than an editor's note and contents page before moving into a rhythm of one scholarly or literary freight car following another. Short items—book reviews and letters—are relegated to the rear, although poetry (if included) is interspersed with articles because it is deemed to be of high importance. Although they may do some subject-specific organization (dividing fiction from nonfiction, for example), there is little visual cajoling of readers.

Cinematic

Over the years, there have been a number of attempts to make magazines that are primarily photo- or art-driven. Without the DNA of written structure to guide form, these magazines have looked to more visual ways to build a structure, often based on thematic relationships. It's unlikely that there will ever be room in the marketplace for more than a few of these, but the best—*Esopus*, a sumptuous magazine named after a river in upstate New York, is a current example—offer valuable lessons in building visual narratives. *Lodown*, *Source*, and some photography magazines are also well-done examples of this approach.

Fanzines

Fanzines—small magazines based around a special interest such as skateboarding, monster films, pro wrestling, or the doings within a genre of music—often confront the uninitiated with a cacophony of tiny, murky pictures, a sea of difficult-to-read text, and a structure best described as no structure. In these magazines, shoehorning as much text as possible into the pages is often the main objective. Little items are squeezed into random nooks and crannies as space allows. It is a mistake to guess that there is no broader intent behind this approach, however. Many fan magazines—labors of love, written and designed from within the community they serve—are specifically, if not necessarily intentionally, laid out to repel those outside of the in-group. The baffling structure and uninviting pages serve as proof of authenticity. Sometimes, however, magazines that look like they were designed on a Mac Plus in Mom's basement were actually produced by a large publisher looking to cash in on a trend. A classic example was the slacker bible *Big Brother* (later *Big Brother Skateboarding*), which LFP shuttered in 2004. But many enthusiast magazines that appear as if they come from within diverse communities are actually published by a single parent company. *LowRider* and *Canoe and Kayak* are both published by Primedia.

Advertising: The Designer's Friend (and Enemy)

Advertising presents both challenges and opportunities for the periodical designer. While designers often curse the necessity of ads—especially the ugly ones and the ones that are unchanged month after month—it is unquestionably easier to design an effective publication if advertisements take up at least 30 percent of the space, and it is possible to design effectively when advertising goes as high as the 55 percent to 60 percent range. More than that, and the reader will have to search for editorial content.

Advertisements can work like levees, guiding the flow of text. All ads come in at fixed shape—with luck, mostly full pages—but whatever they are, they cannot be altered to fit a layout. Articles can take any shape, flowing around advertising as needed. The designer's emphasis, however, should be on placing advertising to achieve a text flow that aids both effective design and visual storytelling.

English readers read left to right and top to bottom, so it seems counterintuitive that advertisers generally prefer to be on right-hand pages, but they do. It is fine to give advertisers right-hand pages as a matter of course, but there are times when the right-hand page must be used for editorial purposes. Just as the front cover signals the start of the magazine, a right-hand position—even deep inside the magazine—signals a beginning. When you're starting a new section on a single page, the right-hand side is always the best choice. Using the right-hand side also has the advantage of helping a multipage section or story seem contiguous—the reader does not have to visually jump over an ad to keep reading—assuming the second page of text is in the usual left-hand position. One-page features such as columns generally work well on the left.

Because the first pages of sections are generally considered destinations within a magazine, most advertisers are willing to sacrifice right-hand placement for what is an otherwise preferred position, on the facing left-hand page.

The opening spread is a billboard for the story: The principal goal of those two pages is to get the reader reading. This is achieved in part by not confronting the reader with a daunting amount of text or distracting ads. Once the reader is committed to the story, the text can stretch out like the Sahara desert before her and she'll keep going, barely noticing as the pages (and ads) float by. But starting with pages that are too businesslike (too much text, too many ads) is likely to turn off readers.

Advertisements are valuable for pacing feature stories. Generally, the ratio of advertising to edit can go up as a feature story progress. Features should start on a spread, if possible, and continue on a full page or second spread. Eventually, if the article is long enough or the magazine carries lots of fractional ads (such as those seen in the *New Yorker*), the reader may find himself confronting one column of text and five columns of ads.

There may be times when a designer may wish to bend these rules—for example, if a feature story includes an effective photograph or photo essay that doesn't have full impact until the reader has background information that comes late in the text. Ideally, that story can stay relatively clear of advertising. Or, if that's not a possibility, it can "open up" again at the appropriate place in the narrative. It's also important to build secondary opportunities to hook the reader after the opening spread. Effective supporting photographs, informational graphics, pull quotes, sidebars, and captions can all help accomplish this.

While advertising can help pace edit, when it doesn't, the culprit is the variety of side deals that magazines are willing to make with advertisers. Advertisers sometimes want their ads to be in the front of the book; others want to be in a specific section or feature, while some would rather that theirs not be closer than ten pages to those of a direct competitor. As a result, the decision to move or flip ads midway through the production process may have implications beyond the pages in question.

Nevertheless, the staff should carefully look at each spread to make sure that the editorial side and the advertising side—or both ads in an all-ad spread—are compatible. The desired relationship between the two sides is a sort of friendly indifference. A severe clash of colors—say, hot purples on one side, cool greens on the other—is jarring and off-putting. On the other hand, if the ad and edit side are too similar, there is a danger of melting the wall between them. Identical or nearly identical colors, elements that seem to continue from one part of the page to the other, or conceptual relationships—the review of a Canon camera opposite a full-page ad for Canon—all harm both advertisers and the magazine. Readers will assume an overly cozy relationship, even if none exists.

Most magazines reserve the right to reject ads for aesthetic reasons, but for many publications this is a toothless policy. However, advertisements that are ugly, dated, or overly familiar—some agencies provide the same "creative" for months or years on end—all make the magazine look tired. Bad advertising has the power to reflect badly on the content around it. When combined with guaranteed placement, a bad ad becomes a shark that bites right where it is least welcome. A compromise policy is to make placement guarantees contingent on the quality of the submitted materials—something production art directors should lobby for.

Fractionals

Some magazines and most newspapers get lots of advertisements that take up less than a full page, some nearly none.

A designer who does not need to consider fractionals has an easier path—ads and edit never become too intimate. However, the many designers who work with partial-page ads must learn how to make them work with editorial. Fractionals can create awkward interactions and make it hard to create high-impact pages. They limit the size of photographs, for one thing, and they are often an unattractive element that must be reconciled into the page structure. However, many advertisers like them for reasons other than their comparatively modest cost. They are likely put on a page with editorial content, which means they may be seen for a longer period of time, and they are useful for serious topics that don't benefit from lavish illustration, such as issue advocacy and conference announcements.

There are many strategies for integrating fractional advertising into the magazine. For the most part, these suggestions, codifed as policy, would benefit advertisers and the publication alike.

DON'T PERMIT GOOFY SHAPES. These are seen more in newspapers than magazines—a roofing contractor whose ad is shaped like a little house, or an accountant whose ad is a fat pencil. One of these can poison an entire page, even if quite small, to the detriment of other advertisers and editorial content. Require that all ads have a minimum of a one-point square frame, or at least a rule at top and bottom to define the space.

CREATE FULL COLUMNS AND EVEN AD LINES WHENEVER POSSIBLE BY COMBINING FRACTIONALS. Many magazines, particularly trade and association titles, maintain a one-ad-per-page policy—a practice that is overly accommodating to the desires of advertisers and not accommodating enough to the needs of readers. Such a policy actively discourages full-page ads because, while fractional ads will share a page with other material, they will almost certainly be the dominant element on that page. A fractional opposite a full-page ad competes with that ad to the detriment of the wealthier customer. A spread with two fractionals (a double dogleg, as the reverse L-shaped layout is derisively called in newspaper circles) is nearly impossible to design in a way that will engage the reader. If the spread encourages the reader to flip past it, neither ad nor editorial is served.

DO NOT ACCEPT ADS THAT VIOLATE THE MAGAZINE'S GRID STRUCTURE—unless you get enough of them to build lines or full pages. Many magazine pages employ a three-column structure. A single standard quarter-page ad on such a page requires that the text wrap around it, creating a skinny "leg" of text. Skinny legs often have awkward breaks, and the short line length makes them less pleasant to read than wider columns.

DO NOT PUT AN AD ON TOP OF EDITORIAL CONTENT. To most professionals this will be obvious, but some magazines, particularly start-ups, experiment with offering advertisers the tops of pages. This policy undermines readers' expectations, creates top-heavy layouts, and suggests a rather too-close relationship with advertisers. Like the one-ad-per-page policy, top placement also makes fractionals overly desirable, possibly to detriment of sales of full-page ads.

CONSIDER A DESTINATION SECTION FOR FRACTIONALS. Many magazines only allow fractional ads in a classified or marketplace section in the back, or at least they offer a lower price for such fractionals. These sections—which can become destinations in their own right for comparison shoppers—offer an attractive option for many advertisers and help keep the body of the magazine free of difficult-to-place small ads.

At any publication, advertising can be a source of conflict. The representative who sold the ad will likely want to ensure that it is shepherded successfully onto a printed page. Designers will be more concerned that ads and editorial mix successfully. Editors don't want anything that compromises editorial integrity. Publishers, who must balance the long- and short-term interests of the business, often have the most balanced perspective. However, they need input from all three departments to make an informed decision if questions are raised about an ad or its suitability. It's the designer's job, when questions about advertising arise, to support editorial integrity and to defend the needs of the reader. When advertising exists in a free-for-all competition with content, reading the magazine becomes a chore rather than a pleasure.

The ABCs of ASFs

DENISE REAGAN

ALTERNATIVE STORY FORM FEVER IS SPREADING through magazines and newspapers like the sniffles. Business magazines like *Forbes* and *Money*, news magazines like *Time* and *Newsweek*, and newspapers like the *Star Tribune, Red Eye* and the *Boston Globe* are all increasing their use of nonnarrative and nonlinear storytelling approaches. Even city and lifestyle magazines have caught the bug. I recently talked with a designer at the *Abilene Reporter-News* in Texas where they are trying many forms of storytelling. Here are some of the tips I shared with her.

Make Text Scannable

This is the key ingredient that makes a story form "alternative." They are not narratives, so they shouldn't be written that way. Complete sentences are not always necessary. Readers should be able to glide through text and find what's interesting or important to them. Headlines, subheads, and bold text should create hierarchy.

BEST LOUNGER
Lee Industries Chair #5325 in adras blue, $1,968 (37"h x 29"w x 38"d) A classic armchair so comfortable and generously proportioned that once you've curled up, it'll be difficult to convince yourself there's reason to move. Also in more than 1,400 other prints; Lee Industries, 800-892-7150 for stores.

BEST MODERN FORMAL DINING
Disfigure "The Esoteric Character of Concealment" Chair, $1,900 (39"h x 24"w x 22"d) This vintage Louis XV–style chair brings colorful conversation to the dinner table—after all, the camouflage-pattern fabric is emblazoned with quotes from the Bill of Rights in graffiti-style print (courtesy of the late, iconoclastic designer Stephen Sprouse). The elegance of the distressed frame provides a courtly contrast; The Future Perfect, NY, 718-599-6276.

BEST KITCHEN DINING
✱ Brilliant Buy: West Elm "Overlapping Squares" Chair in chocolate, $169 (36"h x 21"w x 19"d) The geometric motif adds an instant Art Deco seating arrangement to the kitchen. Also in stem (green) and white; West Elm, 866-937-8356, or westelm.com.

BEST SHOWSTOPPER
Chair Couture "Billy" Chair, $1,695 (37"h x 19"w x 18"d) Not just another pretty face, this vintage French mahogany side chair adds a funky, cheeky touch to the bedroom or living room. Sherbet-bright chartreuse lacquer and aqua upholstery ensure there'll never be a dull moment; Distant Origin, NY, 212-941-0024, or distantorigin.com.

BEST VANITY SEAT
ABC Home Suzani Slipper Chair, $1,895 (30"h x 21"w x 19"d) Vintage Lebanese tapestries and suzanis render this classic slipper chair almost too adorable to perch on. But the low seat and impossible-to-resist rounded curves will make this your seat of choice when you're slipping on those new Manolos; ABC Carpet & Home, NY, 212-473-3000.

BEST FOR A LIBRARY
Weego Home "Jude" Chair in pink and brown stripe, $730 (33"h x 29"w x 31"d) Stripe it up and spice it up with this unabashedly playful armless lounge chair. The wide seat and broad back practically beg to be put to use, whether you're curling up with a good book or looking for a place to deposit shopping bags after indulging in a little retail therapy. Also in troika blue ($615); Weego Home, 800-659-3346.

Etc.
Don't relegate a striking, colorful chair to the corner of a room. To best display intricate woodwork or dramatic upholstery, make sure it can be viewed from all sides.

BEST CLASSIC DINING
Jonathan Adler Chippendale Chair in chocolate brown, $499 (36"h x 18"w x 21"d) Pulled up to the table or placed against the wall, this chair makes an ideal companion. The classic Chinese Chippendale style—open fretwork back, upholstered seat—adapts itself to most any room. Also in dove white and lime green; jonathanadlerfurniture.com for stores.

BEST FOR A BEDROOM
Circa Furniture "Trousdale" Chair, $3,936 (38"h x 27"w x 32"d) This chair's elegant sloping arms and sturdy barrel back beckon you to lean back and relax. The black-and-white graphic print and cut-velvet fabric demand attention—and compliments—be paid; Circa Furniture, CA, 310-289-6872, or circafurniture.com.

HOME ESSENTIALS

92 SHOPETC.COM 10.2006 SHOPETC.COM 10.2006 93

Shop, Etc., *2006*

Hands On | TECHNOLOGY

TOOLS

THE ROAD WARRIOR'S ARSENAL
TAKE YOUR OFFICE WITH YOU WHEN YOU GO

Thanks to the ubiquity of high-speed wireless networks and smart phones that can run even the most sophisticated business applications, life for traveling executives is increasingly like life in the office; the only thing that's different is the view from the window. It's a far cry from the days when road warriors had to pack an additional suitcase to carry extra cables, wires, and phone jacks. Serious techies, especially those traveling internationally, even were known to throw in a pair of wire cutters and a soldering iron. These days, companies are working hard to make sure all of their applications can work on the small displays of cell phones. The future? More of the same. Working from the road is getting downright convenient. Here are six technologies that can make it even more so. —*Michael Fitzgerald*

BEST FOR...
Keeping the power on

Kensington Universal 120-watt Notebook AC/DC Power Adapter
us.kensington.com/html/6368.html

What it does: Packed with 120 watts of power, this AC/DC adapter has enough juice to run a high-performance notebook. But it weighs just six ounces and measures 5.6 by 3.1 inches, so it's 40 percent smaller and lighter than other power supplies.

What's cool: Offers both AC and DC power supplies. It also comes with an adapter for airplane-seat outlets. Purchase an additional $25 cable and it can charge up to six different devices simultaneously.

Drawbacks: The cable to split the devices is short—just 5.6 inches long—and you'll need to buy different connectors to support things such as music players, portable DVD players, and certain kinds of notebooks.

Price: $140

BEST FOR...
Avoiding traffic jams

Rand McNally Traffic
randmcnally.com/traffic

What it does: Download this software to your cell phone and watch as it feeds you up-to-date traffic data for up to 94 cities.

What's cool: With Rand McNally Traffic, your cell phone or BlackBerry screen can supply current information about traffic accidents, congestion, and average road speeds as soon as they're updated in the traffic network.

Drawbacks: The software does not connect to a global positioning system, so you can't get alternative directions without using a different tool. In many cities, traffic systems don't report accidents as they happen, and the lag time can vary widely.

Price: $3.99 a month

BEST FOR...
Collecting business cards

CardScan Personal Version 8
cardscan.com

What it does: Scans business cards and drops the information directly into your address book or contact manager. At 4 1/2 by 3 1/8 inches, it's not much bigger than the stack of cards you accumulate after a week on the road.

What's cool: CardScan synchronizes with Microsoft Outlook and Outlook Express as well as with personal digital assistants like the Palm; it also has its own contact management software. Free online backup is available.

Drawbacks: CardScan works only with Windows. It cannot scan in color, and non-Microsoft e-mail systems, such as Lotus Notes, require a more expensive version.

Price: $160

BEST FOR...
Protecting your data

Synchronica MobileManager 1.0
synchronica.com

What it does: Synchronica's software lets people who use smart phones update their devices wirelessly without having to go to the office. That means salespeople don't have to return to the home office, and people on the road get the latest software, updates, and other key data.

What's cool: The software can be set to send things like weekly price lists automatically. If the device is reported stolen, Synchronica's software automatically wipes its data, locks it, and directs the device to emit a screeching sound that might help catch the thief—or, at the very least, seriously annoy the culprit.

Drawbacks: Works only with Windows Mobile, Pocket PC devices, and Symbian-based smart phones. It does not work with any notebook computers.

Price: About $75 per device per year

BEST FOR...
Staying connected

Kyocera Passport KPC650
kyocera-wireless.com

What it does: The Passport KPC650 is a PC card that you plug into your notebook computer to connect directly to a cellular network. Network providers for the Passport are Verizon and Alltel. Other carriers offer similar cards, and some notebook computers now come with built-in cellular modems.

What's cool: Essentially, the Passport puts you in a Wi-Fi hot spot almost no matter where you are. So you really can work in the park on a nice day, or get access on the Acela train. What's more, the cost of access is built into your data plan; most Wi-Fi hot spots, by contrast, charge by the day or the hour.

Drawbacks: Cellular networks have their dead spots, and the Passport works only where the network does; data speeds may be slower outside the Verizon network. And data access plans can be costly, compared with simple voice access plans.

Price: $150 after rebates from Verizon; $99 after rebates from Alltel

BEST FOR...
Reporting expenses

SamePageSolutions ExpenseWire
expensewire.com

What it does: Takes the hassle out of expense reporting. This Web-based application has reporting, tracking, and management tools to let people file expenses from the road and be reimbursed automatically, sometimes even before they've returned home.

What's cool: Traveling employees can call up their credit cards online and drag-and-drop expenses directly into the reports they file. The software can be customized so your accounting department can set rules to warn people when an entry exceeds company expense policies. For international travelers, it converts foreign currency to U.S. dollars and supports electronic funds transfer for faster reimbursements.

Drawbacks: Firefox users cannot gain access to all the features.

Price: $9.95 per user per month

48 | INC. MAGAZINE | OCTOBER 2006

Illustration by Ulla Puggaard

OCTOBER 2006 | INC. MAGAZINE | 49

Inc., *2006*

Use Parallel Construction

Many ASFs emphasize comparing and contrasting items, such as grids, muglets—small headshots—chronologies, and so on. This only works if the elements use parallel construction. If the idea is to compare things, make it easy. Use the same kind of information for each item, such as name, price, store, materials, and the like. And use the same sentence structure.

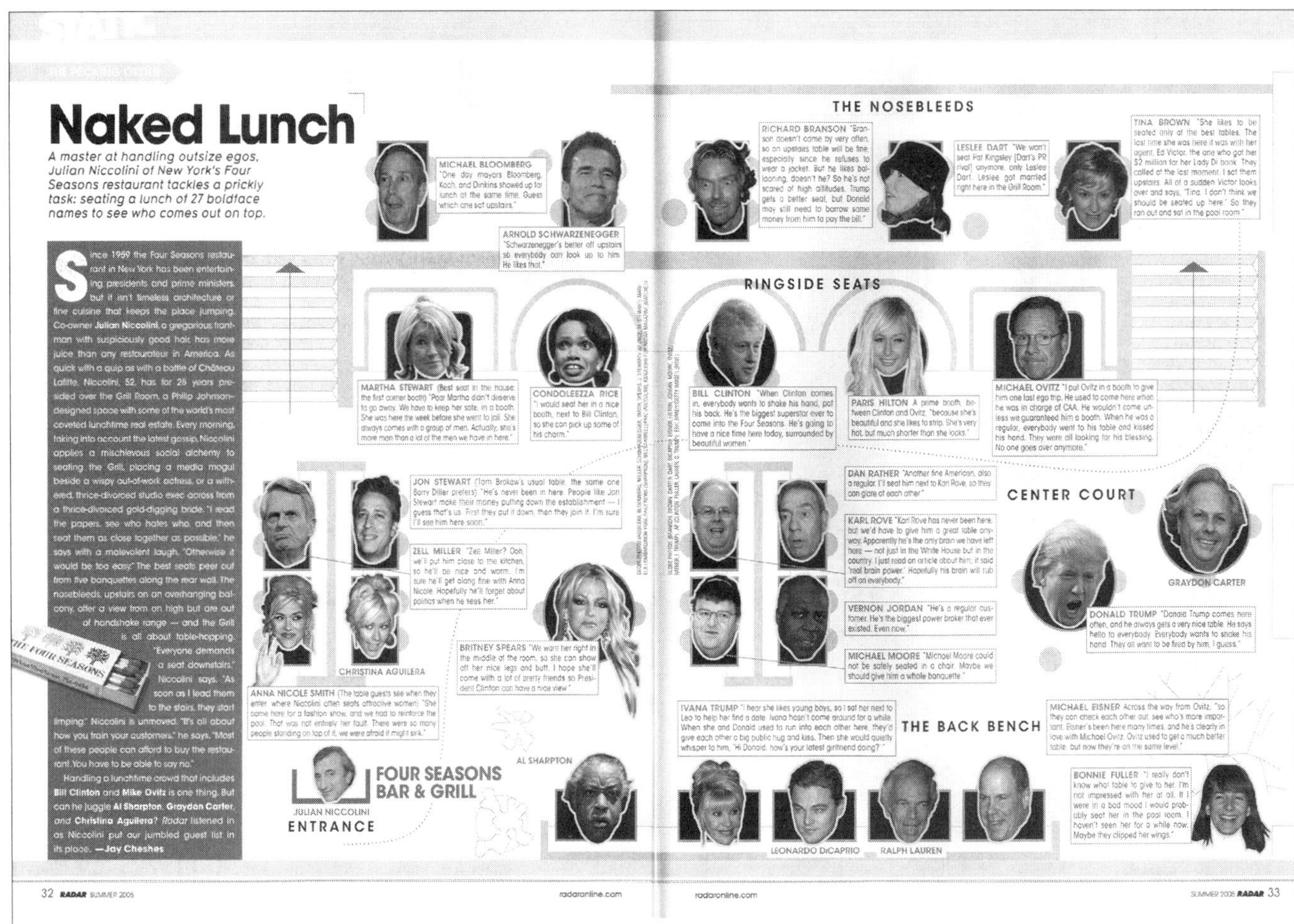

Naked Lunch

A master at handling outsize egos, Julian Niccolini of New York's Four Seasons restaurant tackles a prickly task: seating a lunch of 27 boldface names to see who comes out on top.

Since 1959 the Four Seasons restaurant in New York has been entertaining presidents and prime ministers, but it isn't timeless architecture or fine cuisine that keeps the place jumping. Co-owner **Julian Niccolini**, a gregarious frontman with suspiciously good hair, has more juice than any restaurateur in America. As quick with a quip as with a bottle of Château Lafitte, Niccolini, 52, has for 25 years presided over the Grill Room, a Philip Johnson-designed space with some of the world's most coveted lunchtime real estate. Every morning, taking into account the latest gossip, Niccolini applies a mischievous social alchemy to seating the Grill, placing a media mogul beside a wispy out-of-work actress, or a withered, thrice-divorced studio exec across from a thrice-divorced gold-digging bride. "I read the papers, see who hates who, and then seat them as close together as possible," he says with a malevolent laugh. "Otherwise it would be too easy." The best seats peer out from five banquettes along the rear wall. The nosebleeds, upstairs on an overhanging balcony, offer a view from on high but are out of handshake range — and the Grill is all about table-hopping. "Everyone demands a seat downstairs," Niccolini says. "As soon as I lead them to the stairs, they start limping." Niccolini is unmoved. "It's all about how you train your customers," he says. "Most of these people can afford to buy the restaurant. You have to be able to say no."

Handling a lunchtime crowd that includes **Bill Clinton** and **Mike Ovitz** is one thing. But can he juggle **Al Sharpton**, **Graydon Carter**, and **Christina Aguilera**? *Radar* listened in as Niccolini put our jumbled guest list in its place. **—Jay Cheshes**

MICHAEL BLOOMBERG "One day mayors Bloomberg, Koch, and Dinkins showed up for lunch at the same time. Guess which one sat upstairs."

ARNOLD SCHWARZENEGGER "Schwarzenegger's better off upstairs so everybody can look up to him. He likes that."

MARTHA STEWART (Best seat in the house: the first corner booth) "Poor Martha didn't deserve to go away. We have to keep her safe, in a booth. She was here the week before she went to jail. She always comes with a group of men. Actually, she's more man than a lot of the men we have in here."

CONDOLEEZZA RICE "I would seat her in a nice booth, next to Bill Clinton, so she can pick up some of his charm."

JON STEWART (Tom Brokaw's usual table, the same one Barry Diller prefers) "He's never been in here. People like Jon Stewart make their money putting down the establishment — I guess that's us. First they put it down, then they join it. I'm sure I'll see him here soon."

ZELL MILLER "Zell Miller? Ooh, we'll put him close to the kitchen, so he'll be nice and warm. I'm sure he'll get along fine with Anna Nicole. Hopefully he'll forget about politics when he sees her."

CHRISTINA AGUILERA

ANNA NICOLE SMITH (The table guests see when they enter, where Niccolini often seats attractive women) "She came here for a fashion show, and we had to reinforce the pool. That was not entirely her fault. There were so many people standing on top of it, we were afraid it might sink."

BRITNEY SPEARS "We want her right in the middle of the room, so she can show off her nice legs and butt. I hope she'll come with a lot of pretty friends so President Clinton can have a nice view."

AL SHARPTON

FOUR SEASONS BAR & GRILL

JULIAN NICCOLINI

ENTRANCE

THE NOSEBLEEDS

RICHARD BRANSON "Branson doesn't come by very often, so an upstairs table will be fine, especially since he refuses to wear a jacket. But he likes ballooning, doesn't he? So he's not scared of high altitudes. Trump gets a better seat, but Donald may still need to borrow some money from him to pay the bill."

LESLEE DART "We won't seat Pat Kingsley [Dart's PR rival] anymore, only Leslee Dart. Leslee got married right here in the Grill Room."

TINA BROWN "She likes to be seated only at the best tables. The last time she was here it was with her agent, Ed Victor, the one who got her $2 million for her Lady Di book. They called at the last moment. I sat them upstairs. All of a sudden Victor looks over and says, 'Tina, I don't think we should be seated up here.' So they ran out and sat in the pool room."

RINGSIDE SEATS

BILL CLINTON "When Clinton comes in, everybody wants to shake his hand, pat his back. He's the biggest superstar ever to come into the Four Seasons. He's going to have a nice time here today, surrounded by beautiful women."

PARIS HILTON A prime booth, between Clinton and Ovitz, "because she's beautiful and she likes to strip. She's very hot, but much shorter than she looks."

MICHAEL OVITZ "I put Ovitz in a booth to give him one last ego trip. He used to come here when he was in charge of CAA. He wouldn't come unless we guaranteed him a booth. When he was a regular, everybody went to his table and kissed his hand. They were all looking for his blessing. No one goes over anymore."

DAN RATHER "Another fine American, also a regular. I'll seat him next to Karl Rove, so they can glare at each other."

KARL ROVE "Karl Rove has never been here, but we'd have to give him a great table anyway. Apparently he's the only brain we have left here — not just in the White House but in the country. I just read an article about him; it said 'real brain power.' Hopefully his brain will rub off on everybody."

VERNON JORDAN "He's a regular customer. He's the biggest power broker that ever existed. Even now."

MICHAEL MOORE "Michael Moore could not be safely seated in a chair. Maybe we should give him a whole banquette."

CENTER COURT

GRAYDON CARTER

DONALD TRUMP "Donald Trump comes here often, and he always gets a very nice table. He says hello to everybody. Everybody wants to shake his hand. They all want to be fired by him, I guess."

THE BACK BENCH

IVANA TRUMP "I hear she likes young boys, so I sat her next to Leo to help her find a date. Ivana hasn't come around for a while. When she and Donald used to run into each other here, they'd give each other a big public hug and kiss. Then she would quietly whisper to him, 'Hi Donald, how's your latest girlfriend doing?'"

MICHAEL EISNER Across the way from Ovitz, "so they can check each other out, see who's more important. Eisner's been here many times, and he's clearly in love with Michael Ovitz. Ovitz used to get a much better table, but now they're on the same level."

BONNIE FULLER "I really don't know what table to give to her. I'm not impressed with her at all. If I were in a bad mood I would probably seat her in the pool room. I haven't seen her for a while now. Maybe they clipped her wings."

LEONARDO DiCAPRIO

RALPH LAUREN

32 **RADAR** SUMMER 2005 radaronline.com

radaronline.com SUMMER 2005 **RADAR** 33

Radar, *2005*

Have a Voice

Use attitude or humor if the subject calls for it. This piece from *Radar* shows where "boldface names" would be seated in the Four Season's sought-after lunchtime dining room. The "information" takes the form of amusing ministories about interplays between celebrities and co-owner Julian Niccolini. Also, active voice keeps sentence structures simple and makes the piece easy to read.

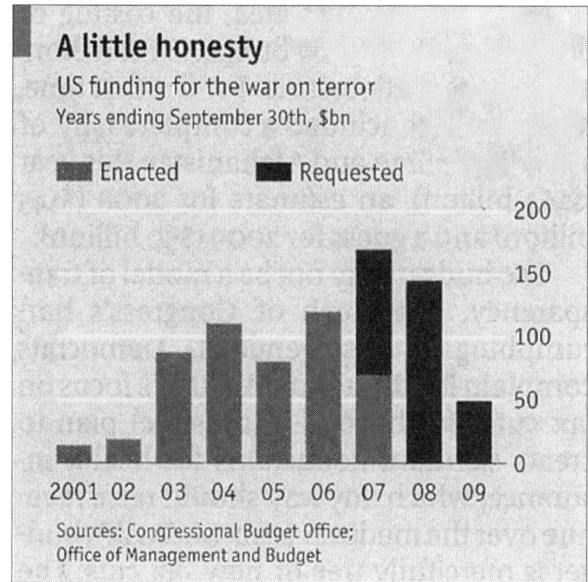

The Economist, *2007*

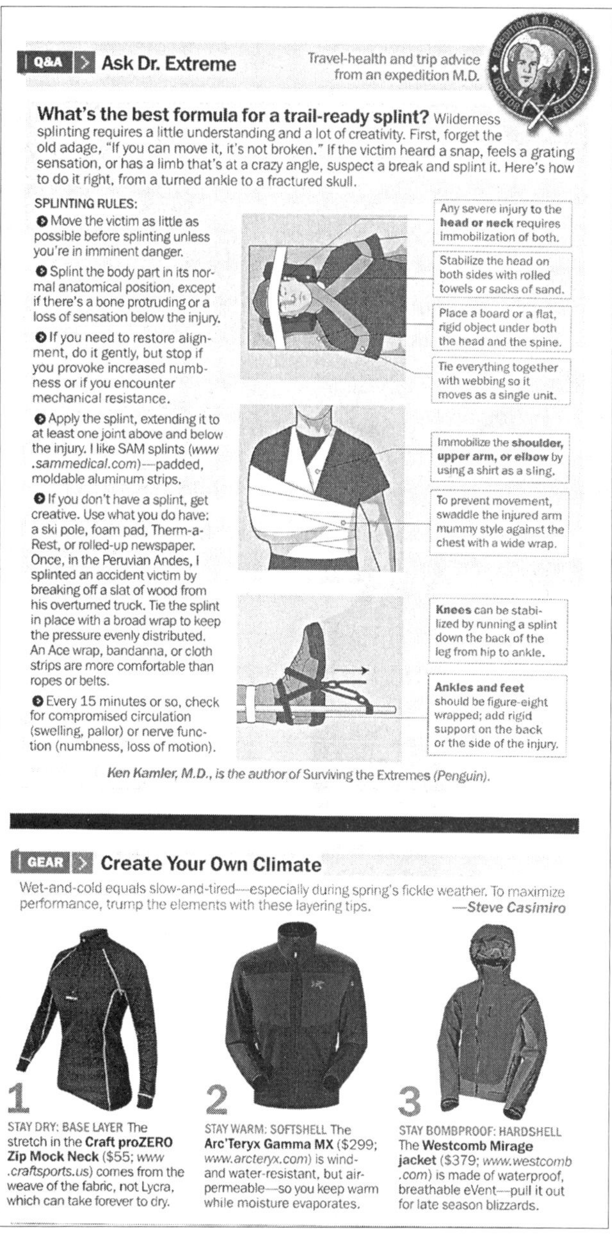

Q&A > **Ask Dr. Extreme**

Travel-health and trip advice from an expedition M.D.

What's the best formula for a trail-ready splint? Wilderness splinting requires a little understanding and a lot of creativity. First, forget the old adage, "If you can move it, it's not broken." If the victim heard a snap, feels a grating sensation, or has a limb that's at a crazy angle, suspect a break and splint it. Here's how to do it right, from a turned ankle to a fractured skull.

SPLINTING RULES:

- Move the victim as little as possible before splinting unless you're in imminent danger.
- Splint the body part in its normal anatomical position, except if there's a bone protruding or a loss of sensation below the injury.
- If you need to restore alignment, do it gently, but stop if you provoke increased numbness or if you encounter mechanical resistance.
- Apply the splint, extending it to at least one joint above and below the injury. I like SAM splints (*www.sammedical.com*)—padded, moldable aluminum strips.
- If you don't have a splint, get creative. Use what you do have: a ski pole, foam pad, Therm-a-Rest, or rolled-up newspaper. Once, in the Peruvian Andes, I splinted an accident victim by breaking off a slat of wood from his overturned truck. Tie the splint in place with a broad wrap to keep the pressure evenly distributed. An Ace wrap, bandanna, or cloth strips are more comfortable than ropes or belts.
- Every 15 minutes or so, check for compromised circulation (swelling, pallor) or nerve function (numbness, loss of motion).

Any severe injury to the **head or neck** requires immobilization of both.

Stabilize the head on both sides with rolled towels or sacks of sand.

Place a board or a flat, rigid object under both the head and the spine.

Tie everything together with webbing so it moves as a single unit.

Immobilize the **shoulder, upper arm, or elbow** by using a shirt as a sling.

To prevent movement, swaddle the injured arm mummy style against the chest with a wide wrap.

Knees can be stabilized by running a splint down the back of the leg from hip to ankle.

Ankles and feet should be figure-eight wrapped; add rigid support on the back or the side of the injury.

Ken Kamler, M.D., is the author of Surviving the Extremes *(Penguin).*

GEAR > **Create Your Own Climate**

Wet-and-cold equals slow-and-tired—especially during spring's fickle weather. To maximize performance, trump the elements with these layering tips. —*Steve Casimiro*

1 STAY DRY: BASE LAYER The stretch in the **Craft proZERO Zip Mock Neck** ($55; *www.craftsports.us*) comes from the weave of the fabric, not Lycra, which can take forever to dry.

2 STAY WARM: SOFTSHELL The **Arc'Teryx Gamma MX** ($299; *www.arcteryx.com*) is wind- and water-resistant, but air-permeable—so you keep warm while moisture evaporates.

3 STAY BOMBPROOF: HARDSHELL The **Westcomb Mirage jacket** ($379; *www.westcomb.com*) is made of waterproof, breathable eVent—pull it out for late season blizzards.

National Geographic Adventure, *2007*

Focus

Make every word and image count. This is not the time to repeat information. Focus on why people should care. Provide the right details, not just any details.

Start Strong

Headlines, intros, and graphics must do triple duty. They must capture readers with their content and style and take the place of the traditional story lead. Headlines must be to the point. Intros must quickly tell readers why this matters.

Be Reader-Centric

The best ASFs are "reader-friendly" in the truest sense of the term—they put readers first. How will this issue affect you? Can you solve this quiz? Why should you or shouldn't you buy this product? How can you grill a pizza?

Show and Sketch

ASFs don't come off without lots of planning. The only way to make sure that everyone is on the same page is to sketch out ideas so everyone can see them. You can also show examples of that story form from other publications. It is crucial that everyone know how a piece will be written so that no one has to edit narrative text into an ASF on deadline.

Cover Up

30

STEVEN HELLER

THE PERSON WHO INVENTED MAGAZINE COVERLINES should be dragged out in full public view, stripped naked, and, before being tarred and feathered, have the following message tattooed on his or her body: Inside: Special Report: I Made Magazine Covers Ugly, Exclusive: Page 2.

I would consider this just retribution. Coverlines have done more to lower the aesthetic standards of magazine design than any other malady affecting late twentieth-century periodical publishing.

Also known as teasers or reefers (because they invite the reader to "refer" to a designated article), coverlines announce the lead stories of a magazine. Except for the *New Yorker*, which prints its coverlines on flaps attached to newsstand copies, so as not to mar the cover art, every commercial magazine uses them in one vile form or another.

Well, OK, not all magazine coverlines are grossly handled. *Metropolis* seamlessly integrates copy into the overall cover design; *Atlantic Monthly*'s are sparse and tastefully composed so as not to interfere with the cover image; and *Rolling Stone*, though laden with coverlines, routinely changes typefaces to express the mood of the cover photograph. But these are exceptions to a practice that has turned the most valuable piece of editorial real estate into a waste dump of intrusive typography.

Fashion, lifestyle, and shelter magazines, such as *Vogue*, *Elle*, *Cosmopolitan*, *Vanity Fair*, *Condé Nast*

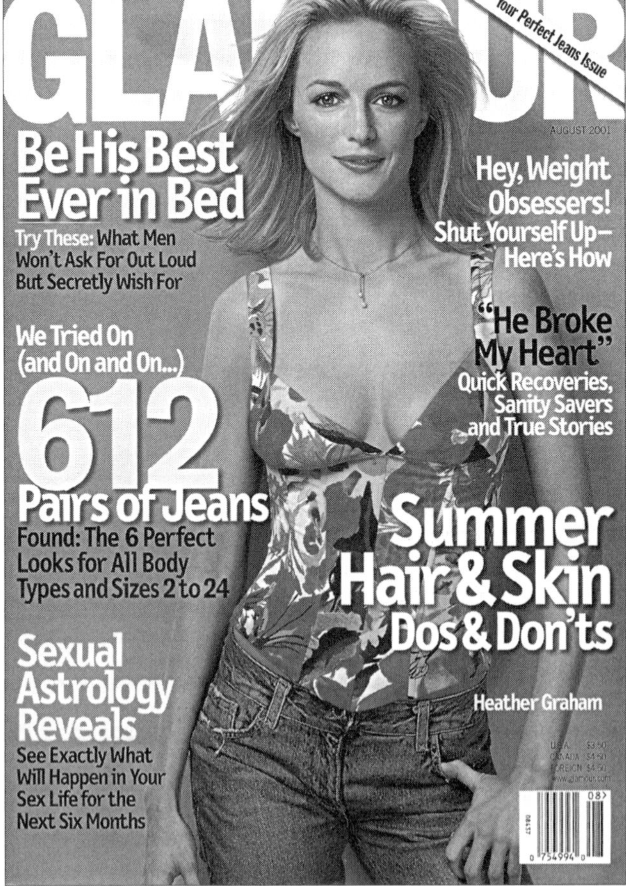

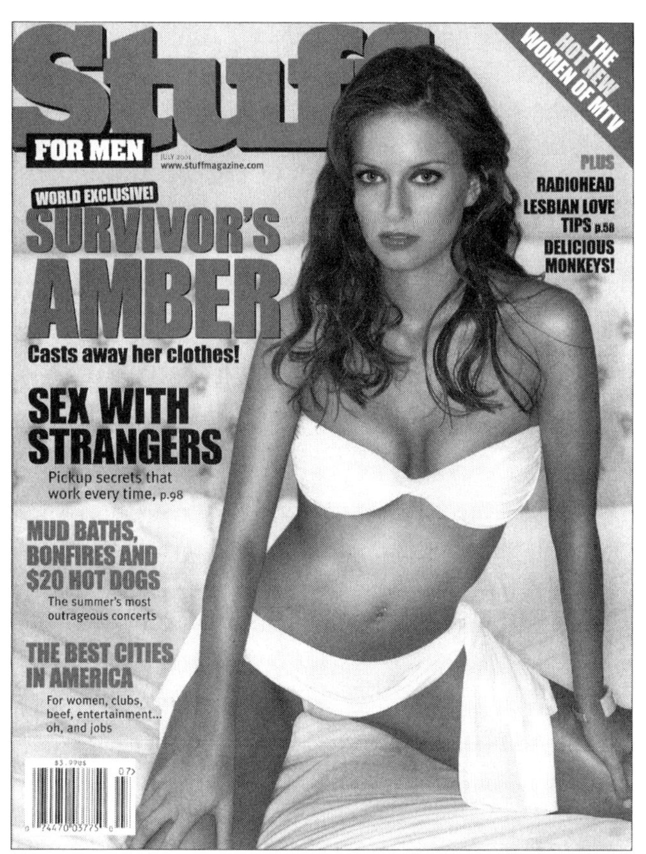
Stuff
FOR MEN
THE HOT NEW WOMEN OF MTV
www.stuffmagazine.com
PLUS
RADIOHEAD
LESBIAN LOVE TIPS p.58
DELICIOUS MONKEYS!
WORLD EXCLUSIVE!
SURVIVOR'S AMBER
Casts away her clothes!
SEX WITH STRANGERS
Pickup secrets that work every time, p.98
MUD BATHS, BONFIRES AND $20 HOT DOGS
The summer's most outrageous concerts
THE BEST CITIES IN AMERICA
For women, clubs, beef, entertainment... oh, and jobs

OUR BIGGEST CELEBRITY ISSUE EVER!
COSMO girl!
YOUR SUMMER LOVE HOROSCOPE (See Page 170)
301 WAYS TO LOOK AMAZING THIS SUMMER
+ Swimsuits You'll Love
Find the Best One for Your Body on Page 132
HEY, FASHION ADDICTS
TEXT2SHOP
ONLY IN CG!
Nicole Richie
The Price She Paid to Be the Coolest Girl in Hollywood
JUNE/JULY 2006
GUYS' SECRET FANTASIES—REVEALED!
CELEB SHOCKER!
Being Too Skinny Almost Ruined Her Career
cosmogirl.com

TAKE THIS TO THE BEACH
His BODY
(A USER'S MANUAL)
The Touch, the Tickle, the Pinch—We Guarantee They'll Tantalize Him
The Cosmo Way to Meet a Man
30 Genius Opening Lines
What's Sexy Now
Try It. Taste It. Grab It. Ride It.
SEDUCTIVE SUMMER BEAUTY
Eyes+Lips+Nails
Reese Witherspoon
What She's Never Revealed...Until Now
FEEL SEXIER NAKED
Bashful in the Buff? 4 Steps to Total Body Confidence
Don't Bend Over Backward for Him!
The Shocking Secret of Women Whose Boyfriends Are Beyond Hooked
7 Ways to Outsmart a Rapist
www.cosmopolitan.com

THE WORLD'S FASTEST GROWING MEN'S MAGAZINE!
FHM
SPACE BABE BONANZA!
ALMOST INFINITE FOLDOUT COVER!
FOR HIM MAGAZINE
July/August 2001
FUNNY!
Johnny Knoxville shares his pain!
SEXY!
The mesmerizing Brooke Burke!
USEFUL!
Stud or dud? Your sex skills analyzed
THE GIRLS OF...
SCI-FI!
A GIFT FROM THE UNIVERSE–NINE WOMEN WHO MAKE OUR PLANET TREMBLE!
www.fhmus.com
an emap-usa magazine

Traveler, *Mademoiselle*, *Redbook*, *McCall's*, *Brides*, and *Better Homes and Gardens*, are among the worst offenders. Headlines crisscross the covers of these magazines like scaffolding in front of a construction site. When displayed in newsstand or supermarket racks, the critical mass of covers forms a typographic jumble. Whatever strategic benefit might be gained by a glut of copy on the cover is reduced because almost every other magazine is glutted too.

The practice of squeezing words on a cover began in the late 1970s, when former Condé Nast design czar Alexander Liberman ordered designers of the fashion and lifestyle magazines he controlled to turn away from elegant design and adopt some of the techniques common to supermarket tabloids, such as the *National Enquirer*. (These tropes had already been put to use by underground press and punk publications.) The strategy suited marketing departments, which believed that coverlines would increase a magazine's visibility in a highly competitive field. In theory, the visual chaos mirrored the growing informality of social attitudes. But the shift from elegance to controlled sensationalism marked the first step in an erosion of design standards and a shift in emphasis from concept- to advertising-driven presentations.

Covers were once designed with a strong image. In the 1930s, magazines such as *Vanity Fair*, *Vogue*, and *Harper's Bazaar* avoided cover copy entirely. When newsstand competition became more intense in the fifties and sixties, coverlines were more common, but they were usually short headlines that introduced a magazine's lead story with possibly a few B-heads signaling off-leads placed unobtrusively in a corner. By the eighties, when the balance between image and text shifted, aesthetics also changed. Billboards composed of discordant typefaces dropped out of black boxes or primary color bands, mortised around photographs, and printed in fluorescent colors became the norm. Condé Nast's covers were more cluttered than most, but its competitors soon sank to the same level. Even as the size of magazines shrank owing to rising paper costs, the number of coverlines grew. Now serious magazines, such as *Newsweek* and *Time*, have become coverline dependent.

Coverlines are now seen as a necessary evil. Cover images are wallpaper against which copy is hung, and few are as memorable as the advertising inside. Coverlines, like the covers themselves, are designed by committees in the same way that a broadsheet newspaper is planned, with editors vying to have their own stories out front. The designer's role is no longer to solve conceptual visual problems, but to arrange or compose type for maximum impact. And even here the task is often usurped by editors. A designer for a high-circulation style magazine described one such cover-approval procedure: "The cover subject is decided upon by the editor, usually a portrait of a celebrity who is hot at that moment. After the image is shot and selected, I am given a file of headlines in order of their importance, which I must then lay out so as to highlight sometimes as many as three lead and three off-lead stories, while retaining the integrity of the photograph. After I've managed to solve the puzzle more or less to my satisfaction, the comp is noodled to death with comments like, 'This headline is too large, this one isn't large enough. Why not use a color band here, or drop out the color there?' The cover has to smack the reader in the eye at the expense of design standards."

Of course, one can't blame only coverlines or their makers for the cheesy look of periodicals. But the way they've been used—and their increasing use—brings down the quality of magazines and the reputations of those who design them. As the designer quoted in the previous paragraph put it: "It's almost impossible to develop into a really good designer when the acceptable standard is so poor."

SECTION 9

Is the Editorial Format Obsolete?

Is there a place for magazines in modern society? These days, that question might have two separate meanings and two separate answers. First, are the creative possibilities of the serial publication exhausted? And second, even if not, will the Web, with its immediacy and low cost, make paper magazines obsolete as a way of delivering information?

There's no doubt that magazines are flourishing right now; the local racks offer more, not fewer, options than there were a few years ago, and while magazines have spawned Web sites, Web sites have also spawned plenty of magazines. Media company earnings look sparse only when compared with the phenomenal profits of the late-nineties economic boom. But that doesn't assuage concerns about the future. Are the magazine racks of large bookstores vestigial? (For that matter, are the bookstores themselves vestigial?)

This section looks at ways the Web and digital culture have influenced periodical design, and the ways magazines have adapted to contemporary circumstances. The deaths of various media have been predicted before, going back to Walter Benjamin, who believed that print would obviate the need for original art, but so far no means of human creative expression has vanished in favor of another. Rather, the methods and technologies have changed, but the essences of the expressions have remained the same.

Beyond Zines

31

PETE MORELEWICZ

THE SAME TECHNOLOGY RESPONSIBLE FOR TODAY'S blog revolution brought us the zine revolution some twenty years prior. Desktop publishing ushered in a new breed of mass communication. No longer encumbered by the cost of production, self-publishing a zine was within the grasp of almost anyone. Early adapters who were unsatisfied with the mainstream press published subversive missives that became the foundation for the zine movement.

Somewhere between small zines (with double- or triple-digit circulation) and big media's offerings are what I'll term "small magazines." In this context, they are titles that were born as zines, and over time acquired a widespread readership and an ad sales base that justifies their continuance. Generally they are still run by their founder(s) and adhere to their original editorial spirit despite their growth. Many of these titles follow the same soul of their punk forebears in the zine world, even if their editorial message more closely meshes with today's mainstream.

You can conceive that successful small magazines like *Adbusters* and *Bark* emerged from the same zine pool as titles like *2600* and *Ben is Dead.* But you can also as easily conceive that they were hatched from an enterprising mind at Wenner Media or Hearst. While these are quality titles befitting their circulation numbers, they tend to exist safely within the fringe of existing niches; the beefy market for cultural reporting can easily subsume a title like *Adbusters.*

But zines that are a bit more out of line with the mainstream—those that tend toward the counterculture—can't as easily blend into the existing fringes. For these publishers, reaching a wider audience often doesn't follow the well-trod path other aspiring titles have followed. So how does a subversive title with a punk attitude survive a growth spurt?

It's no surprise that the success of any small publication escaping the sandlot of zinedom depends largely on its design. Sure, they'll have to compete with magazines whose art budgets are orders of magnitude larger. Photo shoots for a zine generally don't involve scores of models, a staff of assistants, and on-site caterers. Success for a small publication isn't measured by the size of the design budget; it is measured by its ability to convey the editorial mission. And if ad sales are enough to cover the production costs, that's gravy.

No matter what the size of a publication, the harmonic relationship between design and editorial has been carved out through years of success and failure. The magazine whose cover features a tasteful Noguchi-inspired living room will carry more gravitas than the one fronted by a tricked-out lowrider. In our quick-hit, image-driven culture, the design of a publication transmits its sensibility more quickly than the written word. This assertion can be tested every month simply with a visit to Barnes & Noble.

Defining yourself as alternative used to mean following the visual tradition of a cut-and-paste, hard-edge, punk aesthetic. But like so many elements of the underground, mainstream media co-opted and exhausted that look eons ago. Competition on the newsstand dictates both polish and panache, so zine publishers have completed the circle: now they appropriate the aesthetic of mainstream media. But what if that aesthetic deviates from their street-level editorial so much that there becomes a rift between the visual voice and the text inside? Copping the look of big media is a route that often seduces zine publishers looking to broaden their audience. But will new readers understand—and current readers forgive—this discordance?

Once I tried to put out a small magazine. After exchanging favorite zines for the better part of two years with my brother James, we decided to dive into self-publishing. Our aim was to embody the best of the indie media we were digesting: subversive information, pop culture, raw energy, and a dash of humor. Our zine, *POPsmear*, based in New York City and Washington, D.C., published five thousand copies quarterly, largely self-funded with some assistance from ad sales. Using stolen computer time from a nearby college, a rented post office box for headquarters, and all the art supplies we could find, we were able to birth that first issue in just over a week.

Issue 1 of *POPsmear* was an uneven fifty-two pages of black-and-white newsprint. The actual page count is debatable, as the folios tend to wander aimlessly; some-

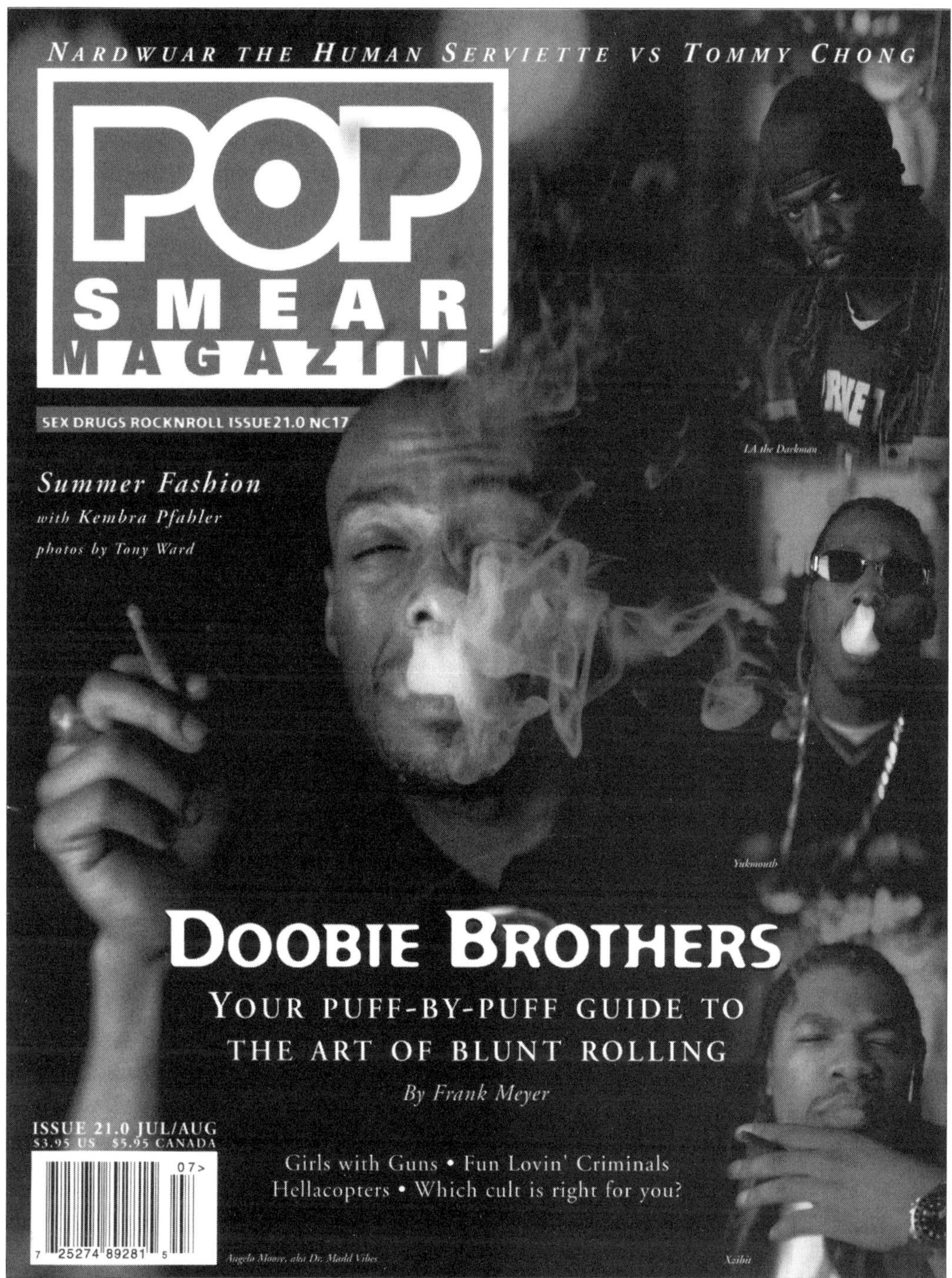

NARDWUAR THE HUMAN SERVIETTE VS TOMMY CHONG
POP
SMEAR
MAGAZINE
SEX DRUGS ROCKNROLL ISSUE21.0 NC17
Summer Fashion
with Kembra Pfahler
photos by Tony Ward
DOOBIE BROTHERS
YOUR PUFF-BY-PUFF GUIDE TO
THE ART OF BLUNT ROLLING
By Frank Meyer
ISSUE 21.0 JUL/AUG
$3.95 US $5.95 CANADA
Girls with Guns • Fun Lovin' Criminals
Hellacopters • Which cult is right for you?

POPsmear, *1998*

times the odd pages are on the left, sometimes the right. The design was nearly as fickle as the pagination, with varying degrees of cut-and-paste prowess, some questionable typography choices, and all the refinement of a "missing cat" flyer. A minefield of ideas, mixed media, and raw expression, it has an energy that I find enviable even today. In an era of clean typography and flawless letterspacing, this baby certainly defies convention. The content, poorly written and absent editing, was as cobbled together as the design. Stories of how to scam free Franklin Mint commemorative board games, selling gravesites over the phone, and a smattering of live music reviews were all included with no clear direction. This unbridled editorial and the obviously amateurish design made a great pair. What *POPsmear* lacked in varnish, it made up for with

I was thinking about this whole Geffen/Speilberg/Katzenburg alliance and how much hype they've gotten as a mastermind dream team. I've heard all the predictions and expectations of how they, more than anyone have the potential to change the face of entertainment media. Granted, they are immensely successful in the entertainment field- immensely- but I have yet to hear the following spin on the matter. This is probably due to the myopic and often vapid spin of entertainment writers, but shit- I would expect more from people who make a living analyzing others. As a side note, I want to mention that I do enjoy more than anything sitting in a bar and bullshitting about stuff, and this was a topic that was quite blankly received by my cohorts one weekday evening (God bless the "open-collar" workers!) at the AKA lounge....

BIG THOUGHTS BY A SMALL MAN

uh....that's James

There is very little that needs to be said about the powerful sway these three hold in the movie/music/entertainment field. Whether or not you personally enjoy or respect what they have done on an individual basis, it is clear that a large number of American consumers have bought into their visions. Now they are at the point of amazing power: a lemming-like sychophant public will pay for whatever they create, while a media-paranoid government, that will kiss any ass that will garner them a positive image (i.e. more votes), courts them at any number of fundraisers and high-profile functions. They have nowhere to go but up, and a hero-hungry America will support no matter what they do. My point is: why don't they use this power in a truly constructive manner? (personal note to Job from Red Flag- read on: this is your big bitch, albiet on a major league level...)

They have already made it financially- why not use this mesmorizing power to truly make difference in our country? They have the ability as successful businessmen and proven spin doctors to both shift public opinion and use things to create a success story. They are the only individuals in this media-reliant country who have the real POWER to make a positive change. They, more than any pathetic Politcal Action Commitee and whiney paranoid political advisor, have the resources to make thing happen. The media (which quite obviously controls the thought of the majority of America- and don't even try to deny it all you media savvy hipsters- I'm talking about the 90% of idiots out there) can truly convince people to get off their asses and make a positive change. These three have done it before for financial gain- and now they can do it for something that really matters. They (hopefully) aren't mired in all the political back-and-forth bullshit that stalls all proposed societal advancement in the government sector.

I don't have the answers as to what they should do- I am only proposing that they are the only ones that have the power to really do something. Wouldn't it be nice if they took advantage of that? Hell, if they were only looking for a spot in history as an egotistical thing that would be fine- just as long as they utilized their position to do something for the good of humanity. I ask a lot of them, but they may be the only ones who can do it.

UPC: (underground press conference, not [barcode] !)

THE FOLLOWING IS A PRESS RELEASE THAT WE GOT VIA EMAIL, AND WERE TOO LAZY TO RETYPE IN OUR STYLE. IT READS KINDA BORING, BUT IT IS AN IMPORTANT AND COOL EVENT TO ATTEND:

CHICAGO, MAY 1, 1995 - Due to the overwhelming success of the First Annual Underground Press Conference, Mary Kuntz Press announced today that it is organizing a Second Annual Underground Press Conference ("UPC"), to be held during the weekend of August 18, 19 and 20, 1995, at De Paul University Lincoln Park Campus, Chicago, Illinois. Last year's conference gathered over 250 editors, publishers, writers, educators, artists and activists from 20 states.

UPC '95 will feature two full days of seminars to discuss issues of importance to the underground press, including production of 'zines and chaps, fundraising, marketing and distribution, censorship, and electronic publishing. Panelists will include such nationally known figures as R. Seth Friedman, editor of Factsheet Five, the Bible of the 'zine scene; Abe Peck, editor of the Chicago Seed, a 1960s radical newspaper; Paul Weinman, Ron Androia and Cheryl Townsend, three legends of the underground poetry press; David Hernandez, founder of Street Sounds poetry/music workshop Michael Basinski, archivist of rare materials at SUNY-Buffalo, (and James from POPsmear).

One very special event new to this year's UPC is the Gallery of 'Zines, an exhibition of participants' publications curated by Ashley Parker Owens, publisher of Global Mail. At the conclusion of the conference, the items on exhibit will be donated to the Chicagoland Great Lakes Underground Press Collection under development at DePaul University's John T. Richardson Library. Also new in 1995 is the establishment of a mentoring program designed to assist 15 to 21 year-olds interested in writing for and producing 'zines.

The Saturday Night Underground Ball, an extremely popular event last year, will be held at The Bop Shop in Chicago's lively Wicker Park neighborhood. This event will feature poetry, music and revelry. The Great Underground Lit Sale, where publishers display their books, magazines and other literary wares, will take place both Saturday and Sunday at the DePaul University campus.

Conference organizers are actively soliciting proposals for seminar topics of interest to writers, publishers, educators and other supporters of the underground press. The deadline for seminar proposals is June 1, 1995. Registration is on-going, and reservations will be taken by mail until August 5, 1995 and in person up to and including the days of the conference. The basic fee for attending the three-day event is $25, and dormitory rooms will be available at discount rates to out-of-town registrants.

To obtain further information about UPC or to receive a registration packet, interested parties should write to Mary Kuntz Press, P.O. Box 476617, Chicago, Illinois 60647. For information by phone, fax or e-mail, call 312/486-0685 (voice), 312/486 9001 (fax), or mkuntz@aol.com

REPRESSION: A bunch of stupid losers

The group that is Repression Records and Stupid Loser computerzine is putting together one of the coolest fucking projects out there. First, a major league indie resource database. It will be easy to use and will contain the following catagories: record labels, fanzines, band addresses, fan clubs, distributors, mail order, freelance artists, cartoonists, publishers, producers, venues, stores, radio stations, useful phone #'s, mail artists, and a bunch more.

Also, they have somehow managed to convince a very silly bank to contribute moolah to start what sounds like a great new online service- not a text based BBS, mind you- but a full on graphically based interface. This will be totally dedicated to independent and underground music. All your shit can go on for free- even your fanzine with pictures n' stuff (watch for POPsmear, probably). There will be label and band info, resource guides, and even a pen pal section for other stupid losers.

Help these guys out- they're not making any money at this- send your info or ask for theirs: Repression Records, 22 Dorchester Ave, Geneva, NY 14456-2315, or email 102041,2546@compuserve.com

You all should know by now what we think of poetry, but we'll make an exception for anything that sounds like a transcript from a Bellvue intake interview! This wonderful bit was slipped to us by one ***Robbie Gennet.*** *Enjoy......*

LYNCHINGRIMACE

What exactly
does it mean,
"to grimace"?
The good book talks
of twisting the face,
convulsions of disgust,
expressions of pain.
And in the alternaate world of MacDonald's
resides a
friendlychubbypurplehappygoluckything
called "The Grimace"

And wouldn't you know it makes me think of
all these children fooled again.

Ronald, you should be ashamed.
Hamburgler, a pox on you.
Mayor McCheese, may your arteries fill
themselves
with the sludge and slime
you bring, you fat cheesy fuck.
And you, Grimace,
May you explode like a hornet's nest of
purple puke,
to knock those silly eyes about
and feed the starving masses.

Take your order, please?

A sincerly uttered, but funny quote from someone I know:
"Isn't 'indie' another word for 'not as good'?"

1-SS 5501016-1
MR HOWIE FELTERSNATCH, PARTNER
LICHTER & HADDER
3117 7TH ST NE
WASHINGTON DC 20017-1410

Ship to:

IVAN IBICHICOCKOFF
3117 7TH ST NE
WASHINGTON DC 2001

DIXIE WRECT
NBR 2B
3117 7TH ST NE
WASHINGTON, DC 20017-1

637479298
HOWIE AETEROWT
3117 7th St NE
Washington DC 2001714

PETEY says "there's no excuse for not making your mail scam as fun as possible!"

POPsmear 4.0 13

POPsmear, *1995*

verve. This type of start is by no means atypical of the small press. But in a realm where success often means publishing more than two issues of a zine, *POPsmear* was a hit. Its success confounded even its creators.

As its popularity grew, so did the budget for putting together issues. By issue 7.0, an ISBN number appeared for newsstand sales, and a masthead (sometimes labeled as "Blame") adorned the issues. But the organization was still confounding: There was no contents page, no logo, no date on most issues, no departments or feature well, no thought to ad placement. But one thing did change: The folios actually appeared on the proper pages.

POPsmear's third year was marked by a drive for legitimacy. It had overtaken the circulation of many of the zines that had influenced its launch and was attracting mainstream media coverage, mostly through its seemingly endless litany of cease-and-desist orders. Though celebrities didn't appreciate having their unlisted numbers published, the readers seemed to love it, and more and more contributors filled its pages.

One of the most influential of these contributors was a designer, and his work helped redefine *POPsmear*. Issue 10.0 features a spread designed by artist Ryan McGinness, author of *flatnessisgod* and nearly a dozen other art books. McGinness was just starting out at the time, and, as James explains, "We gave him the story and asked him to design it. We got improved design for free, and he got exposure." This first foray into formalized art direction was a step toward professionalizing *POPsmear*'s design.

As *POPsmear* grew, so did my time commitment to it. After eleven issues, I left to concentrate on my day job as a graphic designer. James decided to relaunch *POPsmear* as a four-color glossy with a circulation of fifty thousand. McGinness was tapped to be the art director. The design now focused on luring new readers who otherwise wouldn't pick it up. To do this, *POPsmear* aped the supermarket tabloid aesthetic for the cover, finding it fitting for knocking popular culture. "*POPsmear* was always derivative, but with a different take," James contends, "so why not reinforce that with the tabloid sensibility?"

The easy accessibility and headline-screaming, attention-grabbing nature of tabloids were design conventions that broke with the content inside. "We started to conform design-wise, but not editorially. It was the same piece of poop, just a different wrapper," James says. The scatalogical descriptors he uses are quite fitting for the editorial content of the first redesigned issue, 11.5. It includes a life-size color photo of a gaping butthole and an essay on the joys of analingus. Indeed, the comfort and familiarity one may feel with picking up something so familiar looking may end abruptly when confronted with content that is, quite literally, tongue-in-cheek.

So did this duality—the familiar, if pedestrian, cover design paired with such unconventional content—bother James? Not really. "Nonthreatening design helped people get into the content," he says. "We chose commerce over art. . . . [S]ometimes commerce is about *not* making a statement."

The McGinness era of *POPsmear* turned the corner. The relaunched version of *POPsmear* was no longer a pipsqeak zine. It often shared retail space with larger magazines, despite its decidedly counterculture content. But this marked an important event in *POPsmear*'s evolution, and one that may have sowed the seeds of its demise. The design had become so polished, its covers more in line with the rest of the magazine world, that its message was squandered. Scanning the newsstand, *POPsmear* so fit into the general aesthetic that its individuality was lost in a sea of competitors.

The arrangement with James and McGinness lasted four issues. Several others wore the art-director cap, morphing the design from tabloid toward a more mainstream composition, until the magazine, bowing to financial pressures, folded. The last issues of *POPsmear* are virtually indistinguishable from much of the popular celebrity-driven press. The design polish ultimately belied its editorial mission. What set *POPsmear* apart was no longer evident to the casual newsstand browser. Ultimately, reconciling the refined art and lowbrow writing was too much to ask from the reader.

Tada Burke's twenty-year publishing career began memorably. He started a skate fanzine while his family was stationed in Italy. Lacking better tools, he produced it on a photocopier in his father's office, which happened to be part of the Department of Defense. Each page of the DIY zine has the DOD seal emblazoned in the corner. He caught a lot of flak from his dad for that, but his philosophy hasn't changed. "Self-publishing—it's what I surround myself with. Chix, punk rock, graffiti, skateboarding—and being real good at it."

After a succession of design jobs at traditional advertising agencies, Burke became art director of a slick, four-color, bimonthly skate/grafitti/urban culture magazine, *While You Were Sleeping* (*WYWS*). The magazine was experiencing the growing pains of a zine-turned-magazine, and, according to Burke, the competing interests of the "punk rock, fuck-you philosophy" of the magazine's founding and the business aspirations of a new ownership taxed the magazine. "Visually, you could see the transformation" from one epoch to the other. With those schizophrenic covers, "we successfully alienated our readership." After two years, and a good firsthand look at the workings of the small press, Burke left and launched his own small magazine.

Measuring just 4¼" × 5½", *DC Pulse*'s glossy color pages stood out among the smattering of other free publications in Washington, D.C. The content was a mix of Burke's interests—culture, music, and fashion—both self-generated and courtesy of a corps of contributors.

Burke's overall plan for *DC Pulse* was simple: He told the volunteer contributors that "we won't fuck your shit up." He didn't want a model of "dump-on-the-intern, and screw people over by underpaying them. It's free, so volunteer. We circumvented the traditional send-your-shit-out, wait for a call method." The response was positive. "I didn't know there were so many people in this city who needed this platform."

Along with selling ads, doing promotion, and hunting down talent, Burke had to come up with an aesthetic that could integrate so many diverse contributions. *DC Pulse* served up stories about oversized pizza slices, feminist strippers, and nocturnal meanderings, and included interviews with various artists and musicians. To design around this amalgam, Burke decided to employ a very strict template: Articles would open on a spread, one page devoted to text on a two-column grid, the other page reserved for art. Typefaces would be consistent throughout and the use of color in the text judicious.

Why the simple approach? "For the first year, we wanted to keep things to a template, keep it simple. Let's brand ourselves until we're approved or accepted." According to Burke, business concerns dictate acceptance, while creativity dictates craziness. But the choice to go for the staid, templated look wasn't just economics; it was also for credibility. "We didn't want to come off as 'let's go for the punk look.'"

Despite its popularity, the free quarterly stopped publishing after a year. Burke could no longer sustain the constant commitment it required, and it left him little time to earn a wage as a freelancer. But that doesn't mean *DC Pulse* has closed up shop. "As with any independent project that no one gets paid for, it's as

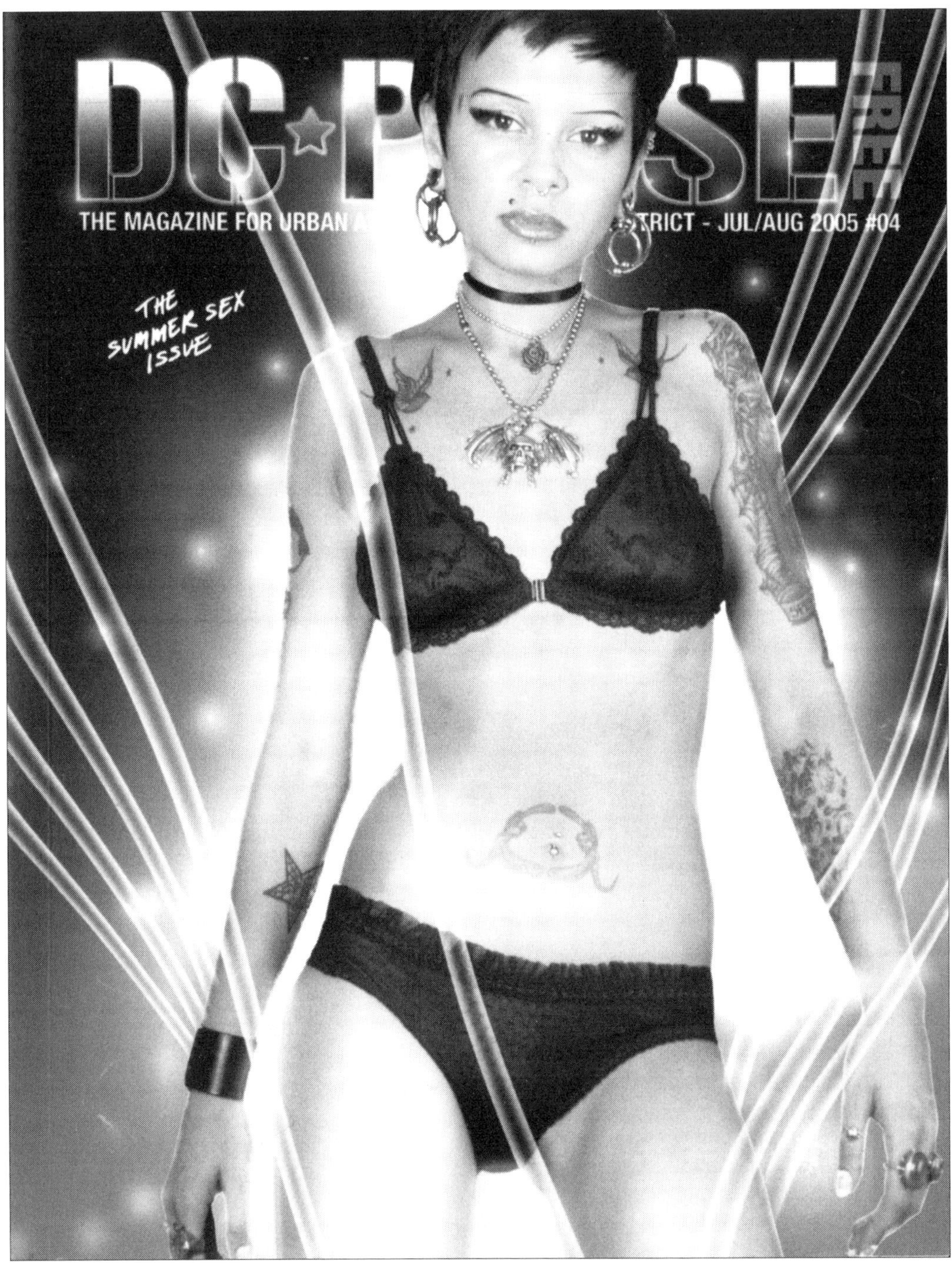

DC Pulse, *2005*

time warrants," says Burke. With typical fiery spirit, he is considering ending the publishing hiatus by relaunching a new incarnation of *DC Pulse*.

The beefy stock, the rich colors, and provocative art all served to entice the reader to pick up those first four issues. Issue 3 sported a stamped metallic cover just beckoning people to fondle it. It's at once a visual and tactile experience, and its polish looks like something produced by the staff of *Metropolis* rather than a mixed band of volunteers. But the content itself is definitely street-level. The editorial couldn't stand up to the refined design. Readers wowed by the seductive wrapping were not expecting the rough-hewn stories they found inside.

So is this disconnect between art and editorial the true hallmark of an alternative small magazine? The lesson

LOULOU GHELECHIKANI

Interview & Photo by Tada Burke

The first time LouLou graced me with her presence, I had never seen a more beautiful woman — except for my Mom of course. Speaking of which, she is a mother herself, with a lovely little munchkin named Shiva. It wasn't many months after I had spoken my first words to LouLou, that I was fortunate enough to run into her again and again. So now, a couple of years later...the multi-talented, extremely independent, free-spirited chanteuse is paving her way to a prosperous and successful career as a recording artist, and is known by thousands around the world as the soothing French vocalist for the Washington, DC band, Thievery Corporation.

DCP: What is the meaning of your birth name?

LouLou: In Farci, it means, "The star of the sharp sword clam."

You grew up in France?

Yes, for about 13 years

Do you come from a musical background?

Not really. My dad was a soccer player, he was Captain of an Iranian soccer team, my mom was a swimmer, but when the Revolution hit, they moved to France. Then my father started a Social, Cultural, Politics, newspaper. So he's been editing, doing some journalism stuff, for the past 10 years. So not really No music I did grow up in a house with all of his friends coming over, a lot of artists, musicians, painters, have always been around so I guess I've always been exposed to that world, you know? I used to listen to my walkman at night,
and pretend I was the singer..

Like a Karaoke machine? (smile)

Yes! Like Fischer Price... You know I always look for those when I go to thrift stores. I want to find those and the record players the plastic ones. Like the ones you just take out and you have this 7" that looks 20 feet long, hanging off the edge with the built-in speaker?! "I did grow up in a

52

DC Pulse

to be learned from the failures of many small press titles is that design is of paramount importance to a growing magazine's success. Zine publishers often aren't indebted to contributors, investors, sponsors, advertisers, and the like. Ironically, the freedom this offers often plagues their design. Whether the concern is to force a commerce-friendly design (in *POPsmear*'s case) or trepidation in unveiling your true self (in *DC Pulse*'s case), the results can be deleterious.

The key is to stay true to the mission. Many out-of-the-mainstream zines end up compromising their own identities to compete with the big boys on their own level. But these small magazines have a distinct advantage: The raw bravado and clear message that drove their creation in the first place can be the key to their success. Stick with it. Representing one ideology with the design and another with the content does nothing but confuse the audience. Ultimately, it's the reader who feels ripped off.

After all, it's human nature to judge a book by its cover.

Are Magazines More Interactive than the Web? 32

JANDOS ROTHSTEIN

THE END OF THE DOT-COM BOOM LEFT US WITH a lot of hard-won lessons, the most vexed of which is that the so-called new economy was really just the old economy ported to a new medium. The most successful business Web sites turned out to be nothing but humble catalogs and brochures in clunky, if instantly obtainable, form. But if Americans have awakened to the reality that the demand for down vests, say, is fairly constant whether you sell them online or out of a cardboard box, the hyperbolic vocabulary of the Internet revolution is still very much with us. Even the most hangdog bankrupt Internet millionaire continues to believe in the medium and that Web design is fundamentally revolutionary because it is interactive.

Nonsense.

While it's true that some Web sites are greatly interactive, the majority require no more input from the user than a paperback requires to switch to a new page. And paper itself has been capable of interactivity since before the dawn of metal type. Playing cards, board games, paper dolls, tax forms, and crossword puzzles, to name but a few examples, can be acted upon, modified, and ordered by users. Timetables and phone books have always used the fundamental, easily understandable principles of alphabetization and categorization to make vast quantities of data quickly navigable—all without electricity or a spare phone line. The Internet merely put a techno gloss on tried-and-true print-design techniques.

No one expects anymore to become magically and instantaneously wealthy due to an ever-so-clever Web scheme (except, perhaps, those involved in fraud and porn). But it is also true that the Web is not going away. And though Borders and Barnes & Noble (not to mention the independently owned bookstore down the street) are no longer panicking due to Amazon, the same cannot be said for the management of the magazines we read—and especially the newspapers. This is where, it would seem, the Web, as a medium for delivering content, rather than as magic money-making pixie dust, can compete with print and even television and win. The Web, after all, brings news and entertainment instantaneously to the reader, it's vaster than a thousand copies of the Sunday *New York Times*, and it's available for free.

The Internet, as a slowly maturing technology, could not really be compared to traditional media until just recently. Over the past few years, the Web has continuously evolved, both in terms of what it can do and what can be found on it. And now that the fuss has died down, and the novelty has finally started to fade, it is possible to actually compare the mature Internet with mature print media and examine the relative merits of each.

Just as it was once assumed that television would supplant movie theaters, many in publishing assume that their Web sites will eventually supplant their printed products. Indeed, some publishers hope that they will. However, the benefits of the Web for print publishers—freedom from the vicissitudes of the paper market and the elimination of distribution costs—are incentives for publishers and not readers. Most printed magazines, too, reach the reader for free or a fraction of their real costs. The Internet is still in less than two-thirds of U.S. homes as of 2004 and broadband is still in less than 20 percent. But as the technology becomes saturated—and growth on the Internet will truly be won at the expense of other media—consumer choice will determine which medium is best for which kinds of information. Neither the Web nor print publications will go away.

Bandwidth

The resolution of the typical computer monitor is 72 dots per inch (dpi); the resolution of a typical color photograph in a magazine is 150 dpi. In short, a square inch of data on paper is roughly four times richer in content than a comparable square inch on a monitor. New technologies will make download times faster, but it is fair to say that download times will never go away because bloat will affect the Web as surely as it affects other forms of software. Put it this way: If you could run a bare-bones but completely adequate copy of Illustrator 88 on your dual-core Intel Apple, it would be blisteringly fast. Instead, you're stuck with overengineered, overfeatured, and oversexed Illustrator CS2. Hundreds of megabytes of data make up a midsized consumer magazine. A reader can graze all that information while waiting five minutes in a dentist's waiting room. A comparable experience is not now available online and may never be.

Variety

Web designers spend a lot of time talking about usability. Although it is possible to design a magazine so poorly that it is impossible to read, the fundamental interface of reading (turn the page) makes this inherently more difficult. With the exception of folios, a contents page, and in some cases signage, the print designer need not concern herself overmuch with navigation. As a result, magazines offer a variety of rich reading (and grazing) experiences that Web sites do not. All Web sites necessarily incorporate a fairly complex interface into the design itself. Web design, for all its gains, is inherently duller and less capable of surprising the reader than print design.

Web aficionados will object that, unlike print, the Web can incorporate motion and sound. This is certainly true—the Web offers a much richer multimedia experience than print. However, this is much like saying that the Web is better at being television than a magazine is. We live in a world where there is room for both reading and watching; subjugating the reading experience to a watching experience does not eliminate the desire to read. Newspapers do a better job at in-depth reporting than television, and that has become increasingly true as television has matured. It is also an open question whether the utility of multimedia Web sites will outlive the novelty. Flash, as its name implies, rarely has much substance.

Elegance

Within the context of a saddle-stitched booklet, a number of factors within the control of the magazine designer affect the way the material will be perceived. Size, length, paper quality, texture, gloss, and the inks used all make a statement about the contents and the advertisers before the consumer reads a single word. It is true that most magazines operate within narrower production constraints than high-end or short-run design projects; nevertheless, a trip to the newsstand will reveal a broad range of production values. The Web is a leveling medium; it is possible for a student to have a Web site that looks and works like BMW's. Furthermore, everything on a Web page is framed by plastic, covered with a patina of dust, and controlled by a coffee-stained keyboard. While magazines can present isolated and self-contained little worlds, Web sites are stuck resolutely in yours.

Timeliness

The Web certainly has the capacity to bring breaking news to readers more quickly than even a daily paper. But, as with television, speed comes with a cost: perspective, editing, and depth. The morning of 9/11, if you are like most people, you turned on the tube, not booted the computer.

"Enhanced" Content

A number of publications are experimenting with what is being called "enhanced content." These adapt the content of the magazine, which has been tailored to the inherently limited real estate in a print vehicle, to the limitless bounds of a Web site. Photographs that would not fit in the print layout are reproduced as Web slide shows; articles are run in longer versions; occasionally the interviews upon which articles are based are run in their entirety. These work essentially like the "cut" scenes included on many DVDs. It's usually possible to see why those scenes were cut, and the same is true for much of this Web content. The editing and streamlining that editors and designers must do, the decisions made for various reasons that ensure that only the highest-caliber content makes it into a published magazine (or, to a lesser extent, newspaper), are a service to the reader. A Web site that is essentially an unedited, bloated version of the magazine is not something most readers would consciously ask for.

Of course, good articles do spark curiosity that does not end on the last page. Web sites can extend the value of the printed magazine, but without a real investment in new content, this service will be of value to a minority of readers.

Portability

I have yet to see anyone happily reading a Web site on the subway; even if your cell phone comes with a browser, the act of reading tiny type on a miniscule screen combined with the vicissitudes of cellular reception makes for a slog. On the other hand, newspapers, magazines, and books all abound on trains, planes, and parks. According to promises made a few years ago, we should all be toting e-paper appliances by now—wireless Internet devices that hold perhaps a book or two in memory and receive the morning paper by wireless transmission every morning, along with updates throughout the day. E-paper failed so quickly you may not have noticed it was ever here. It's now being tried again, and its success is no more likely this time. While publishers would see substantial cost savings if they could eliminate their printing plants and shut down their distribution networks, the per unit cost of a publication to the reader is small. Why trade a paper product that you can throw away, spill coffee on, or forget at the office for an expensive appliance you have to lug around with you? E-paper is a very cool idea—remember the scene in *Minority Report* in which everyone's newspaper changes at once to reflect a breaking story?—but in the real world, when you combine a crude new technology with the unreliability of cellular service to deliver megabytes of info, it seems like a technology that is a long way from prime time.

Customization

One of the former flavors of the month in Web design was customization, the idea that you would visit a site and it would present you with the information you are most interested in. It's true that a Web site is capable of this kind of on-the-fly modification of content. The problem with customization is that it is a solution to a problem that is unique to online content, and as such does not challenge the value of print vehicles. Yes, "your" *New York Times* can present you, upon opening the home page, with sports rather than international headlines. With the print version, you can accomplish the same thing more quickly by pulling the sports section out of the paper. And pulling out the sports section requires no programming on the part of the user.

Proprietary Content

For publishers, the biggest fear of going onto the Web is that they lose control over their content: once an article is on the Web, it can be reproduced without the effort of scanning the page and correcting the resulting text. The advantages are also pretty clear: it can be updated, loaded with hyperlinks, or removed if problematic. Most important, Web content can bridge the gap between print issues and make material available beyond the weeklong or monthlong cycle of a typical magazine. It seems likely that these two impulses—hoarding and sharing—will balance each other for some time. The value of Web content for research will always be limited by the amount of material that isn't up.

Instant Gratification

When I hand someone my business card these days, it no longer contains just my name, address, and phone number; it also has a short code that allows the recipient to access a couple dozen examples of my design work, some of my writing, and assignments for the class I teach. For independent photographers, bloggers, and consultants of every stripe, the Web provides a certain leveling of the commercial landscape. I cannot send a salesman to San Diego to woo a perspective client (or, half the time, even go myself), but I can reach that client with a carefully controlled message. With the exception of blogging, though, these are commercial rather than editorial functions.

Advertising

Finally, as Web advertising has become more profitable for online publishers, it has also become more distracting. The little commercials you have to watch on *Slate*, the obnoxious strobelike blinking banners on many sites—all are more and more like television commercials in that they disrupt and distract from desired content. This interruption extends to bandwidth, too—editorial content waits while ads are downloaded. Sometimes the wait is too long, and the reader moves elsewhere. Yes, advertisers are increasing their spending on the Web because it's perceived as hip and because there is an increasingly large audience. But banners and boxes—because of their diminutive size and the cluttered environment in which they compete—do not serve many products well. Print publications present the only environment where advertising and editorial content exist in harmony—both get a good play, neither has to wait for the other. There will always be a market for print advertising.

Reaching the Modern Reader

33

SAMIR A. HUSNI, PH.D.

THE FIRST MAGAZINES PROVIDED A VERY DIFferent experience from the modern versions. Early magazines were predominantly "storehouses of information." They offered readers a lifeline to the outside world in the same manner as newspapers. Today, neither ink on paper nor frequency can justify the traditional definition of what magazines should and could do. Technology has changed all of our lives and that does not exclude the media we consume. Magazines are unable to keep up with the speed of the Internet, and even the Internet seems slow compared to text messaging. I used to turn to Web sites to get updates on news throughout the day. Now, I receive text messages with headlines and blurbs as soon as the newsrooms release them.

Nevertheless, the print magazine is one creation that technology will never make obsolete. No matter how fancy my next cell phone may be or how much content I can receive on my Blackberry, nothing can ever replace the experience of holding, seeing, and reading a magazine.

Since the advent of movable type, designers and writers have united in their efforts to integrate typography and imagery into a product that you can touch, see, and read. You feel a connection with it that no other media product can provide.

Magazine design is the arrangement of content in an interesting and orderly manner. Some designers focus on pictures and graphics, but for design to truly work for any publication, design must always incorporate the meaning of words on the page. Both text and photos work together to create communication that, if successful, will draw in viewers and get them hooked.

The role of visuals is important in magazines because it captures the attention of the reader. This process starts on the cover. Catching the eye is the first step in the buying process.

Covers are made up of three basic components: color, pictures, and type. According to psychologists, our brain perceives color first, then pictures, and finally words. This hierarchy of recognition must be understood in order to create an effective cover.

First, colors should be simple and meaningful. *Time* uses a bright red border on their cover to brand the magazine. As a result, the magazine is recognizable even if the title cannot be seen. The same is true for *National Geographic*. The yellow of its border is part of its logo—not the shape of the border, but the color. Lesser-known magazines can also bring meaning to their publication through color by simply being simple. Part of developing a magazine is choosing a palette of colors. Over time, this established palette will become more and more recognizable to readers.

Second, cover pictures should be in the customer's face—establishing eye contact with the reader. That "see me" factor of the images is so important because grabbing the reader's attention for a few precious seconds is the first step toward making a sale. What kind of picture is cover-worthy? In most cases it will be one of three types: something to fantasize about (a celebrity or a model to look at, a place where you can add yourself to the picture such as a beachfront or mountaintop), something to relate to (crafts, hobbies, a cake, or things you can do), and last but not least, pictures of real events and real people in the news (the president, September 11, an AIDS victim, or a starving African child). While tragedy and fantasy seem to have little in common, they share the ability to connect to the reader. If you do not have that "wow factor" from the first second, the reader's eye moves to the next cover on the newsstand or coffee table, and the chances of your magazine being picked up diminish.

Third, magazines should use cover type as something readers can skim first and read second. Readers are willing to forgive a technically poor picture, but they will not forgive a limp coverline. The type on the cover must be readable, legible, and short. Editors will tell you that short coverlines are a sign of a confidence. My test for coverlines is always the same. Drop the magazine to the ground, stand straight, and try to read the coverlines. If you can't, they are too small and readers will not be able to see them. Use a page number with one of those coverlines to lead the readers inside the magazine. If readers are intrigued, flip to the story, and like what they find, it will validate the whole magazine. The chances of hearing that cash register ring are now much higher.

Targeting

Whether on the newsstand or in the mailbox, a magazine cover was—until the advent of television in the fifties—regarded as a piece of art. The *Saturday Evening Post* featured a different Norman Rockwell picture each issue, while *Vogue* showed images of well-dressed women on its covers. Less imaginative magazines like *Reader's Digest* and a few others used their covers for the table of contents.

Today covers are designed to draw in the prospective reader. With over fifteen thousand consumer magazines being published in the United States, a cover must scream from the newsstand with large, engaging pictures and enticing coverlines. (I like to call them "sell lines.") The cover is very much like the front window of a store. As shoppers walk by, the displays should catch their eyes and make them want to come inside and shop. Effective coverlines convince readers they will miss out if they do not read what's inside.

While covers bark from the newsstand, they should whisper on the coffee table and in the mailbox. A recent trend has been the widespread use of the split

Home . . .

cover. A split cover is when a publisher uses two, three, or—in the case of *TV Guide*'s celebration of Star Trek's thirty-fifth anniversary—thirty-five different covers for a weekly issue. Many magazines routinely print one cover for subscribers and another for the newsstand. Others add multiple newsstand versions for different regions of the country. Split covers may use completely different pictures or sell lines. Or—in the case of *Good Housekeeping* and *National Geographic Kids*—even different logos. But in either case, the cover remains true to the aim of getting the readers' attention. The home version of a cover may "whisper" because it is free of most of the sell lines of the newsstand edition and the language is toned down. Subscriber covers may use "love" instead of "sex" and may change the focus from "being a better father" to "being a better man" (*Best Life Magazine*).

During the nearly thirty years I have been tracking magazines, I have seen what works and doesn't work, not only from a business perspective but from a visual

. . . and away. Both covers January 2007.

perspective as well. From my observations, I have formulated three postulates that can make the design of interior pages easier for anyone.

My first postulate is to have one and only one focus point for every spread (or single page). Readers can become confused if they do not know where to look. This does not mean that there should be only one picture; it means that one dominant element should anchor every page.

The second postulate is to design from the inside out to avoid trapping white space in the middle of pages. Empty spaces in the middle of a layout serve as natural mental breaks and become distracting for readers—they demand attention but don't offer a payoff. By designing outward you are able to keep consistent spacing between objects and place white space, if wanted, near the margins where it can be a natural border rather than an empty spot in your design. White space on the outside directs attention inward toward the content.

My final postulate is to group pictures together. Seeing images grouped helps readers absorb the story

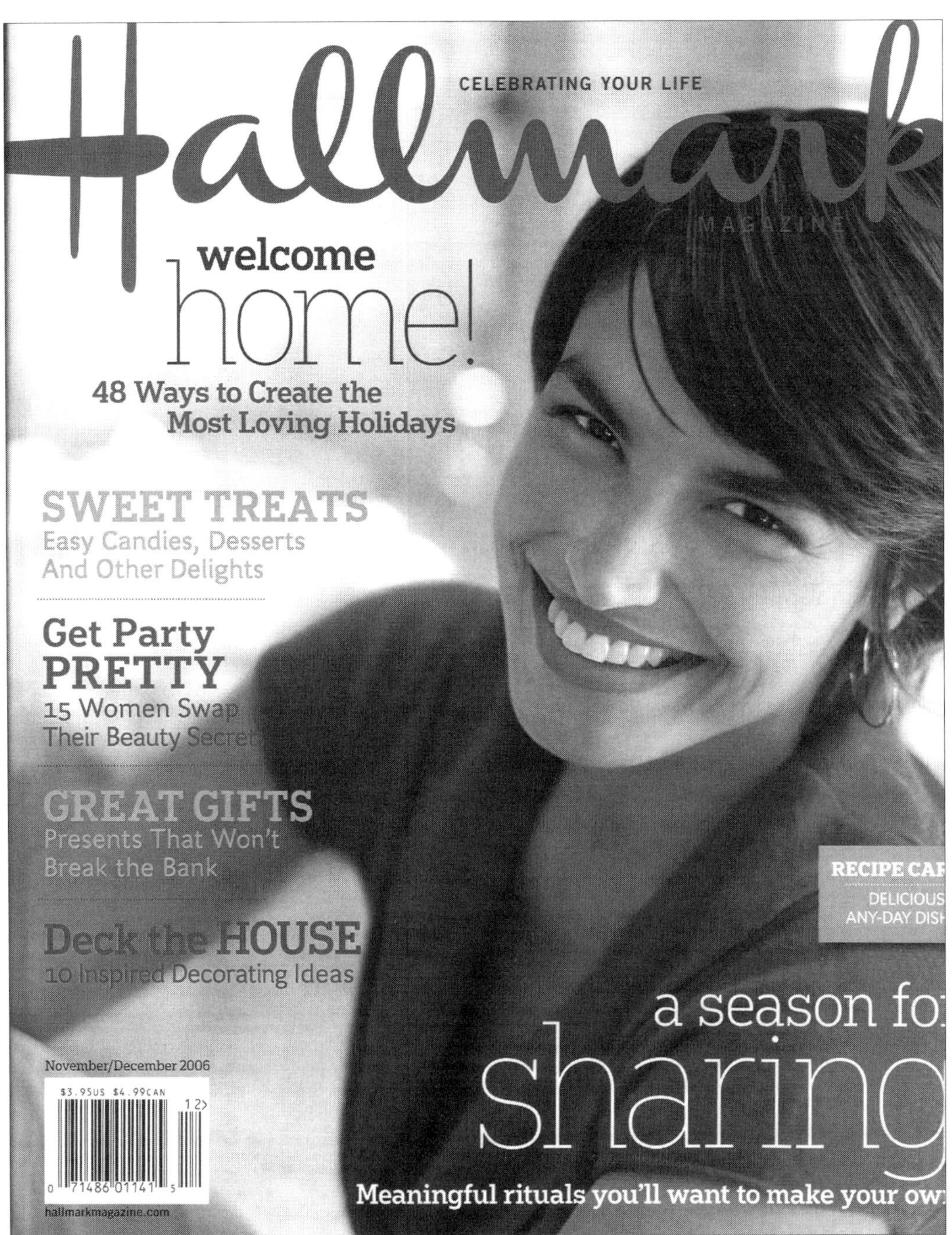

2006

faster through visual narrative and allows designers to create engaging contrasts—big and small, horizontal and vertical. These contrasts lead the reader into the story by providing a sense of direction and a natural flow.

Today's Reader

My basic rules have been applicable to periodical design for a long time, but in the last few years I have seen magazines begin to change the way they do things. More and more designers are dividing (think nuggets of chicken instead of the whole breast), grouping (think putting all the nuggets next to each other), and simplifying (think making the access to the nuggets as easy as possible). The result of this approach is not a happy meal but pages that encourage a ritualized approach to reading: the reader digs in, pulls out something interesting and satisfying, and maybe dives back in for more. The process of reading becomes active and reader-directed rather than editor-directed. What does this kind of addictive page look like? More entry and exit points—short items that pull you in and let you go quickly in the form of sidebars, info graphics, subtitles,

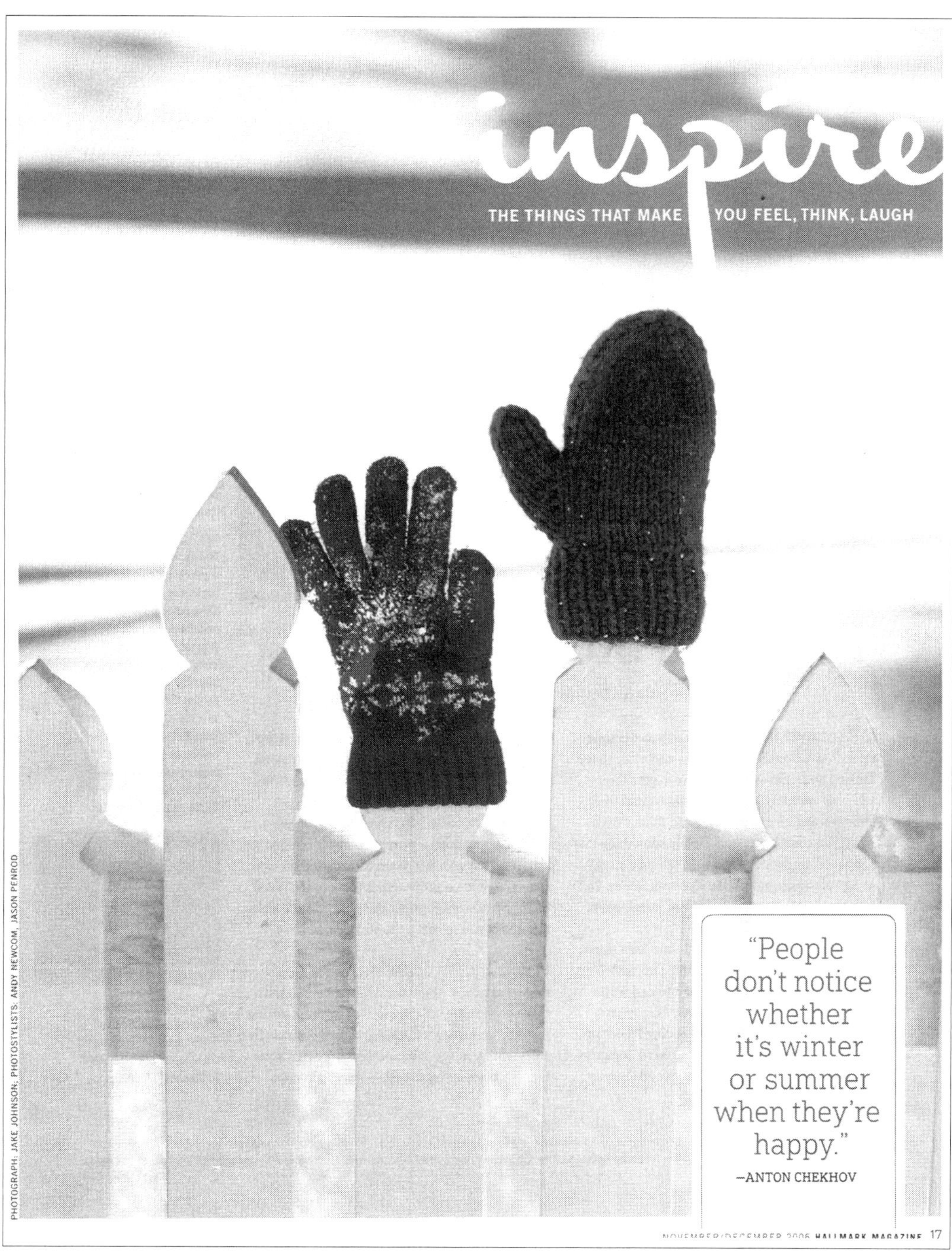

Hallmark, *2006*

informative captions, and a strong headline—each one of which gives the reader something desirable. This provides more places to feed your brain and more places to leave the page satisfied, even if you read only one sidebar rather than the whole spread. Unlike the *New Yorker*, which can pile up in a guilt-inducing heap, magazines with exit points satisfy the need to accomplish something.

In some cases editors and designers have also begun breaking magazines into sections and treating each as a separate editorial entity. No longer are these publications viewing their product as a front advertising well and a back editorial well. The Hallmark Corporation has done this in a very successful way with its new magazine, *Hallmark*. Divided into five sections—"Inspire," "Renew," "Nest," "Connect," and "Nourish"—*Hallmark* magazine begins each section with a splash page that serves as a menu or guide to what the reader should expect on the following pages. Each section's splash page has a large picture and a few words that hint at what is to come. In essence this page serves as a break between courses, and it provides a good piece of real estate for advertisers: opposite the splash page.

Hallmark isn't the only magazine that has abandoned the traditional approach to structuring content and advertising. *Cosmopolitan* groups topics together: if you are looking for beauty and fashion, it will be together in one section of the magazine regardless of article length, and if you are looking for love and lust, it will all be found together in another section, whether in the form of a department or an article. The topic drives the conversation and not the sections.

While some magazines are bought so readers can dream about the luxury homes or high-priced cars that grace their pages, others are successful because they provide useful information to their readers. Readers turn to *Every Day with Rachael Ray*, *Domino*, and *Wood* to find recipes, learn of design trends, and fuel their DIY spirit. With this in mind, more and more publishers are gearing their publications to be approachable by readers. To do this, designers are humanizing not only the overall design but the pictures as well. For many designers this flies against their desire for perfection. Rather than taking a "Martha Stewart" approach to photo styling—a perfect meal on a homemade tablecloth in a lavishly decorated room—many magazines are choosing to reflect the realistic capabilities of working couples in their photographs. *All You*, *Woman's World*, and *Quick & Simple* are examples of magazines that prove it is possible to make a compelling magazine that shows reality rather than fantasy. To humanize those magazines, designers and photographers are going after the imperfection in the design and the pictures rather than old-fashioned straight lines and perfect pictures. The covers of the Wal-Mart-only distributed *All You* shows real life as it happens every day: busy and cluttered.

The ultimate role of magazine design is to immediately tell the readers there is something in it for them. To me, a magazine must be able to whisper to the reader and to start a conversation with him or her. Magazines are far more than ink on paper. Successful magazines are the ones that cater to all five senses and create a brand in the reader's mind, one page at a time.

No matter how technology may change or what flashy, new media may be introduced, magazines will continue to be launched by the hundreds every year. While publishers must keep up with the changing tides of technology and fashion, they must also remain true to the basic principles that made the industry what it is today.

Art and Design Won't Save Publishing 34

GILBERT CRANBERG

A RECENT ROMENESKO ITEM HEADED "DO READERS really care if there are ads on the front page?" noted that *BusinessWeek*'s Jon Fine suspects that "only the most navel-gazing of journalists care about a small ad appearing on Page One." Probably true, but only because those "small ads" are seen in isolation. Do the numbers, and small ads over time aggregate to a large amount of prime space for news switched to advertising.

I did the numbers for the *Des Moines Register*, which recently put one-inch ads daily across the bottom of the front pages of five sections. In the course of a year, those seemingly inconsequential strips will equate to more than ninety pages of news lost to ads.

Ads at least bring in revenue, which pays for paper, salaries, training, travel, and other expenses that can improve quality. The same can't be said for the very large number of column inches that seem increasingly to be devoted to oversized graphics. Call it the Invasion of the Space Snatchers. This problem does not just affect newspapers: Magazines are purchased to be read, but their staffs also seem to have decreasing faith in the value of words.

It's not unusual nowadays for artwork to dwarf, by large margins, the stories they illustrate. The Sunday *New York Times* is a major case in point. The August 6, 2006 "Week in Review" section, for instance, devoted thirty-four column inches of text to a piece about Ariel Sharon but all of fifty-five column inches to two pictures of Sharon.

The Space Snatchers attacked again on another story in the same section with a jumbo graphic that stretched the full length of the page for two columns, and then some. The graphic? Of all things, a tape measure. If editors had utilized one, they would have found the art had gobbled up nearly twice the space taken by the story.

Words are losing to art at magazines as well. *Esquire*, which once devoted only one page to art and ten pages to text for an article about what was wrong with Spiro Agnew, now turns over less than two pages to text and more than three pages to art in a five-page layout on what's swell about Brad Pitt. The Pitt layout (October 2006) includes two murky photographs of the actor riding his 4 × 4.

Even *National Geographic*, long known for excellent reporting and photojournalism, has seen a shift in priorities. The March 1976 issue devotes ten pages to text and twenty to art in an article about Sicily. The September 2006 issue proffers less than six pages of text and more than twenty-four pages to art in a layout on China—and *National Geographic*'s pages now hold fewer words than they once did.

The *Times*' and *National Geographic*'s readers tend to be intensely interested in news and ideas—and once *Esquire*'s readers were too. They are, by and large, the proverbial news junkies. I question whether they have to be lured to stories by having them jazzed up with massive quantities of art.

I am not talking here about graphs and other infographics that help tell the story. What I see, much too often, are inflated illustrations that gobble up space without a payoff in information.

I have a lot of respect for the work of graphic artists. I relied on them extensively to dress up the opinion pages when I was editorial page editor at the *Register*. I believe in making publications attractive, and I was an early user of color on editorial pages. In fact, I recently heard from a former staff member who now heads a very large staff of designers and artists at a major paper who wrote to thank me for inspiring her to do newspaper graphics. I am not against art in an editorial context. That said, too much of what I see nowadays looks to be a mindless effort to overwhelm readers with size and quantity.

Print publications are now larded with too much art in a misguided attempt to compete with television and the Web. While it is understandable that newspapers and magazines are responding to diminishing circulation numbers by looking toward what seem to be the ascendant media, they are making a mistake in doing so. Television and the Internet are always on, always available, and always changing. Editors and print designers alike must face up to the fact that if they attempt to compete with an inherently visual medium by becoming more visual themselves, they will only succeed in making print's graphic limitations all the more stark by comparison and at the cost of what magazines and newspapers do well.

While there are doubtlessly some readers who consciously and consistently notice and appreciate visuals, even for them the amount of time spent with the most well-considered photograph or illustration still pales in comparison to the amount of time spent with the shortest of articles. Any thoughtful critic can come up with exceptions in which generous art is mission critical—*National Geographic* itself would not be what it is without its enterprising (and expensive) photojournalism, the soft-core approach of *Maxim* and its imitators is inherently photo-driven, and for fashion and glamour magazines, images provide information. But, for the majority of publications—which neither have the capability to imitate *National Geographic* or *Vogue*, nor the appeal to the same prurient interests as *Maxim*—big visuals come at a price.

Readers subscribe to periodicals for text, not for artwork. To the extent that publications substitute overly generous graphics for news and ideas, they shortchange readers and alienate them.

When I see splurging on graphics I wonder, "Where was the editor?" Space is an editor's prize possession, but editors who do not hesitate to trim inflated stories seem to put away their red pencils when art is involved. They should no more abdicate to artists than to writers.

At both newspapers and magazines, the efforts to make publications more visual have done little to reduce hemorrhaging readerships—indeed, circulations have become smaller at the same time art has become bigger. Many publications are turning cartwheels to trim costs; it would be a sound investment by both newspaper and magazines to give readers more news and opinion by going easier on the art.

Contributors

DAVID BARRINGER is the author of *American Mutt Barks in the Yard*, copublished by *Emigré* and Princeton Architectural Press. He has written for *I.D. Magazine*, *Eye Magazine*, and AIGA's *Voice*. Contact: davidbarringer.com.

ROGER BLACK has been involved in the design of content-based media since 1970. He's led redesigns at *Newsweek*, *Esquire*, *Fast Company*, *Smart Money*, *Reader's Digest*, and other publications. He was a staff art director at the *New York Times*, *Rolling Stone*, and *Newsweek*. He currently works from a small studio in New York and contributes occasionally to rogerblack.com.

JOHN BRADY is former editor in chief at *Writer's Digest* and *Boston* magazine. He is a partner at Brady & Paul Communications, a publishing consultancy that has redesigned over three hundred magazines. He can be reached at bradybrady@aol.com.

GILBERT CRANBERG is George H. Gallup Professor of Journalism Emeritus at the University of Iowa School of Journalism and Mass Communication. He was associated for thirty-three years with the *Des Moines Register* and *Tribune*, where he was editor of the editorial pages of both papers.

Harp magazine editor in chief and art director **SCOTT CRAWFORD** has been involved in magazines since before he even hit puberty (late last year). At the age of twelve, he published his first fanzine—devoted to the then-burgeoning Washington, D.C. punk scene—and over twenty years later, he still gets a kick out of discovering and turning his readers onto new music. He lives in Silver Spring, Maryland, with his wife, three children, and slobbering mess of a dog, Elvis.

STEVEN HELLER is cochair of the MFA Designer as Author program at The School of Visual Arts and editor of *Voice: AIGA Journal of Design*.

SAMIR HUSNI is the chair of the Journalism Department at the University of Mississippi. He is also professor and Hederman Lecturer of Journalism. Dr. Husni is the author of the annual *Samir Husni's Guide to New Magazines*, which is now in its twenty-first year. He is also the author of *Launch Your Own Magazine: A Guide for Succeeding in Today's Marketplace*, published by Hamblett House, Inc., and *Selling Content: The Step-by-Step Art of Packaging Your Own Magazine*, published by Kendall Hunt. When he is not at newsstands buying magazines, Dr. Husni is at home or in his office reading them.

HANA JUNG is design director of *Northern Virginia Living*.

JOYCE RUTTER KAYE has been the editor in chief of *Print* since 2003, after five years as managing editor. As editor in chief, she has overseen a complete redesign of the sixty-seven-year-old magazine and its Web site, launched *Print*'s annual conferences, and created a minor ruckus for publishing a special issue on sex and design. Since Kaye joined *Print*, the magazine has won two National Magazine Awards for general excellence and a number of additional ASME nominations. Previously Kaye was managing editor of *U&lc*, a reporter for *Advertising Age/Creativity*, and a freelance writer covering design and consumer culture.

ALISSA LEVIN is principal of Point Five Design, a studio and consultancy in New York City. Point Five Design has been recognized for its work for the *Paris Review*, *Legal Affairs*, the *American Prospect*, *Harvard Divinity Bulletin*, and *Lingua Franca*, among other publications.

GREG LINDSAY is a contributing writer to *Fast Company* and an editor at large for *Advertising Age*. He covered the magazine business as a senior correspondent for *Inside.com*, as a contributing editor to *Folio*, and as media editor of *Women's Wear Daily*, and he continues to write about the media business for *Mediabistro.com* and many other magazines.

MARGARET LITTMAN is a Chicago-based writer and editor who shops for magazines more than anything else. Her magazine racks are filled with her clips from *Art & Antiques*, *Ladies Home Journal*, and *Wine Enthusiast* magazines. She was the editor of *Chicago Shops 2006* and is the author of several guidebooks, including *The Dog Lover's Companion to Chicago* and *VegOut Vegetarian Guide to Chicago*.

After *POPsmear*, **PETE MORELEWICZ** went on to design various magazines for big, soulless corporations until he landed at *Washington City Paper*, where he now serves as art director. Along with his wife Christine, he curates a museum devoted to squished pennies from their Washington, D.C., home.

ROBERT NEWMAN has been the design director of *Fortune*, *Real Simple*, *Entertainment Weekly*, *New York*, *Details*, *Vibe*, *Inside*, the *Village Voice*, and *Guitar World*. He was the editor of the music and culture magazine the *Rocket* in Seattle. He is past president of the Society of Publication Designers, has been a frequent guest lecturer at the Poynter Institute, and speaks regularly to groups about design and art direction. His Web site is *robertnewman.com*.

KATHY MARTIN O'NEIL worked at *Outside Magazine* from 1989 to 1995, starting as an intern and finishing as managing editor. Today she is a freelance writer and editor in Indianapolis with three kids.

DENISE M. REAGAN has been making connections between words and visuals since she entered the news design field in 1988. A graduate of the University of Florida journalism school in Gainesville, she has designed and art directed pages at the *News-Sentinel* in Fort Wayne, Indiana; the *Detroit Free Press*; the *Star Tribune* in Minneapolis; the *Savannah Morning News*; and the *South Florida Sun-Sentinel*. She is now the AME/Visuals at the *Florida Times-Union* in Jacksonville. As a consultant with MG Redesign, she has worked on projects such as the redesign of the *Spokesman-Review*.

RON REASON is a publication design consultant and educator based in Chicago and a visiting faculty member (and former director of visual journalism) of the Poynter Institute for Media Studies in St. Petersburg, Florida. He has redesigned large and small magazines and newspapers around the globe. He can be reached by e-mail at ron@ronreason.com. His Web site, with tips, case studies, and other resources, is: *www.ronreason.com*.

DAN ROLLERI was editor and publisher of *Speak Magazine*. He is currently writing a book and living in Sisters, Oregon.

JANDOS ROTHSTEIN is an assistant professor of graphic design at George Mason University, design director of *Governing Magazine*, and a freelance editorial design consultant. He has written for *Print*, *ID*, *Voice: AIGA Journal of Design*, *Design Journal*, and other publications. He lives approximately in Washington, D.C., with his wife and two daughters.

DAN ZEDEK is the design director of the *Boston Globe*. He has worked as an art director or deputy at numerous magazines and weekly newspapers including *Parenting*, *Seattle Weekly*, *Natural Health*, *Guitar World*, and the *Village Voice*. He redesigned many of those publications and has acted as freelance redesign consultant for numerous other newspapers and magazines.

Index

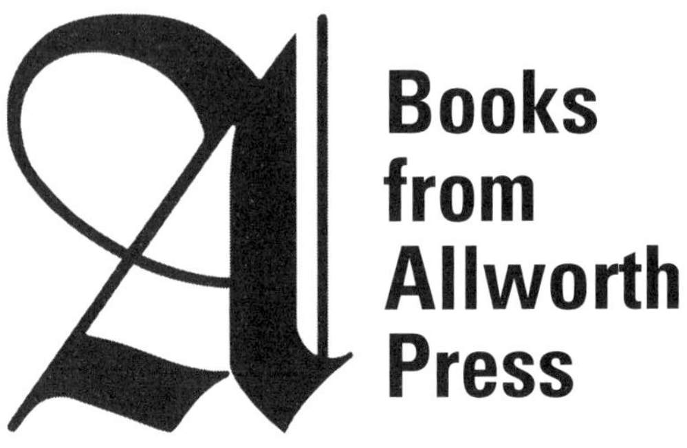

Allworth Press
is an imprint
of Allworth
Communications, Inc.
Selected titles are
listed below.

Editing by Design: For Designers, Art Directors, and Editors—
The Classic Guide to Winning Readers, Third Edition
by Jan V. White (paperback, 8½ × 11, 256 pages, $29.95)

The Elements of Graphic Design: Space, Unity, Page Architecture, and Type
by Alex W. White (paperback, 6⅛ × 9¼, 160 pages, $24.95)

Thinking in Type: The Practical Philosophy of Typography
by Alex W. White (paperback, 6 × 9, 224 pages, $24.95)

How to Think Like a Great Graphic Designer
by Debbie Millman (paperback, 6 × 9, 256 pages, $24.95)

Advertising Design and Typography
by Alex W. White (hardcover, 8¾ × 11¼, 224 pages, $50.00)

The Education of an Art Director
by Steven Heller and Véronique Vienne (paperback, 6 × 9, 240 pages, $19.95)

Looking Closer 5: Critical Writings on Graphic Design
edited by M. Bierut, W. Drenttel, and S. Heller (paperback, 6¾ × 9⅞, 304 pages, $21.95)

Looking Closer 4: Critical Writings on Graphic Design
edited by M. Bierut, W. Drenttel, and S. Heller (paperback, 6¾ × 9⅞, 304 pages, $21.95)

Looking Closer 3: Classic Writings on Graphic Design
edited by M. Bierut, J. Helfand, S. Heller, and R. Poynor (paperback, 6¾ × 9⅞, 304 pages, $21.95)

Design Literacy, Second Edition
by Steven Heller (paperback, 6 × 9, 464 pages, $24.95)

Citizen Designer: Perspectives on Design Responsibility
by Steven Heller and Véronique Vienne (paperback, 6 × 9, 272 pages, $19.95)

Design Literacy (continued): Understanding Graphic Design
by Steven Heller (paperback, 6¾ × 9⅞, 296 pages, $19.95)

Graphic Design and Reading
edited by Gunnar Swanson (paperback, 6¾ × 9⅞, 240 pages, $19.95)

The Education of a Graphic Designer, Second Edition
by Steven Heller (paperback, 6 × 9, 368 pages, $24.95)

To request a free catalog or order books by credit card, call 1-800-491-2808. To see our complete catalog on the World Wide Web, or to order online for a 20 percent discount, you can find us at ***www.allworth.com***.